Math 2XX3

TABLE OF CONTENTS
& ACKNOWLEDGEMENTS

PAGE

MATH 2XX3 - Advanced Calculus II

Prof. S. Alama [1]

◇

Class notes recorded, adapted, and illustrated
by Sang Woo Park

◇

Revised April 2, 2019

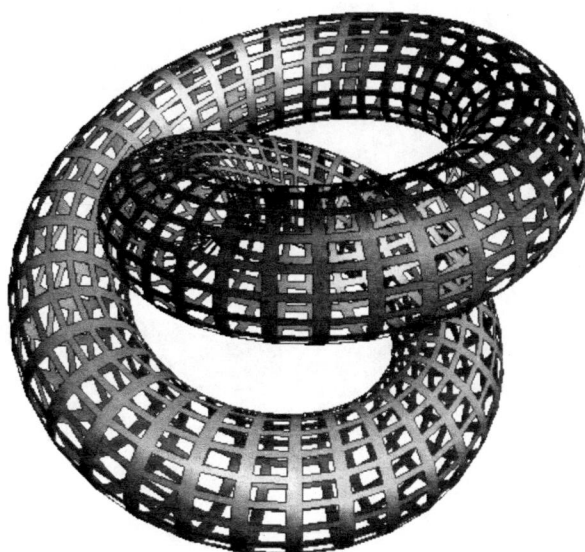

Contents

Preface

These notes are intended as a kind of organic textbook for a class in advanced calculus, for students who have already studied three terms of calculus (from a standard textbook such as Stewart [Stew],) and one or two terms of linear algebra.

Typically, these two subjects (calculus and linear algebra) have been introduced as separate areas of study, and aside from some small intersection the true intertwined nature of multivariable and vector calculus with linear algebra has been hidden. For example, in Stewart the derivative of multivariable functions is only discussed in special cases, introducing only the partial derivatives and certain physically important combinations (curl and divergence,) but avoiding the discussion of the derivative as a linear transformation (ie, a matrix.) As a consequence, the notion of differentiability is not properly presented. In addition, the chain rule is presented as an ad hoc collection of separate formulas dealing with specific cases of composite functions, together with some visual tricks to make them easier to calculate. There are many other instances where mysterious looking calculation techniques are introduced in order to avoid a more powerful and general formulation via matrices and linear maps. This is because standard calculus books cannot assume that students have linear algebra as a prerequisite or corequisite course.

A second issue which we address here is the level and mathematical content of the multivariable calculus introduced in the first three terms. In a mixed audience with not only mathematics students but also physicists, engineers, biologists, economists, etc, the emphasis in the calculus class is on formulas, calculation, and problem solving directed to the applications of calculus, and less stress is put on the actual mathematics. This can lead to a shock when students encounter higher level mathematics, such as real and complex analysis or topology, where calculational proficiency becomes secondary to an understanding of when and why mathematical facts are true. In this course we will pay careful attention to precise definitions, and the need to verify that they are satisfied in specific examples. Facts will be presented as Theorems, and students will need to understand the hyptheses and the conclusions, how they apply (or not) to specific cases, and what their consequences are. Some computation will be needed to do examples, but we will make a step up in mathematical rigor and the emphasis will be on understanding the definitions and theorems.

The topics presented here begin with the foundations of multivariable calculus: a discussion of the structure of Euclidean space $\mathbb{R}^n$, followed by limits and continuity, the derivative, and important properties of the derivative. This covers Chapters 1–3. The succeeding chapters are more or less independent of each other and may be covered in any order (and some may be deemed optional.) Chapter 4 concerns the differential geometry of curves in $\mathbb{R}^3$, with the Frenet frame and curvature. The Implicit and Inverse Function Theorems are the subject of Chapter 5. Chapter 6 introduces the second-order Taylor's Theorem in order to understand the role of the second derivative matrix in classifying critical points. Chapter 7 is an introduction to the Calculus of Variations, which puts together many aspects of the previous material in the study of extremal problems in spaces of functions. And finally, in Chapter 8 we introduce Fourier Series and orthogonal decompositions, a field which is too important to mathematics and its applications to be relegated to more specialized classes in partial differential equations. (An inexpensive paperback Dover book by Tolstov [Tol] is also used for this segment of the course.)

Why write these notes when there are so many calculus textbooks on the market? It's true that there are some excellent books dealing with advanced calculus in a way which introduces correct mathematical definitions and statements of theorems, without introducing the difficulties of rigorously proving all of the (fairly complex) theorems of vector calculus; the book by Marsden & Tromba [MT] is one. However, these books are intended as a replacement for Stewart, and spend many pages on developing the calculation techniques which students have already learned in the 3-term calculus sequence. And the linear algebra background presumend by [MT] is actually much less than what students learn in the 2-semester linear algebra sequence 1B03–2R03. More advanced books, such as Marsden & Hoffman [MH], are really analysis books and the level is too high for a second-year course. And so we have a need for an intermediate level text.

Fortunately, a student, Sang Woo Park, made a LaTeX transcription of his class notes for Math 2XX3 in the Winter 2017 term, which he generously offered to his fellow students on his personal web page as the document evolved. Sang Woo then added some graphics to illustrate various concepts, and this text was born!

Finally, I will be keeping a corrected copy and a list of corrections on the course web page. If you find an error, or some place where the text is unclear, (and it doesn't already appear on the list of corrections,) please send me email at `alama@mcmaster.ca` so I can make the correction.

Prof. S. Alama, McMaster University, October 2017. Revised April 2, 2019

Bibliography

[AR]   H. Anton and C. Rorres. *Elementary Linear Algebra: Applications Version, 11th Edition:*. Wiley Global Education, 2013.

[MH]   J. Marsden and M. Hoffman. *Elementary Classical Analysis*. W. H. Freeman, 1993.

[MT]   J. E. Marsden and A. Tromba. *Vector calculus*. Macmillan, 2003.

[Stew] J. Stewart. *Calculus: Early Transcendentals*. Cengage Learning, 2015.

[Tol]   G. Tolstov. *Fourier Series*. Dover Books on Mathematics. Dover Publications, 2012.

Chapter 1

Space, vectors, and sets

Over the last three terms you've studied (at least) two flavors of mathematics: calculus and linear algebra. They have been taught separately, and probably feel very different to you. Linear Algebra is about vectors and matrices, and how you use them to solve linear algebraic equations. Calculus is about functions, continuity, and rates of change. The main goal of this course is to bring these two subjects together. Indeed, to understand calculus in more than one dimension it is essential to use concepts from linear algebra. And the constructions from linear algebra (which may have seemed strange and arbitrary to you when you learned them) are then motivated by their use in understanding calculus in the plane and in space.

We begin by a brief discussion of space,

$$\mathbb{R}^n = \{(x_1, x_2, \ldots, x_n) : x_1, x_2, \ldots, x_n \in \mathbb{R}\},$$

where it all happens.

1.1 Vector norms

To connect linear algebra to calculus we need to talk about lengths and distance. This is done via a *norm*.

Definition 1.1. Euclidean norm *of* $\vec{x} = (x_1, x_2, \ldots, x_n)$ *is given as*

$$\|\vec{x}\| = \sqrt{\vec{x} \cdot \vec{x}} = \sqrt{\sum_{j=1}^{n} x_j^2}$$

Using the norm we can then define the *distance* between any two points $\vec{p}$ and $\vec{q}$ in $\mathbb{R}^n$,

$$\text{dist}(\vec{p}, \vec{q}) = \|\vec{p} - \vec{q}\|.$$

Notice that this also suggests that the "norm" of a "'vector" $x \in \mathbb{R}^1 = \mathbb{R}$ (and $\mathbb{R}$ is a vector space!) should be defined by

$$\|x\| = \sqrt{x^2} = |x|,$$

1

so in one dimension the distance is defined via the absolute value,

$$\text{dist}(p, q) = |p - q|, \qquad \forall p, q \in \mathbb{R}.$$

In dimension $n \geq 2$ the Euclidean norm is intimately related to the dot product of vectors,

$$\vec{x} \cdot \vec{y} = \sum_{i=1}^{n} x_i\, y_i,$$

which gives us the useful concept of *orthogonality*: $\vec{x} \perp \vec{y}$ when $\vec{x} \cdot \vec{y} = 0$. More generally, the dot product enables us to calculate angles between vectors:

$$\vec{x} \cdot \vec{y} = \|\vec{x}\|\, \|\vec{y}\|\, \cos\theta,$$

where θ is the angle between $\vec{x}$ and $\vec{y}$, drawn in the plane determined by the two vectors. Since $|\cos\theta| \leq 1$ for any angle, we also have the famous

Theorem 1.2 (Cauchy-Schwartz Inequality).

$$|\vec{x} \cdot \vec{y}| \leq \|\vec{x}\|\, \|\vec{y}\|$$

The Euclidean norm has certain properties, which are intuitively clear if we think about it as measuring the length of a vector:

Theorem 1.3 (Properties of a norm).

1. *$\|\vec{x}\| \geq 0$ and $\|\vec{x}\| = 0$ iff $\vec{x} = \vec{0} = (0, 0, \ldots, 0)$.*

2. *For all scalars $a \in \mathbb{R}$, $\|a\vec{x}\| = |a| \cdot \|\vec{x}\|$.*

3. *(Triangle inequality) $\|\vec{x} + \vec{y}\| \leq \|\vec{x}\| + \|\vec{y}\|$.*

Proof. (i) If $\vec{x} = \vec{0}$, then by the formula $\|\vec{0}\| = \sqrt{0} = 0$. On the other hand, if $\|\vec{x}\| = 0$, then

$$0 = \|\vec{x}\|^2 = \sum_{i=1}^{n} x_i^2.$$

This is a sum of squares, so each term in the sum is non-negative, and thus each must equal zero. This proves (i).

For (ii), this is just factoring (and being careful that $\sqrt{a^2} = |a|$!!)

$$\|a\vec{x}\| = \sqrt{a^2 \sum_{i=1}^{n} x_i^2} = |a| \sqrt{\sum_{i=1}^{n} x_i^2} = |a| \|\vec{x}\|.$$

For (iii), we look at the square of the norm, which is easier than that norm itself:

$$\|\vec{x} + \vec{y}\|^2 = (\vec{x} + \vec{y}) \cdot (\vec{x} + \vec{y}) = \vec{x} \cdot \vec{x} + \vec{y} \cdot \vec{y} + 2\vec{x} \cdot \vec{y} = \|\vec{x}\|^2 + \|\vec{y}\|^2 + 2\vec{x} \cdot \vec{y}$$
$$\leq \|\vec{x}\|^2 + \|\vec{y}\|^2 + 2\|\vec{x}\|\,\|\vec{y}\|$$
$$= (\|\vec{x}\| + \|\vec{y}\|)^2.$$

Since each term is non-negative, we can take the square root of each side to obtain the triangle inequality (iii). □

Remark. It is easy to verify that in $\mathbb{R}^1 = \mathbb{R}$, $\|x\| = |x|$ satisfies all the above properites of the norm. The first two conditions are immediate. To verify the triangle inequality, we use the fact that $|x|^2 = x^2$, so

$$|x + y|^2 = (x + y)^2 = x^2 + y^2 + 2xy \leq x^2 + y^2 + 2|x|\,|y| = |x|^2 + |y|^2 + 2|x|\,|y| = (|x| + |y|)^2.$$

As above, each term is non-negative, so we take the square root to obtain the triangle inequality for the absolute value,

$$|x + y| \leq |x| + |y| \tag{1.1}$$

We separate out the properties in this way to point out that there may be many other ways of measuring the length of a vector in $\mathbb{R}^n$ (which give different numerical values) which would be equally valid as norms.

Example 1.4 (A non-Euclidean norm - *The Taxi Cab Norm*). Consider the vector $\vec{p} = (p_1, p_2) \in \mathbb{R}^2$. The euclidean norm gives the length of the diagonal line joining $\vec{0}$ to $\vec{p}$. On the other hand,

$$\|\vec{p}\|_1 = |p_1| + |p_2|$$

gives us the length traveled in a rectangular grid system, like the number of blocks traveled in a car in a city of streets meeting at right angles. We can define a taxi cab norm in any dimension: for $\vec{p} = (p_1, p_2, \ldots, p_n) \in \mathbb{R}^n$, $\|\vec{p}\|_1 = \sum_{j=1}^{n} |p_j|$.

As with the Euclidean norm, we may define the distance between two points $\vec{p}, \vec{q} \in \mathbb{R}^n$ as the taxi cab norm length of the vector joining them, $\text{dist}_1(\vec{p}, \vec{q}) = \|\vec{p} - \vec{q}\|_1$. In the plane, this is the number of city blocks (east-west plus north-south) you need to drive to get from one point to the other. Unless the two points lie on the same street (and can be joined by a segment parallel to one of the axes), the distance will be larger than the Euclidean distance, which is the distance "as the bird flies" from one point to the other along the (diagonal) straight line path. □

The Taxi Cab norm is a valid norm because it satisfies all properties of a norm above. (You will show this as an exercise!) So it also gives us a valid alternative way to measure *distance* in $\mathbb{R}^n$, $\text{dist}(\vec{p}, \vec{q}) = \|\vec{p} - \vec{q}\|$. This way of measuring distance gives $\mathbb{R}^n$ a *different geometry*, as we will see below. (However, this norm is not compatible with the dot product, as you will also see from the exercise below.)

Definition 1.5. *The* Neighborhood *of radius $r > 0$ about a point $\vec{p}$ is the set*

$$D_r(\vec{p}) = \left\{ \vec{x} \in \mathbb{R}^n \,\middle|\, \|\vec{x} - \vec{p}\| < r \right\}$$

We may also call this the disk *of radius $r > 0$ in $\mathbb{R}^2$, or the* ball *of radius $r > 0$ in $\mathbb{R}^3$.*

Remark. Different books use different notations for a neighborhood, and so depending on which of the calculus books you read, the neighborhood around $\vec{a}$ of radius r may be written using any of the following notations:

$$D_r(\vec{a}) = B_r(\vec{a}) = B(\vec{a}, r)$$

Definition 1.6. *The sphere of radius $r > 0$ about $\vec{p}$ is defined as*

$$S_r(\vec{p}) = \left\{ \vec{x} \in \mathbb{R}^n \,\middle|\, \|\vec{x} - \vec{p}\| = r \right\}$$

The shape of the neighborhood and sphere depends strongly on which norm you choose. First, let's start with the familiar Euclidean norm. Then, the sphere is given by

$$\|\vec{x} - \vec{p}\| = r$$

$$\iff \sqrt{\sum_{j=1}^{n} (x_j - p_j)^2} = r,$$

which is equivalent to

$$\sum_{j=1}^{n} (x_j - p_j)^2 = r^2.$$

When $n = 3$, we have

$$(x_1 - p_1)^2 + (x_2 - p_2)^2 + (x_3 - p_3)^2 = r^2,$$

the usual sphere in $\mathbb{R}^3$ with center $\vec{p} = (p_1, p_2, p_3)$

When $n = 2$, we have

$$(x_1 - p_1)^2 + (x_2 - p_2)^2 = r^2,$$

the usual circle in $\mathbb{R}^n$ with center $\vec{p} = (p_1, p_2)$.

If we replace Euclidean norm by the Taxi Cab norm (for simplicity, take $\vec{p} = \vec{0}$), we have

$$S_r^{\text{taxi}}(\vec{0}) = \left\{ \vec{x} \in \mathbb{R}^n \,\middle|\, \|\vec{x} - \vec{0}\|_1 = r \right\}$$

In other words, we have

$$\vec{x} \in S_r^{\text{taxi}}(\vec{0}) \iff \sum_{j=1}^{n} |x_j| = r$$

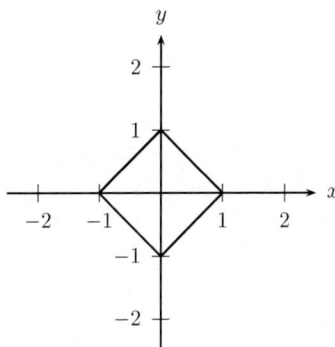

Figure 1.1. Neighborhood around $(0,0)$ of radius 1 using the Taxi Cab norm.

In $\mathbb{R}^2$, we have $\vec{x} = (x_1, x_2)$. Then, $r = |x_1| + |x_2|$, which is a diamond. (See figure 1.1)[1]. Notice that in the first quadrant, $x_1, x_2 \geq 0$, we have $x_1 + x_2 = r$, which is the line segment with slope -1 connecting $(r, 0)$ to $(0, r)$. In the second quadrant, $|x_1| = -x_1$ and so the equation of the taxi cab circle is $-x_1 + x_2 = r$, the segment with slope $+1$ joining $(-r, 0)$ to $(0, r)$. The two other segments (in the third and fourth quadrants) forming the taxi-sphere may be derived in a similar manner.

1.2   Subsets of $\mathbb{R}^n$

Let's introduce some properties of *subsets* in $\mathbb{R}^n$. $A \subset \mathbb{R}^n$ means A is a *collection* of points $\vec{x}$, drawn from $\mathbb{R}^n$.

Definition 1.7. *Let $A \subset \mathbb{R}^n$, and $\vec{p} \in A$. We say $\vec{p}$ is an interior point of A (Figure 1.2) if there exists a neighbourhood of $\vec{p}$, i.e. an open disk disk, which is entirely contained in A:*

$$D_r(\vec{p}) \subset A.$$

So an interior point is one which is "well inside" the set A, in the sense that all of its neighbors up to distance $r > 0$ are elements of the set. It means that one can walk a certain distance r from $\vec{p}$ and stay within the set A.

Example 1.8.
$$A = \left\{ \vec{x} \in \mathbb{R}^n \mid \vec{x} \neq \vec{0} \right\}$$

Take any $\vec{p} \in A$, so $\vec{p} \neq \vec{0}$. Then, let $r = \|\vec{p} - \vec{0}\| > 0$, and $D_r(\vec{p}) \subset A$, since $\vec{0} \notin D_r(\vec{p})$. (Notice: any smaller disk, $D_s(\vec{p}) \subset D_r(\vec{p}) \subset A$, where $0 < s < r$ works to show that $\vec{p}$ is an interior point).

So every $\vec{p} \in A$ is an interior point to A. $\qquad\qquad\square$

---

[1]Note that $|x_1| + |x_2| = r$ is a *circle* in $\mathbb{R}^2$ under the Taxi Cab norm. Then, we have

$$\pi = \frac{\text{circumference}}{\text{diameter}} = \frac{8r}{2r} = 4$$

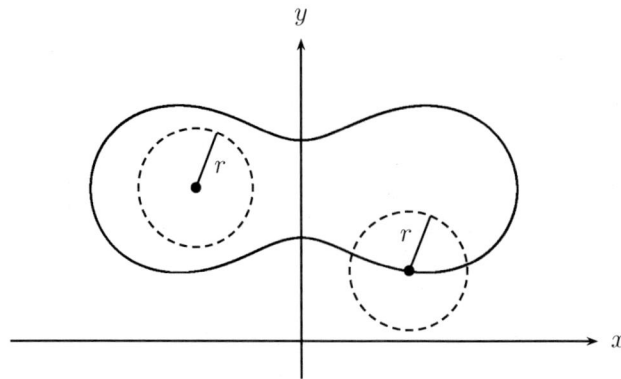

Figure 1.2. The point on the left is an interior point; the point on the right is a boundary point.

Definition 1.9. *If every $\vec{p} \in A$ is an interior point, we call A an* open set.

Example 1.10. $A = \left\{ \vec{x} \in \mathbb{R}^n \mid \vec{x} \neq \vec{0} \right\}$ is an open set. $\square$

Proposition 1.11. $A = D_R(\vec{0})$ *is an open set.*

Proof. If $\vec{p} = \vec{0}$, $D_r(\vec{0}) \subseteq A = D_R(\vec{0})$ provided $r \leq R$. So $\vec{p} = \vec{0}$ is interior to A. Consider any other $\vec{p} \in A$. It's evident that $D_r(\vec{p}) \subset A = D_R(\vec{0})$ provided that $0 \leq r \leq R - \|\vec{p}\|$. Therefore, $A = D_R(\vec{0})$ is an open set. $\square$

Example 1.12 (Figure 1.3). Suppose we use a Taxi Cab disks instead of a Euclidean disk. It does not change which points are interior to A since the diamond is inscribed in a circle. In other words,

$$D_r^{\text{taxi}}(\vec{p}) \subset D_r^{\text{Euclid}}(\vec{p})$$

$\square$

Definition 1.13. *The complement of set A is*

$$A^c = \{\vec{x} \mid \vec{x} \notin A\}$$

That is, A^c consists of all points which are not elements of A. Any point in $\mathbb{R}^n$ must belong either to A or to A^c, but never to both.

Using complements, we define a complementary notion to openness:

Definition 1.14. *A set A is* closed *if A^c is open.*

Notice that this does NOT mean that a set A is closed if it is not open. Sets are not doors: they don't have to be either open or closed. The open and closed sets are special, and not every set falls into one of the two categories. Here is a better way of understanding when a set is closed. First, we define the boundary of a set A:

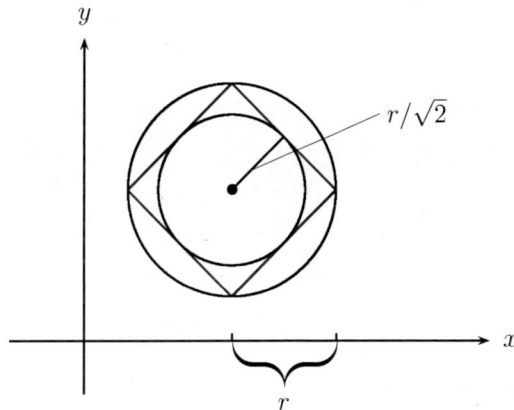

Figure 1.3. A disk with radius r constructed with the Euclidean norm inscribes the same disk constructed with the Taxi Cab norm. Furthermore, the disk constructed with the Taxi Cab norm inscribes a disk with radius $r/\sqrt{2}$ constructed with the Euclidean norm

Definition 1.15. $\vec{b}$ *is a* boundary point *of A (Figure 1.2) if for every* $r > 0$, $D_r(\vec{b})$ *contains both points in A and points not in A:*

$$D_r(\vec{b}) \cap A \neq \emptyset \ \text{ and } \ D_r(\vec{b}) \cap A^c \neq \emptyset$$

The boundary ∂A is the collection of all the boundary points of A.

In the example 1.11, the set of all boundary points of $A = D_R(\vec{0})$

$$\left\{ \vec{b} \,\middle|\, \|\vec{b}\| = R \right\}$$

is a sphere of radius R.

Notice that a boundary point of A can never be an interior point, and an interior point of A can never be in ∂A.

Theorem 1.16. *A is closed if and only if A contains all its boundary points.*

Example 1.17. Consider the following set:

$$A = \{(x_1, x_2) \in \mathbb{R}^2 \,\big|\, x_1 \geq 0, x_2 > 0\}$$

Not every point in A is an interior point. In fact, the interior points are the $\vec{p} = (p_1, p_2)$ where both $p_1 > 0, p_2 > 0$. To see this, apply the definition with $r = \min\{p_1, p_2\}$. Then, $D_r(\vec{p}) \subset A$.

On the other hand, any $\vec{p}$ that lies on either of the axes (including $\vec{0}$) is a boundary point. So none of the points on the segment $x_1 = 0$ (which are included in A are interior points, and hence A is not open.

On the other hand, points lying on the axis $x_2 = 0$ are boundary points of A but are not elements of A, and so A cannot be closed either. $\qquad\square$

1.3 Practice problems

1. Verify that the taxicab norm on $\mathbb{R}^2$, $\|\vec{x}\| = |x_1| + |x_2|$ satisfies the conditions which make it a valid norm, that is:

1. $\|\vec{x}\| = 0$ if and only if $\vec{x} = \vec{0}$;

2. $\|a\,\vec{x}\| = |a|\,\|\vec{x}\|$ for all $a \in \mathbb{R}$ and $\vec{x} \in \mathbb{R}^2$;

3. $\|\vec{x} + \vec{y}\| \le \|\vec{x}\| + \|\vec{y}\|$ for all $\vec{x}, \vec{y} \in \mathbb{R}^2$.

2. (a) Verify that the following identities hold for the Euclidean norm on $\mathbb{R}^n$, defined by:

$$\|\vec{x}\| = \sqrt{\vec{x} \cdot \vec{x}} = \sqrt{\sum_{j=1}^{n} x_j^2}$$

(i) [Paralellogram Law] $\|\vec{x} + \vec{y}\|^2 + \|\vec{x} - \vec{y}\|^2 = 2\|\vec{x}\|^2 + 2\|\vec{y}\|^2$;

(ii) [Polarization Identity] $\vec{x} \cdot \vec{y} = \dfrac{1}{4}\left(\|\vec{x} + \vec{y}\|^2 - \|\vec{x} - \vec{y}\|^2\right)$.

(b) Show that the Parallelogram Law becomes **false** if we replace the Euclidean norm on $\mathbb{R}^2$ by the Taxicab norm (as defined in problem 1.)

3. Let $U = \{(x_1, x_2) \in \mathbb{R}^2 : |x_2| \le x_1, \text{ and } x_1 > 0\}$. Find all interior points of U and all boundary points of U. Is U an open set? Is U a closed set?

4. Show each set is open, by showing every point $\vec{a} \in U$ is an interior point. [So you need to explicitly find a radius $r > 0$ so that $D_r(\vec{a}) \subset U$.]

(a) $U = \{(x_1, x_2) \in \mathbb{R}^2 : x_1^2 + x_2^2 > 0\}$;

(b) $U = \{(x_1, x_2) \in \mathbb{R}^2 : 1 < x_1^2 + x_2^2 < 4\}$.

Chapter 2

Functions of several variables

2.1 Limits and continuity

In this section, we will be considering vector valued functions such that

$$F : A \subseteq \mathbb{R}^n \to \mathbb{R}^k.$$

Using the matrix notation we can write:

$$F(x_1, x_2, \ldots, x_n) = \begin{bmatrix} F_1(x_1, x_2, \ldots, x_n) \\ F_2(x_1, x_2, \ldots, x_n) \\ \vdots \\ F_k(x_1, x_2, \ldots, x_n) \end{bmatrix}.$$

Example 2.1. Given a $(k \times n)$ matrix M, we can define the following function:

$$F(\vec{x}) = M\vec{x}.$$

This looks like a pretty special example, but it turns out to be an important one. And it gives a direct connection between calculus and matrices which we will exploit. □

The first order of business is to define what we mean by the limit of a function, and then we can define the notion of continuity. What does $\lim_{\vec{x} \to \vec{a}} F(\vec{x}) = \vec{L}$ mean? First, we start by noting that it is not sufficient to treat each variable, $x_1, x_2, \ldots x_n$, separately.

Example 2.2. Consider the following function:

$$F(x, y) = \frac{xy}{x^2 + 4y^2},$$

where $(x, y) \neq (0, 0)$.

We can try to find its limit at $(0, 0)$ by treating each variable separately.

$$\lim_{x \to 0} \left(\lim_{y \to 0} F(x, y) \right) = \lim_{x \to 0} \left(\frac{0}{x^2} \right) = \lim_{x \to 0} = 0$$

9

Similarly, we have

$$\lim_{y \to 0} \left(\lim_{x \to 0} F(x, y) \right) = 0$$

However, if we take $(x, y) \to (0, 0)$ along a straight line path with $y = mx$, where m is constant, we have

$$F(x, mx) = \frac{mx^2}{x^2 + 4m^2x^2} = \frac{m}{1 + 4m^2}$$

In this case, we have

$$\lim_{\substack{(x,y) \to (0,0) \\ \text{along } y = mx}} F(x, y) = \frac{m}{1 + 4m^2}$$

Therefore, $F(x, y)$ does not approach any particular value as $(x, y) \to (0, 0)$. $\square$

We can never show that the limit $\lim_{\vec{x} \to \vec{a}} F(\vec{x})$ exists using these kinds of arguments, but we can show that it **does not exist** by showing that the limit does not exist along certain directions, or that it gives different values when approaching $\vec{x} \to \vec{a}$ along different directions. Thus, we can say that $\lim_{\vec{x} \to \vec{a}} \frac{xy}{x^2+y^2}$ does not exist.

Example 2.3. Consider the following function:

$$F(x, y) = \frac{y^2}{x^4 + y^2}.$$

If we approach $(0, 0)$ along $y = mx$, the values of $F(x, y) = F(x, mx) \to 1$. However, if we approach along a parabola, $y = mx^2$, we obtain a limiting value of $m^2/(1 + m^2)$. We get different limits along different parabolas, and so the limit as $(x, y) \to (0, 0)$ does not exist. $\square$

From these examples we conclude that if there is to be a limit

$$\lim_{\vec{x} \to \vec{a}} F(\vec{x}) = \vec{b},$$

we must have a criterion which doesn't depend on the path or the direction in which $\vec{x}$ approaches $\vec{a}$, but only on *proximity*. In other words, we want $\|F(\vec{x}) - \vec{b}\|$ to go to zero as the distance $\|\vec{x} - \vec{a}\|$ goes to zero, regardless of the path taken in getting there.

Definition 2.4. *We say* $\lim_{\vec{x} \to \vec{a}} F(\vec{x}) = \vec{b}$ *if for any given* $\varepsilon > 0$, *there exists* $\delta > 0$ *such that whenever* $0 < \|\vec{x} - \vec{a}\| < \delta$, *we have* $\|F(x) - \vec{b}\| < \varepsilon$. *Therefore,*

$$\lim_{\vec{x} \to \vec{a}} F(x) = \vec{b} \iff \lim_{\vec{x} \to \vec{a}} \|F(\vec{x}) - \vec{b}\| = 0$$

Remark. We can state the definition equivalently in a geometrical form: for any given $\varepsilon > 0$, there exists a radius $\delta > 0$ such that

$$F(\vec{x}) \in D_\varepsilon(\vec{b}),$$

whenever $\vec{x} \in D_\delta(\vec{a})$ and $\vec{x} \neq \vec{a}$. $\square$

Before we look at an example, here's a useful observations. Take $\vec{v} = (v_1, v_2, \ldots, v_n) \in \mathbb{R}^n$. Then, we have

$$\|\vec{v}\| = \sqrt{\sum_{j=1}^{n} v_j^2} \geq \sqrt{v_i^2} = |v_i|$$

for each individual coordinate $i = 1, 2, \ldots, n$. So when applying the definition of the limit, we may use the following inequalities: for any $\vec{x}, \vec{a} \in \mathbb{R}^n$,

$$|x_i - a_i| \leq \|\vec{x} - \vec{a}\|, \tag{2.1}$$

for each $i = 1, \ldots, n$.

Example 2.5. Show

$$\lim_{(x,y)\to(0,0)} \frac{2x^2 y}{x^2 + y^2} = 0$$

Solution: We must set up the definition of the limit. Note that $F : \mathbb{R} \setminus \{\vec{0}\} \to \mathbb{R}$, which is real-valued, so we drop the vector symbols in the range (but not in the domain, which is $\mathbb{R}^2$!) Matching the notation of the definition, we have $b = 0$, $\vec{a} = (0,0)$. Call

$$R = \|\vec{x} - \vec{a}\| = \|\vec{x}\| = \sqrt{x^2 + y^2},$$

the distance from $\vec{x}$ to $\vec{a}$. By the above observation (2.1),

$$|x| \leq R, \qquad |y| \leq R.$$

Since $F(\vec{x}) \in \mathbb{R}$, the norm $\|F(\vec{x}) - \vec{b}\| = |F(\vec{x}) - 0|$ is just the absolute value. We now want to *estimate* the difference $|F(\vec{x}) - 0|$ and show that it is *bounded* by a quantity which depends only on R, and tends to zero as $R \to 0$. To do this, we find an *upper bound* for the numerator, and a *lower bound* for the denominator, as a fraction becomes larger when its numerator is increases, and its denominator is decreased. In this case, the denominator is exactly R^2, and so:

$$\begin{aligned}
|F(\vec{x}) - b| &= \left| \frac{2x^2 y}{x^2 + y^2} - 0 \right| \\
&= \frac{2|x|^2 |y|}{x^2 + y^2} \\
&\leq \frac{2 \cdot R^2 \cdot R}{R^2} \\
&= 2R \\
&= 2\|\vec{x} - \vec{a}\|
\end{aligned}$$

By letting $\|\vec{x} - \vec{a}\| = \|\vec{x}\| < \varepsilon/2$, we get $|F(\vec{x}) - 0| < \varepsilon$. Therefore, the definition is satisfied by choosing $\delta > 0$ to be any value with $0 < \delta \leq \varepsilon/2$ $\qquad \square$

Example 2.6. Consider the following function, $F : \mathbb{R}^3 \setminus \{\vec{0}\} \to \mathbb{R}$:

$$F(x, y, z) = \frac{3z^2 + 2x^2 + 4y^2 + 6z^2}{x^2 + 2y^2 + 3z^2}, \qquad (x, y, z) \neq (0, 0, 0)$$

Prove that

$$\lim_{(x,y,z) \to (0,0,0)} F(x, y, z) = 2.$$

Solution: In analogy with the previous example, let $R = \|(x, y, z) - (0, 0, 0)\| = \sqrt{x^2 + y^2 + z^2}$. We use the "common denominator" to write the desired quantity as a fraction, and estimate as before:

$$\begin{aligned}
\|F(x, y, z) - \vec{b}\| &= |F(x, y, z) - 2| \\
&= \left| \frac{3z^3 + 2x^2 + 4y^2 + 6z^2}{x^2 + 2y^2 + 3z^2} - 2 \right| \\
&= \frac{3|z|^3}{x^2 + 2y^2 + 3z^2} \\
&\leq \frac{3R^3}{x^2 + y^2 + z^2} \\
&= \frac{3R^3}{R^2} \\
&= 3R
\end{aligned}$$

Then,

$$\|F(x, y, z) - \vec{b}\| < 3R < \varepsilon$$

provided that

$$R = \|\vec{x} - \vec{0}\| < \delta = \frac{\varepsilon}{3}$$

$\square$

Example 2.7. Consider the following function, $F : \mathbb{R}^2 \setminus \{\vec{0}\} \to \mathbb{R}$:

$$F(x, y) = \frac{(\sin^3 x)(y + 2)^2}{[x^2 + (y + 2)^2]^2}, \qquad (x, y) \neq (0, -2)$$

Prove that

$$\lim_{(x,y) \to (0,-2)} F(x, y) = 0.$$

In this example $\vec{a} = (0, -2)$, so the important distance is

$$R = \|\vec{x} - \vec{a}\| = \|(x, y) - (0, -2)\| = \sqrt{x^2 + (y + 2)^2},$$

that is we want to show that for any $\epsilon > 0$ we can find $\delta > 0$ so that if $0 < R = \|(x, y) - (0, -2)\| < \delta$, then $|F(x, y) - 0| < \epsilon$. Notice that

$$|x| = \sqrt{x^2} \leq \sqrt{x^2 + (y + 2)^2} \quad \text{and} \quad |y + 2| = \sqrt{(y + 2)^2} \leq \sqrt{x^2 + (y + 2)^2},$$

and also $|\sin x| \leq |x| \leq R$. The denominator is exactly $[x^2+(y+2)^2]^2 = \|\vec{x}-(0,-2)\|^4 = R^4$, and so we may estimate the desired quantity,

$$|F(x,y) - 0| = \left| \frac{(\sin^3 x)(y+2)^2}{[x^2 + (y+2)^2]^2} \right| = \frac{|\sin x|^3 |y+2|^2}{[x^2 + (y+2)^2]^2} \leq \frac{R^3 R^2}{R^4} = R.$$

Taking $\delta = \epsilon$, if $0 < \|\vec{x} - (0,-2)\| = R < \delta = \epsilon$, then $|F(x,y) - 0| < \epsilon$, as needed.

We are now ready to define continuity. A continuous function is one whose limits coincide with the value the function at the limit vector:

Definition 2.8. *Consider a function $F : \mathbb{R}^n \to \mathbb{R}^k$ with domain $A \subseteq \mathbb{R}^n$. For $\vec{a} \in A$, we say F is* continuous *at $\vec{a}$ in the domain of F iff*

$$F(a) = \lim_{\vec{x} \to \vec{a}} F(\vec{x})$$

Example 2.9. Going back to example 2.6, if we redefine F as follows,

$$F(x,y,z) = \begin{cases} \dfrac{3z^2 + 2x^2 + 4y^2 + 6z^2}{x^2 + 2y^2 + 3z^2} & (x,y,z) \neq (0,0,0) \\ 2 & (x,y,z) = (0,0,0) \end{cases}$$

then F is continuous at $(0,0,0)$ (and at all $\vec{x} \in \mathbb{R}$). $\qquad\qquad\qquad\qquad\qquad\square$

If F is continuous at every $\vec{a} \in A$, $(\forall \vec{x} \in A)$, we say F is continuous on the set A. Continuity is always preserved by the usual algebraic operations: sum. product, quotient, and composition of continuous functions is continuous.

2.2   Differentiability

You're used to thinking of the derivative as another function, "derived" from the original one, which gives numerical values of the rate of change (slope of the tangent line) of the function. But having a derivative is a property of the function, a measure of how smoothly the values of the function vary, and so we talk about "differentiability", the ability of the function to be differentiated at all.

Let's recall how the derivative was defined for functions of one variable, because it's the basic idea which we'll return to:

Definition 2.10. *For a function $f : \mathbb{R} \to \mathbb{R}$, its* derivative *is defined as*

$$f'(x) = \lim_{h \to 0} \frac{f(x+h) - f(x)}{h}.$$

If it exists, we say f is differentiable *at x.*

Differentiability is a *stronger* property than continuity:

Theorem 2.11. *If $f : \mathbb{R} \to \mathbb{R}$ is differentiable at x, then $f(x)$ is also continuous at x.*

Differentiable functions, $f(x)$, are well approximated by their tangent lines (also known as linearization). We wish to extend this idea to $F : \mathbb{R}^n \to \mathbb{R}^m$.

First, we can try dealing with independent variables, $x_1, x_2, \ldots, x_n$, one at a time by using partial derivatives. We start by introducing the standard basis in $\mathbb{R}^n$:

$$\vec{e}_1 = (1, 0, 0, \ldots, 0)$$
$$\vec{e}_2 = (0, 1, 0, \ldots, 0)$$
$$\vdots$$
$$\vec{e}_n = (0, 0, 0, \ldots, 1)$$

In particular, we have the usual $\vec{e}_1 = \vec{i}, \vec{e}_2 = \vec{j}, \vec{e}_3 = \vec{k}$ in $\mathbb{R}^3$.

For any $\vec{x} \in \mathbb{R}^n$, and $h \in \mathbb{R}$, $(\vec{x} + h\vec{e}_j)$ moves from $\vec{x}$ parallel to the x_j axis by distance h. In other words,

$$\vec{x} + h\vec{e}_j = (x_1, x_2, \ldots, x_j + h, x_{j+1}, \ldots, x_n).$$

Definition 2.12. *A partial derivative of $f(x)$ with respect to x_j is defined as*

$$\frac{\partial f}{\partial x_j}(\vec{x}) = \lim_{h \to 0} \frac{f(\vec{x} + h\vec{e}_j) - f(\vec{x})}{h},$$

for all $j = 1, 2, \ldots, n$ (provided the limit exists.)

A partial derivative of function is calculated by treating of $\vec{x}_j$ as the only variable, and all others treated as constants. For a vector valued function $F : \mathbb{R}^n \to \mathbb{R}^m$,

$$F(\vec{x}) = \begin{bmatrix} F_1(\vec{x}) \\ F_2(\vec{x}) \\ \vdots \\ F_m(\vec{x}) \end{bmatrix},$$

we treat each component $F_i(\vec{x}) : \mathbb{R}^n \to \mathbb{R}$ separately as a real valued function. Each has n partial derivatives, and so $F : \mathbb{R}^n \to \mathbb{R}^m$ has $(m \times n)$ partial derivatives, which form an $(m \times n)$ matrix, the <u>Jacobian matrix</u> or <u>total derivative</u> matrix,

$$DF(\vec{x}) = \left(\frac{\partial F_i}{\partial x_j} \right)_{\substack{i=1,2,\ldots,m \\ j=1,2,\ldots,n}}.$$

Be careful: each row (with fixed i and $j = 1, \ldots, n$) corresponds to the partial derivatives of one component $F_i(\vec{x})$. Each column (with fixed j and $i = 1, \ldots, m$) corresponds to differentiating the vector $F(\vec{x})$ with respect to one independent variable, x_j. That is, we count the components of F top to bottom, and the independent variables' derivatives left to right.

Example 2.13. Consider a function $F : \mathbb{R}^2 \to \mathbb{R}^3$:

$$F(\vec{x}) = \begin{bmatrix} x_1^2 \\ x_1 x_2 \\ x_2^4 \end{bmatrix}.$$

Jacobian of the function is given by

$$DF(\vec{x}) = \begin{bmatrix} \frac{\partial F_1}{\partial x_1} & \frac{\partial F_1}{\partial x_2} \\ \frac{\partial F_2}{\partial x_1} & \frac{\partial F_2}{\partial x_2} \\ \frac{\partial F_3}{\partial x_1} & \frac{\partial F_3}{\partial x_2} \end{bmatrix}$$

$$= \begin{bmatrix} 2x_1 & 0 \\ x_2 & x_1 \\ 0 & 4x_2^3 \end{bmatrix}$$

$\square$

The question now is whether the derivative matrix $DF(\vec{x})$ gives us the same information and properties as the ordinary derivative did in single-value calculus. The following example shows that we must be more careful with functions of several variables:

Example 2.14. Consider the following function:

$$f(x,y) = \begin{cases} \frac{xy}{(x^2+y^2)^2}, & (x,y) \neq (0,0) \\ 0, & (x,y) = (0,0) \end{cases}$$

Do partial derivatives exist at $(0,0)$?

By definition,

$$\frac{\partial f}{\partial x}(0,0) = \lim_{h \to 0} \frac{f(0+h,0) - f(0,0)}{h}$$

$$= \lim_{h \to 0} \frac{\frac{h \cdot 0}{(h^2+0^2)^2} - 0}{h}$$

$$= \lim_{h \to 0} \frac{0}{h} = 0$$

Similarly, $\frac{\partial f}{\partial y}(0,0) = 0$ by symmetry of x, y. Therefore,

$$Df(0,0) = \begin{bmatrix} 0 & 0 \end{bmatrix}$$

Although partial derivatives exist, f is not cotinuous at $(0,0)$. (For example, $f(x, mx) \to \pm\infty$ as $x \to 0^{\pm}$ for $m \neq 0$). $\square$

By the previous example, we see that the mere existence of the partial derivatives is not a very strong property for a function of several variables; despite the existence of the partial derivatives, the function isn't even continuous at $\vec{x} = \vec{0}$. So it's doubtful that the partial derivatives are giving us very significant information as to the smoothness of the function in this example. A "differentiable" function should at least be continuous.

To get a reasonable information from $Df(\vec{x})$, we need to ask for more than just its existence. To understand what is needed, let's go back to $f : \mathbb{R} \to \mathbb{R}$. We rewrite the derivative at $x = a$, making the substitution $h = x - a$ in the definition, so that

$$f'(a) = \lim_{x \to a} \frac{f(x) - f(a)}{x - a}.$$

Equivalently, we have:

$$0 = \lim_{x \to a} \left(\frac{f(x) - f(z)}{x - a} - f'(x) \right)$$

$$= \lim_{x \to a} \left(\frac{f(x) - \overbrace{[f(a) + f'(x)(x - a)]}^{L_a(x)}}{x - a} \right) = 0,$$

where $L_a(x) = f(a) + f'(x)(x - a)$ is the *linearization* of f at a, the equation of the tangent plane to $y = f(x)$ at $x = a$. Thus, the difference between the value of $f(x)$ and its tangent plane $L_a(x)$ is very small compared to the distance $(x - a)$ of x to a. In other words, f is differentiable at x if its linear approximation gives an estimate of the value $f(x + h)$ to within an error which is small compared to $\Delta x = x - a$.

This is the attribute of the one-dimensional derivative which we want to extend to higher dimensions. Let's make the analogy. For $F : \mathbb{R}^n \to \mathbb{R}^m$, $F(\vec{x})$ has $(m \times n)$ partial derivates (see definition 2.12). Then, the linearization of F at $\vec{a}$ is

$$L_{\vec{a}}(\vec{x}) = \underbrace{F(\vec{a})}_{m \times 1} + \underbrace{DF(\vec{a})}_{m \times n} \underbrace{(\vec{x} - \vec{a})}_{n \times 1}.$$

So, $L : \mathbb{R}^n \to \mathbb{R}^m$, just like F. The derivative matrix $DF(\vec{a})$ is a *linear transformation* of $\mathbb{R}^n \to \mathbb{R}^m$.

Notice that when $n = 2$ and $m = 1$, For $F : \mathbb{R}^2 \to \mathbb{R}$, we have

$$DF(\vec{a}) = \begin{bmatrix} \frac{\partial F}{\partial x_1}(\vec{a}) & \frac{\partial F}{\partial x_2}(\vec{a}) \end{bmatrix},$$

a (1×2) row vector and

$$\vec{x} - \vec{a} = \begin{bmatrix} x_1 - a_1 \\ x_2 - a_2 \end{bmatrix},$$

so we have

$$L_{\vec{a}}(\vec{x}) = F(\vec{a}) + \frac{\partial F}{\partial x_1}(x_1 - a_1) + \frac{\partial F}{\partial x_2}(x_2 - a_2),$$

a familiar equation of the tangent plane to $z = F(x_1, x_2)$.

We're now ready to introduce the idea of differentiability:

Definition 2.15 (Differentiability). *We say $F : \mathbb{R}^n \to \mathbb{R}^m$ is differentiable if*

$$\lim_{\vec{x} \to \vec{a}} \frac{\|F(\vec{x}) - F(\vec{a}) - DF(\vec{a})(\vec{x} - \vec{a})\|}{\|\vec{x} - \vec{a}\|} = 0.$$

Equivalently,

$$\lim_{\vec{h} \to \vec{0}} \frac{\|F(\vec{x} + \vec{h}) - F(\vec{x}) - DF(\vec{x})\vec{h}\|}{\|\vec{h}\|} = 0$$

In summary, F is differentiable if $\|F(\vec{x}) - L_{\vec{a}}(\vec{x})\|$ is small compared to $\|\vec{x} - \vec{a}\|$, or if $F(\vec{x})$ is approximated by $L_{\vec{a}}(\vec{x})$ with an error which is much smaller than $\|\vec{x} - \vec{a}\|$.

There is a very useful notation to express this idea that one quantity is very small compare to another, the "little-o" notation. We write $o(h)$, "little-oh of h", for a quantity which is small compred to h., in the sense

$$g(h) = o(h) \iff \lim_{h \to 0} \frac{g(h)}{h} = 0.$$

Using this notation, differentiability can be written as

$$\|F(\vec{x}) - [F(\vec{a}) + DF(\vec{a})(\vec{x} - \vec{a})]\| = o(\|\vec{x} - \vec{a}\|). \tag{2.2}$$

Example 2.16. Is the following function differentiable at $\vec{a} = \vec{0}$?

$$F(x_1, x_2) = \begin{cases} \dfrac{x_2^2 \sin x_1}{\sqrt{x_1^2 + x_2^2}}, & \vec{x} \neq \vec{0} \\ 0, & \vec{x} = \vec{0} \end{cases}$$

Solution: First, we have

$$\frac{\partial F}{\partial x_1}(\vec{0}) = \lim_{h \to 0} \frac{F(\vec{0} + h\vec{e}_1) - F(\vec{0})}{h}$$
$$= \lim_{h \to 0} \frac{0 - 0}{h} = 0$$

Similarly, we have

$$\frac{\partial F}{\partial x_2}(\vec{0}) = 0$$

So we have

$$DF(\vec{0}) = \begin{bmatrix} \frac{\partial F}{\partial x_1} & \frac{\partial F}{\partial x_2} \end{bmatrix} = \begin{bmatrix} 0 & 0 \end{bmatrix}$$

For differentiability, we have to look at:

$$\left| \frac{x_2^2 \sin x_1}{\sqrt{x_1^2 + x_2^2}} - 0 - \begin{bmatrix} 0 & 0 \end{bmatrix} \cdot \begin{bmatrix} x_1 \\ x_2 \end{bmatrix} \right|$$
$$= \frac{x_2^2 |\sin x_1|}{\sqrt{x_1^2 + x_2^2}}$$

Then,

$$\frac{|F(\vec{x}) - L_{\vec{0}}(\vec{x})|}{\|\vec{x} - \vec{0}\|} = \frac{x_2^2 |\sin x_1|}{\left(\sqrt{x_1^2 + x_2^2} \right)^2} = \frac{x_2^2 |\sin x_1|}{x_1^2 + x_2^2}$$
$$\leq \frac{R^2 \cdot R}{R^2} = R = \|\vec{x} - \vec{0}\|$$

By the squeeze theorem, we have

$$\lim_{\vec{x} \to \vec{0}} \frac{|F(\vec{x}) - L_{\vec{0}}(\vec{x})|}{\|\vec{x} - \vec{0}\|} = 0$$

Therefore, F is differentiable at $\vec{x} = \vec{0}$ □

Example 2.17. Verify that F is differentiable at $\vec{a} = \vec{0}$.

$$F(\vec{x}) = \begin{bmatrix} 1 + x_1 + x_2^2 \\ 2x_2 - x_1^2 \end{bmatrix}$$

First, note that

$$F(\vec{a}) = F(\vec{0}) = \begin{bmatrix} 1 \\ 0 \end{bmatrix}$$

We also need to compute the Jacobian at $\vec{0}$:

$$DF(\vec{0}) = \begin{bmatrix} 1 & 0 \\ 0 & 2 \end{bmatrix}$$

Then, we get the following linearization of the function:

$$\begin{aligned} L_{\vec{0}}(\vec{x}) &= F(\vec{0}) + DF(\vec{x})(\vec{x} - \vec{0}) \\ &= \begin{bmatrix} 1 \\ 0 \end{bmatrix} + \begin{bmatrix} 1 & 0 \\ 0 & 2 \end{bmatrix} \begin{bmatrix} x_1 \\ x_2 \end{bmatrix} \\ &= \begin{bmatrix} 1 + x_1 \\ 2x_2 \end{bmatrix} \end{aligned}$$

Then, to verify the definition of differentiabiility we estimate the quotient,

$$\frac{\|F(\vec{x}) - L_{\vec{0}}(\vec{x})\|}{\|\vec{x} - \vec{0}\|} = \frac{\left\| \begin{bmatrix} x_2^2 \\ -x_1^2 \end{bmatrix} \right\|}{\|\vec{x}\|} = \frac{\sqrt{x_2^4 + x_1^4}}{\sqrt{x_1^2 + x_2^2}} \leq \frac{\sqrt{R^4 + R^4}}{R} = \sqrt{2}R = \sqrt{2}\|\vec{x} - \vec{0}\|,$$

where we have used $x_1^4 \leq R^4$ and $x_2 \leq R^4$, with $R = \sqrt{x_1^2 + x_2^2}$.

As $\vec{x} \to \vec{0}$, $\|\vec{x} - \vec{0}\| = R \to 0$, by the squeeze theorem, the desired limit goes to 0. Therefore, F is differentiable at $\vec{0}$.   □

Verifying differentiability can involve quite a bit of work, but fortunately there is a powerful theorem which makes differentiability much easier to show.

Theorem 2.18. *Suppose $F : \mathbb{R}^n \to \mathbb{R}^m$, and $\vec{a} \in \mathbb{R}^n$. If there exists a disk $D_r(\vec{a})$ in which* **all** *the partial derivatives $\partial(F_i(\vec{x}))/\partial x_j$ exist and are continuous, then F is differentiable at $\vec{x} = \vec{a}$.*

So it's enough to calculate the partial derivatives and verify that each one is a continuous function, and then we can conclude that the function is differentiable, without going through the definition! It's convenient to give this property a name:

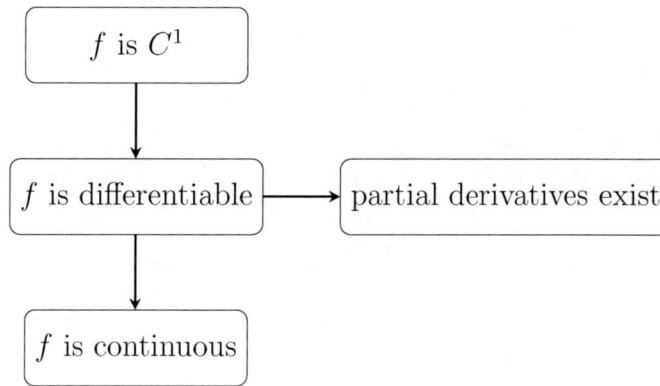

Figure 2.1. Relationship between differentiability and continuity

Definition 2.19. *Suppose* $F : \mathbb{R}^n \to \mathbb{R}^m$, *and* $\vec{a} \in \mathbb{R}^n$. *If there exists a disk* $D_r(\vec{a})$ *in which* **all** *the partial derivatives* $\partial(F_i(\vec{x}))/\partial x_j$ *exist and are continuous, then we say that* F *is* continuously differentiable, *or* C^1, *at* $\vec{x} = \vec{a}$. *If* F *is continuously differentiable at all points* $\vec{x} \in A$, *we say that* F *is continuously differentiable on* A, *or* $F \in C^1(A)$.

So far as our example, we calculate the partial for $\vec{x} \neq \vec{0}$:

$$\frac{\partial F}{\partial x_1} = x_2^2 \left(\cos x_1 \left(x_1^2 + x_2^2 \right)^{-\frac{1}{2}} + \left(-\frac{1}{2} \left(x_1^2 + x_2^2 \right)^{-\frac{3}{2}} 2x_1 \right) \sin x_1 \right)$$

$$= \frac{x_2^2}{(x_1^2 + x_2^2)^{3/2}} \left[\cos x_1 \left(x_1^2 + x_2^2 \right) - x_1 \sin x_1 \right].$$

This is a quotient of sums, products, and compositions of continuous functions as long as the denominator is not zero (that is, when $(x_1, x_2) \neq (0,0)$,) and therefore it is continuous. I invite you to calculate $\frac{\partial F}{\partial x_2}$, which has a similar form and is also continuous for all $(x_1, x_2) \neq (0,0)$. By definition, F is C^1 at all $\vec{x} \neq \vec{0}$, so by Theorem 2.18 we conclude that F is differentiable at all points in its domain.

We summarize the ideas in this chapter in Figure 2.1. A function which is continuously differentiable is automatically differentiable (by Theorem 2.18.) A function which is differentiable must be continuous. However, none of these definitions are equivalent. There are continuous functions which are not differentiable. There are also functions with partial derivatives existing but the function is discontinuous. And there are differentiable functions which are not C^1.

2.3   Chain rule

As in single-variable calculus, the composition of differentiable functions is differentiable, and we have a convenient formula for calculating the derivative.

Let's be a little careful about domains. Suppose $A \subseteq \mathbb{R}^n$ and $B \subseteq \mathbb{R}^m$ are open sets, $F : A \subseteq \mathbb{R}^n \to \mathbb{R}^m$ with $F(A) \subseteq B$, that is

$$F(\vec{x}) \in B \text{ for all } \vec{x} \in A,$$

and $G : B \subset \mathbb{R}^m \to \mathbb{R}^p$. Then, we define the *composition* $H : A \subset \mathbb{R}^n \to \mathbb{R}^p$ via

$$H(\vec{x}) = G \circ F(\vec{x}) = G\left(F(\vec{x})\right).$$

As in single-variable calculus, the composition of continuous functions is continuous:

Theorem 2.20. *Let* $F : A \subseteq \mathbb{R}^n \to \mathbb{R}^m$ *be continuous at* $\vec{a} \in A$, *and* $G : B \subseteq \mathbb{R}^m \to \mathbb{R}^p$ *be continuous at* $\vec{b} = F(\vec{a}) \in B$. *Then the function* $H = G \circ F$ *is continuous at* $\vec{a}$.

This is not hard to show, using the $\delta - \epsilon$ definition of the derivative, but we leave it for a later course. Here we are more concerned with differentiation of vector-valued functions.

Example 2.21. This may seem like a overly simple example, but it is an important one. Consider the case where F and G are *linear* maps,

$$\begin{cases} F(\vec{x}) = M\vec{x} & M \text{ an } (m \times n) \text{ matrix} \\ G(\vec{y}) = N\vec{y} & N \text{ an } (p \times m) \text{ matrix} \end{cases}$$

Then,

$$H(\vec{x}) = G\left(F(\vec{x})\right) = NM\vec{x}$$

is also a linear function, which is represented by the product NM. (Recall that the order of multiplication matters a lot!) $\qquad\square$

In fact this example leads right into the general form of the chain rule for compositions in higher dimensions. Recall that however nonlinear the functions F and G are, their derivatives are matrices!

Theorem 2.22. *Assume* $F : \mathbb{R}^n \to \mathbb{R}^m$ *is differentiable at* $\vec{x} = \vec{a}$ *and* $G : \mathbb{R}^m \to \mathbb{R}^p$ *is differentiable at* $\vec{b} = F(\vec{a})$. *Then,* $H = G \circ F$ *is differentiable at* $\vec{x} = \vec{a}$ *and*

$$DH(\vec{a}) = \underbrace{DG(\vec{b})}_{DG(F(\vec{a}))} DF(\vec{a})$$

The product above is matrix multiplication, so be careful of the order of multiplication. Unless the matrices are both square (which will only happen when the dimensions $n = m = p$,) you may not be able to multiply them in the wrong order, but be very careful anyway.

Note that all of the various forms of chain rule done in first year calculus (and explained by complicated tree diagrams) can be derived directly from this general formula. So the tree diagrams used in Stewart are just imitating the natural structure of matrix multiplication!

Finally, we point out that the Chain Rule is more than just a formula: it also contains the information that the composition $H = G \circ F$ is differentiable at $\vec{a}$, provided F is differentiable at $\vec{a}$ and G is differentiable at $\vec{b} = F(\vec{a})$.

Example 2.23. Consider the following functions, $F : \mathbb{R}^3 \to \mathbb{R}^2$ and $G : \mathbb{R}^2 \to \mathbb{R}^2$:

$$F(\vec{x}) = \begin{bmatrix} x_1^2 + x_2 x_3 \\ x_1^2 + x_3^2 \end{bmatrix}, G(\vec{y}) = \begin{bmatrix} -y_2^3 \\ y_1 + y_2 \end{bmatrix}$$

Let $H = G \circ F(\vec{x})$. Find $DH(\vec{a})$ where $\vec{a} = (1, -1, 0)$.

First, when $\vec{a} = (1, -1, 0)$, $\vec{b} = F(\vec{a}) = (1, 1)$. Now,

$$DF(\vec{x}) = \begin{bmatrix} 2x_1 & x_3 & x_2 \\ 2x_1 & 0 & 2x_3 \end{bmatrix}, DF(1, -1, 0) = \begin{bmatrix} 2 & 0 & -1 \\ 2 & 0 & 0 \end{bmatrix}$$

Similarly, we have

$$DG(\vec{y}) = \begin{bmatrix} 0 & -3y_2 \\ 1 & 1 \end{bmatrix}, DG(1, 1) = \begin{bmatrix} 0 & -3 \\ 1 & 1 \end{bmatrix}$$

As each entry of $DF(\vec{x})$, $DG(\vec{y})$ (the partial derivatives of F, G) is a continuous function for every $\vec{x}, \vec{y}$, both F, G are C^1 and hence are differentiable, by Theorem 2.18 they are differentiable. By Chain Rule, we get

$$DH(1, -1, 0) = DG(1, 1)DF(1, -1, 0)$$

$$= \begin{bmatrix} 0 & -3 \\ 1 & 1 \end{bmatrix} \begin{bmatrix} 2 & 0 & -1 \\ 2 & 0 & 0 \end{bmatrix}$$

$$= \begin{bmatrix} -6 & 0 & 0 \\ 4 & 0 & -1 \end{bmatrix}$$

$\square$

A complete proof of the Chain Rule is a bit complicated, but we can give an idea of why it works by using the definition of the derivative, written in the form (2.2). Call $\vec{u} = F(\vec{x})$, for $\vec{x}$ in a neighborhood of $\vec{a}$. Since G is differentiable at $\vec{b} = F(\vec{a})$, we have

$$H(\vec{x}) = G(F(\vec{x}) = G(\vec{u})$$

$$= G(\vec{b}) + DG(\vec{b}) \left[\vec{u} - \vec{b} \right] + E_1, \tag{2.3}$$

with an error $E_1 = o(\|\vec{u} - \vec{b}\|)$. Now, since F is differentiable at $\vec{a}$, we have

$$\vec{u} - \vec{b} = F(\vec{x}) - F(\vec{a}) = DF(\vec{a}) \left[\vec{x} - \vec{a} \right] + E_2, \tag{2.4}$$

with an error $E_2 = o(\|\vec{x} - \vec{a}\|)$. This is where we have to be a little tricky: from (2.4) we do two things. The first is that $E_1 = o(\|\vec{u} - \vec{b}\|) = o(\|\vec{x} - \vec{a}\|)$ is also small compared with $\|\vec{x} - \vec{a}\|$, and the second is that we can substitute into (2.3) to obtain:

$$H(\vec{x}) = G(\vec{b}) + DG(\vec{b}) \left[DF(\vec{a}) (\vec{x} - \vec{a}) + E_2 \right] + E_1$$

$$= H(\vec{a}) + DG(\vec{b}) DF(\vec{a}) (\vec{x} - \vec{a}) + o(\|\vec{x} - \vec{a}\|),$$

that is,

$$H(\vec{x}) - H(\vec{a}) - DG(\vec{b}) DF(\vec{a}) (\vec{x} - \vec{a}) = o(\|\vec{x} - \vec{a}\|).$$

By the definition of the derivative, H is differentiable at $\vec{a}$, with Jacobian (total derivative) given by the matrix product, $DH(\vec{a}) = DG(\vec{b}) DF(\vec{a})$.

2.4 Practice problems

1. Prove each of the following using the definition of the limit. (To show the limit does not exist, it is enough to consider the limit along different paths.)

(a) $\displaystyle\lim_{\vec{x}\to\vec{0}} \frac{x_1^6}{x_1^6 + 3x_2^2}$ does not exist.

(b) $\displaystyle\lim_{\vec{x}\to\vec{0}} \frac{x_1^3 x_2^2}{[x_1^2 + x_2^2]^2} = 0.$

(c) $\displaystyle\lim_{\vec{x}\to(1,2)} \frac{(x_1-1)^2(x_2-2)^2}{[(x_1-1)^2 + (x_2-2)^2]^{\frac{3}{2}}} = 0$

2. Let $F(x,y) = \dfrac{xy^2}{(x^2+y^2)^2}$ for $(x,y) \neq (0,0)$ and $f(0,0) = 0$.

(a) Show that $\dfrac{\partial f}{\partial x}(0,0), \dfrac{\partial f}{\partial y}(0,0)$ both exist.

(b) Show that f is not continuous at $(0,0)$.

3. Let M be a $k \times n$ matrix, and define $F(\vec{x}) = M\vec{x}$ (ie, via matrix multiplication, with $\vec{x}$ as a column vector.) Use the definition of differentiability to show that F is differentiable at all $\vec{x} \in \mathbb{R}^n$, and $DF(\vec{x}) = M$.

4. Let $F : \mathbb{R}^2 \to \mathbb{R}^3$ be defined by

$$F(\vec{x}) = \begin{bmatrix} x_1 \cos x_2 \\ x_1 x_2^2 \\ e^{-x_2} x_1 \end{bmatrix}$$

Find $DF(\vec{x})$. Calculate the linearization $L_{\vec{a}}(\vec{x})$ around $\vec{a} = (1,0)$.

5. Let $F : \mathbb{R}^2 \to \mathbb{R}^2$, $G : \mathbb{R}^2 \to \mathbb{R}^2$, defined by

$$F(r,\theta) = \begin{bmatrix} r\cos\theta \\ r\sin\theta \end{bmatrix}, \qquad G(x,y) = \begin{bmatrix} 2xy \\ y^2 - x^2 \end{bmatrix}$$

and let $H = G \circ F$. Explain why F, G, and H are all differentiable, and use the chain rule to calculate $DH(\sqrt{2}, \frac{\pi}{4})$.

6. Justify the approximation

$$\ln(1 + 2x_1 + 4x_2) = 2x_1 + 4x_2 + o(\|\vec{x}\|)$$

for $\vec{x}$ close to $\vec{0}$.

Chapter 3

Paths, directional derivative, and gradient

In this section we use the chain rule to explore two very common (and complementary) situations,

- parametrized paths, $\vec{c} : \mathbb{R} \to \mathbb{R}^n$, for which the domain is one-dimensional;

- real-valued $f : \mathbb{R}^n \to \mathbb{R}$, which are functions of $n \geq 2$ variables but are scalar-valued.

In fact, we will use paths as a tool to derive some qualitative facts about functions of several variables.

3.1   Paths and curves

We start with paths, which parametrize curves in $\mathbb{R}^n$. First, recall that an *interval* is a connected set in the real line, which includes the open intervals (a, b), $(-\infty, b)$, (a, ∞), or $(-\infty, \infty) = \mathbb{R}$; the closed intervals $[a, b]$, $[a, \infty)$, $(-\infty, b]$ (which include endpoints); or intervals like $(a, b]$ which are neither open nor closed.

Definition 3.1. *Let $I \subseteq \mathbb{R}$ be an interval. A* path *$\vec{c} : I \subseteq \mathbb{R} \to \mathbb{R}^n$ is a vector-valued function of a scalar independent variable, usually, t:*

$$\vec{c}(t) = \begin{bmatrix} c_1(t) \\ c_2(t) \\ \vdots \\ c_n(t) \end{bmatrix}$$

The path $\vec{c}(t)$ can be thought of as a vector (or a point, representing the tip of the vector) moving in time t. The moving point traces out a **curve** in $\mathbb{R}^n$ as t increases, and thus we use paths to attach functions (the moving coordinates) to a geometrical object, a curve in space. Note that this is not the only way to describe a curve:

23

Example 3.2. A unit circle in $\mathbb{R}^2$ described as a path is

$$\vec{c}(t) = (\cos t, \sin t),$$

where $t \in [0, 2\pi)$. But we could also describe the unit circle *non-parametrically* as

$$x^2 + y^2 = 1$$

We will talk about such non-parametric curves and surfaces in a later chapter.

Note that the same curve can be described by different paths. Going back to unit circle, we can also write

$$\vec{b}(t) = \left(\sin(t^2), \cos(t^2)\right), \qquad t \in [0, \sqrt{2\pi}).$$

Using different paths can change (1) time dynamics and (2) direction of the curve. This curve has a non-constant speed and reversed *orientation*, that is, the path $\vec{c}(t)$ traces the circle counter-clockwise while $\vec{b}(t)$ draws it clockwise. $\qquad\square$

If $\vec{c}$ is differentiable, $D\vec{c}(t)$ is an $(n \times 1)$ matrix. Since each component $\vec{c}_j(t)$ is a real-valued function of only one variable, the *partial-derivative* is the usual (or ordinary) derivative:

$$\frac{\partial c_j}{\partial t} = \frac{dc_j}{dt} = c'_j(t) = \lim_{h \to 0} \frac{c_j(t + h) - c_j(t)}{h}$$

So $D\vec{c}(t) = \vec{c}'(t)$ is written as a column vector:

$$D\vec{c}(t) = \begin{bmatrix} c'_1(t) \\ c'_2(t) \\ \vdots \\ c'_3(t) \end{bmatrix}$$

$$= \lim_{h \to 0} \frac{\vec{c}(t + h) - \vec{c}(t)}{h}$$

which is a vector which is tangent to the curve traced out at $\vec{x} = \vec{x}(t)$. Physically, $\vec{c}'(t)$ is the velocity vector for motion along the path (Figure 3.1).

Example 3.3 (Lines). Given two points, $\vec{p}_1, \vec{p}_2 \in \mathbb{R}^n$, there is a unique line connecting them. One path which represents this line is

$$\vec{c}(t) = \vec{p}_1 + t\vec{v},$$

where $\vec{v} = \vec{p}_2 - \vec{p}_1$. Velocity is then given by $\vec{c}'(t) = \vec{v}$, a constant. $\qquad\square$

A path, $\vec{c}(t)$, is continuous (or differentiable, or C^1,) provided that each of the components $c_j(t)$, $j = 1, 2, \ldots, n$ is continuous (or differentiable, or C^1.) Note that $\{\vec{c}(t) : t \in [a, b]\}$ traces out a curve in $\mathbb{R}^n$, with initial endpoint, $\vec{a}$, and final endpoint, $\vec{b}$. The path $\vec{c}(t)$ *parameterizes* the curve drawn out.

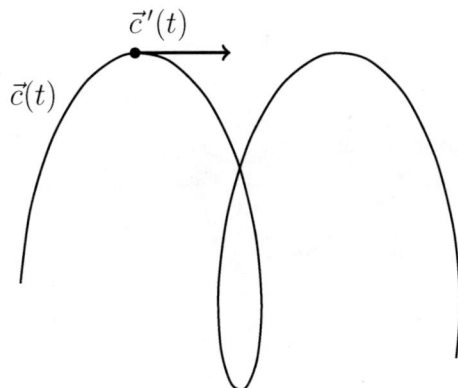

Figure 3.1. $\vec{c}'(t)$ is the velocity vector for motion along the path $\vec{c}(t)$. It is always tangent to $\vec{c}(t)$.

Recall that for any function $F : \mathbb{R}^k \to \mathbb{R}^n$, differentiability means that linearization at $\vec{a} \in \mathbb{R}^k$ gives a good approximation to the function itself. For a differentiable path, the linearization at $t = a \in \mathbb{R}$ is the path

$$\ell_a(t) = \vec{c}(a) + D\vec{c}(a)\,[t-a] = \vec{c}(a) + \vec{c}'(a) \cdot [t-a],$$

which is a straight line through the point $\vec{c}(a)$ in the direction of the vector $\vec{v}(a) = \vec{c}'(a)$, which is the <u>velocity vector</u> for a particle moving along the path. We call $\vec{v}(t) = \vec{c}'(t)$ the velocity vector. When $\vec{c}'(a) \neq \vec{0}$, this is the tangent line to the curve at $\vec{c}(a)$, and so $\vec{c}'(a)$ indeed represents a tangent vector to the curve at that point. The velocity is a vector, and so it carries both magnitude and direction. The magnitude (norm) of velocity $\|\vec{v}(t)\| = \|\vec{c}'(t)\|$ is called the <u>speed</u> of the path. If the velocity $\vec{v}(t) \neq 0$, we can also determine the direction of motion via the <u>unit tangent</u> vector:

Definition 3.4. *Let $\vec{c}(t)$ be a differentiable path, with $\|\vec{c}'(t)\| \neq 0$. The* **unit tangent vector** *is defined as*

$$\vec{T}(t) = \frac{\vec{\mathrm{v}}}{\|\vec{\mathrm{v}}(t)\|} = \frac{\vec{c}'(t)}{\|\vec{c}'(t)\|}$$

All this suggests that things may go wrong when the path has points with zero speed, as the following example illustrates:

Example 3.5. Consider the "astroid", parametrized by $\vec{c} : \mathbb{R} \to \mathbb{R}^2$:

$$\vec{c}(t) = \left(\cos^3 t, \sin^3 t\right), \ t \in [-\pi, \pi].$$

This is a C^1 path (in fact, it is C^∞, differentiable to all orders!) Its velocity vector is given by

$$\vec{c}'(t) = \left(-3\cos^2 t \sin t, 3\sin^2 t \cos t\right).$$

To find the unit tangent, we have to find its speed first:

$$v = \sqrt{9\cos^4 t \sin^2 t + 9\sin^4 t \cos^2 t} = \sqrt{9\cos^2 t \sin^2 t(\sin^2 t + \cos^2 t)}$$
$$= 3|\sin t \cos t|,$$

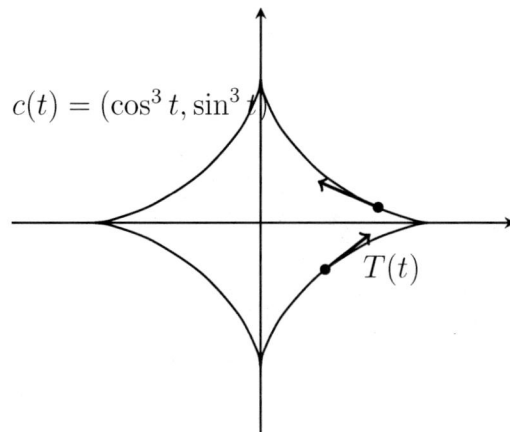

Figure 3.2. For $\vec{c}(t) = (\cos^3 t, \sin^3 t)$, unit tangent suddenly changes its direction at the cusp.

remembering that $\sqrt{x^2} = |x|$, because we always choose the positive square root. Then, the unit tangent is given by

$$\vec{T}(t) = \frac{\vec{v}(t)}{\|\vec{v}(t)\|} = \left(-|\cos t| \frac{\sin t}{|\sin t|}, |\sin t| \frac{\cos t}{|\cos t|} \right)$$

Note that its tangent is undefined when $\sin t = 0$ or $\cos t = 0$, i.e. at multiples of $\frac{\pi}{2}$. Worse, $\frac{\sin t}{|\sin t|}, \frac{\cos t}{|\cos t|}$ flip discontinuously as t crosses a multiple of $\pi/2$ from -1 to $+1$, or vice versa. Although the path is C^1, the curve is not smooth! When $\vec{v}(t) = \vec{c}'(t) = 0$, it allows the curve to have cusps (Figure 3.2). □

Note that it is possible to have a nice tangent direction even when $\vec{c}'(t) = 0$:

Example 3.6. For constant vectors $\vec{p}, \vec{w} \neq \vec{0}$ in $\mathbb{R}^n$, define the two paths

$$\vec{c}(t) = \vec{p} + \vec{w}t^2, \qquad t \in \mathbb{R}, \vec{b}(t) = \vec{p} + \vec{w}t^3, \qquad t \in \mathbb{R}.$$

Each is continuously differentiable for all $t \in \mathbb{R}$. First, $\vec{c}'(t) = 2t\vec{w}$, with speed $\|\vec{c}'(t)\| = 2|t| \|\vec{w}\|$. The unit tangent vector,

$$\vec{T}(t) = \frac{2t\vec{w}}{2|t| \|\vec{w}\|} = \begin{cases} +\frac{\vec{w}}{\|\vec{w}\|}, & \text{if } t > 0, \\ -\frac{\vec{w}}{\|\vec{w}\|}, & \text{if } t < 0, \end{cases}$$

and is undefined at $t = 0$. Notice that $\vec{c}(t)$ traces out a half-line, starting at $t = 0$ at the point $\vec{c}(0) = \vec{p}$, and moving along the ray in the direction of positive multiples of $\vec{w}$, for $t < 0$. When $t < 0$ it moves along the same line, but in the opposite direction, *towards* $\vec{p}$ as $t \to 0^-$. The path is not smooth, since velocity is zero at $t = 0$, and the unit tangent jumps at that time.

The path $\vec{b}(t)$ is also not smooth, since $\vec{b}'(0) = \vec{0}$. But the difficulty here is artificial: $\vec{b}'(t) = 3t^2\vec{w}$, with speed $\|\vec{b}'(t)\| = 3t^2\|\vec{w}\|$. Although the speed is also zero at $t = 0$, we can still define a unit tangent vector, $\vec{T}(t) = \frac{\vec{w}}{\|\vec{w}\|}$ when $t \neq 0$ has a removable discontinuity. It's simply a bad choice to parametrize the line; the curve (straight line) is smooth even though the path $\vec{b}(t)$ is not! □

Although it's possible to have a continuously varying tangent vector even when the speed of the path can vanish, we wish to avoid such tricky cases. So we will only call a curve "smooth" if the speed is never zero, and so the unit tangent $\vec{T}(t)$ may be defined, and will be continuous:

Definition 3.7. *We say a path $\vec{c}(t)$, $t \in I$, is* smooth *(or regular) if $\vec{c}$ is a C^1 path with $\|\vec{c}'(t)\| \neq 0$ for any $t \in I$. We call a geometrical curve* smooth *if can be parametrized by a C^1 path $\vec{c}(t)$ which is smooth (ie, C^1 with nonvanishing speed.)*

For a smooth curve the unit tangent vector $\vec{T}(t)$ is continuous, and so we eliminate the bad behavior of the astroid example above.

Specializing to curves in space $\vec{c}(t) \in \mathbb{R}^3$, we will want to use vector operations to study the velocity and tangent vectors associated to the paths. The following product rules will be useful:

Theorem 3.8.

1. If $f : \mathbb{R} \to \mathbb{R}$, $\vec{c} : \mathbb{R} \to \mathbb{R}^n$, both differentiable,

$$\frac{d}{dt}\Big(f(t)\vec{c}(t)\Big) = f(t)\vec{c}'(t) + f'(t)\vec{c}(t)$$

2. If $\vec{c}, \vec{d} : \mathbb{R} \to \mathbb{R}^n$ are differentiable,

$$\frac{d}{dt}\Big(\vec{c}(t) \cdot \vec{d}(t)\Big) = \vec{c}'(t) \cdot \vec{d}(t) + \vec{c}(t) \cdot \vec{d}'(t)$$

3. If $\vec{c}, \vec{d} : \mathbb{R} \to \mathbb{R}^3$ are differentiable,

$$\frac{d}{dt}\Big(\vec{c}(t) \times \vec{d}(t)\Big) = \vec{c}(t) \times \vec{d}'(t) + \vec{c}'(t)\vec{d}(t),$$

where $\vec{c} \times \vec{d} = \sum_{i,j,k=1}^{3} c_i d_j \vec{e}_k \varepsilon_{ijk}$[1].

To prove these, we write them in components,

$$\vec{c}(t) = (c_1(t), c_2(t), \ldots, c_n(t)) = \sum_{i=j}^{n} c_j \vec{e_j},$$

---

[1] $\varepsilon_{ijk} = \begin{cases} 0 & \text{if } i = j \text{ or } j = k \text{ or } \text{k} = \text{i} \\ 1 & \text{if } (i, j, k) \text{ is positively ordered} \\ -1 & \text{if } (i, j, k) \text{ is negatively ordered} \end{cases}$

using the standard basis $\{\vec{e_1}, \ldots, \vec{e_n}\}$ of $\mathbb{R}^n$, and do the ordinary derivative. For example,

$$
\begin{aligned}
\frac{d}{dt}\Big(f(t)\vec{c}(t)\Big) &= \frac{d}{dt}\Big(\sum_{j=1}^{n} f(t)\vec{c}_j(t)\vec{e}_j\Big) \\
&= \sum_{j=1}^{n} \frac{d}{dt}\Big(f(t)\vec{c}_j(t)\Big)\vec{e}_j \\
&= \sum_{j=1}^{n} \Big(f'(t)\vec{c}_j(t) + f(t)\vec{c}_j{}'(t)\Big)\vec{e}_j \\
&= f'(t)\vec{c}(t) + f(t)\vec{c}'(t).
\end{aligned}
$$

The verification of the other two formulae are left as an exercise.

Example 3.9. Suppose $\vec{c}$ is a twice differentiable path and its acceleration vector $\vec{a}(t) = \vec{c}''(t)$ satisfies the equation

$$\vec{a}(t) = k\vec{c}(t)$$

for some constant $k \neq 0$. Show that $\vec{c}(t)$ describes a motion in a fixed plane. $\square$

Define a vector,

$$\vec{n}(t) = \vec{c}(t) \times \vec{v}(t) = \vec{c}(t) \times \vec{c}'(t).$$

Notice $\vec{n}(t) \perp \vec{c}(t)$ and $\vec{n}(t) \perp \vec{v}(t)$, i.e. $\vec{n}(t)$ is normal to the plane containing the vectors $\vec{c}, \vec{v}$ (drawn with common endpoint.) Our goal is to show that $\vec{n}$ is a constant, independent of t, in which case the path $\vec{c}(t)$ always lies in the same plane which is normal to $\vec{n}$. To do this, we differentiate the equation defining $\vec{n}$,

$$
\begin{aligned}
\frac{d\vec{n}}{dt} = \frac{d}{dt}\left(\vec{c}(t) \times \vec{c}'(t)\right) &= \vec{c}(t) \times \underbrace{\vec{c}''(t)}_{\vec{a}(t)} + \underbrace{\vec{c}'(t) \times \vec{c}'(t)}_{\vec{0}} \\
&= \vec{c}(t) \times k\vec{c}(t) \\
&= \vec{0}
\end{aligned}
$$

Therefore, $\vec{n}$ is constant in time.

As $\vec{n}$ is a constant vector, it defines a fixed plane,

$$P = \{\vec{w} \mid \vec{w} \cdot \vec{n} = 0\}$$

passing through the origin, which contains the moving vector $\vec{c}(t)$ for all t. We have just shown that the path moves in the plane P.

Definition 3.10 (Arc length). *The arc length (or distance traveled along the parameterized curve) for $a \leq t \leq b$ is given by*

$$\int_a^b \underbrace{\|\vec{c}'(t)\|}_{speed}\, dt$$

We are also interested in keeping track of how much distance we travel along a path, starting at a fixed time $t = a$. Think of the trip odometer in a car, which you set to zero at the start of a road trip and keeps track of how far you've driven since you started out.

Definition 3.11 (Arc length function). *The arc length function associated to the path $\vec{c}(t)$, with starting time $t = a$ is*

$$s(t) = \int_a^t \|\vec{c}'(u)\| du$$

We use the dummy variable u in the integral since the independent variable t is one of the limits of integration. So the arclength function $s(t)$ is an *antiderivative* of the speed $\|\vec{c}'(t)\|$,

$$\frac{ds}{dt} = \|\vec{c}'(t)\|,$$

but with the constant of integration chosen to make $s(0) = 0$. If this seems mysterious, you should review the First Fundamental Theorem of Calculus from Stewart.

Example 3.12. Consider the following path:

$$\vec{c}(t) = (3\cos t, 3\sin t, 4t), \ t \in [0, 4\pi].$$

Its velocity vector is given by

$$\vec{v}(t) = (-3\sin t, 3\cos t, 4).$$

It follows that its speed $\|\vec{c}'(t)\| = \sqrt{3^2 + 4^2} = 5$. Then, we can compute the arc length function:

$$s(t) = \int_0^t v(t)dt = \int_0^t 5du = 5t$$

In particular, the total arc length over $t \in [0, 4\pi]$ is $s(4\pi) = 20\pi$. □

Definition 3.13. *When the path $\vec{c}(t)$ traces out the curve with speed $\|\vec{v}(t)\| = 1$ for all t, we say that the curve is* arc length parameterized.

We note that a C^1 arclength parametrized path is smooth. If a curve is arc length parameterized, its arc length function becomes

$$s(t) = t$$

In this case it is conventional to use the letter s instead of t as the parameter in the path.

Theorem 3.14. *Let $\vec{c}(t)$, $t \in I$, be a smooth path. Then, there is an arclength reparametrization for the curve, $\vec{\gamma}(s)$, with $\|\vec{\gamma}'(s)\| = 1$ for all s.*

Example 3.15. In example 3.12, the helix is not arc length parameterized but we can reparameterize it so that it is. To do so, we need to solve for $t = \varphi(s)$ to invert the function, $s(t)$.

Going back the example, we had $s(t) = 5t$. It follows that $t = \frac{1}{5}s$. Then,

$$\vec{c}(s) = \vec{c}(\varphi(s)) = \vec{c}\left(\frac{s}{5}\right) = \left(3\cos\left(\frac{s}{5}\right), 3\sin\left(\frac{s}{5}\right), \frac{4s}{5}\right)$$

is an arc length parameterization of the original helix, i.e. $\|\vec{c}'(s)\| = 1$, $\forall s$. □

3.2 Directional derivatives and gradient

Now let's use curves to explore functions defined on $\mathbb{R}^n$. We restrict our attention here to *real (scalar) valued functions*, that is $f : \mathbb{R}^n \to \mathbb{R}$. Think of $f(\vec{x})$ as describing a quantity such as temperature or air pressure in a room, and an insect or drone moving around the room along the path $\vec{c}(t)$, measuring the value of f as it moves. In other words, it measures the composition, $h(t) = f(\vec{c}(t))$.

If $f : \mathbb{R}^n \to \mathbb{R}$ is differentiable, $Df(\vec{x})$ is a $(1 \times n)$ matrix:

$$Df(\vec{x}) = \begin{bmatrix} \frac{\partial f}{\partial x_1} & \frac{\partial f}{\partial x_2} & \cdots & \frac{\partial f}{\partial x_n} \end{bmatrix}$$

We use *paths* $\vec{c}(t)$ to explore $f(x)$ by looking at

$$h(t) = f \circ \vec{c}(t) = f\left(\vec{c}(t)\right).$$

where $h : \mathbb{R} \to \mathbb{R}$, By chain rule,

$$Dh(t) = h'(t) = \underbrace{Df(\vec{c}(t))}_{1 \times n} \underbrace{D\vec{c}(t)}_{n \times 1}$$

$$= Df\left(\vec{c}(t)\right) \vec{c}'(t)$$

$$= \begin{bmatrix} \frac{\partial f}{\partial x_1} & \frac{\partial f}{\partial x_2} & \cdots & \frac{\partial f}{\partial x_n} \end{bmatrix} \begin{bmatrix} c_1' \\ c_2' \\ \vdots \\ c_n' \end{bmatrix}$$

We can think of this as a dot product of $\vec{c}'(t)$ with a vector $Df^T = \nabla f$, the gradient vector:

$$h'(t) = \nabla f(\vec{c}(t)) \cdot \vec{c}'(t)$$

Suppose $f : \mathbb{R}^n \to \mathbb{R}$ is differentiable at $\vec{a} \in \mathbb{R}^n$, and we have a path $\vec{c} : \mathbb{R}^n \to \mathbb{R}$ with $\vec{c}(0) = \vec{a}$. Let $\vec{v} = \vec{c}'(0)$. Then, $h'(0)$ measures rate of change of f along the path, $\vec{c}$, as we cross through $\vec{a}$:

$$h'(0) = \nabla f(\vec{c}(0)) \cdot \vec{c}'(0)$$

$$= \nabla f(\vec{c}(0)) \cdot \vec{v}$$

Note that we get the same value for $h'(0)$ for *any* path $\vec{c}(t)$ going through $\vec{a}$ with velocity $\vec{c}'(0) = \vec{v}$: other than insisting that the path pass through the point $\vec{a}$ with velocity vector $\vec{v}$, this quantity is *path-independent*. In other words, $h'(0)$ says something about f at $\vec{a}$, and not the past or future trajectory of the path $\vec{c}(t)$. In particular, we get the same value for the derivative $h'(0)$ if we take the simplest possible path which passes through $\vec{a}$ with velocity $\vec{v}$ at $t = 0$, a straight line,

$$\vec{c}(t) = \vec{a} + t\vec{v}, \qquad t \in \mathbb{R}.$$

When we use the straight line to calculate $h'(0)$, it means that we can write $h(t) = f(\vec{c}(t)) = f(\vec{a} + t\vec{v})$, and so

$$h'(0) = \lim_{t \to 0} \frac{h(t) - h(0)}{t - 0} = \lim_{t \to 0} \frac{f(\vec{a} + t\vec{v}) - f(\vec{a})}{t}.$$

This is an important quantity to calculate for any function f, and so we give it a name:

Definition 3.16 (Directional derivative). *The directional derivative of f at $\vec{a}$ in direction $\vec{v}$ is given by*

$$D_{\vec{v}}f(\vec{a}) = \lim_{t \to 0} \frac{f(\vec{a} + t\vec{v}) - f(\vec{a})}{t}.$$

If the function f is differentiable at $\vec{a}$, then we may apply the chain rule as above and obtain:

Theorem 3.17. *Let $f : \mathbb{R}^n \to \mathbb{R}$ be differentiable at $\vec{x} = \vec{a}$, and $\vec{v} \in \mathbb{R}^n$ a nonzero constant vector. Then,*

$$D_{\vec{v}}f(\vec{a}) = \frac{d}{dt}f(\vec{a} + t\vec{v})\Big|_{t=0} = \nabla f(\vec{a}) \cdot \vec{v}.$$

Now, we can make some observations. Since the shape of the path $\vec{c}(t)$ doesn't matter, only that it passes through $\vec{a}$ with velocity $\vec{v}$, we might as well choose a straight line path when calculating directional derivatives, $\vec{c}(t) = \vec{a} + t\vec{v}$, with $\vec{c}(0) = \vec{a}$ and $\vec{c}'(0) = \vec{v}$. Using the Chain Rule as above, the directional derivative can be rewritten as

$$D_{\vec{v}}f(\vec{a}) = Df(\vec{a})\vec{v} = \nabla f(\vec{a}) \cdot \vec{v}.$$

From this formula we recognize that the partial derivatives are just special cases of directional derivatives, obtained by choosing $\vec{v} = \vec{e}_j$. That is,

$$\frac{\partial f}{\partial x_j}(\vec{a}) = D_{\vec{e}_j}f(\vec{a}).$$

There is one little problem with our definition of directional derivatives: $D_{\vec{v}}f(\vec{a})$ depends not only on the "direction" of the vector $\vec{v}$, but also its magnitude. To see this, notice that although $\vec{v}$ and $2\vec{v}$ are parallel (and thus have the same direction,) $D_{2\vec{v}}f(\vec{a}) = \nabla f(\vec{a}) \cdot (2\vec{v}) = 2D_{\vec{v}}f(\vec{a})$. To get the information on how fast f is changing at $\vec{a}$, we need to restrict to unit vectors $\|\vec{v}\| = 1$. So we often use the term "directional derivative" only when $\vec{v}$ is a unit vector.

Directional derivatives also give a geometrical interpretation of the gradient vector, $\nabla f(\vec{a})$, when $\nabla f(\vec{a}) \neq \vec{0}$. Applying the Cauchy-Schwartz inequality (Theorem 1.2), we have:

$$|D_{\vec{v}}f(\vec{a})| = |\nabla f(\vec{a}) \cdot \vec{v}| \leq \|\nabla f(\vec{a})\|\|\vec{v}\| = \|\nabla f(\vec{a})\|,$$

and equality holds if and only if $\vec{v}$ is parallel to $\nabla f(\vec{a})$. Therefore, we can conclude that the length of the gradient vector, $\|\nabla f(\vec{a})\|$, gives the largest of $D_{\vec{v}}f(\vec{a})$ among all choices of unit directions $\vec{v}$,

$$\|\nabla f(\vec{a})\| = \max\left\{D_{\vec{u}}f(\vec{a}) : \vec{u} \in \mathbb{R}^n \text{ with } \|\vec{u}\| = 1\right\}.$$

In other words, the direction $\vec{v}$ in which $f(\vec{x})$ increases most rapidly is the direction of $\nabla f(\vec{a})$, i.e.

$$\vec{v} = \frac{\nabla f(\vec{a})}{\|\nabla f(\vec{a})\|},$$

provided that $\nabla f(\vec{a}) \neq \vec{0}$.

Similarly, $-\nabla f(\vec{a})$ points in the direction of the least (most negative) $D_{\vec{v}} f(\vec{a})$, i.e.

$$\vec{v} = -\frac{\nabla f(\vec{a})}{\|\nabla f(\vec{a})\|},$$

gives the direction in which f decreases fastest at $\vec{a}$.

3.3 Gradients and level sets

We recall that if $G : \mathbb{R}^n \to \mathbb{R}$, the *level set* of G at level $k \in \mathbb{R}$ (a constant) is

$$S = \{\vec{x} \in \mathbb{R}^n : G(\vec{x}) = k\}.$$

For example, in $\mathbb{R}^2$, the function $f(x, y) = x^2 + y^2$ has level sets $x^2 + y^2 = k$ which define circles of radius $\sqrt{k}$ when $k > 0$. When $k = 0$ the level set consists only of the origin, and for $k < 0$ the level set is empty, $S = \emptyset$. This suggests that generically (that is, for all but a few values of k,) when it is non-empty the level set of a C^1 function of 2 variables is a curve, but that it can be lower dimensional (a point.) (Later on, with the Implicit Function Theorem we will understand why this is so.)

What does the gradient ∇G tell us in this situation? The graph of $G(\vec{x})$ lies in the higher dimensional space $\mathbb{R}^{n+1}$, and so when $n \geq 3$ we can't really visualize the graph. However, we know from the last section that G increases most rapidly if we move $\vec{x}$ along the direction of $\nabla G(\vec{x})$. Moving $\vec{x}$ along the level set S doesn't change the value of G at all, so this suggests that the directional derivatives "along" the level set are zero.

A more precise description uses the concept of the *tangent plane* to the surface. As we did in the last section, we use paths $\vec{c}(t)$ to explore the surface (or curve, in 2D) defined by the level set. To do this, we only consider smooth paths $\vec{c}(t)$ which remain on the surface S for all time $t \in \mathbb{R}$. Since "remaining on the surface" means that the coordinates of $\vec{c}(t) = (x_1(t), \ldots, x_n(t))$ must solve the equation $G(\vec{x}) = k$ at all times, we have

$$G(\vec{c}(t)) = k, \qquad \forall t \in \mathbb{R}.$$

Taking such a path, assume it passes through the point $\vec{a} \in S$ at time $t = 0$, with velocity vector $\vec{v} = \vec{c}'(0)$. Then, $\vec{v}$ must be a *tangent vector* to the surface S at the point $\vec{a} \in S$. In fact, this is how we define a *tangent plane* (or tangent line, in 2D) to the surface S, as the collection of all possible velocity vectors corresponding to paths lying along the surface S.

Using implicit differentiation and the chain rule, since $G(\vec{c}(t)) = k$ is constant,

$$0 = \frac{d}{dt}(k) = \frac{d}{dt} G(\vec{c}(t)) = \nabla G(\vec{c}(t)) \cdot \vec{c}'(t). \tag{3.1}$$

Evaluating at $t = 0$, we get

$$\nabla G(\vec{a}) \cdot \vec{v} = 0,$$

so the vector $\nabla G(\vec{a})$ is orthogonal to the tangent vector $\vec{v}$. Since this is true for any path $\vec{c}(t)$ with any velocity vector $\vec{v}$, it follows that $\nabla G(\vec{a})$ is either the zero vector or it is a normal vector to the plane containing all tangent vectors.

Theorem 3.18. *Assume $G : \mathbb{R}^n \to \mathbb{R}$ is a C^1 function, $\vec{a} \in \mathbb{R}^n$, $k = G(\vec{a})$, and $S = \{\vec{x} \in \mathbb{R}^n : G(\vec{x}) = k\}$ is the level set.*

If $\nabla G(\vec{a}) \neq \vec{0}$, then $\nabla G(\vec{a})$ is a normal vector to the tangent plane of S at $\vec{a}$.

Example 3.19. Suppose $g : \mathbb{R} \to \mathbb{R}$ is C^1 with $g'(r) \neq 0$ for all $r > 0$, and $G : \mathbb{R}^3 \to \mathbb{R}$ is defined by $G(x, y, z) = g(x^2 + y^2 + z^2)$. If the orgin does not lie on the level set $S = \{(x, y, z) : G(x, y, z) = k\}$, then its normal vector is parallel to the vector $\vec{x} = (x, y, z)$.

To see this, use the chain rule to calculate the gradient of G: define $r = f(x, y, z) = x^2 + y^2 + z^2$, and then

$$DG(x, y, z) = Dg(r)\, Df(x, y, z) = [g'(r)] \begin{bmatrix} 2x & 2y & 2z \end{bmatrix} = 2g'(r) \begin{bmatrix} x & y & z \end{bmatrix}$$

Writing this as a gradient vector, $\nabla G = 2g'(r)\vec{x}$, which is parallel to $\vec{x}$ as long as $g'(r) \neq 0$, which is true since the origin ($r = 0$) does not lie on the level set. $\qquad \square$

3.4 Lagrange multipliers

As an application of these ideas we present the method of Joseph-Louis Lagrange (1736-1813) for finding constrained maxima and minima. Here's the setup: we want to minimize or maximize a function $F : \mathbb{R}^n \to \mathbb{R}$, but only over those vectors which satisfy a constraint condition, given as the level set of $G : \mathbb{R}^n \to \mathbb{R}$. That is, we want to

$$\text{maximize (or minimize) } F(\vec{x}) \text{ for all } \vec{x} \text{ with } G(\vec{x}) = k, \tag{3.2}$$

where k is a fixed constant. Such optimization problems arise naturally in fields such as economics, where fixed resources or capacities restrict our choice when optimizing.

The way that Lagrange solves this problem is to introduce a new unknown scalar λ, the "Lagrange multiplier", into the problem:

Theorem 3.20 (Lagrange multipliers). *Assume $F, G : \mathbb{R}^n \to \mathbb{R}$ are C^1 functions. If the constrained optimization problem (3.2) is attained at $\vec{x} = \vec{a}$, and $\nabla G(\vec{a}) \neq \vec{0}$, then there is a constant $\lambda \in \mathbb{R}$ with*

$$\nabla F(\vec{a}) = \lambda \nabla G(\vec{a}).$$

Proof of Theorem 3.20. Assume F has a maximum at $\vec{a} \in S$, that is, with $G(\vec{a}) = k$. Consider any path $\vec{c}(t)$ which lies on the surface S and passes through $\vec{a}$, so $G(\vec{c}(t)) = k$ is constant for all t, with $\vec{c}(0) = \vec{a}$ and $\vec{c}'(0) = \vec{v}$ is a tangent vector to S at $\vec{a}$. The function

$h(t) = F(\vec{c}(t))$ has its maximum at $t = 0$ (when $\vec{c}(0) = \vec{a}$,) and so by first year calculus $h'(0) = 0$. As in the derivation of (3.1), by implicit differentiation and the chain rule we have

$$0 = h'(0) = \nabla F(\vec{c}(0)) \cdot \vec{c}'(0) = \nabla F(\vec{a}) \cdot \vec{v},$$

for any tangent vector $\vec{v}$ to S at $\vec{a}$. In other words, $\nabla F(\vec{a})$ is orthogonal to all of the vectors in the tangent plane to S, so it must point parallel to the normal vector of S. But by Theorem 3.18 that is given by $\nabla G(\vec{a})$, and so there is a constant λ of proportionality for which $\nabla F(\vec{a}) = \lambda \nabla G(\vec{a})$. $\square$

So the gradients of F and G are *parallel* at a solution of the constrained extremal problem. Geometrically, since $\nabla F(\vec{a})$ is a normal vector to the level set of F, and similarly $\nabla G(\vec{a})$ is a normal vector to the constraint set S (which is a level set of G), a maximum or minimum value of F on S where a level set of F is *tangent* to the constraint set S. See Figure 3.3 below.

In practice, this means solving a system

$$\nabla F(\vec{x}) = \lambda \nabla G(\vec{x}), \qquad G(\vec{x}) = k, \tag{3.3}$$

with $(n + 1)$ equations in the $(n + 1)$ unknowns, $\vec{x} = (x_1, \ldots, x_n)$ and λ, for the $(n + 1)$ unknowns $\vec{x} = (x_1, \ldots, x_n)$ and λ. This may be a linear system, but in most cases it will be *nonlinear*. So typically, Gaussian elimination is not applicable and we must be clever and crafty to combine the equations and hope to be able to find the solutions.

Notice what the Theorem does *not* say: it does not say that there must exist points where the maximum or minimum of F on the surface $S = \{\vec{x} \mid G(\vec{x}) = k\}$. Nor does it exclude the possibility that the maximum and/or minimum occurs at points where F or G fails to be C^1 or even at points where $\nabla G(\vec{a}) = \vec{0}$. So our best hope is to find the solutions to the Lagrange Multiplier equation (3.3), check if there are any points on S with $\nabla G = \vec{0}$, and reason out whether they are minima or maxima (or neither!) We are aided by the following fact (which you encountered in first year calculus):

Theorem 3.21. *Let $F : \mathbb{R}^n \to \mathbb{R}$ be a continuous function, and $S \subset \mathbb{R}^n$ be a set which is both <u>closed</u> and <u>bounded</u>. Then $F(\vec{x})$ attains both its maximum and minimum values on the set S.*

The case $f : \mathbb{R} \to \mathbb{R}$ is continuous on the closed and bounded interval $[a, b]$ is in Stewart, p. 278 in Chapter 4 (the "Extreme Value Theorem".) If the constraint set is unbounded we may not have a maximum or minimum value at all.

Example 3.22. Find the closest and furthest point from the origin to the surface $4x^2 + 2xy + 4y^2 + z^2 = 1$.

First we need to set this up as a problem with level set constraint. The function to be optimized is the distance to the origin, which is $\|\vec{x}\|$. However, it is equivalent (and much easier) to instead minimize/maximize the square of the distance, $F(\vec{x}) = \|\vec{x}\|^2 = x^2 + y^2 + z^2$, since the square is a monotone increasing function of positive numbers. The constraint is $G(x, y, z) = 1$, with $G(x, y, z) = 4x^2 + 2xy + 4y^2 + z^2$. These are C^1 functions, so by Theorem 3.2 at an extrema we must satisfy the equations (3.3), which in this example gives:

$$2x = \lambda(8x + 2y), \qquad 2y = \lambda(2x + 8y), \qquad 2z = 2\lambda z, \qquad 4x^2 + 2xy + 4y^2 + z^2 = 1,$$

to be solved for (x, y, z) and λ. Note that these equations are nonlinear, but with a bit of care we will use linear algebra anyway. But be very careful not to let solutions go unnoticed!

The easiest equation is the third one, $2z = 2\lambda z$ or $(1 - \lambda)z = 0$. So there are two possibilities (both of which must be dealt with!) $z = 0$ or $\lambda = 1$. First, assume $\boxed{z = 0}$. We rewrite the first two equations as a system,

$$\begin{cases} 4x + y = \dfrac{1}{\lambda}x \\ x + 4y = \dfrac{1}{\lambda}y \end{cases} \quad \text{or, equivalently,} \quad \begin{cases} \left(4 - \dfrac{1}{\lambda}\right)x + y = 0 \\ x + \left(4 - \dfrac{1}{\lambda}\right)y = 0. \end{cases}$$

If this looks familiar it's because it's an eigenvalue problem (except the eigenvalue is called $1/\lambda$.) To find a nonzero solution we need the determinant of the matrix of coefficients to vanish (as in the eigenvalue problem!), that is

$$0 = \det \begin{bmatrix} \left(4 - \frac{1}{\lambda}\right) & 1 \\ 1 & \left(4 - \frac{1}{\lambda}\right) \end{bmatrix} = \left(4 - \frac{1}{\lambda}\right)^2 - 1 = \left(5 - \frac{1}{\lambda}\right)\left(3 - \frac{1}{\lambda}\right).$$

So we can solve for $\lambda = \frac{1}{5}, \frac{1}{3}$; that is, there are two different possibilites for λ when $z = 0$. When $\lambda = \frac{1}{5}$, substituting into the first equation of the system gives $y = x$. Then, plugging into the constraint equation,

$$1 = 4x^2 + 2xy + 4y^2 + z^2 = 4x^2 + 2x^2 + 4x^2 + 0 = 10x^2,$$

and so $x = \pm\sqrt{\frac{1}{10}}$. This gives our pair of solutions to the equations,

$$(x, y, z) = \left(\sqrt{\frac{1}{10}}, \sqrt{\frac{1}{10}}, 0\right), \qquad (x, y, z) = \left(-\sqrt{\frac{1}{10}}, -\sqrt{\frac{1}{10}}, 0\right).$$

(Be careful: since $y = x$ we don't get all the permutations of the signs!) For the other Lagrange multiplier $\lambda = \frac{1}{3}$, we again use the first equation to get $y = -x$, and then the constraint gives us

$$1 = 4x^2 + 2xy + 4y^2 + z^2 = 4x^2 - 2x^2 + 4x^2 + 0 = 6x^2,$$

and so $x = \pm\sqrt{\frac{1}{6}}$. This gives our pair of solutions to the equations,

$$(x, y, z) = \left(\sqrt{\frac{1}{6}}, -\sqrt{\frac{1}{6}}, 0\right), \qquad (x, y, z) = \left(-\sqrt{\frac{1}{6}}, \sqrt{\frac{1}{6}}, 0\right).$$

This exhausts all the possibilites for the case $z = 0$.

The other case was $\lambda = 1$, in which case the equations for (x, y) become

$$3x + y = 0 \qquad x + 3y = 0,$$

which has only the trivial solution $(x, y) = (0, 0)$ (check the determinant of the coefficient matrix!) Plugging into the constraint,

$$1 = 4x^2 + 2xy + 4y^2 + z^2 = 0 + 0 + 0 + z^2 = 1,$$

so $z = \pm 1$, and we get

$$(x, y, z) = (0, 0, 1), \qquad (x, y, z) = (0, 0, -1).$$

Thus, we have 6 points which satisfy the Lagrange multiplier equations. The maximum and minimum must be attained among these, so test them in $F(x, y, z)$:

$$F\left(\pm\left(\sqrt{\frac{1}{10}}, \sqrt{\frac{1}{10}}, 0\right)\right) = \frac{1}{5}, \quad F\left(\pm\left(\sqrt{\frac{1}{6}}, -\sqrt{\frac{1}{6}}, 0\right)\right) = \frac{1}{3}, \quad F(0, 0, \pm 1) = 1.$$

The minimum value is $\frac{1}{5}$, attained at the points $(x, y, z) = \pm\left(\sqrt{\frac{1}{10}}, \sqrt{\frac{1}{10}}, 0\right)$, and the maximum value is 1, attained at the points $(x, y, z) = (0, 0, \pm 1)$.

$\square$

Example 3.23. Find the point on $S = \{(x, y) \in \mathbb{R}^2 \mid x^2 y = 2\}$ which is closest to $(0, 0)$.

As in the above example, the function which we wish to optimize is $F(x, y) = \|(x, y) - (0, 0)\|^2 = x^2 + y^2$, as the square of the distance is minimized (or maximized) whenever the distance is. The constraint $G(x, y) = x^2 y$ has level sets which may be expressed as graphs in the plane, $y = k/x^2$, $x \neq 0$, when $k \neq 0$. The level sets are not closed curves, and are *unbounded* sets, and hence we are not guaranteed to have either maximum or minimum values of $F(x, y)$ for given functions F. In particular, for this choice $F(x, y) = x^2 + y^2$, there can be no maximum value, since $(x, 2x^{-2}) \in S$ for each $x \neq 0$, and $F(x, 2x^{-2}) = x^2 + 4x^{-4} \longrightarrow +\infty$ diverges as $x \to 0$.

Let's see if we can find a minimum value, which seems to exist given the graph in Figure 3.3 below. We seek solutions to the Lagrange Multiplier equations, (3.3),

$$\nabla F(x, y) = (2x, 2y) = \lambda \nabla G(x, y) = \lambda\left(2xy, x^2\right).$$

That is,

$$2x = 2\lambda y x, \qquad 2y = \lambda x^2, \qquad x^2 y = 2.$$

The first equation gives us $x(1 - \lambda y) = 0$, so either $x = 0$ or $1 - \lambda y = 0$. Since $x = 0$ is impossible (we can't satisfy the constraint!) we must have $y = 1/\lambda$. From the second equation, $\frac{2}{\lambda} = \lambda x^2$, or $x^2 = 2/\lambda^2$. Now we plug this into the constraint,

$$2 = x^2 y = \left(\frac{2}{\lambda^2}\right)\left(\frac{1}{\lambda}\right) = \frac{2}{\lambda^3},$$

and so $\lambda = 1$ is the only solution. Returning to the other variables, we have

$$x^2 = \frac{2}{\lambda^2} = 2 \implies x = \pm\sqrt{2}, \quad y = \frac{1}{\lambda} = 1,$$

and so we get two constrained critical points, $(x, y, \lambda) = (\pm\sqrt{2}, 1, 1)$. The points $(x, y) = (\pm\sqrt{2}, 1) \in S$ are closest to $(0,0)$, with distance $\sqrt{F(x, y)} = \sqrt{3}$.

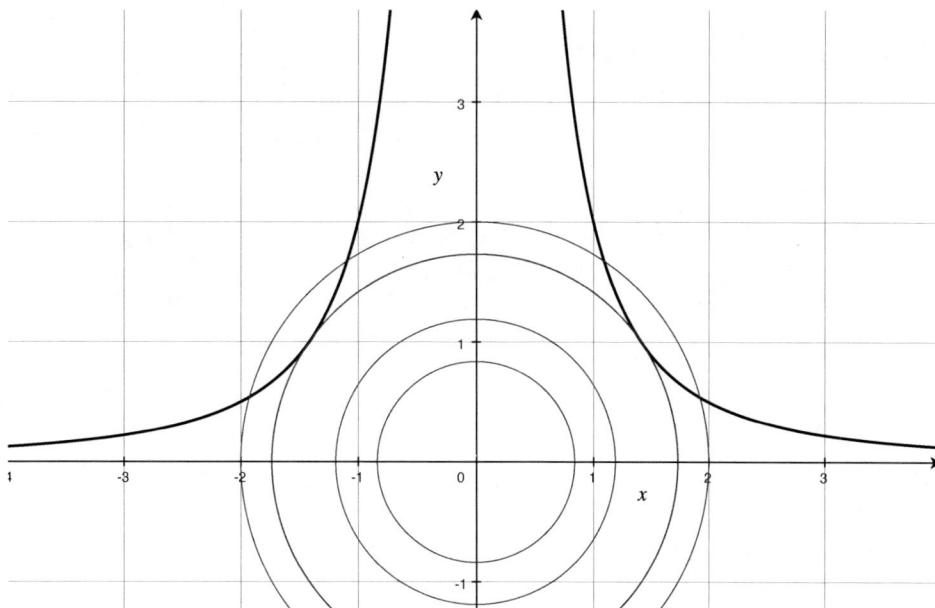

Figure 3.3. The constraint set $S = \{(x, y) \mid x^2 y = 2\}$ is shown in bold. The level sets of $F(x, y) = x^2 + y^2$ are the purple circles. The constrained extremum (a minimum in this example) is attained when the level set of F is tangent to the constraint set S.

What does the Lagrange Multiplier λ tell us? One might expect that it has something to do with whether the critical point obtained is a maximum or minimum, but this is not the case. Since the extremum is obtained when $\nabla F(\vec{a}) = \lambda \nabla G(\vec{a})$, when $\lambda > 0$ the two vectors $F(\vec{a}), G(\vec{a})$ point in the same direction, and when $\lambda < 0$ they point along the same line but in opposite directions. This suggests that it tells us what happens as we move *orthogonally* to the level set, that the value of $F(\vec{x})$ will increase or decrease as we move off of the level set, to higher or lower values of G. In fact, if we think of the solution to the constrained optimization problem as a function of both $\vec{x}$ and the constraint value k, we can understand the role of λ. Call

$$M(k) = \max\{F(\vec{x}) \mid \forall \vec{x} \text{ with } G(\vec{x}) = k\},$$

which is maximized by $\vec{x}(k)$ with Lagrange Multiplier $\lambda(k)$. Then, $\frac{dM}{dk}(k) = \lambda(k)$. This is particularly important in economics, in defining the "shadow price", the additional amount earned by increasing one's budget (the constraint value k) by one dollar.

3.5   Practice Problems

1. Consider the path $\vec{c}: \mathbb{R} \to \mathbb{R}^2$ defined by $\vec{c}(t) = (\cos t,\ \sin^2 t)$.

(a) What curve is traced out by $\vec{c}(t)$ for $t \in \mathbb{R}$?

[Careful! $|\sin t|, |\cos t| \leq 1$ for all t.]

(b) Verify that the path is smooth (or regular) for $0 < t < \pi$, but not for any larger interval. What goes wrong at $t = 0, \pi$?

(c) Find a smooth reparametrization $\vec{r}(u)$, $u \in [-1, 1]$, which traces out the entire curve.

2. Assume $\vec{c}(t)$ is a smooth parametrized curve.

(a) If $\vec{c}(t)$ lies on the surface of the sphere of radius $R > 0$ for all $t \in \mathbb{R}$, show that the velocity $\vec{c}\,'(t)$ is always orthogonal to the position $\vec{c}(t)$.

[Hint: the sphere of radius $R > 0$ can be described as all vectors with $\|\vec{x}\|^2 = R^2$. Plug in $\vec{c}(t)$ and do implicit differentiation in t.]

(b) Conversely, show that if the position and velocity are always orthogonal, $\vec{c}(t) \cdot \vec{c}\,'(t) = 0$ for all $t \in \mathbb{R}$, then the path $\vec{c}(t)$ always remains on a sphere.

3. Let $f(x, y) = \cos(xy)$ and $\vec{a} = (\frac{1}{2}, \pi)$.

(a) Find $\nabla f(\vec{a})$.

(b) Find a unit vector which is normal to the level set $\{(x, y) : f(x, y) = 0\}$ at the point $\vec{a}$.

(c) For the unit vector $\vec{u} = (\frac{3}{5}, -\frac{4}{5})$, find the directional derivative $D_{\vec{u}} f(\vec{a})$.

(d) What is the largest possible value for $D_{\vec{v}} f(\vec{a})$ among all unit vectors $\vec{v}$? What is the least possible value?

(e) Consider the path $\vec{c}(t) = (\frac{1}{2}, \pi) + t (\frac{3}{5}, -\frac{4}{5})$, and the composition $g(t) = f \circ \vec{c}(t)$. Find $g'(0)$.

4. Let $f(x, y) = \sqrt[3]{xy}$. Show that both $\frac{\partial f}{\partial x} = 0 = \frac{\partial f}{\partial y}$, (and therefore $\nabla f(0, 0) = \vec{0}$,) but the directional derivatives $D_{\vec{v}} f(0, 0)$ do not exist for any $\vec{v}$ which is not parallel to $\mathbf{i} = (1, 0)$ or $\mathbf{j} = (0, 1)$. Why can't we apply Theorem 3.17?

5. Let $F: \mathbb{R}^3 \to \mathbb{R}$ be a C^1 function, and S the level set defined by $F(\vec{x}) = 4$. Assume that the origin lies inside the level surface S, and there is a point $\vec{a} \in S$ at which the distance to the origin is maximized. Show that the normal vector to the surface S at $\vec{a}$ is parallel to $\vec{a}$.

[Hint: the distance is maximized means that $\|\vec{x}\| \leq \|\vec{a}\|$ holds for all $\vec{x} \in S$, which also means that $G(\vec{x}) := \|\vec{x}\|^2$ has a maximum at $\vec{a}$.]

Chapter 4

The geometry of space curves

In this chapter we look more in detail at curves in $\mathbb{R}^3$, and the relationship between the dynamics (how they are traced out in time) and the geometry (their shape.) This is an introduction to the field of differential geometry, and is based on finding a moving basis of vectors which is carried by the space curve along the trajectory.

4.1 The Frenet frame and curvature

A path, or moving vector,

$$\vec{c}(t) = \begin{bmatrix} x(t) \\ y(t) \\ z(t) \end{bmatrix} = (x, y, z)(t),$$

traces out a curve, for $t \in [a, b]$, in space. We recall that its velocity vector and speed are given by $\vec{v}(t) = \vec{c}'(t)$ and $\frac{ds}{dt} = \|\vec{c}'(t)\|$, respectively. Recall also that we have a smooth parameterization if $\vec{c} \in C^1$ and $\|\vec{c}'(t)\| \neq 0$ for any $t \in [a, b]$.

In the previous chapter we introduced the arc length function,

$$s(t) = \int_a^t \|\vec{c}'(u)\| du,$$

the total distance along the curve up to time t. We also introduced the idea of arc length parameterization, in which $s(t) = t$. Then, since $\frac{ds}{dt} = \|\vec{c}'(t)\|$, arc length parameterization is a path that travels along the curve with unit speed, $ds/dt = 1$, throughout. In fact, any path with $\|\vec{c}'(t)\| \neq 0$ can be parameterized by arc length by inverting $s = s(t)$ such that $t = \varphi(s)$. Note that we can always do this for a smooth path ($ds/dt > 0$ so $s(t)$ is monotonically increasing). In practice, however, you may not be able to find an explicit formula for the arc length parameterization!

Example 4.1. Consider the following path:

$$\vec{c}(t) = (x(t), y(t)) = \left(t, \frac{1}{2}t^2 \right):$$

Since $y = x^2/2$, it's a parabola. Then, we observe that

$$\vec{c}'(t) = (1, t), \|\vec{c}'(t)\| = \sqrt{1 + t^2} \geq 1 > 0.$$

So the path is smooth. Then, we have

$$s(t) = \int_0^t \|\vec{c}'(u)\| du = \int_0^t \sqrt{1 + u^2} du = \frac{1}{2} \left(\ln \left| \sqrt{1 + t^2} + t \right| + t\sqrt{1 + t^2} \right).$$

Clearly, there's no way we can *explicitly* solve for t as a function of s. The way out of this trouble is to treat all $\vec{c}$ as if they were parameterized by arc length and use Chain rule with $ds/dt = \|\vec{c}'(t)\|$ to compensate. $\qquad\qquad\square$

Recall that unit tangent vector to $\vec{c}(t)$ is

$$\vec{T}(t) = \frac{\vec{c}'(t)}{\|\vec{c}'(t)\|}.$$

We wish to understand how the shape of the curve changes over its length: how curved is it?

Definition 4.2. *The* curvature *of a curve is defined as rate of change of the unit tangent vector with respect to arc length:*

$$\kappa = \left\| \frac{d\vec{T}}{ds} \right\|.$$

By chain rule,

$$\frac{d\vec{T}}{dt} = \frac{d\vec{T}}{ds} \cdot \frac{ds}{dt}$$

So, in the original time parameter, t,

$$\kappa(t) = \left\| \frac{1}{\frac{ds}{dt}} \frac{d\vec{T}}{dt} \right\| = \frac{\|\vec{T}'(t)\|}{\|\vec{c}'(t)\|}$$

While the curvature is naturally defined in terms of the arclength function s (because it is a *geometrical* quantity, and shouldn't depend on the speed at which the curve is traced out,) this formula is more practical for finding κ in specific examples.

We've understood the magnitude of derivative of the unit tangent $\|\vec{T}'(s)\|$ as a measure of curvature; what does its direction tell us? Since $\|\vec{T}(s)\| = 1$ is a unit vector for all s, by implicit differentiation,

$$0 = \frac{d}{ds}(1) = \frac{d}{ds} \left(\|\vec{T}(s)\|^2 \right) = \frac{d}{ds} \left(\vec{T}(s) \cdot \vec{T}(s) \right) = 2\vec{T}(s) \cdot \vec{T}'(s),$$

using the product rule for dot products, Theorem 3.8. Therefore, we have $\vec{T}'(s) \perp \vec{T}(s)$ at all points on the curve.

Definition 4.3. *The* principal normal vector *to a smoothly parametrized curve* $\vec{c}(s)$ *is*
$$\vec{N}(s) = \frac{\vec{T}'(s)}{\|\vec{T}'(s)\|}.$$

Looking at the equation satisfied by the derivative of the unit tangent,

$$\vec{T}'(s) = \|\vec{T}'(s)\|\vec{N} = \kappa\vec{N},$$

so the tangent turns in the direction of $\vec{N}$. Note that $\vec{N}$ is only defined when $\|\vec{T}'(s)\| \neq 0$, that is, when the curvature is nonzero! When the curvature is zero there is no preferred direction apart from the unit tangent; this is easy to understand for a straight line path. If $\vec{c}(s)$ is a straight line, the curvature $\kappa(s) = 0$ for all s, and there is no second direction in which the tangent turns.

As we don't always want to express our paths with arclength parametrization, we should have a formula for $\vec{N}(t)$ in terms of an arbitrary parameter t. As usual, this is easily done, using the chain rule. Since $\vec{T}'(t) = \vec{T}'(s)\frac{ds}{dt}$, the term $\frac{ds}{dt}$ cancels out in the fraction, and we have the easy formula,

$$\vec{N}(t) = \frac{\vec{T}'(t)}{\|\vec{T}'(t)\|},$$

again provided $\vec{T}'(t) \neq \vec{0}$.

Example 4.4. Consider a circle of radius $R > 0$ in xy-plane:

$$\vec{c}(t) = (R\sin t, R\cos t, 0).$$

Now, we can easily find its velocity vector and speed:

$$\vec{c}'(t) = (R\cos t, -R\sin t, 0)$$
$$\|\vec{c}'(t)\| = R$$

Notice that this travels with constant speed (clockwise) but is not arc length parameterized (unless the radius $R = 1$.)

Its unit tangent is

$$\vec{T}(t) = \frac{\vec{c}'(t)}{\|\vec{c}'(t)\|} = \frac{\vec{c}'(t)}{R} = (\cos t, -\sin t, 0)$$

Then,

$$\vec{N}(t) = \vec{T}'(t) = (-\sin t, -\cos t, 0)$$

Again, notice that $\vec{N}(t)$ is perpendicular to $\vec{T}(t)$, but lies in the same plane as the curve itself.

Finally, we have

$$\kappa(t) = \frac{\|\vec{T}'(t)\|}{\|\vec{c}'(t)\|} = \frac{1}{R}.$$

Therefore, circles with larger radii have smaller curvature. □

Example 4.5. Consider the following helix:

$$\vec{c}(t) = (3\cos t, 3\sin t, 4t).$$

Following the same approach as shown in the previous example, we get

$$\vec{c}'(t) = (-3\sin t, 3\cos t, 4)$$
$$\|\vec{c}'(t)\| = 5$$
$$\vec{T}(t) = \left(-\frac{3}{5}\sin t, \frac{3}{5}\cos t, \frac{4}{5}\right)$$
$$\vec{T}'(t) = \left(-\frac{3}{5}\cos t, -\frac{3}{5}\sin t, 0\right)$$

Then,

$$\kappa(t) = \frac{\|\vec{T}'(t)\|}{\|\vec{c}'(t)\|} = \frac{3/5}{5} = \frac{3}{25}$$

This curve also has a constant curvature, like the circle, although it is not planar. □

As long as the curvature $\kappa(s) \neq 0$, $\vec{T}, \vec{N}$ determines a plane in $\mathbb{R}^3$, the *osculating plane*. The normal vector to the osculating plane is given by

$$\vec{B} = \vec{T} \times \vec{N},$$

the *Binormal vector* to the curve. We observe that $\vec{B} \perp \vec{T}$, $\vec{B} \perp \vec{N}$, and

$$\|\vec{B}\| = \|\vec{T}\|\|\vec{N}\| |\sin\theta| = 1 \cdot 1 \cdot \sin(\pi/2) = 1$$

Therefore, $\{\vec{T}(s), \vec{N}(s), \vec{B}(s)\}$ is a moving *orthonormal basis* for $\mathbb{R}^3$ at each point along the curve. This plane is also referred to as *moving frame* or *Frenet frame*.

Remark. • If curvature $\kappa(s) = 0$ for all s, then the curve is a straight line. This is easy to see, since then $\vec{T}'(s) = 0$ for all s, which may be integrated to get $\vec{T}(s) = \vec{u}$, a constant, for all s. But $\vec{c}'(s) = \vec{T}(s) = \vec{u}$ is integrated to $\vec{c}(s) = s\vec{u} + \vec{a}$, where $\vec{u}, \vec{a}$ are constants, which is the parametric equation of a line.

• When $\kappa = 0$, $\vec{N}$ and $\vec{B}$ cannot be defined.

• If $\vec{B}(s)$ is a constant vector, then $\vec{c}(t)$ lies in a fixed plane, with normal vector $\vec{B}$.

Now, suppose $\vec{B}(s)$ isn't constant. First, its norm is constant, since $\|\vec{B}(s)\| = 1$ for all s. By now we know that by differentiating implicitly we should get some geometrical information about $\vec{B}(s)$ and its derivative:

$$1 = \|\vec{B}(s)\|^2 = \vec{B}(s) \cdot \vec{B}(s)$$

holds for all s. So we can apply implicit differentiation:

$$0 = \frac{d}{dS}(1) = \frac{d}{dS}\left(\vec{B} \cdot \vec{B}\right) = 2\vec{B}' \cdot \vec{B}.$$

Then, it follows that $\vec{B}' \perp \vec{B}$, for every s.

Next, since $\vec{B}(s) \perp \vec{T}(s)$ for all s, we have $\vec{B} \cdot \vec{T} = 0$ for all s. Then,

$$\frac{d}{ds}\left(\vec{B} \cdot \vec{T}\right) = \vec{B}'(s) \cdot \vec{T}(s) + \vec{B}(s) \cdot \vec{T}'(s) = 0.$$

Since $\vec{T}' = \kappa \vec{N}$ and $\vec{B} \cdot \vec{N} = 0$, it follows that

$$\vec{B}'(s) \cdot \vec{T}(s) = 0 \iff \vec{B}'(s) \perp \vec{T}(s)$$

Since $\left\{\vec{T}, \vec{N}, \vec{B}\right\}$ form a orthonormal basis for $\mathbb{R}^3$, we must have $\vec{B}'(s)$ parallel to $\vec{N}$. Therefore,

$$\vec{B}'(s) = -\tau(s)\vec{N}(s)$$

for a function $\tau(s)$ called the *torsion*. Since $\tau = \|d\vec{B}/ds\|$, it measures how fast the normal $\vec{B}$ to the osculating plane is twisting.

Definition 4.6 (Torsion).

$$\tau = \left\|\frac{d\vec{B}}{ds}\right\| = \frac{\|\vec{B}'(t)\|}{\|\vec{c}'(t)\|}$$

Putting all the information together we get *Frenet formulas*:

Theorem 4.7 (Frenet formulas). *Let $\vec{c}(t)$ be a smoothly parametrized curve. Then the Frenet frame $\{\vec{T}, \vec{N}, \vec{B}\}$ satisfy the system of equations,*

$$\begin{cases} \dfrac{d\vec{T}}{ds} = \kappa\vec{N} \\[2mm] \dfrac{d\vec{B}}{ds} = -\tau\vec{N} \\[2mm] \dfrac{d\vec{N}}{ds} = -\kappa\vec{T} + \tau\vec{B} \end{cases}$$

Example 4.8. Consider the following helix:

$$\vec{c}(t) = (3\cos t, 3\sin t, 4t)$$

Then, we have

$$\|\vec{c}\,'(t)\| = 5,$$

$$\vec{T}(t) = \left(-\frac{3}{5}\sin t, \frac{3}{5}\cos t, \frac{4}{5}\right),$$

$$\vec{T}\,'(t) = \left(-\frac{3}{5}\cos t, -\frac{3}{5}\sin t, 0\right),$$

$$\kappa = \frac{3}{25},$$

$$\vec{N}(t) = (-\cos t, -\sin t, 0),$$

$$\vec{B}(t) = \vec{T} \times \vec{N} = \left(\frac{4}{5}\sin t, -\frac{4}{5}\cos t, \frac{3}{5}\right),$$

$$\vec{B}\,' = \left(\frac{4}{5}\cos t, \frac{4}{5}\sin t, 0\right),$$

$$\tau = \frac{4}{25}.$$

$\square$

4.2   Dynamics

How do the geometrical quantities $\{\vec{T}, \vec{N}, \vec{B}\}$, κ, τ relate to dynamical quantities, velocity $\vec{c}\,'(t) = \vec{v}(t)$, speed $\|\vec{c}\,'(t)\| = ds/dt$, and acceleration $\vec{a}(t) = \vec{v}\,'(t) = \vec{c}\,''(t)$?

First, observe that

$$\vec{v}(t) = \vec{c}\,'(t) = \frac{ds}{dt} \cdot \vec{T}(t)$$

Then,

$$\vec{a}(t) = \frac{d}{dt}\left(\frac{ds}{dt} \cdot \vec{T}(t)\right) = \frac{d^2 s}{dt^2} \cdot \vec{T}(t) + \frac{ds}{dt} \cdot \vec{T}\,'(t)$$

$$= \frac{d^2 s}{dt^2} \cdot \vec{T} + \frac{ds}{dt} \cdot \left(\frac{d\vec{T}}{ds} \cdot \frac{ds}{dt}\right)$$

So we have

$$\vec{a}(t) = \underbrace{\frac{d^2 s}{dt^2} \cdot \vec{T}}_{\text{Linear acceleration}} + \underbrace{\kappa \left(\frac{ds}{dt}\right)^2 \vec{N}}_{\text{Steering-term}}$$

So there are two orthogonal components to the acceleration vector $\vec{a}(t)$. One is due to *linear acceleration*, changing speed by rate $\frac{d^2 s}{dt^2}$ in the tangent (forward) direction. This is acceleration by pushing down on the gas pedal when driving (or deceleration by braking.) It changes speed but not direction. The other term is in the direction of the principal normal, and it changes direction, like turning the steering wheel. Notice that it is proportional to the curvature κ of the path, and also proportional to the square of the speed (so steering gets much harder at high speeds!)

Example 4.9. Consider the following path

$$\vec{c}(t) = (e^t \cos t, e^t \sin t, e^t)$$

that drwas a spiral in xy direction and monotonically increases along the z coordinate.

First, observe that

$$\vec{v}(t) = \vec{c}\,'(t) = (-e^t \sin + e^t \cos t, e^t \cos t + e^t \sin t, e^t)$$
$$\frac{ds}{dt} = \|\vec{c}\,'(t)\| = \sqrt{3}e^t$$

Then, we have

$$\vec{T}(t) = \frac{\vec{c}\,'(t)}{\|\vec{c}\,'(t)\|} = \frac{1}{\sqrt{3}}(-\sin t + \cos t, \cos t + \sin t, 1),$$
$$\vec{T}\,'(t) = \frac{\vec{c}\,'(t)}{\|\vec{c}\,'(t)\|} = \frac{1}{\sqrt{3}}(-\cos t - \sin t, -\sin t + \cos t, 0).$$

Since $\|\vec{T}\,'(t)\| = \sqrt{2/3}$, we can easily find the principal normal vector:

$$\vec{N}(t) = \frac{\vec{T}\,'(t)}{\|\vec{T}\,'(t)\|} = \frac{1}{\sqrt{2}}(-\cos t - \sin t, -\sin t + \cos t, 0)$$

Then,

$$\kappa = \frac{\|\vec{T}\,'(t)\|}{\|\vec{c}\,'(t)\|} = \frac{\sqrt{2}}{3}e^{-t}.$$

Furthermore,

$$\vec{B}(t) = \vec{T}(t) \times \vec{N}(t) = \cdots = \frac{1}{\sqrt{6}}(\cos t - \sin t, -\sin t - \cos t, 2)$$
$$\vec{B}\,'(t) = \frac{1}{\sqrt{6}}(-\sin t - \cos t, -\cos t + \sin t, 0)$$

Therefore, torsion of the curve is given by

$$\tau(t) = \frac{\|\vec{B}\,'(t)\|}{\|\vec{c}\,'(t)\|} = \frac{1}{3}e^{-t}$$

We can then veriy formula for $\vec{a}$ in terms of $\vec{T}, \vec{N}, \kappa$, (and verify that it agrees with $\vec{a} = \vec{v}\,'(t)$ calculated directly). $\qquad\square$

Now, we present an alternative equation for curvature using dynamical quantities:

Theorem 4.10.
$$\kappa(t) = \frac{\|\vec{c}\,'(t) \times \vec{c}\,''(t)\|}{\|\vec{c}\,'(t)\|^3} = \frac{\|\vec{v}(t) \times \vec{a}(t)\|}{\|\vec{v}(t)\|^3}$$

Proof. To verify it, we use the decomposition of $\vec{a}$:

$$\vec{v} \times \vec{a} = \vec{v} \times \left(\frac{d^2s}{dt^2} \cdot \vec{T} + \kappa \left(\frac{ds}{dt} \right)^2 \vec{N} \right)$$

$$= \frac{d^2s}{dt^2} \left(\vec{v} \times \vec{T} \right) + \kappa \left(\frac{ds}{dt} \right)^2 \left(\vec{v} \times \vec{N} \right)$$

$$= \kappa \left(\frac{ds}{dt} \right)^3 \left(\vec{T} \times \vec{N} \right)$$

$$= \kappa \left(\frac{ds}{dt} \right)^3 \vec{B}$$

Then, $\kappa(ds/dt)^3 \|\vec{B}\| = \|\vec{v} \times \vec{a}\|$. Since $\vec{B}$ is a unit vector, we get the desired identity by taking the norm on each side of the equation. $\qquad\square$

4.3 Practice problems

Practice problems will be given from Stewart [Stew].

Chapter 5

Implicit functions

5.1 The Implicit Function Theorem I

Often, we have an *implicit* relationship between variables,

$$F(x_1, x_2, \ldots, x_n) = 0,$$

rather than an *explicit* function relation, such as

$$x_n = f(x_1, x_2, \ldots, x_{n-1}).$$

Example 5.1. Look at a familiar example in $\mathbb{R}^2$ (See Figure 5.1), the unit circle,

$$x^2 + y^2 = 1.$$

This fails vertical line test $(y \neq f(x))$ as well as horizontal line test $(x \neq g(y))$; globally, this relation does not define a function. Locally, we can write this as a function, i.e. by restricting attention to small pieces of the curve.

First, define

$$F(x, y) = x^2 + y^2 - 1$$

If $y_0 > 0$, $x_0^2 + y_0^2 = 1$, i.e. $F(x_0, y_0) = 0$, and we look at a window (or *neighborhood*) around (x_0, y_0), which lies entirely in the upper half plane, we can solve for $y = f(x)$,

$$y = \underbrace{\sqrt{1 - x^2}}_{f(x)}$$

We could calculate $y' = f'(x)$ from the explicit formula but we can also get it via *implicit differentiation*:

$$\frac{d}{dx}\left(F(x, f(x))\right) = \frac{\partial F}{\partial x} \cdot \frac{dx}{dx} + \frac{\partial F}{\partial y} \cdot f'(x)$$
$$= 2x + 2yf'(x),$$

so $f'(x) = -x/y$. $\qquad\qquad\square$

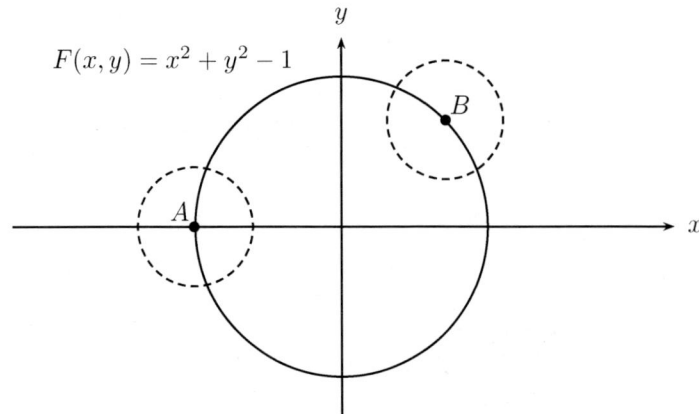

Figure 5.1. Near the neighborhood around point A, vertical line test fails as single x value corresponds to two y values. On the other hand, neighborhood around point B can be solved as $y = \sqrt{1 - x^2}$.

For a general $F(x, y) = 0$, we can solve for $f'(x)$ if

$$\frac{\partial F}{\partial y}(x_0, y_0) \neq 0,$$

where y is the variable we want to solve for. This gives the limitation on which we can solve for $y = f(x)$ locally. For the circle example, we had

$$\frac{\partial F}{\partial y} = 2y.$$

When $y = 0$, the vertical line test fails in every neighborhood of $(x_0, y_0) = (\pm 1, 0)$, which is exactly when the partial derivative with respect to y vanishes.

In general, suppose we have a C^1 function,

$$F : \mathbb{R}^{n+1} \to \mathbb{R},$$

and consider all functions of $F(\vec{x}, y) = 0$. In order to write $y = g(\vec{x})$ – i.e. we can solve for y as a differentiable function of $\vec{x}$ – we do the same implicit differentiation, with the chain rule,

$$\frac{\partial}{\partial x_i}\left(F\left(x_1, x_2. \ldots .x_n, f(\vec{x})\right)\right) = \frac{\partial F}{\partial x_i} + \frac{\partial F}{\partial y}\frac{\partial f}{\partial x_i}$$

for each $i = 1, 2, \ldots, n$. We can then solve for each

$$\frac{\partial f}{\partial x_i} = \frac{-\dfrac{\partial F}{\partial x_i}}{\dfrac{\partial F}{\partial y}},$$

provided $\partial F/\partial y \neq 0$. This is a sufficient condition to solve for $y = f(\vec{x})$.

Theorem 5.2 (Implicit Function Theorem I). *Assume $F : \mathbb{R}^{n+1} \to \mathbb{R}$ is C^1 in a neighborhood of $(\vec{x}_0, y_0)$ with $F(\vec{x}_0, y_0) = 0$. If $\frac{\partial F}{\partial y}(\vec{x}_0, y_0) \neq 0$, then there exists neighborhood $\mathcal{U}$ of $\vec{x}_0$ and $\mathcal{V}$ of y_0 and a C^1 function*

$$f : \mathcal{U} \subset \mathbb{R}^n \to \mathcal{V} \subset \mathbb{R},$$

for which $F(\vec{x}, f(\vec{x})) = 0$ for all $\vec{x} \in \mathcal{U}$. In addition,

$$Df(\vec{x}) = \frac{-1}{\frac{\partial F}{\partial y}(\vec{x}, y)} D_{\vec{x}} F(\vec{x}, y),$$

where

$$D_{\vec{x}} F(\vec{x}, y) = \begin{bmatrix} \frac{\partial F}{\partial x_1} & \frac{\partial F}{\partial x_2} & \cdots & \frac{\partial F}{\partial x_n} \end{bmatrix}.$$

Example 5.3. Consider the following function:

$$xy + y^2 z + z^3 = 1.$$

For which part on this surface can we write $z = f(x, y)$, i.e.

$$F : \mathbb{R}^3 \to \mathbb{R}, F(x, y, z) = xy + y^2 z + z^3 - 1$$

is C^1? □

We want to solve for z, so we look at

$$\frac{\partial F}{\partial z} = y^2 + 3z^2.$$

We observe that $\partial F/\partial z = 0$ iff $y = 0$ and $z = 0$. However, $y = 0$ and $z = 0$ is not defined on this surface. At all points on this surface, $\partial F/\partial z \neq 0$. So at every (x_0, y_0, z_0) with $F(x_0, y_0, z_0) = 0$, we can solve for $z = f(x, y)$ locally near (x_0, y_0).

We can then use the implicit differentiation formula in the theorem to calculate $Df(x, y)$:

$$D_{(x,y)}F = \begin{bmatrix} y & (x + 2yz) \end{bmatrix},$$

so we get

$$Df(x, y) = \frac{-D_{(x,y)}F}{\partial F/\partial z} = \begin{bmatrix} -\dfrac{y}{y^2 + 3z^2} & -\dfrac{x + 2yz}{y^2 3z^2} \end{bmatrix}$$

or

$$\nabla f(x, y) = \left(-\frac{y}{y^2 + 3z^2}, -\frac{x + 2yz}{y^2 + 3z^2} \right).$$

Example 5.4. Consider the following equation:

$$x^4 + xz^2 + z^4 = 1.$$

Show that we can solve for $z = g(x)$ near $(x_1, z_1) = (-1, 1)$ but not near $(x_2, z_2) = (1, 0)$. □

Proof. First, let

$$F(x, z) = x^4 + xz^2 + z^4 - 1.$$

Clearly, $F : \mathbb{R}^2 \to \mathbb{R}$ is C^1 for all $(x, z) \in \mathbb{R}^2$. Observe that

$$\frac{\partial F}{\partial z} = 2xz + 4z^3,$$

and so $\partial F(-1, 1)/\partial z \neq 0$.

By the Implicit Function Theorem, we can solve for $z = g(x)$ locally near $(x_1, z_1) = (-1, 1)$. In addition, we can get an explicit formula for its derivative:

$$Dg(x) = g'(x) = -\frac{\partial F(x, z)/\partial x}{\partial F/\partial z} = -\frac{4x^3 + z^2}{2xz + 4z^3}$$

Finally, since $\partial F(1, 0)/\partial z = 0$, the Implicit Function Theorem does not apply near $(1, 0)$. This **does not** mean that you cannot solve for z as a function of (x, z) locally near $(1, 0)$ (see Example 5.5 below.) Nevertheless, in this example it is the case that we can't solve for $z = g(x)$ locally near $(1, 0)$. Notice that F is even symmetric in z, that is $F(x, -z) = F(x, z)$ for all (x, z). So for every point (x, z) which solves $F(x, z) = 0$, it's also true that $F(x, -z) = 0$. This means that for every x there are two values $\pm z$ lying on the curve described by $F(x, z) = 0$. (So we can not solve $x = g(z)$ *globally*, as the vertical line rule fails unless $z = 0$.) When $z \neq 0$ this is all right, since the points (x, z) and $(x, -z)$ are far apart, so we can solve locally, but in any neighborhood of $(x, z) = (1, 0)$ there are always two points $(x, \pm z)$ and the curve is not a function locally near $(1, 0)$. $\square$

Example 5.5. As mentioned above, it's possible that the hypotheses of the Implicit Function Theorem are not satisfied, but it is still possible to solve for $z = g(x)$ with C^1 function g anyway. This may seem silly, but it's a legitimate example: take $F : \mathbb{R}^2 \to \mathbb{R}$ as $F(x, z) = (z - x^2)^2$. Then F is C^1, and $F(x, z) = 0$ is equivalent to $(z - x^2) = 0$, which is equivalent to $z = x^2$, and the curve is globally described by the C^1 graph of $g(x) = x^2$. The Implicit Function Theorem does not apply at any (x, z) on the curve, since $\frac{\partial F}{\partial z} = 2(z - x^2) = 0$ at every point.

Example 5.6. Intermediate situations are also possible when the hypotheses of the Implicit Function Theorem fail to hold. Consider the following equation:

$$x - z^3 = 0$$

Clearly, $F(x, z) = x - z^3$ is C^1 for all $(x, z) \in \mathbb{R}^2$. Note that

$$\frac{\partial F}{\partial z} = -3z^2.$$

Clearly, $\partial F/\partial z = 0$ at $(x, z) = (0, 0)$. However, we can write $z = x^{1/3}$ globally. So an explicit representation of z as a function of x exists, $z = g(x) = x^{1/3}$. On the other hand, $g(x)$ isn't differentiable at $(x_0, z_0) = (0, 0)$, so the vanishing of the partial derivative $\frac{\partial F}{\partial z}$ is making itself felt in a more subtle way. $\square$

5.2   The Implicit Function Theorem II

We also have a version of the Implicit Function Theorem which applies to under-determined systems of (nonlinear) equations.

Example 5.7. Suppose we have a system of equations with more unknowns:

$$\begin{cases} u^2 - v^2 - x^3 = 0 \\ 2uv - y^5 = 0 \end{cases}$$

Can we solve for (u, v) as functions of (x, y)?

First, consider a C^1 function, $F : \mathbb{R}^4 \to \mathbb{R}^2$, that is defined as follows:

$$\begin{cases} F_1(x, y, u, v) = u^2 - v^2 - x^2 = 0 \\ F_2(x, y, u, v) = 2uv - y^5 = 0 \end{cases}$$

Following what we did before, we can assume $(u, v) = g(x, y)$ and see when we can calculate Dg. Note that

$$0 = \frac{\partial}{\partial x} F_1(x, y, u(x, y), v(x, y)) = \frac{\partial F_1}{\partial x} + \frac{\partial F_1}{\partial u}\frac{\partial u}{\partial x} + \frac{\partial F_1}{\partial v}\frac{\partial v}{\partial x}$$
$$0 = \frac{\partial}{\partial x} F_2(x, y, u(x, y), v(x, y)) = \frac{\partial F_2}{\partial x} + \frac{\partial F_2}{\partial u}\frac{\partial u}{\partial x} + \frac{\partial F_2}{\partial v}\frac{\partial v}{\partial x}$$

Then, we can solve for $\partial u/\partial x$ and $\partial v/\partial x$. Rearranging,

$$\begin{bmatrix} \dfrac{\partial F_1}{\partial u} & \dfrac{\partial F_1}{\partial v} \\ \dfrac{\partial F_2}{\partial u} & \dfrac{\partial F_2}{\partial v} \end{bmatrix} \begin{bmatrix} \dfrac{\partial u}{\partial x} \\ \dfrac{\partial v}{\partial x} \end{bmatrix} = \begin{bmatrix} -\dfrac{\partial F_1}{\partial x} \\ -\dfrac{\partial F_2}{\partial x} \end{bmatrix}$$

This can be solved if $D_{(u,v)}F$ is invertible, i.e. $\det\left[D_{(u,v)}F\right] \neq 0$.

Similarly, we can also solve for $\partial u/\partial y$ and $\partial v/\partial y$. As a result, we get a different linear system to solve but with the same matrix $\left[D_{(u,v)}F\right]$. The second version of the Implicit Function Theorem says that this is the correct condition to solve for $g(x)$ in this setting.   □

Let's see how this works in general. The notation is a bit complicated, but the basic idea is the same as in the example. Given the following system of functions,

$$F_1(x_1, \ldots, x_n, u_1, \ldots u_m) = 0$$
$$F_2(x_1, \ldots, x_n, u_1, \ldots u_m) = 0$$
$$\vdots$$
$$F_m(x_1, \ldots, x_n, u_1, \ldots u_m) = 0$$

we want to solve for $\vec{u} = (u_1, \ldots, u_m) \in \mathbb{R}^m$ as a function, $\vec{u} = g(\vec{x})$, of $\vec{x} = (x_1, \ldots, x_n) \in \mathbb{R}^n$. Via implicit differentiation, for the case of $n = m = 2$, we arrived at an appropriate condition where this is possible.

Theorem 5.8 (Implicit Function Theorem II - General Form). *Let*

$$F : \mathbb{R}^{n+m} \to \mathbb{R}^m$$

be a C^1 function in a neighborhood of $(\vec{x}_0, \vec{u}_0) \in \mathbb{R}^{n+m}$, with $F(\vec{x}_0, \vec{u}_0) = \vec{0}$. If, in addition, $D_{\vec{u}}F(\vec{x}_0, \vec{u}_0)$ is invertible, then there exists neighborhoods $\mathcal{V}$ of $\vec{x}_0$ and $\mathcal{U}$ of $\vec{u}_0$, for which solutions of $F(\vec{x}, \vec{u}) = \vec{0}$ lie on a C^1 graph, $\vec{u} = g(\vec{x})$,

$$g : \mathcal{V} \subset \mathbb{R}^n \to \mathcal{U} \in \mathbb{R}^m$$

Example 5.9. Consider the following set of equations:

$$\begin{cases} 2xu^2 + yv^4 = 3 \\ xy(u^2 - v^2) = 0 \end{cases}$$

Can we solve for $(u, v) = g(x, y)$ near $(x_0, y_0, y_0, v_0) = (1, 1, -1, -1)$?   □

Let

$$F = \begin{bmatrix} F_1 \\ F_2 \end{bmatrix}, \vec{x} = (x, y), \vec{u} = (u, v),$$

where F is defined as

$$\left. \begin{aligned} F_1(\vec{x}, \vec{u}) &= 2xu^2 + yv^4 - 3 = 0 \\ F_2(\vec{x}, \vec{u}) &= xy(u^2 - v^2) = 0) \end{aligned} \right\} \tag{5.1}$$

Then, we get the following Jacobian

$$D_{\vec{u}}F = \frac{\partial(F_1, F_2)}{\partial(u, v)}$$

$$= \begin{bmatrix} \dfrac{\partial F_1}{\partial u} & \dfrac{\partial F_1}{\partial v} \\ \dfrac{\partial F_2}{\partial u} & \dfrac{\partial F_2}{\partial v} \end{bmatrix}$$

$$= \begin{bmatrix} 4xu & 4yv^3 \\ 2uxy & -2vxy \end{bmatrix}$$

Substituting the given values, we have

$$D_{\vec{u}}F(1, 1, -1, -1) = \begin{bmatrix} -4 & -4 \\ -2 & 2 \end{bmatrix}$$

Since $\det D_{\vec{u}}F = -16 \neq 0$, the Implicit Function Theorem does apply, and we can solve for $\vec{u} = (u, v) = g(\vec{x}) = g(x, y)$ near $(x_0, y_0, u_0, v_0) = (1, 1, -1, -1)$.

In general, we can't get an explicit formula for g, but we can get a formula for $Dg(x, y)$, i.e. its partial derivatives, using implicit differentiation. For the above example, we may calculate $\frac{\partial u}{\partial x}, \frac{\partial v}{\partial x}$ by implicitly differentiating the equations (5.1) with respect to x, remembering that u, v are functions of (x, y):

$$0 = \frac{\partial F_1}{\partial x} = \frac{\partial}{\partial x}\left[2xu^2 + yv^4 - 3\right] = 2u^2 + 4xu\,u_x + 4yv^3\,v_x$$

$$0 = \frac{\partial F_1}{\partial x} = \frac{\partial}{\partial x}\left[xy(u^2 - v^2)\right] = y(u^2 - v^2) + xy(2u\,u_x - 2v\,v_x).$$

At $(x, y, u, v) = (1, 1, -1, -1)$ we obtain the system of equations,

$$-4u_x - 4v_x = -2$$
$$-2u_x + 2v_x = 0.$$

Notice that the coefficient matrix is exactly $D_{\vec{u}}F(1, 1, -1, -1)$. This is not an accident! Using Cramer's Rule[1] the system may be easily solved using determinants, and we have $u_x(1, 1) = v_x(1, 1) = \frac{1}{4}$. To find $u_y(1, 1), v_y(1, 1)$, do the same thing but take the implicit derivative with respect to y.

5.3   Inverse Function Theorem

In general, suppose we have a C^1 function, $f : \mathbb{R}^n \to \mathbb{R}^n$, where $\vec{x} = f(\vec{u})$. Is it possible to solve for $\vec{u} = g(\vec{x})$?

In single-variable calculus, a function $f : \mathbb{R} \to \mathbb{R}$ is *one-to-one* on an interval $[a, b]$ if and only if f is strictly monotone on $[a, b]$. For these functions, f has an inverse $g = f^{-1}$,

$$g(f(x)) = x, \quad \forall x \in [a, b]$$

If f is differentiable on $[a, b]$, and $f'(x) > 0$ on $[a, b]$ (or $f'(x) < 0$ on $[a, b]$), then the inverse $g(x)$ is also differentiable, and

$$g'(f(x)) = \frac{1}{f'(x)}, \quad \forall x \in [a, b]$$

If, for example, $f'(x) > 0$ for all $x \in \mathbb{R}$, then it's globally invertible, i.e. $g(f(x)) = x$ for all $x \in \mathbb{R}$. How do we apply this for $f : \mathbb{R}^n \to \mathbb{R}^n$ with $n \geq 2$? There's no such thing as a monotone function of several variables!

Let's look at a simple example for guidance.

Example 5.10. Consider the following set of equations:

$$\begin{cases} x = u^2 - v^2 \\ y = 2uv \end{cases}$$

---

[1] **Cramer's Rule.** Given a system of linear equations that is represented by 2×2 matrices,

$$\begin{cases} ax + by = s \\ cx + dy = t \end{cases},$$

solution of the system is given by

$$x = \frac{\det \begin{pmatrix} s & b \\ t & d \end{pmatrix}}{\det \begin{pmatrix} a & b \\ c & d \end{pmatrix}}, y = \frac{\det \begin{pmatrix} a & s \\ c & t \end{pmatrix}}{\det \begin{pmatrix} a & b \\ c & d \end{pmatrix}}$$

Note that this example fits the form of the Implicit Function Theorem, but it's a special case. We want to invert this relation, i.e. given, $\vec{x} = f(\vec{u})$, we want to solve for $\vec{u} = g(\vec{x})$.

To get a nice theorem for this special case, we can use the framework of the Implicit Function Theorem:

$$\begin{cases} F_1(\vec{x}, \vec{u}) = f_1(\vec{u}) - x = 0 \\ F_2(\vec{x}, \vec{u}) = f_2(\vec{u}) - y = 0 \end{cases}$$

Since

$$D_{\vec{u}} F(\vec{x}, \vec{u}) = Df(\vec{u}),$$

we can do this locally near a point $(\vec{x}_0, \vec{u}_0)$ provided that

$$\det (Df(\vec{u})) \neq 0$$

$\square$

This is a very satisfying result, because it's a direct extension of the linear algebra case. If we had a linear change of variables, $\vec{x} = M\vec{u}$ with a constant matrix M, we can solve $\vec{u} = M^{-1}\vec{x}$ provided $\det M \neq 0$. So while it makes no sense to calculate the determinant of a nonlinear function, it turns out that the nonlinear function is invertible (at least locally) when its derivative matrix is invertible!

Theorem 5.11 (Inverse Function Theorem). *Suppose $f : \mathbb{R}^n \to \mathbb{R}^n$ which is C^1 in a neighborhood of $\vec{u}_0$, with $f(\vec{u}_0) = \vec{x}_0$. If $\det (Df(\vec{u}_0)) \neq 0$, then there exist neighborhoods $\mathcal{U}$ of $\vec{u}_0$ and $\mathcal{V}$ of $\vec{x}_0$ and a C^1 function $g : \mathcal{V} \to \mathcal{U}$, with*

$$\underset{\text{with } \vec{u} \in \mathcal{U}}{\vec{x} = f(\vec{u})} \iff \underset{\text{with } \vec{x} \in \mathcal{V}}{\vec{u} = g(\vec{x})},$$

i.e. near $\vec{x}_0$ and $\vec{u}_0$, g is the inverse of f.

Moreover,

$$Dg(\vec{x}) = [Df(\vec{u})]^{-1}. \tag{5.2}$$

The formula for the derivative matrix of the inverse function follows directly from the Chain Rule: since $\vec{x} = f(\vec{u}) = f(g(\vec{x}))$, ignore the middle equality and differentiate with respect to $\vec{x}$. Since the function $h(\vec{x}) = \vec{x} = I\vec{x}$, with I the identity matrix, $Dh(\vec{x}) = I$. So

$$I = Dh(\vec{x}) = D(f \circ g(\vec{x})) = Df(\vec{u}) \, Dg(\vec{x}).$$

Since we are assuming in the theorem that $\det(Df(\vec{u})) \neq 0$, the matrix is invertible, and the above formula (5.2) is verified.

Example 5.12. Apply the Inverse Function Theorem to the function that was defined in the previous example:

$$\begin{cases} x = u^2 - v^2 \\ y = 2uv \end{cases}$$

$\square$

Observe that
$$\det\left(Df(u,v)\right) = \det\begin{bmatrix} 2u & -2v \\ 2v & 2u \end{bmatrix} = 4u^2 + 4v^2 \neq 0$$

as long as $(u_0, v_0) \neq (0,0)$. So we can invert the variables and solve for $(u,v) = g(x,y)$, locally near any $(u_0, v_0) \neq (0,0)$.

Notice that
$$f_1(-u, -v) = x = f_1(u, v)$$
$$f_2(-u, -v) = y = f_2(u, v)$$

So in any neighborhood of $(0,0)$ there are 2 values of (u,v) corresponding to each (x,y). Therefore, f is not invertible near $(u,v) = (0,0)$.

Example 5.13. Consider the following equations:

$$\begin{cases} x = e^y \cos v \\ y = e^u \sin v \end{cases}$$

For which (u,v,x,y) can we solve for u, v as functions of x, y? □

Let
$$f(u,v) = \begin{bmatrix} e^u \cos v \\ e^u \sin v \end{bmatrix}.$$

Then, we have
$$Df(u,v) = \begin{bmatrix} e^u \cos v & -e^u \sin v \\ e^u \sin v & e^u \cos v \end{bmatrix}$$

Then, we can compute $\det(Df(u,v))$, (or $\det\left(\frac{\partial(x,y)}{\partial(u,v)}\right)$):

$$\det(Df(u,v)) = e^{2u}.$$

Clearly, $\det(Df(u,v)) > 0$ for all u, v. By the Inverse Function Theorem, we can invert and solve for $(u,v) = g(x,y)$, near any (u_0, v_0).

We can invert locally near any point; can we find a global inverse, i.e. a g for which $(u,v) = g(x,y)$ for every $(u,v) \in \mathbb{R}^2$? If so, then f would have to be a one-to-one function. However,

$$f(u, v + 2\pi k) = f(u,v)$$

for all $k \in \mathbb{Z}$. Therefore, f can't be globally inverted.

Example 5.14. Consider the following equations:

$$\begin{cases} x = f_1(u,v) = u^3 - 3uv^2 \\ y = f_2(u,v) = -v^3 + 3u^2v \end{cases}$$

Since they're polynomials, $f : \mathbb{R}^2 \to \mathbb{R}^2$ is C^1. Then, we have

$$\frac{\partial(x,y)}{\partial(u,v)} = \begin{bmatrix} 3u^2 - 3v^2 & -6uv \\ 6uv & -3v^2 + 3u^2 \end{bmatrix}$$

$$\det\left(\frac{\partial(x,y)}{\partial(u,v)}\right) = (3u^2 - 3v^2)^2 + (6uv)^2$$

Clearly, $\det(\partial(x,y)/\partial(u,v)) = 0$ iff $u = v = 0$. So, Inverse Function Theorem holds for all $(u_0, v_0) \neq (0,0)$, and we can solve for $(x,y) = g(u,v)$ around any $(u_0, v_0) \neq (0,0)$. $\square$

5.4   Practice problems

1. [MT, p. 210] Show that the equation $x+y-z+\cos(xyz) = 1$ can be solved for $z = g(x,y)$ near the origin. Find $\frac{\partial g}{\partial x}$ and $\frac{\partial g}{\partial y}$ at $(0,0)$.

2. [MT, p. 210] Show that $xy + z + 3xz^5 = 4$ is solvable for z as a function of (x,y) near $(1,0,1)$. Compute $\partial z/\partial x$ and $\partial z/\partial y$ at $(1,0)$.

3. [MT, p. 210]

   (a). Check directly where we can solve the equation

$$F(x,y) = y^2 + y + 3x + 1 = 0$$

for y in terms of x.

   (b). Check that your answer in part (a) agrees with the answer you expect from the implicit function theorem. Compute dy/dx.

4. [MT, p. 210] Repeat problem 3 with

$$F(x,y) = xy^2 - 2y + x^2 = 0.$$

5. [MT, p. 210] Let $F(x,y) = 0$ define a curve in the xy plane through the point (x_0, y_0), where F is C^1. Assume that $(\partial F/\partial y)(x_0, y_0) \neq 0$. Show that this curve can be locally represented by the graph of a function $y = g(x)$. Show that (i) the line orthogonal to $\nabla F(x_0, y_0)$ agrees with (ii) the tangent line to the graph of $y = g(x)$.

6. [MT, p. 210] Show that $x^3z^2 - z^3yx = 0$ is solvable for z as a function of (x,y) near $(1,1,1)$, but not near the origin. Compute $\partial z/\partial x$ and $\partial z/\partial y$ at $(1,1)$.

7. [MT, p. 210] Investigate whether or not the system

$$u(x,y,z) = x + xyz$$
$$v(x,y,z) = y + xy$$
$$w(x,y,z) = z + 2x + 3z^2$$

can be solved for x, y, z in terms of u, v, w near $(x,y,z) = (0,0,0)$.

8. [MT, p. 210] Let (x_0, y_0, z_0) be a point of the locus defined by $x^2 + xy - a = 0$, $z^2 + x^2 - y^2 - b = 0$, where a and b are continuous.

(a) Under what conditions may the part of the locus near (x_0, y_0, z_0) be represented in the form $x = f(z), y = g(z)$?

(b) Compute $f'(z)$ and $g'(z)$.

9. [MT, p. 211] Let $F(x, y) = x^3 - y^2$ and let $\mathcal{C}$ denote the level curve given by $F(x, y) = 0$.

(a) Without using the implicit function theorem, show that we can describe $\mathcal{C}$ as the graph of x as a function of y near any point.

(b) Show that $F_x(0,0) = 0$. Does this contradict the implicit function theorem?

10. [MT, p. 211] Consider the system of equations

$$x^5 v^2 + 2y^3 u = 3$$
$$3yu - xuv^3 = 2.$$

Show that near the point $(x, y, u, v) = (1, 1, 1, 1)$, this system defines u and v implicitly as functions of x and y. For such local functions u and v, define the local function f by $f(x, y) = (u(x, y), v(x, y))$. Find $Df(1, 1)$.

11. [MT, p. 211] Consider the equations

$$x^2 - y^2 - u^3 + v^2 + 4 = 0$$
$$2xy + y^2 - 2u^2 + 3v^4 + 8 = 0.$$

(a) Show that these equations determine functions $u(x, y)$ and $v(x, y)$ near the point $(x, y, u, v) = (2, -1, 2, 1)$.

(b) Compute $\frac{\partial u}{\partial x}$ at $(x, y) = (2, -1)$.

Chapter 6

Taylor's Theorem and critical points

6.1 Taylor's Theorem in one dimension

Consider a one-dimensional function:

$$g : \mathbb{R} \to \mathbb{R},$$

which is C^{k+1}, i.e. it is $(k+1)$ times continuously differentiable; i.e., each derivative,

$$\frac{d^j g}{dx^j}(t),\ j = 1, 2, \ldots, k+1,\ (\text{of order up to and including the } (k+1)^{\text{st}}),$$

exists and is a continuous function (in some interval). Then, we can approximate $g(x)$ locally near $t = a$ by a polynomial of degree k, *Taylor's polynomial*, $P_k(t)$:

$$P_k(t) = g(a) + g'(a)(t - a) + \frac{1}{2!}g''(a)(t - a)^2 + \cdots + \frac{1}{k!}\frac{d^k g}{dt^k}(a)(t - a)^k$$

The Taylor coefficients are chosen to match $g(t)$ up to the kth derivative at $t = a$,

$$\frac{d^j P_k}{dt^j}(a) = \frac{d^j g}{dt^j}(a),\ j = 0, 1, 2, \ldots, k.$$

To review this material, look back to section 11.11 in Stewart [Stew]. There, the emphasis was on the Taylor Series, and questions of its convergence, but here we are interested in truncating the series for the purpose of approximation. And in any question of approximation the error made (the remainder term) is of the highest importance.

For example, $P_1(t) = g(a) + g'(a)(t - a)$ is the tangent line. Since we know that g is differentiable,

$$\lim_{t \to a} \frac{|g(t) - P_1(t)|}{|t - a|} = 0 \text{ or } g(t) = P_1(t) + o(|t - a|)$$

Theorem 6.1 (Taylor's Theorem, 1D version). *Assume $g : \mathbb{R} \to \mathbb{R}$ is C^{k+1} in a neighborhood of $t = a$. Then, for each t, there exists c between a and t for which*

$$g(t) = P_k(t) + R_k(a, t),$$

with <u>remainder</u> $R_k(a, t) = \frac{d^{k+1}g}{dt^{k+1}}(c)(t - a)^{k+1}$.

Since we assumed that $\frac{d^{k+1}g}{dt^{k+1}}$ is continuous, the remainder term is very small when $t \to a$,

$$\lim_{t \to a} \frac{R_k(a, t)}{|t - a|^k} = 0,$$

i.e. $R_k(a, t) = o\left(|t - a|^k\right)$. So $R_k(a, t)$ is small compared with each of the terms appearing in $P_k(t)$.

Remark. Locally, $g(t)$ is well approximated by its Taylor polynomial, but only near $x = a$.

Example 6.2. For $g(t) = \cos t$ at $a = 0$, we look at the 3rd order Taylor polynomial:

$$g(0) = \cos 0 = 1, \quad g'(0) = -\sin 0 = 0, \quad g''(0) = -\cos(0) = -1, \quad g'''(0) = \sin 0 = 0.$$

Therefore, Taylor's Theorem implies that for t near 0, and

$$g(t) = \cos t = \underbrace{1 - 0t - \frac{1}{2}t^2 + 0t^3}_{P_3(t)} + R_3(0, t) = 1 - \frac{1}{2}t^2 + o(t^3).$$

This tells us that $\cos t$ is approximately quadratic near $a = 0$, with an error which is very small compared to t^3 (it is of the order of t^4.) This is *local* information, as the graph of $\cos t$ doesn't look in the least like an inverted parabola when t is large, since the cosine oscillates periodically between ± 1 while the parabola diverges to $-\infty$ for $t \to \pm\infty$. (See Figure 6.1.) $\qquad\square$

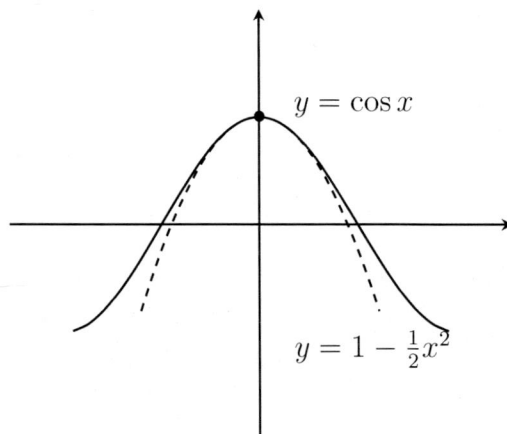

Figure 6.1. Third degree Taylor expansion of $\cos x$ tells us that the curve is locally quadratic near $x = 0$.

6.2 Taylor's Theorem in higher dimensions

To obtain a version of Taylor's Theorem in several variables we apply the one-dimensional version in a careful way, by restricting our attention to each line, $\vec{x} = \vec{a} + t\vec{u}$, through $\vec{a}$ in direction $\vec{u}$.

Assume $f \in C^3$ near $\vec{a} \in \mathbb{R}^n$. Let's sample $f(\vec{x})$ along a line running through x_0. Take a unit vector $\vec{u}$, $\|\vec{u}\| = 1$, and the line,

$$\vec{l}(t) = \vec{a} + t\vec{u},$$

that goes through $\vec{a}$ at $t = 0$ in the direction of $\vec{u}$. Then, we let

$$g(t) = f(\vec{l}(t)) = f(\vec{a} + t\vec{u}),$$

so $g : \mathbb{R} \to \mathbb{R}$. By the chain rule, if f is C^3 near $\vec{a}$, then g is C^3 near $t = 0$, and so we may apply Taylor's Theorem to g to approximate its values near $t = 0$. In doing so, we will generate a Taylor expansion for $f(\vec{x})$ with $x = \vec{a} + t\vec{u}$.

We calculate the terms in the Taylor polynomial for g, which has the form,

$$g(t) = g(0) + g'(0)(t - 0) + \frac{1}{2}g''(0)(t - 0)^2 + R_2, \quad \text{with } R_2 = o(t^2).$$

We begin with:

$$g(0) = f(\vec{a}),$$
$$g'(t) = Df(\vec{a} + t\vec{u}) \cdot \vec{l}'(t) = Df(\vec{a} + t\vec{u})\vec{u}.$$

So $g'(0) = Df(\vec{a})\vec{u} = \nabla f(\vec{a}) \cdot \vec{u}$. Using the definition $\vec{x} = \vec{l}(t) = \vec{a} + t\vec{u}$, we have $t\vec{u} = \vec{x} - \vec{a}$, and so the first derivative term may be rewritten as

$$g'(0)(t - 0) = Df(\vec{a})[\vec{x} - \vec{a}].$$

Finding the second derivative is a little tricky. We write the first derivative out in its coordinates,

$$g'(t) = \sum_{i=1}^{n} \frac{\partial f}{\partial x_i}(\vec{a} + t\vec{u})u_i.$$

Then we use the Chain Rule in the form you learned last year to calculate

$$g''(t) = \sum_{i=1}^{n} \frac{d}{dt}\left(\frac{\partial f}{\partial x_i}(\vec{a} + t\vec{u})\right)u_i = \sum_{i=1}^{n}\sum_{j=1}^{n} \frac{\partial^2 f}{\partial x_i \partial x_j}(\vec{a} + t\vec{u})u_j u_i$$

Therefore,

$$g''(0) = \sum_{i=1}^{n}\sum_{j=1}^{n} \frac{\partial^2 f}{\partial x_i \partial x_j}(\vec{a})u_j\, u_i,$$

which is a *quadratic form* with matrix

$$H(\vec{x}) = \left[\frac{\partial^2 f}{\partial x_i \partial x_j}(\vec{a})\right]_{i,j=1,\ldots,n},$$

the *Hessian matrix* of f at $\vec{a}$. We will also write $H(\vec{x}) = D^2 f(\vec{x})$, as it is the matrix of all second partial derivatives of f. For f a C^2 function, $f_{x_i x_j} = f_{x_j x_i}$, so $H(\vec{a})$ is a **symmetric** matrix. Again using $t\vec{u} = \vec{x} - \vec{a}$, we may then write

$$g''(0)(t - 0)^2 = t\vec{u} \cdot H(\vec{a})t\vec{u} = [\vec{x} - \vec{x_0}] \cdot H(\vec{a})[\vec{x} - \vec{a}].$$

In this equation, the matrix $H(\vec{a})$ multiplies $[\vec{x} - \vec{a}]$, and the result (a vector) is dotted with $[\vec{x} - \vec{a}]$.

Finally, the remainder term in the expansion of g is $o(t^2)$, but notice that $|t| = \|\vec{x} - \vec{a}\|$, so the remainder is very small compared to the square distance, $\|\vec{x} - \vec{a}\|^2$.

We now have all the ingredients for the one-dimensional Taylor's Theorem for g, and so applying it we get the following theorem:

Theorem 6.3 (Second order Taylor's approximation). *Assume $f : \mathbb{R}^n \to \mathbb{R}$ and is C^3 in a neighborhood of $\vec{a}$. Then,*

$$f(\vec{x}) = f(\vec{a}) + Df(\vec{a})(\vec{x} - \vec{a}) + \frac{1}{2}(\vec{x} - \vec{a}) \cdot H(\vec{a})(\vec{x} - \vec{a}) + R_2(\vec{a}, \vec{x}),$$

where

$$H(\vec{a}) = D^2 f(\vec{a}) = \left[\frac{\partial^2 f}{\partial x_i \partial x_j} \right]_{i,j=1,2,\dots,n}$$

is the Hessian and

$$\lim_{\vec{x} \to \vec{a}} \frac{R_2(\vec{a}, \vec{x})}{\|\vec{x} - \vec{a}\|^2} = 0,$$

i.e. $R_2(\vec{a}\vec{x}) = o(\|\vec{x} - \vec{a}\|^2)$.

Alternatively, we may write $\vec{x} = \vec{a} + \vec{h}$, and then the second order Taylor's approximation can be written as

$$f(\vec{a} + \vec{h}) = f(\vec{a}) + Df(\vec{a})\vec{h} + \frac{1}{2}\vec{h} \cdot D^2 f(\vec{a})\vec{h} + R_2(\vec{a}, \vec{h}),$$

with

$$\lim_{\vec{h} \to \vec{0}} = \frac{R_2(\vec{a}, \vec{h})}{\|\vec{h}\|^2} = 0.$$

We will find this form to be more useful at times in the next section.

Example 6.4. Find the second order Taylor polynomial of the following functions:

$$f(x, y) = \cos\left(xy^2\right)$$

near $\vec{a} = (\pi, 1)$.   □

First, we compute the derivatives:

$$f(\vec{a}) = f(\pi, 1) = \cos(\pi) = 1,$$

$$\frac{\partial f}{\partial x} = -y^2 \sin\left(xy^2\right), \qquad \frac{\partial f}{\partial y} = -2xy \sin\left(xy^2\right),$$

$$\frac{\partial^2 f}{\partial x^2} = -y^2 \cos\left(xy^2\right) y^2, \qquad \frac{\partial^2 f}{\partial x \partial y} = -2y \sin\left(xy^2\right) - 2xy^3 \cos\left(xy^2\right),$$

$$\frac{\partial^2 f}{\partial y^2} = -2x \sin\left(xy^2\right) - 2xy \cos\left(xy^2\right).$$

Then, at $\vec{a} = (\pi, 1)$, we find that

$$Df(\vec{a}) = \begin{bmatrix} 0 & 0 \end{bmatrix}$$

$$D^2 f(\vec{a}) = \begin{bmatrix} 1 & 2\pi \\ 2\pi & 4\pi^2 \end{bmatrix}$$

So, we have

$$f(\vec{a} + \vec{h}) = -1 + \frac{1}{2}\vec{h} \cdot \begin{bmatrix} 1 & 2\pi \\ 2\pi & 4\pi^2 \end{bmatrix} \vec{h} + R_2$$

$$f(\pi + h_1, 1 + h_2) = -1 + \frac{1}{2} \begin{bmatrix} h_1 \\ h_2 \end{bmatrix} \cdot \begin{bmatrix} h_1 + 2\pi h_2 \\ 2\pi h_1 + 4\pi^2 h_2 \end{bmatrix}$$

$$= -1 + \frac{1}{2}\left(h_1^2 + 4\pi h_1 h_2 + 4\pi^2 h_2^2 \right) + o(\|\vec{h}^2\|)$$

In terms of a point $\vec{x}$ (near $\vec{a}$), we can write $\vec{x} = \vec{a} + \vec{h}$, so $\vec{h} = \vec{x} - \vec{a}$, and then

$$\cos\left(xy^2\right) = -1 + \frac{1}{2}\left((x - a_1)^2 + 4\pi(x - a_1)(y - a_2) + 4\pi^2(y - a_2)^2 \right) + R_2,$$

and $R_2 = o(\|\vec{x} - \vec{a}\|^2$. The advantage of the $f(\vec{a} + \vec{h})$ form is that it is easier to guess the behaviour of $f(\vec{x})$ near $\vec{x} = \vec{a}$. This is what we will do in the next section, to classify critical points as maxima and minima!

6.3   Local minima/maxima

This is exactly the same definition as in Stewart [Stew], only generalized to $\mathbb{R}^n$. (So if you were paying attention to the definitions last year, this is old news!)

Definition 6.5. *We say $\vec{a}$ is a* local minimum *for f if there exists an open disk $D_r(\vec{a})$ for which*

$$f(\vec{a}) \leq f(\vec{x})$$

for all $\vec{x} \in D_r(\vec{a})$. $\vec{a}$ is a strict local minimum *if*

$$f(\vec{a}) < f(\vec{x})$$

for all $\vec{x} \neq \vec{a}, \vec{x} \in D_r(\vec{a})$.

Definition 6.6. *We say $\vec{a}$ is a local maximum for f if $\exists r > 0$ with $f(\vec{a}) \geq f(\vec{x})$, $\forall \vec{x} \in D_r(\vec{a})$. $\vec{a}$ is a strict local max if $f(\vec{a}) > f(\vec{x})$, $\forall \vec{x} \in D_r(\vec{a}) \setminus \{\vec{a}\}$.*

Example 6.7. As you have seen from your previous multivariable course, $f(x, y) = x^2 + y^2$ has a local minimum (in fact, the global minimum) at $(x, y) = (0, 0)$, and $g(x, y) = -x^2 - y^2$ has a local maximum (in fact, the global maximum) at $(x, y) = (0, 0)$. Verifying this directly is not hard, since a sum of squares is always non-negative, and so

$$f(0, 0) = 0 \leq x^2 + y^2 = f(x, y), \quad \text{for all } (x, y) \in \mathbb{R}^2.$$

We leave the verification for $g(x, y)$ as an exercise.   □

Note that if f is differentiable, we have a necessary condition for local maxima and minima: they can only occur at a *critical point* of f:

Theorem 6.8. *If f has a local maxima or minima at $\vec{a}$ and is differentiable at $\vec{a}$, then $Df(\vec{a}) = \vec{0}$.*

Proof. Again, we start by restricting to line through $\vec{a}$:

$$g(t) = f(\vec{a} + t\vec{u}),$$

where $\vec{u}$ is a unit vector. If f has a local minima at $\vec{a}$, then

$$g(0) = f(\vec{a}) \leq f(\vec{a} + t\vec{u}) = g(t),$$

for all t with $|t| < r$. So $g(t)$ has a local minima at $t = 0$. By a calculus theorem, $g'(0) = 0$. But,

$$0 = g'(0) = Df(\vec{a})\vec{u},$$

for all $\vec{u}$. Then, by taking $\vec{u} = \vec{e}_1, \vec{e}_2 \ldots, \vec{e}_n$, we get

$$\frac{\partial f}{\partial x_j}(\vec{a}) = 0,$$

for each $j = 1, 2, 3, \ldots, n$. Therfore, $Df(\vec{a}) = 0$. $\qquad\square$

Definition 6.9. *An $\vec{a}$ for which $Df(\vec{a}) = 0$ is called a* critical point.

Example 6.10. In Example 6.4 , $\vec{a} = (\pi, 1)$ was a critical point. $\qquad\square$

Recall that not all critical points must be local maxima or minima, even in one dimension. But in higher dimensions the possible variety of critical point behavior is much larger.

Now, we want to combine Taylor's Theorem and linear algebra to classify critical points as local minima, maxima, or other. Taylor's theorem states that for $\vec{x} = \vec{a} + \vec{h}$, if $\|\vec{h}\|$ is small,

$$f(\vec{x}) = f(\vec{a} + \vec{h}) = f(\vec{a}) + \underbrace{Df(\vec{a})\vec{h}}_{0} + \underbrace{\frac{1}{2}\vec{h} \cdot D^2 f(\vec{a})\vec{h}}_{\text{quadratic form}} + \underbrace{R_2(\vec{a}, \vec{h})}_{o(\|\vec{h}\|^2)} \qquad (6.1)$$

So we expect the behaviour of $f(\vec{x})$ near $\vec{a}$ to be determined by the quadratic term.

Recall that the Hessian matrix, $M = D^2 f(\vec{a})$, is a *symmetric* matrix. This allows us to apply the following theorem:

Theorem 6.11 (The Spectral Theorem). *Assume M is a symmetric $(n \times n)$ matrix. Then,*

- *All eigenvalues of M are real, $\lambda_i \in \mathbb{R} \, \forall i = 1, 2, \ldots, n$.*

- *There is an orthonormal basis $\{\vec{u}_1, \vec{u}_2, \ldots, \vec{u}_n\}$ of $\mathbb{R}^n$ composed ot eigenvalues of M,*

$$M\vec{u}_i = \lambda_i \vec{u}_i, \qquad \|\vec{u}_i\| = 1, \qquad \vec{u}_i \cdot \vec{u}_j = 0 \;\; for \;\; i \neq j$$

- *In the basis of eigenvalues, M is a diagonal matrix. In other words, if we let U be the matrix whose columns are the $\vec{u}_i$; then*

$$MU = U\Lambda,$$

where $\Lambda = \operatorname{diag}(\lambda_1, \lambda_2, \ldots, \lambda_n)$.

Remark. Note that since the eigenvalues are real, they can be ordered, smallest to largest:

$$\lambda_1 \le \lambda_2 \le \cdots \le \lambda_n.$$

However, they may not be necessarily distinct. (For example, the identity matrix I has each $\lambda_j = 1$.)

Written in the orthonormal basis of eigenvalues, the quadratic form, $\vec{h} \cdot M\vec{h}$, has an easy expression. First, since the $\vec{u}_i$ form a basis, any vector may be expressed as a linear combination,

$$\vec{h} = \sum_{i=1}^{n} c_i \vec{u}_i,$$

with coefficients $c_i \in \mathbb{R}$, $i = 1, 2, \ldots, n$. Notice that

$$\vec{h} \cdot u_j = \sum_{i=1}^{n} c_i \vec{u}_i \cdot \vec{u}_j = c_j, \tag{6.2}$$

since $\vec{u}_i \cdot \vec{u}_j = 0$ if $i \ne j$ and $\vec{u}_i \cdot \vec{u}_j = 1$ if $i = j$. In particular, we can evaluate the norm of $\vec{h}$ in terms of the coefficients c_i,

$$\|\vec{h}\|^2 = \vec{h} \cdot \vec{h} = \vec{h} \cdot \left(\sum_{j=1}^{n} c_j \vec{u}_j \right)$$

$$= \sum_{j=1}^{n} c_j \, \vec{h} \cdot \vec{u}_i$$

$$= \sum_{j=1}^{n} c_j^2, \tag{6.3}$$

using (6.2).

To evaluate the quadratic form we make a similar calculation, using the orthogonality of the normalized eigenvectors:

$$\vec{h} \cdot M\vec{h} = \vec{h} \cdot \sum_{i=1}^{n} c_i M\vec{u}_i$$

$$= \vec{h} \cdot \sum_{i=1}^{n} \lambda_i c_i \vec{u}_i$$

$$= \sum_{i=1}^{n} \lambda_i c_i (\underbrace{\vec{h} \cdot \vec{u}_i}_{c_i})$$

$$= \sum_{i=1}^{n} \lambda_i c_i^2 \tag{6.4}$$

Note the similarity of the two forms (6.3) and (6.4). The fundamental difference is that the sum in (6.4) is weighted by the eigenvalues λ_i. Using these calculations, we prove the following fact about quadratic forms and eigenvalues:

Theorem 6.12. *Suppose M is a symmetric matrix with eigenvalues*

$$\lambda_1 \le \lambda_2 \le \cdots \le \lambda_n.$$

Then, for any vector $\vec{h} \in \mathbb{R}^n$,

$$\lambda_1 \|\vec{h}\|^2 \le \vec{h} \cdot M\vec{h} \le \lambda_n \|\vec{h}\|^2$$

Proof. First, we apply (6.4) and use the fact that $\lambda_n \ge \lambda_i$ for any i, and so:

$$\vec{h} \cdot M\vec{h} = \sum_{i=1}^{n} \lambda_i c_i^2$$
$$\le \sum_{i=1}^{n} \lambda_n c_i^2$$
$$= \lambda_n \sum_{i=1}^{n} c_i^2 = \lambda_n \|\vec{h}\|^2,$$

by (6.3), which proves the right hand inequality. For the left hand side, we use the fact that $\lambda_1 \le \lambda_i$ for all i, so

$$\vec{h} \cdot M\vec{h} = \sum_{i=1}^{n} \lambda_i c_i^2 \ge \sum_{i=1}^{n} \lambda_1 c_i^2 = \lambda_1 \|\vec{h}\|^2.$$

This proves both sides of the inequality. $\square$

Definition 6.13. *We say the quadratic form $q(\vec{h}) = \vec{h} \cdot M\vec{h}$ is* positive definite *if $q(\vec{h}) > 0$ for all $\vec{h} \ne \vec{0}$. Similarly, $q(\vec{h})$ is* negative definite *if $q(\vec{h}) < 0$ for all $\vec{h} \ne \vec{0}$. If $q(\vec{h}) \ge 0$ $\forall \vec{h} \in \mathbb{R}^n$ we call the quadratic form* positive semi-definite, *and* negative semi-definite *if $q(\vec{h}) \le 0$ $\forall \vec{h} \in \mathbb{R}^n$.*

The quadratic form is indefinite *if it takes on both positive and negative values.*

From Theorem 6.12 we may conclude that:

- $q(\vec{h})$ is positive definite if and only if all the eigenvalues of M are strictly positive; that is when $0 < \lambda_1 \le \lambda_2 \le \cdots \le \lambda_n$.

- $q(\vec{h})$ is positive semi definite if and only if all the eigenvalues of M are nonnegative; that is when $0 \le \lambda_1 \le \lambda_2 \le \cdots \le \lambda_n$.

- $q(\vec{h})$ is negative definite if and only if all the eigenvalues of M are strictly negative; that is when $\lambda_1 \le \lambda_2 \le \cdots \le \lambda_n < 0$.

- $q(\vec{h})$ is negative semi definite if and only if all the eigenvalues of M are nonpositive; that is when $\lambda_1 \leq \lambda_2 \leq \cdots \leq \lambda_n \leq 0$.

- $q(\vec{h})$ is indefinite if and only if M has both positive and negative eigenvalues.

Now we apply this idea to the Hessian via Taylor's Theorem to get the following theorem:

Theorem 6.14 (Second derivative test). *Suppose f is C^3 in a neighborhood of a critical point $\vec{a}$. Let $\lambda_1 \leq \lambda_2 \leq \cdots \leq \lambda_n$ be the eigenvalues of $D^2 f(\vec{a})$. Then,*

(1) If all eigenvalues are positive, then $\vec{a}$ is a strict local minimum of f.

(2) If all eigenvalues are negative, then $\vec{a}$ is a strict local maximum of f.

(3) If $D^2 f(\vec{a})$ has at least one positive and at least one negative eigenvalue, then $\vec{a}$ is a saddle point.

We note that if there are zero eigenvalues we might still have a local max or a local min; in that case, the behavior of $f(\vec{x})$ near the critical point will be determined by higher order terms in the Taylor expansion. A matrix M with zero eigenvalues is called <u>degenerate</u>, as is a critical point $\vec{a}$ with Hessian $D^2 f(\vec{a})$ having one or more zero eigenvalue.

Proof. We prove (1); parts (2) and (3) will be for you to do as Exercises! So assume $\vec{a}$ is a critical point for f, and the Hessian $D^2 f(\vec{a})$ has all strictly positive eigenvalues, $0 < \lambda_1 \leq \lambda_2 \leq \cdots \leq \lambda_n$.

The idea is to show that the quadratic term is much more important than the error term when we're close to $\vec{a}$. Since $R_2(\vec{a}, \vec{h}) = o(\|\vec{h}\|^2)$, there exists $r > 0$ for which

$$\frac{|R_2(\vec{a}, \vec{h})|}{\|\vec{h}\|^2} < \frac{1}{4}\lambda_1, \qquad \text{whenever } \|\vec{h}\| < r.$$

In other words, $|R_2(\vec{a}, \vec{h})| < \frac{1}{4}\lambda_1 \|\vec{h}\|^2$ when $\|\vec{h}\| < r$. (In fact, what we'll need here is $R_2(\vec{a}, \vec{h}) > -\frac{1}{4}\lambda_1 \|\vec{h}\|^2$, so the remainder term isn't very negative.)

For any $\vec{x} \in D_r(\vec{a}) \setminus \{\vec{a}\}$, let $\vec{h} = \vec{x} - \vec{a}$, so $\|\vec{h}\| < r$, and by (6.1) and Proposition 6.12,

$$f(\vec{x}) = f(\vec{a} + \vec{h}) = f(\vec{a}) + 0 + \frac{1}{2}\vec{h} \cdot D^2 f(\vec{a})\,\vec{h} + R_2(\vec{a}, \vec{h})$$

$$\geq f(\vec{a}) + \frac{1}{2}\lambda_1 \|\vec{h}\|^2 - \frac{1}{4}\lambda_1 \|\vec{h}\|^2$$

$$> f(\vec{a}),$$

which shows that $\vec{a}$ is a strict local minimum.

[*To prove (b), do the same thing but choose your $r > 0$ based on the remainder being smaller (in absolute value) than $\frac{1}{4}|\lambda_n|\|\vec{h}\|^2$. To do (c), look at points near $\vec{a}$ along an eigenvector u_i direction, $\vec{h} = t\vec{u}_i$, and apply the same idea as in (a) or (b), depending on whether λ_i is positive or negative.*] $\qquad\square$

Are conditions (a) and (b) necessary conditions to have a local minimum or a local maximum? Not quite (see example 2 below!) but almost:

Theorem 6.15. *Suppose* $f : \mathbb{R}^n \to \mathbb{R}$ *is a* C^3 *function.*

(i) *If* $\vec{a}$ *is a local minimum of* f, *then every eigenvalue of* $D^2 f(\vec{a})$ *satisfies* $\lambda_i \geq 0$, $i = 1, \ldots, n$;

(ii) *If* $\vec{a}$ *is a local maximum of* f, *then every eigenvalue of* $D^2 f(\vec{a})$ *satisfies* $\lambda_i \leq 0$, $i = 1, \ldots, n$.

So at a local minimum we have no negative eigenvalues, and at a local maximum there are no positive eigenvalues of the Hessian.

Proof. We only show (i); (ii) is similar (but upside down!) Suppose $\vec{a}$ is a local minimizer of f, but (for a contradiction) assume $\lambda_1 < 0$. Let $\vec{u}$ be the eigenvector, $D^2 f(\vec{a})\vec{u} = \lambda_1 \vec{u}$, with $\|\vec{u}\| = 1$. Then $Df(\vec{a}) =$ and the quadratic form $\vec{u} \cdot D^2 f(\vec{a})\vec{u} = \lambda_1 < 0$, so applying Taylor's Theorem,

$$f(\vec{a} + t\vec{u}) = f(\vec{a}) + 0 + \frac{1}{2}t\vec{u} \cdot D^2 f(\vec{a})(t\vec{u}) + o(\|t\vec{u}\|^2)$$

$$= f(\vec{a}) + \frac{t^2 \lambda_1}{2} + o(t^2)$$

$$< f(\vec{a}),$$

for all sufficiently small $|t|$ (ie, for $|t| < r$ where r is chosen so that $\frac{|R_2|}{t^2} < \frac{1}{4}|\lambda_1|$.) So $\vec{a}$ cannot be a local minimum, which contradicts our initial assumption. In conclusion, $\lambda_1 \geq 0$ so all the eigenvalues are nonnegative. $\square$

Example 6.16. Consider

$$f(x, y, z) = x^3 - 3xy + y^3 + \cos z$$

Find all critical points and classify them using the Hessian.

First, we calculate the gradient,

$$\begin{cases} \frac{\partial f}{\partial x} = 3x^2 - 3y \\ \frac{\partial f}{\partial y} = -3x + 3y^2 \\ \frac{\partial f}{\partial z} = -\sin z \end{cases}$$

Critical points are defined as $\nabla f(\vec{a}) = \vec{0}$ so we get the following critical points

$$(x, y, z) = (0, 0, n\pi) \text{ and } (1, 1, n\pi),$$

where $n \in \mathbb{Z}$.

Then, we want to compute the Hessian at each point.

$$D^2 f(\vec{x}) = \begin{bmatrix} 6x & -3 & 0 \\ -3 & 6y & 0 \\ 0 & 0 & -\cos z \end{bmatrix}$$

Notice that at $(0,0,n\pi)$, the Hessian depends on whether n is even or odd:

$$D^2 f(0,0,2k\pi) = \begin{bmatrix} 0 & -3 & 0 \\ -3 & 0 & 0 \\ 0 & 0 & -1 \end{bmatrix}$$

$$D^2 f(0,0,(2k+1)\pi) = \begin{bmatrix} 0 & -3 & 0 \\ -3 & 0 & 0 \\ 0 & 0 & 1 \end{bmatrix}$$

When n is even, we find the eigenvalues of the Hessian are

$$\lambda = -3, -1, 3$$

so we get a saddle at $(0,0,2k\pi)$, $k \in \mathbb{Z}$. Similarly, when n is odd, we find that its eigenvalues are

$$\lambda = -3, 1, 3$$

which is also a saddle. Thus, we get a saddle at $(0,0,n\pi)$ for all $n \in \mathbb{Z}$.

At $(1,1,n\pi)$, we get

$$D^2 f(1,1,n\pi) = \begin{bmatrix} 6 & -3 & 0 \\ -3 & 6 & 0 \\ 0 & 0 & (-1)^{n+1} \end{bmatrix}$$

By observation, we find that $\vec{e}_3 = \begin{bmatrix} 0 \\ 0 \\ 1 \end{bmatrix}$ is an eigenvector with $\lambda = (-1)^{n+1}$. Then, the two remaining eigenvalues are eigenvalues of the 2×2 submatrix, $\begin{bmatrix} 6 & -3 \\ -3 & 6 \end{bmatrix}$. Since its trace is 12 and determinant is 27, its characteristic equation is given by

$$\lambda^2 - 12\lambda + 27 = 0.$$

So we find that two other eigenvalues are $\lambda = 3, 9$. Therefore, $(1,1,(2k+1)\pi)$ is a local minima, and $(1,1,2k\pi)$ are saddles. $\square$

Remark. When $D^2 f(\vec{a})$ has zero as an eigenvalue, things can get complicated. For example, if $\lambda_i \geq 0$ for all i, you *could* still have a local minima. In this case, the behaviour would be determined by higher order terms in Taylor Series. We call this *Degenerate critical point.*

Example 6.17. Consider

$$f(x,y) = x^2 + y^4$$

We find that
$$\nabla f(x, y) = \begin{bmatrix} 2x \\ 4y^3 \end{bmatrix}$$
so we get only one critical point, $(x, y) = (0, 0)$. Ntice that
$$D^2 f(x, y) = \begin{bmatrix} 2 & 0 \\ 0 & 12y^2 \end{bmatrix} \text{ so } D^2 f(0, 0) = \begin{bmatrix} 2 & 0 \\ 0 & 0 \end{bmatrix}$$

So we get $\lambda = 2, 0$. We call this a *degenerate* case, as the quadratic form is not positive definite and the Theorem doesn't apply.

Still, $f(0, 0) < f(x, y)$ for all $(x, y) \neq (0, 0)$ so its a minimum even if the Hessian test doesn't tell us so. □

Example 6.18. Consider
$$g(x, y) = x^2 - y^4$$

This has the same second order Taylor expansion as the previous example but has a different ramainder, $R_2 = -y^4$. This is a degenerate saddle.

Notice that both g and f from the previous example have exactly the same Taylor expansion to second order,
$$g(\vec{0} + \vec{h}), f(\vec{0} + \vec{h}) = 0 + \vec{0} \cdot \vec{h} + \frac{1}{2} \vec{h} \cdot \begin{bmatrix} 2 & 0 \\ 0 & 0 \end{bmatrix} + R_2(\vec{h})$$
$$= h_1^2 + R_2(h_1, h_2).$$

The only difference is in the remainder term, $R_2 = \pm h_2^4$, and so for a degenerate case (ie, an eigenvalue $\lambda = 0$) the quadratic form does not control the remainder term, and the character of the critical point (min, max, saddle) could be determined by the remainder and not the Hessian! □

Notice that for the converse, eigenvalues don't have to be strictly larger or smaller than 0. In other words, if $\vec{a}$ is a local minima, then $\vec{a}$ is a critical point and all the eigenvalues of $D^2 f(\vec{a})$ must be greater than equal to 0 (not necessarily strictly greater than 0).

Where does the 2nd derivative test in Stewart come from?

For $f : \mathbb{R}^2 \to \mathbb{R}$, we're looking at the eigenvalues of a 2×2 matrix $M = D^2 f(x_0, y_0)$. Call
$$a = f_{xx}(x_0, y_0), \quad b = f_{xy}(x_0, y_0) = f_{yx}(x_0, y_0), \quad c = f_{yy}(x_0, y_0),$$
so the eigenvalue equation is
$$0 = \det \begin{bmatrix} a - \lambda & b \\ b & c - \lambda \end{bmatrix} = \lambda^2 - (a + c)\lambda + (ac - b^2) = \lambda^2 - T\lambda + D,$$

where $T = a + c$ is the <u>trace</u> and $D = ab - c^2$ the <u>determinant</u> of M. If the two eigenvalues are λ_1, λ_2, then those are the roots of this polynomial, so it factors as
$$\lambda^2 - T\lambda + D = (\lambda - \lambda_1)(\lambda - \lambda_2).$$

Multiplying out the product and matching powers of λ,

$$D = \lambda_1 \lambda_2, \quad T = \lambda_1 + \lambda_2.$$

So $D > 0$ if and only if both eigenvalues have the <u>same sign</u> (and neither is zero.) Note also that if $D > 0$, the product $ac > b^2 \geq 0$ also, so a and c have the same sign. Since $T = a + c = \lambda_1 + \lambda_2$, each of $T, a, c, \lambda_1, \lambda_2$ must have the same sign. In conclusion, if $D > 0$ and $a = f_{xx}(x_0, y_0) > 0$, then both eigenvalues $\lambda_1, \lambda_2 > 0$, and we get a local minimum. If $D > 0$ and $a = f_{xx}(x_0, y_0) < 0$, then both eigenvalues $\lambda_1, \lambda_2 < 0$, and we get a local maximum. If $D < 0$, then the product of the eigenvalues is negative, and they have opposite signs, and (x_0, y_0) is a saddle point. (The case $D = 0$ is the degenerate case, (d).)

6.4   Practice problems

1. Assume $f : \mathbb{R}^n \to \mathbb{R}$ is C^3, $\vec{a}$ is a critical point of f, and the Hessian is strictly negative definite, $\vec{h} \cdot D^2 f(\vec{a}) \vec{h} < 0$ for all $\vec{h} \in \mathbb{R}^n$. Prove that $\vec{a}$ is a strict local maximum of f, that is: there exists $r > 0$ so that $f(\vec{x}) < f(\vec{a})$ for all $\vec{x} \in D_r(\vec{a}) \setminus \{\vec{a}\}$.

2. For each function, find all critical points and use the Hessian to determine whether they are local maxima, minima, or saddle points.

    (a) $f(x, y, z) = x - 2\sin x - 3yz$

    (b) $g(x, y, z) = \cosh x + 4yz - 2y^2 - z^4$

    (c) $u(x, y, z) = (x - z)^4 - x^2 + y^2 + 6xz - z^2$

3. Let M be a positive definite, symmetric $(n \times n)$ matrix. Show that

$$\lambda_n = \max \left\{ \frac{\|M \vec{x}\|}{\|\vec{x}\|} \ \middle| \ \vec{x} \neq \vec{0} \right\}$$

is the largest eigenvalue of the matrix M.

    [Hint: do it in two steps. First, show $\frac{\|M \vec{x}\|}{\|\vec{x}\|} \leq \lambda_n$ for all $\vec{x} \neq \vec{0}$, then find a particular $\vec{x}$ for which equality holds.]

4. [MT, p. 166] Determine the second-order Taylor formula for the given function about the given point (x_0, y_0).

    (a) $f(x, y) = e^{x+y}$, where $x_0 = 0, y_0 = 0$.

    (b) $f(x, y) = \sin(xy) + \cos(x)$, where $x_0 = 0, y_0 = 0$.

5. [MT, p. 166] Calculate the second-order Taylor approximation to $f(x, y) = \cos x \sin y$ at the point $(\pi, \pi/2)$.

Chapter 7

Calculus of Variations

7.1 One-dimensional problems

The calculus of variations studies extremal (minimization or maximization) problems where the quantity to be optimized is a *function*, and not just a number or a vector in finite dimensional space. A typical set-up is to consider all possible C^1 functions $u : [a,b] \subset \mathbb{R} \to \mathbb{R}$, connecting given fixed endpoints $P_1 = (a,c)$ and $P_2 = (b,c)$, that is

$$u(a) = c, \quad u(b) = d. \tag{7.1}$$

Denote by $\mathcal{A}$ the collection of all such $u \in C^1([a,b])$ satisfying the endpoint condition (or boundary condition) given above in (7.1). We then try to find $u \in \mathcal{A}$ which minimizes (or maximizes, or is a critical point of) an integral expression,

$$I(u) = \int_a^b F(u'(x), u(x), x) \, dx, \tag{7.2}$$

where $F : \mathbb{R}^3 \to \mathbb{R}$ is a given C^2 function. *[It will be convenient write $F(p, u, x)$, with the letter p holding the place of the derivative u'.]* We call such $I : \mathcal{A} \to \mathbb{R}$ a *functional*; it is a real-valued function whose domain is a set of functions!

Whether we can actually find an extremum for I and what properties it has depends strongly on the form of the function F. Let's start with some common examples:

Example 7.1. Set $[a,b] \subset \mathbb{R}$ and choose values $c, d \in \mathbb{R}$. Consider all C^2 functions, $u(x)$, joining $P_1 = (a,c)$ and $P_2 = (b,d)$, i.e. $u(a) = c$ and $u(b) = d$. Among all C^2 curves, $u(x)$, connecting P_1 to P_2, find the one with shortest arclength. $\qquad \square$

Let $\vec{c}(t) = (t, u(t))$. Then, we have

$$\|\vec{c}'(t)\| = \sqrt{1 + u'(t)^2}.$$

This allows us to compute the arc length:

$$I(u) = \int_a^b \sqrt{1 + u'(x)^2} dx.$$

Now, call $\mathcal{A} = \{u : [a, b] \to \mathbb{R} \,|\, u \in C^2, u(a) = c, u(b) = d\}$. Then, $I : \mathcal{A} \to \mathbb{R}$ is a function of functions, or *functional*. We want to minimize $I(u)$ over all $u \in \mathcal{A}$.

Example 7.2. For the same class $\mathcal{A}$ of functions, take $u \in \mathcal{A}$ and rotate around the x axis, creating a surface of revolution. We would then like to choose $u(x)$ for which the surface of revolution has the least area.

This surface can be parametrized using cylindrical coordinates around the x-axis, $r = \sqrt{y^2 + z^2}$ and θ measured in the (y, z) plane, by $r = u(x)$, $x \in [a, b]$. The surface area is then given by

$$I(u) = \int_a^b 2\pi\, u(x) \sqrt{1 + (u'(x))^2}\, dx,$$

corresponding to $F(p, u, x) = 2\pi u \sqrt{1 + p^2}$. The surface of revolution determined by a u which minimizes $I(u)$ is called a *minimal surface* $\qquad\square$

Example 7.3. Same setup, we fix two endpoints P_1, P_2 and look at all graphs $y = u(x)$ connecting them, but now we imagine that the graph describes a track with a marble rolling down it, and we want to choose the graph $y = u(x)$ so that the marble spends the least time to roll downhill from one point to the other. To make things a little easier, we take $P_1 = (0, 0)$, orient the y-axis downward, and let $P_2 = (b, d)$ with $b, d > 0$ (so it's below the $x - axis$ and to the right of P_1.) Doing a little mechanics (see the chapter in Simmons' book), the total time taken in rolling down hill is:

$$I(u) = \int_0^b \frac{\sqrt{1 + (u'(x))^2}}{\sqrt{2gu(x)}}dx, \quad u \in \mathcal{A}, \tag{7.3}$$

where g is the (constant) acceleration due to gravity. So this fits the standard pattern, with $F(p, u, x) = \frac{\sqrt{1+p^2}}{\sqrt{2gu}}$. *[You may notice that the denominator vanishes when $u(x) = 0$, but we won't let it worry us, although it should.]*

This is one of the oldest variational problems, the "Brachistochrone" problem, posed by Johann Bernoulli in 1696 in a journal as a challenge to other mathematicians to solve (partly to show off the fact that he knew the solution, and to embarrass his brother, Jacob.) In the end, it was solved by at least 4 others, Jacob Bernoulli, Newton, L'Hôpital, and Leibnitz.

The First Variation.   We use the analogy to finding critical points of a function $f : \mathbb{R}^n \to \mathbb{R}$. At a local extremum $\vec{a}$ of f, we know that the one-dimensional restrictions $g(t) = f(\vec{a} + t\vec{v})$ must have critical points $g'(0) = 0$ at $t = 0$. The Chain Rule then asserts,

$$0 = g'(t) = Df(\vec{a})\vec{v}, \quad \text{for all } \vec{v} \in \mathbb{R}^n.$$

That is, all directional derivatives of f at $\vec{a}$ vanish, for all directons $\vec{v}$. In particular, the partial derivatives of f, which are the directional derivatives with $\vec{v} = \vec{e}_j$, the standard basis vectors, are all zero, so the matrix $Df(\vec{a})$ is the zero matrix, and f has a critical point at $\vec{a}$.

Unfortunately, there is no clear meaning of "partial derivative" for $I(u)$ in (7.2), but we can use the idea of one-dimensional reduction as above to make sense of the derivative $DI(u)$ via directional derivatives. To do this, we introduce the idea of a <u>variation</u> of $u \in \mathcal{A}$. As above, we want to look at $I(u + tv)$ and compare it's value to that of $I(u)$. To do that, we need $u(x) + tv(x)$ to be $C^1([a, b])$ and have the same fixed endpoints (7.1) as $u(x)$. This is accomplished by choosing variations v which are C^1 and vanish on the endpoints. We write $v \in \mathcal{A}_0$, with

$$\mathcal{A}_0 = \left\{ v \in C^1([a, b]) \mid v(a) = 0 = v(b) \right\}. \tag{7.4}$$

So then we will always have $u + tv \in \mathcal{A}$ for all t. See Figure 7.1

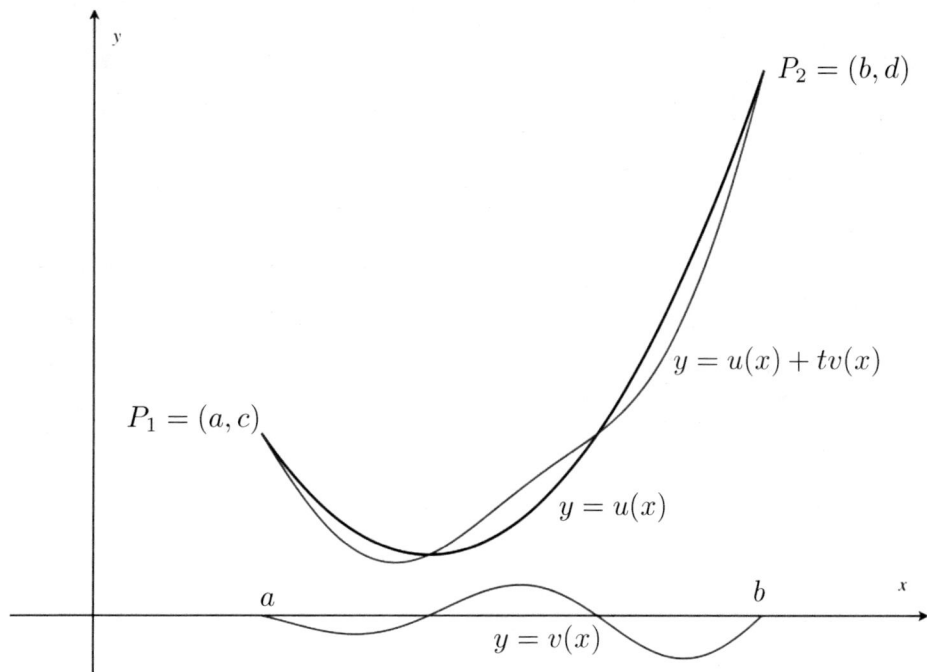

Figure 7.1. An admissible curve, $y = u(x)$, $u \in \mathcal{A}$ connecting P_1 to P_2. For $v \in \mathcal{A}_0$ (vanishing at both $x = a, b$,) we create the variations $u + tv$.

Now we proceed as in the vector case, and look at $g(t) = I(u + tv)$ for any $v \in \mathcal{A}_0$; if u is an extremal of I, then $g'(0) = 0$ for all variations $v \in \mathcal{A}_0$, that is

$$0 = \frac{d}{dt} I(u + tv) \Big|_{t=0}. \tag{7.5}$$

Let's see how this works in Example 7.1, the shortest arclength problem. Since $I(u) =$

$\int_a^b \sqrt{1 + (u'(x))^2}$, we calculate:

$$0 = \frac{d}{dt}I(u+tv)\bigg|_{t=0} = \frac{d}{dt}\int_a^b \sqrt{1 + (u'(x) + tv'(x))^2}\,dx\bigg|_{t=0}$$

$$= \int_a^b \frac{d}{dt}\left[\sqrt{1 + (u'(x) + tv'(x))^2}\right] dx\bigg|_{t=0}$$

$$= \int_a^b \frac{(u'(x) + tv'(x))\,v'(x)}{\sqrt{1 + (u'(x) + tv'(x))^2}}dx\bigg|_{t=0}$$

$$= \int_a^b \frac{u'(x)\,v'(x)}{\sqrt{1 + (u'(x))^2}}dx,$$

for every $v \in \mathcal{A}_0$. Compare with the vector case: this is supposed to be the analogue of the equation $0 = Df(\vec{a})\vec{v}$. But in the above integral, we have $v'(x)$ rather than just $v(x)$. We fix this by integrating by parts: for every $v \in \mathcal{A}_0$,

$$0 = \int_a^b \frac{u'(x)}{\sqrt{1 + (u'(x))^2}}v'(x)\,dx$$

$$= \frac{u'(x)}{\sqrt{1 + (u'(x))^2}}v'(x)\bigg|_a^b - \int_a^b \frac{d}{dx}\left[\frac{u'(x)}{\sqrt{1 + (u'(x))^2}}\right]v(x)\,dx$$

$$= -\int_a^b \frac{d}{dx}\left[\frac{u'(x)}{\sqrt{1 + (u'(x))^2}}\right]v(x)\,dx,$$

since $v \in \mathcal{A}_0$ implies that at the endpoints, $v(a) = 0 = v(b)$. Now, an integral can be zero without the integrand being the zero function, but here we are saying that the integral vanishes for **every** $v \in \mathcal{A}_0$, and this can only happen when the integrand is flat zero for all $x \in [a, b]$:

Lemma 7.4 (The Fundamental Lemma of the Calculus of Variations). *Assume h is continuous on $[a, b]$, and for every $v \in \mathcal{A}_0$ we have $\int_a^b h(x)\,v(x)\,dx = 0$. Then $h(x) = 0$ for all $x \in [a, b]$.*

Accepting the FLCoV for the moment, let's continue with the Example. We may then conclude that the integrand is always zero, and obtain a 2nd order ODE, the <u>Euler–Lagrange equation</u> for the functional I,

$$\frac{d}{dx}\left[\frac{u'(x)}{\sqrt{1 + (u'(x))^2}}\right] = 0.$$

This may be solved by integration: first, $\frac{u'(x)}{\sqrt{1+(u'(x))^2}} = C$ for some constant of integration C. After some algebra, $u'(x) = C_1 = \pm\sqrt{\frac{C}{1-C^2}}$, another constant. So $y = u(x) = C_1 x + C_2$, a linear function. (The values of C_1, C_2 may be chosen to match the endpoints (7.1).) So we've reconfirmed that the shortest distance in the plane between two points is a straight line segment!

Proof of FLCoV. Suppose (for a contradiction) that there is a point x_0 with $h(x_0) \neq 0$. By considering $-h(x)$ instead if necessary, we can assume $h(x_0) > 0$. Since h is continuous, there is an open interval around x_0, (α, β) on which $h(x) > 0$. Now choose v to be a C^1 function with $v(x) > 0$ in (α, β) and $v(x) = 0$ outside that interval. An example of such a function is:

$$v(x) = \begin{cases} (x - \alpha)^2 (\beta - x)^2, & \text{if } x \in (\alpha, \beta), \\ 0, & \text{otherwise.} \end{cases}$$

Such a function is depicted in Figure 7.2. This $v \in \mathcal{A}_0$, and $h(x)v(x) > 0$ in (α, β) and vanishes outside. Therefore, there is positive area under the graph, and so

$$0 = \int_a^b h(x)\, v(x)\, dx = \int_\alpha^\beta h(x)\, v(x)\, dx > 0,$$

which is a contradiction. What went wrong? We assumed h was not always zero; this proves that $h(x) = 0$ for all $x \in (a, b)$. $\qquad\square$

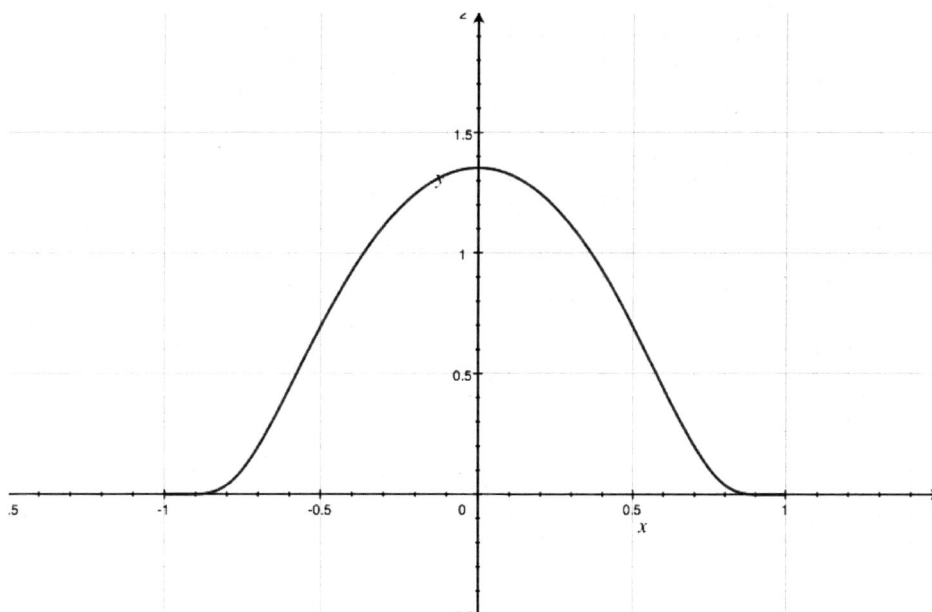

Figure 7.2. One of the functions v as described in the proof of Lemma 7.4, which is positive in $(-1, 1)$ and zero outside of that interval. It attaches to zero smoothly; the derivatives $v'(\pm 1) = 0$, and so $v \in C^1$.

Before doing the other two examples, let's develop a general formula for the first variation and Euler-Lagrange equations for I of the form (7.2). We proceed as above:

$$0 = \frac{d}{dt} I(u + tv)\Big|_{t=0}$$

$$= \frac{d}{dt} \int_a^b F(u'(x) + tv'(x), u(x) + tv(x), x)\, dx\Big|_{t=0}$$

$$= \int_a^b \frac{d}{dt} \left[F(u'(x) + tv'(x), u(x) + tv(x), x) \right] dx\Big|_{t=0}$$

$$= \int_a^b \left[\frac{\partial F}{\partial p}(u' + tv', u + tv, x)\, v'(x) + \frac{\partial F}{\partial u}(u' + tv', u + tv, x)\, v(x) \right] dx\Big|_{t=0}$$

$$= \int_a^b \left[\frac{\partial F}{\partial p}(u'(x), u(x), x)\, v'(x) + \frac{\partial F}{\partial u}(u'(x), u(x), x)\, v(x) \right] dx$$

$$= \frac{\partial F}{\partial p}(u'(x), u(x), x)\, v(x)\Big|_a^b - \int_a^b \frac{d}{dx}\left(\frac{\partial F}{\partial p}(u', u, x) \right) v(x)\, dx + \int_a^b + \frac{\partial F}{\partial u}(u', u, x)\, v(x)\, dx$$

$$= \int_a^b \left[-\frac{d}{dx}\left(\frac{\partial F}{\partial p}(u'(x), u(x), x) \right) + \frac{\partial F}{\partial u}(u'(x), u(x), x) \right] v(x)\, dx,$$

for all $v \in \mathcal{A}_0$. Note that we integrated the first term by parts, and used $v(a) = 0 = v(b)$ to eliminate the term coming from the endpoints, as in the first example. Applying the FLCoV, we conclude that the integrand must always be zero, and obtain the Euler–Lagrange equation,

$$\frac{d}{dx}\left(\frac{\partial F}{\partial p}(u'(x), u(x), x) \right) - \frac{\partial F}{\partial u}(u'(x), u(x), x) = 0, \tag{7.6}$$

which is a 2nd order ODE, and usually a nonlinear one!! This equation may be very difficult to solve, as we'll see in Example 3. In Example 1, F depended only on $p = u'(x)$, and in that case it was easy to solve by direct integration. (In fact, if $F = F(p)$ is independent of u, x, the solutions are always straight lines– check it yourself as an exercise!)

There is an interesting special case, which is when $F = F(p, u)$ and does not depend explicitly on x. In that case, we can integrate the EL equation using a trick: by a careful application of the Chain Rule,

$$\frac{d}{dx}\left(u'(x)\frac{\partial F}{\partial p}(u', u) - F(u', u) \right) = u'\frac{d}{dx}\left(\frac{\partial F}{\partial p} \right) + u''\frac{\partial F}{\partial p} - \left(\frac{\partial F}{\partial p}u'' + \frac{\partial F}{\partial u}u' \right)$$

$$= \left[\frac{d}{dx}\left(\frac{\partial F}{\partial p} \right) - \frac{\partial F}{\partial u} \right] u'(x)$$

$$= 0,$$

for any solution of the EL equation. In conclusion, for $F = F(p, u)$, the Euler–Lagrange equation is equivalent to

$$u'(x)\frac{\partial F}{\partial p}(u', u) - F(u', u) = C_1, \tag{7.7}$$

with C_1 a constant, which is only a first order ODE!

Now let's apply this same procedure in the minimal surface of revolution, Example 7.2, for which $F(p,u) = 2\pi u\sqrt{1+p^2}$. Then the EL equation is,

$$\frac{d}{dx}\left(\frac{2\pi u(x)u'(x)}{\sqrt{1+(u'(x))^2}}\right) - 2\pi\sqrt{1+(u'(x))^2} = 0,$$

a 2nd order nonlinear ODE, which is pretty ugly. Instead we recognize that $F(p,u)$ has no explicit x-dependence, and use the reduced form (7.7), to get:

$$C = 2\pi\frac{u(x)[u'(x)]^2}{\sqrt{1+(u'(x))^2}} - 2\pi u(x)\sqrt{1+(u'(x))^2} = -\frac{2\pi u(x)}{\sqrt{1+(u'(x))^2}}.$$

Call $C_1 = C/(2\pi)$. So $-u/C_1 = \sqrt{1+(u'(x))^2}$, and squaring both sides and solving for u' gives $u'(x) = \pm\sqrt{\frac{u^2}{C_1^2}-1}$, which is a separable ODE. By resisting the temptation to do trig substitution with a secant function and instead doing hyperbolic substitution with cosh, we get:

$$x + C_2 = \int dx = \int \frac{du}{\sqrt{\frac{u^2}{C_1^2}-1}} \qquad \textit{[substitute } u = C_1\cosh\theta,\ du = C_1\sinh\theta d\theta,\textit{]}$$

$$= \int \frac{C_1\sinh\theta\, d\theta}{\sinh\theta}$$

$$= \int C_1\, d\theta = C_1\theta = C_1\cosh^{-1}\left(\frac{u}{C_1}\right).$$

So the general solution to the EL equations is

$$u(x) = C_1\cosh\left(\frac{x+C_2}{C_1}\right).$$

To find the constants C_1, C_2 we should plug in the endpoints (7.1), but in general this is not very pretty. The main interest here is in the shape and not the specific values of the constants. We have shown that the surface of revolution with the least area for given boundary conditions, a "minimal surface", is called the <u>catenoid</u>; it is generated by one of this family of cosh graphs, and is drawn in Figure 7.3.

Finally, we return to the Brachistochrone, the original problem posed by Bernoulli to determine the marble track which leads to the shortest time of descent. (This was discussed in Example 7.3.) This example is also of the special form, $F(p,u) = \frac{\sqrt{1+p^2}}{\sqrt{2gu}}$, independent of x, so the same reduction of order will be useful. Doing the partial derivatives as in (7.7), we get a constant C for which

$$C = u'\frac{\partial F}{\partial p}(u',u) - F(u',u) = \frac{(u')^2}{\sqrt{1+(u')^2}\sqrt{2gu}} - \frac{\sqrt{1+(u')^2}}{\sqrt{2gu}} = \frac{1}{\sqrt{1+(u')^2}\sqrt{2gu}}.$$

Simplifying somewhat, we get

$$u(x)\left[1+(u'(x))^2\right] = k, \qquad \text{with } k = \frac{1}{2gC^2}.$$

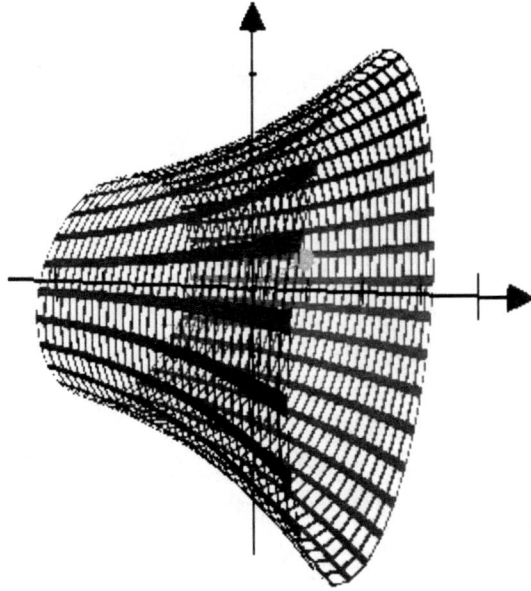

Figure 7.3. A surface of revolution, the catenoid.

Although we could write this as a separable first order ODE, it has no closed-form (explicit) solution! However, by a method which will remain mysterious, we can exhibit a solution in the form of a parametrized curve, $x = \frac{k}{2}(t - \sin t)$, $y = \frac{k}{2}(1 - \cos t)$, for parameter $t \in \mathbb{R}$. This is a famous curve, the <u>cycloid</u>, obtained by following a point on the rim of a wheel!

7.2   Problems in higher dimensions

We can also consider variational problems in higher dimensions, looking for an unknown function $u : \overline{D} \subset \mathbb{R}^n \to \mathbb{R}$ which minimizes a multiple integral over the domain D,

$$I(u) = \int_D F(\nabla u, u, \vec{x})\, dx_1 \ldots dx_n,$$

among C^1 functions u with given values on the boundary ∂D, $u(\vec{x}) = g(\vec{x})$ for all $\vec{x} \in \partial D$, where g is a given function. A common choice is to take $g(\vec{x}) = 0$, and that's what we'll assume in this section: $u \in \mathcal{A}_0$, that is, u is C^1 inside D and on its boundary ∂D, with

$$u(\vec{x}) = 0 \text{ for all } \vec{x} \in \partial D. \tag{7.8}$$

(This boundary condition is often called *Dirichlet's condition.*)

Rather than develop formulas for a general form of $F(\vec{p}, u, \vec{x})$, let's look at a specific example. Imagine a very thin membrane, represented by the planar domain $D \subset \mathbb{R}^2$, which is attached to the boundary ∂D (like a drum skin attached to its rim, although the rim ∂D need not be circular.) If we weigh the membrane down with a load, exerting a pressure $f(x, y)$ on the surface of the membrane, it will stretch and take a new form $z = u(x, y)$, $(x, y) \in D$. Since the membrane is attached to the rim, we have $u(x, y) = 0$

for all $(x,y) \in \partial D$, so such a $u \in \mathcal{A}_0$. From linear elasticity theory, the shape of the loaded membrane minimizes the elastic energy,

$$I(u) = \iint_D \left[\frac{1}{2}|\nabla u(x,y)|^2 + f(x,y)u(x,y) \right] dx\, dy,$$

among all $u \in \mathcal{A}_0$.

As we have done before, we look at variations of u by $v \in \mathcal{A}_0$: expanding the square,

$$\begin{aligned}
I(u+tv) &= \iint_D \left[\frac{1}{2}|\nabla u + t\nabla v|^2 + f(x,y)(u+tv) \right] dx\, dy \\
&= \iint_D \left[\frac{1}{2}|\nabla u|^2 + f(x,y)u + t\left(\nabla u \cdot \nabla v + f(x,y)v\right) + \frac{t^2}{2}|\nabla v|^2 \right] dx\, dy \\
&= I(u) + t\iint_D \left(\nabla u \cdot \nabla v + f(x,y)v\right) dx\, dy + \frac{t^2}{2}\iint_D |\nabla v|^2 dx\, dy. \quad (7.9)
\end{aligned}$$

We notice in passing that this is a Taylor expansion– we'll come back to that later!

First, let's do the usual thing for the first variation:

$$0 = \frac{d}{dt}I(u+tv)\bigg|_{t=0} = \iint_D \left(\nabla u \cdot \nabla v + f(x,y)v\right) dx\, dy, \quad (7.10)$$

for all $v \in \mathcal{A}_0$. As before, we must integrate by parts to express the integral in terms of $v(x,y)$ and not ∇v. For that, we need to go back to vector calculus, and use the Divergence Theorem!

Theorem 7.5 (Multiple Integration by Parts). *Let $D \subset \mathbb{R}^n$ $(n=2,3)$ be an open set with smooth boundary ∂D and unit normal vector $\vec{n}$. Suppose $v: \overline{D} \in \mathbb{R}^n \to \mathbb{R}$, $(n=2,3,)$ is a C^1 function, and $\vec{A}: \mathbb{R}^n \to \mathbb{R}^n$ $(n=2,3)$ is a C^1 vector field. Then, for $D \subset \mathbb{R}^2$,*

$$\iint_D \vec{A} \cdot \nabla v\, dx\, dy = \int_{\partial D} v\vec{A} \cdot \vec{n}\, ds - \iint_D v\nabla \cdot \vec{A}\, dx\, dy,$$

and for $D \subset \mathbb{R}^3$,

$$\iiint_D \vec{A} \cdot \nabla v\, dx\, dy\, dz = \iint_{\partial D} v\vec{A} \cdot \vec{n}\, dS - \iiint_D v\nabla \cdot \vec{A}\, dx\, dy\, dz.$$

Recall that $\nabla \cdot \vec{A} = \mathrm{div}\,(\vec{A}) = \mathrm{trace}(D\vec{A})$ is the divergence, the trace of the derivative matrix (I bet you never thought of it like that before!) In 2D, the boundary integral is a line integral around the curve ∂D; in 3D it is a surface integral on the surface ∂D.

Proof. We do it in 2D; 3D is basically the same, plus one more integral sign all around. Integration by parts is the product rule plus the Fundamental Theorem of Calculus; in higher dimension, that means the Divergence Theorem (Green's in 2D, Gauss' in 3D.) By a vector identity (valid in any dimension,)

$$\nabla \cdot (v\vec{A}) = \nabla v \cdot \vec{A} + v\nabla \cdot \vec{A}.$$

We integrate both sides (double in 2D, triple in 3D), and apply the Divergence Theorem (a variant of Green's theorem in 2D, Gauss' Theorem in 3D),

$$\iint_D \left[\nabla v \cdot \vec{A} + v \, \nabla \cdot \vec{A} \right] dx \, dy = \iint_D \nabla \cdot (v\vec{A}) \, dx \, dy = \int_{\partial D} v \, \vec{A} \cdot \vec{n} \, ds,$$

which is the same thing as what we want. $\qquad\qquad\qquad\qquad\qquad\qquad$ $\square$

Let's get back to what we were doing, trying to get the Euler–Lagrange equation for our elastic energy functional. Applying the Integration by Parts Theorem with $\vec{A} = \nabla u$ to the first term in (7.10), we have:

$$\begin{aligned} 0 &= \iint_D \nabla u \cdot \nabla v \, dx \, dy + \iint_D f(x,y) v \, dx \, dy \\ &= \int_{\partial D} v \, \nabla u \cdot \vec{n} \, ds - \iint_D \operatorname{div}(\nabla u) \, v \, dx \, dy + \iint_D f(x,y) v \, dx \, dy \\ &= \iint_D \left(-\Delta u + f(x,y) \right) v \, dx \, dy, \end{aligned}$$

for all $v \in \mathcal{A}_0$. In the above, we have used the fact that $v = 0$ on ∂D to eliminate the line integral, and written the Laplacian $\Delta u = \operatorname{div}(\nabla u)$ (also written as $\nabla^2 u$ by physicists.) We apply our old friend the Fundamental Lemma of the Calculus of Variations (which is true in any dimension, for pretty much the same reasons as in 1D,) to conclude that the term multiplying v must always be zero. Thus, we get the Euler–Lagrange equation, which is a linear 2nd order partial differential equation (PDE),

$$\Delta u(x, y, z) = f(x, y, z),$$

which in this case is *Poisson's equation*, which appears in many different physical contexts.

As a last remark, note that the equation (7.9) really is the second order Taylor polynomial for the functional $I(u)$; if u solves the EL equation (Poisson's equation above,) then (as in the case of vector functions at a critical point,) we have

$$I(u + tv) = I(u) + \frac{t^2}{2} \iint_D |\nabla v|^2 \, dx \, dy > I(u)$$

for all $t \neq 0$, as long as $v \not\equiv 0$. Thus, the solution to Poisson's equation represents the global minimizer of $I(u)$ among all $u \in \mathcal{A}_0$.

7.3   Practice problems

1. Let $I(u) = \int_0^1 F(u'(x), u(x), x) \, dx$. Find the first variation and Euler-Lagrange equations for each choice of F below. Then solve the equations to find a general solution for extremals of $I(u)$.

[Note: your solutions should have two constants of integration.]

(a) $F(p, u, x) = \frac{\sqrt{1+p^2}}{u}$

(b) $F(p, u, x) = \sqrt{p^2 + u^2}$

(c) $F(p, u, x) = \frac{1}{2}u^2 - \frac{1}{2}p^2$

2. Let $I(u) = \int_0^4 [(u')^2 - xu'] \, dx$, for $u \in C^1$ satisfying $u(0) = 0$ and $u(4) = 3$. Find the first variation and the Euler-Lagrange equation, and then solve it to find the (unique) solution (which gives the minimizer of $I(u)$ over the admissible set.)

3. Consider the surface of the right circular cylinder, $x^2 + y^2 = a^2$, in $\mathbb{R}^3$. Using cylindrical coordinates, this surface may be parametrized by the polar angle θ and z, $\Phi(\theta, z) = (a \cos \theta, a \sin \theta, z)$.

A <u>geodesic</u> on a surface is a curve of shortest length joining two points. Take two points on the cylinder, identified by local coordinates (θ_1, z_1) and (θ_2, z_2) with $\theta_1 < \theta_2$, and consider the collection of all paths of the form

$$\vec{r}(\theta) = (a \cos \theta, a \sin \theta, z(\theta)), \quad \theta \in [\theta_1, \theta_2],$$

with $z(\theta)$ a C^1 function, $z(\theta_1) = z_1$ and $z(\theta_2) = z_2$.

(a) Show that the arclength of the curve $\vec{r}(\theta)$ equals: $I(z) = \int_{\theta_1}^{\theta_2} \sqrt{a^2 + [z'(\theta)]^2} \, d\theta$.

(b) Find the first variation and Euler-Lagrange equations for $I(z)$.

(c) Solve the differential equation, and show that the extremals ("geodesics") are helices, ie, the z-coordinate is a linear function of the polar angle θ.

4. Let $D \subset \mathbb{R}^2$ be a bounded open set with smooth boundary curve ∂D. Define the admissible class $\mathcal{A}_0$ of C^1 functions $u : \overline{D} \subset \mathbb{R}^2 \to \mathbb{R}$, which vanish on the boundary, $u(x, y) = 0$ for all $(x, y) \in \partial D$. Find the first variation and Euler-Lagrange equation for the functional

$$I(u) = \iint_D \left[\frac{1}{2}|\nabla u|^2 - \frac{1}{3}u^3 \right] dx \, dy.$$

(Do not try to solve the resulting PDE! Just the form of the equation will do.)

5. Let $D \subset \mathbb{R}^3$ be a bounded open set with smooth boundary surface ∂D. Define the admissible class $\mathcal{A}_0$ of C^1 functions $u : \overline{D} \subset \mathbb{R}^3 \to \mathbb{R}$, which vanish on the boundary, $u(x, y, z) = 0$ for all $(x, y, z) \in \partial D$. Let $\vec{E} : \mathbb{R}^3 \to \mathbb{R}^3$ be a C^1 vector field, and consider the functional

$$I(u) = \iiint_D \frac{1}{2}|\nabla u - \vec{E}(x, y, z)|^2 \, dx \, dy \, dz.$$

(a) Expand out $I(u + tv)$ for $u, v \in \mathcal{A}_0$, in powers of t.

(b) Use part (a) to find the Euler-Lagrange equation. *(Do not try to solve it!)*

(c) Explain why any solution u of the Euler–Lagrange equation must be a strict minimizer of $I(u)$ among functions in $\mathcal{A}_0$.

6. Let $D \subset \mathbb{R}^2$ as in problem 1, but now think of points in $\mathbb{R}^2$ representing space and time, $(x,t) \in \mathbb{R}^2$, and $u(x,t): D \subset \mathbb{R}^2 \to \mathbb{R}$ a C^1 function. For a constant $c > 0$, consider the functional

$$I(u) = \frac{1}{2} \iint_D \left[(u_t(x,t))^2 - c^2(u_x(x,t))^2 \right] dx\, dt.$$

Calculate the first variation, but to avoid confusion write it as $\frac{d}{ds}I(u+sv)|_{s=0}$ for $v \in \mathcal{A}_0$ (as before, $v(x,t) = 0$ on ∂D), and find the Euler–Lagrange equation *(A.K.A. the Wave Equation.)*

[*You can still apply the Integration by Parts, by writing* $\nabla v = (v_x, v_t)$, *treating* t *as if it were* y.]

Chapter 8

Fourier Series

8.1   Fourier's Crazy, Brilliant Idea

In 1807, Jean-Baptiste Joseph Fourier (1768–1830) published his research on solutions of the heat equation, the partial differential equation describing heat flow in a solid object. An important part of his work involved linear combinations of special solutions of the form

$$e^{-kt}\sin(\omega x).$$

At this point, Fourier makes what looks like a ridiculous claim: that *any* continuous function may be represented as a *series* of terms of this form, that is

$$\sum_{n=1}^{\infty} \sin(\omega_n x),$$

for an appropriate choice of frequencies ω_n. On the face of it, this is absurd. The sine functions oscillate periodically, with period $2\pi/\omega_n$, so how could they represent any continuous function?

In the end Fourier was essentially right, almost any function (even discontinuous ones) can be represented (on bounded intervals) in terms of convergence series of sines (or cosines,) which we now call Fourier Series,

$$\alpha_0 + \sum_{n=1}^{\infty}\left[\alpha_n \cos(n\omega_0 x) + \beta_n \sin(n\omega_0 x)\right].$$

However, it is not entirely clear in what sense we should interpret the series; being an infinite series there is an important (and difficult) question of *convergence*. The question of which functions can be obtained as convergent Fourier Series, and in what sense the convergence takes place, have been keeping mathematicians busy since Fourier's time. The study of Fourier Series and its applications has also stimulated a huge amount of mathematical research in analysis, which has contributed to solving many, many other important problems in mathematics and in applications (which include data transmission, audio and video compression, medical scanning, and image processing!)

Let's begin by reviewing the properties of the sine (and cosine) functions. Consider a function of the form

$$f_1(x) = A\sin(\omega x + \varphi). \tag{8.1}$$

The constant ω is the *angular frequency*, and φ is called the *phase*. f_1 is a periodic function with period $T = 2\pi/\omega$, in other words,

$$f_1(x + T) = f_1(x) \quad \text{for all } x \in \mathbb{R}.$$

Similarly, if $k \in \mathbb{N}$, then $f_k(x) = A\sin(k\omega x + \varphi)$ is also T-periodic. This may be verified easily, since

$$f_k(x + T) = A\sin(k\omega(x + T) + \varphi) = A\sin(k\omega x + \varphi + 2\pi k) = A\sin(k\omega x + \varphi) = f_k(x).$$

Since any linear combination of these $f_k(x)$ is T-periodic, we can't hope to represent non-periodic function by Fourier series, at least not on the whole real line $\mathbb{R}$. So the solution is to restrict our attention to functions defined on an interval of length T.

Next, by the angle addition identity from trigonometry, we have the identity,

$$A\sin(\omega x + \varphi) = \alpha\cos(\omega x) + \beta\sin(\omega x),$$

where $A = \sqrt{\alpha^2 + \beta^2}$ and $\alpha = A\sin\varphi, \beta = A\cos\varphi$. So we see that using both sines and cosines with the same angular frequency ω produces the exact same family of wave forms as (8.1) with phase angle. And so we will make our series in both sines and cosines, rather than using the phase angle. It will also be convenient to define our functions on a *symmetric* interval of length $T = 2L$, and take $x \in [-L, L]$. The symmetry will help us understand the different roles of the sine and cosine terms, and simplify the expressions of the series. We follow Fourier and consider integer multiple of the fundamental frequency, $\omega = \pi/L$, i.e.

$$\alpha_k \cos\left(\frac{k\pi x}{L}\right) + \beta_k \sin\left(\frac{k\pi x}{L}\right),$$

where $k = 1, 2, 3, \ldots$ as our basic building blocks. Using these building blocks, we want to answer two questions: (1) given a function $f(x)$ on $[-L, L]$, can we choose the coefficients α_k, β_k such that f is represented by the following form,

$$\alpha_0 + \sum_{k=1}^{\infty}\left(\alpha_k \cos\left(\frac{k\pi x}{L}\right) + \beta_k \sin\left(\frac{k\pi x}{L}\right)\right),$$

and (2) does the series converge to $f(x)$ and in what sense does it converge?

8.2   Orthogonality

Fourier Series are so useful because they are related to a natural sense of orthogonality in a vector space whose "points" are functions. Again, we restrict our attention to T-periodic functions, but for convenience we choose a symmetric interval of length T, $[-L, L]$ with $T = 2L$. Then, the collection of all continuous, $2L$-periodic functions $f : \mathbb{R} \to \mathbb{R}$ form a *vector space* which we call C_L. We introduce an inner product (or scalar product) on C_L:

Definition 8.1 (Inner product). *Let f, g be continuous functions on $[-L, L]$. Their L^2 inner product (or scalar product) is $\langle f, g \rangle = \int_{-L}^{L} f(x)g(x)dx$*

We can easily verity the symmetry and linearity of the inner product. Now, we also define an associated norm:

Definition 8.2 (Norm). *Let f, g be continuous functions on $[-L, L]$. Their L^2 norm is*

$$\|f\| = \sqrt{\langle f, f \rangle} = \sqrt{\int_{-L}^{L} (f(x))^2 \, dx}.$$

The term "L^2" inner product and norm comes from the square (and square root) appearing in the form of the norm $\|f\|$. One may define a whole family of norms on functions $f \in C_L$,

$$\left[\int_{-L}^{L} |f(x)|^p \, dx \right]^{\frac{1}{p}},$$

for any $p \geq 1$, the so-called L^p norms. We won't deal with these here, but you will run into them later on in your analysis courses!

Using the L^2 definition of norm, we can define distance between f and g as $\|f(x) - g(x)\|$, which is equal to square root of area under the graph of $(f(x) - g(x))^2$.

This definition of norm should have the property that $\|f\| = 0$ iff $f(x) = 0$. This is true by an argument which is similar to the proof of the FLCoV (and which we omit here.)

Example 8.3. With this definition of inner product, we find that

$$\left\{ 1, \cos\left(\frac{k\pi x}{L}\right), \sin\left(\frac{k\pi x}{L}\right) | k = 1, 2, 3, \ldots \right\}$$

form an orthogonal family of functions. In other words,

$$\left\langle \cos\left(\frac{k\pi x}{L}\right), \cos\left(\frac{m\pi x}{L}\right) \right\rangle = 0, \qquad \text{for } m \neq k;$$

$$\left\langle \sin\left(\frac{k\pi x}{L}\right), \sin\left(\frac{m\pi x}{L}\right) \right\rangle = 0, \qquad \text{for } m \neq k;$$

$$\left\langle \sin\left(\frac{k\pi x}{L}\right), \cos\left(\frac{m\pi x}{L}\right) \right\rangle = 0, \qquad \text{for } m = 0, 1, \ldots, \text{ and } k = 1, 2, \ldots$$

(Note that $1 = \cos(0 \cdot \pi x)$ is included in the formulas for the cosine!)

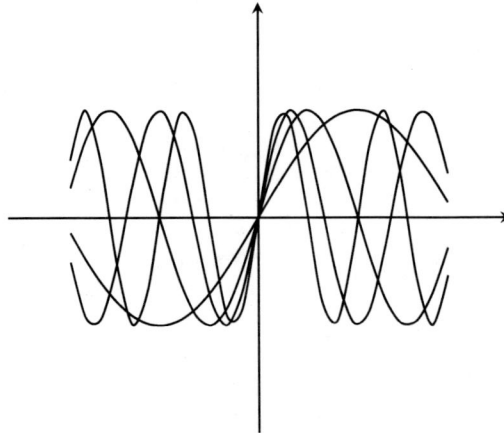

Figure 8.1. $y = sin(kx)$, where $k = 1, 2, 3, 4$. As k increases, period decreases.

To derive these we use the angle addition formulas (this was done in section 7.2 of Stewart!) to calculate the integrals explicity. For example,

$$\int_{-L}^{L} \cos\left(\frac{k\pi x}{L}\right) \cos\left(\frac{m\pi x}{L}\right) dx \tag{8.2}$$

$$= \int_{-L}^{L} \frac{1}{2}\left[\cos\left(\frac{(k-m)\pi x}{L}\right) + \cos\left(\frac{(k+m)\pi x}{L}\right)\right] dx$$

$$= \frac{1}{2}\left[\frac{L}{(k-m)\pi}\sin\left(\frac{(k-m)\pi x}{L}\right) + \frac{L}{(k+m)\pi}\sin\left(\frac{(k+m)\pi x}{L}\right)\right]_{-L}^{L}$$

$$= 0,$$

if $k \neq m$. (Notice that the first term would divide by zero if $k = m$!) The others are done in a similar way. We also notice that the family is orthogonal, but generally is is not orthonormal, in the sense that the norms are not equal to one. For each $k = 1, 2, \ldots$,

$$\left\|\cos\left(\frac{k\pi x}{L}\right)\right\|^2 = \int_{-L}^{L} \cos^2\left(\frac{k\pi x}{L}\right) dx = \int_{-L}^{L}\left[\frac{1}{2} + \frac{1}{2}\cos\left(2\frac{k\pi x}{L}\right)\right] dx = L, \tag{8.3}$$

so $\left\|\cos\left(\frac{k\pi x}{L}\right)\right\| = \sqrt{L}$. A similar calculation shows $\left\|\sin\left(\frac{k\pi x}{L}\right)\right\| = \sqrt{L}$ also, but $\|1\| = \sqrt{2L}$. $\quad\square$

8.3 Fourier Series

The idea is to take a function $f(x)$ defined on an interval of length $T = 2L$, typically $(-L, L)$, and associate to it a series of trigonometric function of period $T = 2L$:

$$f(x) \sim S(x) = \frac{a_0}{2} + \sum_{k=1}^{\infty}\left(a_k \cos\left(\frac{k\pi x}{L}\right) + b_k \sin\left(\frac{k\pi x}{L}\right)\right)$$

(We do not write this as an equality, since we have no idea if the infinite series converges!) Further, we want to derive the coefficients a_k and b_k from $f(x)$ and test whether the series converges or not.

To find the coefficients, we use orthogonality. We use the L^2 inner product on C_L, the set of continuous periodic functions defined on $[-L, L]$:

$$\langle f, g \rangle = \int_{-L}^{L} f(x)g(x).$$

Then, $f \perp g$ when $\langle f, g \rangle = 0$ and we found in Example 8.3 that

$$\left\{ \frac{1}{2}, \cos\left(\frac{k\pi x}{L}\right), \sin\left(\frac{k\pi x}{L}\right) \,\middle|\, k = 1, 2, 3, \ldots \right\}$$

is an orthogonal family on C_T. By calculating the inner product when $k = m$ as in (8.2), (8.3), we find that

$$\left\langle \cos\left(\frac{k\pi x}{L}\right), \cos\left(\frac{m\pi x}{L}\right) \right\rangle = \begin{cases} \sqrt{L} & m = k = 1, 2, 3, \ldots \\ \sqrt{2L} & m = k = 0, \\ 0 & m \neq k. \end{cases}$$

$$\left\langle \sin\left(\frac{k\pi x}{L}\right), \sin\left(\frac{m\pi x}{L}\right) \right\rangle = \begin{cases} \sqrt{L} & m = k = 1, 2, 3, \ldots \\ 0 & m \neq k. \end{cases}$$

Recall for vectors $u, v \in \mathbb{R}^n$, the projection of v onto u is

$$\frac{v \cdot u}{\|u\|^2} u.$$

By analogy, we define the Fourier Sine and Cosine series coefficients as the orthogonal projections on to the basis functions,

$$\left. \begin{aligned} a_0 &= \frac{\langle f, \frac{1}{2} \rangle}{\|\frac{1}{2}\|^2} = \frac{1}{L} \int_{-L}^{L} f(x)dx \\ a_k &= \frac{\langle f, \cos\left(\frac{k\pi x}{L}\right) \rangle}{\|\cos\left(\frac{k\pi x}{L}\right)\|^2} = \frac{1}{L} \int_{-L}^{L} f(x) \cos\left(\frac{k\pi x}{L}\right) dx \\ b_k &= \frac{\langle f, \sin\left(\frac{k\pi x}{L}\right) \rangle}{\|\sin\left(\frac{k\pi x}{L}\right)\|^2} = \frac{1}{L} \int_{-L}^{L} f(x) \sin\left(\frac{k\pi x}{L}\right) dx \end{aligned} \right\} \tag{8.4}$$

(Note that the formula for a_0 is the same as that for a_k with $k = 0$; this is why we choose the constant function $\frac{1}{2}$ in our orthogonal family, and not 1, for instance.) So for each finite $n \in \mathbb{N}$ we obtain a *trigonometric polynomial* which represents the projection of $f(x)$, $x \in [-L, L]$ onto the first n sine and cosine terms,

$$S_n(x) = \frac{a_0}{2} + \sum_{k=1}^{n} \left(a_k \cos\left(\frac{k\pi x}{L}\right) + b_k \sin\left(\frac{k\pi x}{L}\right) \right).$$

This is a *partial sum* of the complete Fourier Series for $f(x)$, in other words, a truncation to n terms of the infinite series

$$S(x) \sim \frac{a_0}{2} + \sum_{k=1}^{\infty} \left(a_k \cos\left(\frac{k\pi x}{L}\right) + b_k \sin\left(\frac{k\pi x}{L}\right) \right).$$

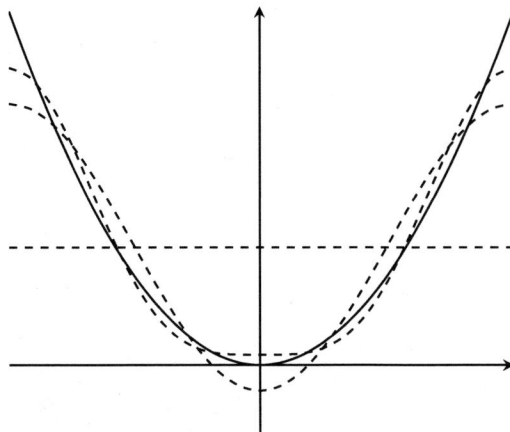

Figure 8.2. Dashed curves represent the first three partial sums of Fourier series for $f(x) = x^2$ for $x \in (-\pi, \pi)$. As the number of terms increase, the sum converges to x^2 in the interval. Solid curve represents $f(x) = x^2$

If the series converges, then for large n, the partial sum $S_n(x)$ should be a good approximation to $f(x)$ on $(-L, L)$.

Example 8.4. Consider $f(x) = \cos^2 x = \frac{1}{2} + \frac{1}{2}\cos(2x)$ with $L = \pi$ on $[-\pi, \pi]$. Then,

$$\begin{cases} a_0 = 1, a_1 = 0, a_2 = 1/2, a_{k \geq 3} = 0 \\ b_k = 0, \forall k \end{cases}$$

It turns out that any function of the form $\cos^m x, \sin^m x$ or $\cos^m x \sin^k x$ is a trig polynomial and it can be written as a linear combination using trigonometric identities. And so this function is *exactly equal* to its Fourier Series! Since the series is actually a finite sum, there is no convergence question to deal with. $\square$

Example 8.5. Consider $f(x) = x^2$ for $x \in (-\pi, \pi)$. Now, x^2 is not a periodic function, but the Fourier Series in $(-\pi, \pi)$ will be periodic outside that interval, so what the series generates is *not* equal to x^2 outside of that interval, but the *periodic extension* of the piece of x^2 inside $(-\pi, \pi)$: see Figure 8.2.

To calculate the coefficients, we think for a minute before jumping into the integrals. Since $f(x) = x^2$ is an *even* function, $f(-x) = f(x)$, and $\sin(kx)$ is an odd function, $\sin(-kx) = -\sin(kx)$, the product $f(x)\sin(kx)$ is *odd*. Since we are integrating over a symmetric interval $x \in [-L, L]$, the $b_k = 0$ for all $k = 1, 2, 3, \ldots$ On the other hand, $f(x)\cos(kx)$ is even, and so we have to actually do an integral! We integrate by parts, twice, to get:

$$
\begin{aligned}
a_k &= \frac{1}{\pi} \int_{-\pi}^{\pi} x^2 \cos(kx)dx = \frac{2}{\pi} \int_0^{\pi} x^2 \cos(kx)dx \\
&= \frac{2}{\pi}\left[x^2 \frac{\sin(kx)}{k}\bigg|_0^{\pi} - \int_0^{\pi} 2x \frac{\sin(kx)}{k}dx \right] \\
&= \frac{2}{\pi}\left[2x \frac{\cos(kx)}{k^2}\bigg|_0^{\pi} - \int_0^{\pi} 2\frac{\cos(kx)}{k^2}dx \right] \\
&= \frac{2}{\pi}\left[\frac{2\pi}{k^2}\cos(k\pi) + \frac{2}{k^3}\sin(kx)\bigg|_0^{\pi} \right] \\
&= \frac{4}{k^2}(-1)^k,
\end{aligned}
$$

for $k = 1, 2, 3, \ldots$ Note that $\sin(k\pi) = 0$ and $\cos(k\pi) = (-1)^k$ for integer values of k. We still need to look at $k = 0$ separately,

$$
a_0 = \frac{1}{2\pi} \int_{-\pi}^{\pi} x^2\, dx = \frac{1}{\pi} \int_0^{\pi} x^2\, dx = \frac{2\pi^2}{3}.
$$

We then conclude that the Fourier Series for $f(x) = x^2$ is purely a cosine series,

$$
f(x) \sim S(x) = \frac{\pi^2}{3} + \sum_{k=1}^{\infty} \frac{4(-1)^k}{k^2}\cos(kx)
$$

$\square$

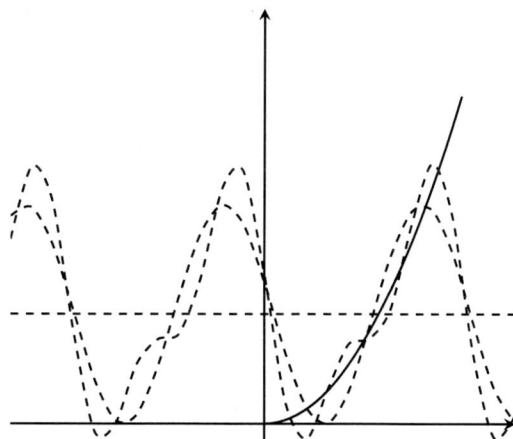

Figure 8.3. Dashed curves represent the first four partial sums of Fourier series for $f(x) = x^2$ for $x \in (0, 2\pi)$. As the number of terms increase, the sum converges to x^2 in the interval. The solid curve represents $f(x) = x^2$

Example 8.6. Consider $g(x) = x^2$ where $x \in (0, 2\pi)$ (Figure 8.3). This periodic extension is different from the one above: it agrees with x^2 on the asymmetrical interval $(0, 2\pi)$ and replicates that shape periodically to the rest of $\mathbb{R}$. Unlike the previous example, this extension is *discontinuous* at all $x = 2\pi m$. So even in the best case, where the series, $S(x)$, converges everywhere, it's discontinuous function at $x = 2\pi m$, for all $m \in \mathbb{Z}$. Still, does it converge there, and if so, to which values?

We calculate the Fourier coefficients, but now over the non-symmetric interval $(0, 2\pi)$. Since the interval is not symmetric, we cannot assume either family of coefficients vanishes, and indeed we have

$$a_0 = \frac{1}{2\pi} \int_0^{2\pi} x^2 dx = 8\pi^2/3,$$

$$a_k = \frac{1}{\pi} \int_0^{2\pi} x^2 \cos(kx)dx = 4/k^2,$$

$$b_k = \frac{1}{\pi} \int_0^{2\pi} x^2 \sin(kx)dx = -4\pi/k,$$

$k = 1, 2, 3, \ldots$ We don't get the same Fourier Series, but then again this is not the same function! The Fourier Series for x^2 depends on the domain, since it only samples x^2 over an interval, and then replicates its values periodically to fill out all of $x \in \mathbb{R}$. $\square$

Example 8.7. Consider $f(x) = x$ where $x \in (-\pi, \pi)$ and $L = \pi$ (Figure 8.4). Then, we get

$$a_k = \frac{1}{\pi} \int_{-\pi}^{\pi} x \cos(kx)dx = 0$$

$$b_k = \frac{1}{\pi} \int_{-\pi}^{\pi} x \sin(kx)dx$$

$$= \frac{2}{\pi} \int_0^{\pi} x \sin(kx)dx$$

$$= \frac{2}{k}(-1)^{k+1}$$

So as $f(x) = x$ on $(-\pi, \pi)$ is odd, we have a sine series:

$$f(x) \sim S(x) = \sum_{k=1}^{\infty} \frac{2(-1)^{k+1}}{k} \sin(kx)$$

$S(x)$ has discontinuities, $f(-\pi) = -\pi \neq \pi = f(\pi)$. So what happens at the discontinuities, $x = (2m-1)\pi$?

$$S(n\pi) = \sum_{k=1}^{\infty} \frac{2(-1)^{k+1}}{k} \sin(kn\pi) = \sum_{k=1}^{\infty} 0 = 0$$

It will be a general fact that at a *jump discontinuity*, the Fourier series, $S(x)$, takes the midpoint value. It does not choose the value of $f(x)$ from either the right or the left at a jump discontinuity. $\square$

8.4 Pointwise and Uniform Convergence

Let's talk with convergence; not only is it interesting and important, but it goes to the heart of what we get when we use Fourier Series to approximate a function. First, let's review

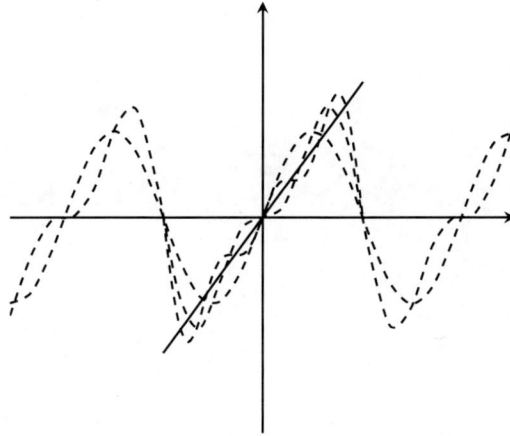

Figure 8.4. Dashed curves represent the first three partial sums of Fourier series for $f(x) = x$ for $x \in (-\pi, \pi)$. As the number of terms increase, the sum converges to x^2 in the interval. The solid curve represents $f(x) = x$. The series converges at each x (by the Pointwise Convergence Theorem), but the accuracy of the approximation by partial sums is poor near the jump discontinuities, $x = (2m - 1)\pi$, $m \in \mathbb{Z}$.

convergence of numerical series, $\sum_{k=1}^{\infty} c_k$, where c_k are real numbers. A series converges to a number s if

$$\lim_{n \to \infty} \sum_{k=1}^{n} c_k = s.$$

We call $S_n = \sum_{k=1}^{n} c_k$, the *n-th partial sum* of the series. If the limit, $\lim_{n \to \infty} S_n$, does not exist, we say the series *diverges*.

We understand convergence in the following way: in finite time we can only ever directly calculate the partial sums, $S_n = \sum_{k=1}^{i} nftyc_k$. If for all sufficiently large numbers n, the partial sums S_n are a good approximation for a single value S, then the series converges to S. Thus, for a convergent series we may evaluate S to high accuracy by taking n sufficiently large.

Notice also that if the series converges, then the "tail" of the series,

$$S - S_n = \sum_{k=n+1}^{\infty} c_k$$

is negligeably small when n is sufficiently large, so the tail tends to zero,

$$\lim_{n \to \infty} \sum_{k=n+1}^{\infty} c_k = 0. \tag{8.5}$$

In fact, the above limit expression is *equivalent* to the convergence of the series (and it is by using this that the "convergence tests" from Stewart are derived.)

From the above criterion (8.5), IF the series converges, THEN it must be true that $\lim_{k \to \infty} c_k = 0$. BE CAREFUL, this is a *necessary* condition for convergence, but not a *sufficient* one. For a series to converge, it is necessary for each term $c_k \to 0$ as $k \to \infty$, but even more, the values of c_k must decrease "fast enough" so that the sum of the values does not accumulate.

Example 8.8 (Harmonic Series). Look at $\sum_{k=1}^{\infty} \frac{1}{k}$, so $c_k = \frac{1}{k}$. Consider the n terms which follow after $c_n = \frac{1}{n}$, from c_{n+1} to c_{2n}:

$$c_{n+1} + c_{n+2} + \cdots + c_{n+(n-1)} + c_{2n} = \frac{1}{n+1} + \frac{1}{n+2} + \cdots \frac{1}{n+(n-1)} + \frac{1}{2n}$$

$$\geq n \cdot \frac{1}{2n} = \frac{1}{2},$$

since each term is larger than the last one in the list, $c_{2n} = \frac{1}{2n}$, and there are n of them. But then we can never have (8.5) for this series, as for any $n \in \mathbb{N}$ the tail

$$\sum_{k=n+1}^{\infty} c_k \geq \sum_{k=n+1}^{2n} \frac{1}{k} \geq \frac{1}{2},$$

by the above estimate. Hence, the Harmonic Series is divergent.

Example 8.9 (Geometric Series). This is the most important example. Consider

$$\sum_{k=0}^{\infty} r^k.$$

This is exceptional, because we can explicitly calculate S_n for these,

$$S_n = \frac{1 - r^{n+1}}{1 - r}, \qquad \text{if } r \neq 1.$$

Since $\lim_{n\to\infty} r^{n+1} = 0$ when $|r| < 1$, the geometric series converges when $|r| < 1$, and

$$S = \lim_{n\to\infty} S_n = \sum_{k=0}^{\infty} r^k = \frac{1}{1-r}, \qquad \text{when } |r| < 1.$$

On the other hand, if $|r| > 1$, then $\lim_{n\to\infty} r^{n+1}$ does not exist, and so the series diverges. The cases $r = \pm 1$ are more delicate and need to be dealt with separately. When $r = -1$, then $r^{n+1} = (-1)^{n+1}$ oscillates between -1 and $+1$, and so it diverges (even though it doesn't tend to $\pm\infty$) and so the series diverges. It doesn't blow up, the values of S_n just oscillate between 1 (when n is even) and 0 (when n is odd.) When $r = 1$, the partial sums $S_n = n$, and these diverge to infinity. In conclusion, the geometric series converges *if and only if $|r| < 1$.*   □

Example 8.10 (p-series). $\sum_{k=1}^{\infty} 1/k^p$ converges iff $p > 1$.

This may be verified using the Integral Test (see Stewart!) Unlike the geometric series, we don't have a value to which the series converges– at least not yet! We will see that using Fourier Series we may derive actual numerical values for some numerical series!   □

Using the comparison test, we can determine convergence and divergence of many series using these examples.

Theorem 8.11 (Comparison Test). *Assume that $0 \leq a_k \leq b_k$ for all $k \in \mathbb{N}$.*

- *If $\sum_{k=1}^{\infty} b_k$ converges, then $\sum_{k=1}^{\infty} a_k$ also converges.*

- *If $\sum_{k=1}^{\infty} a_k$ diverges, then $\sum_{k=1}^{\infty} b_k$ also divverges.*

Example 8.12. The series $\sum_{k=1}^{\infty} \frac{1}{2k^2+k+1}$ converges, since $a_k = \frac{1}{2k^2+k+1} \leq \frac{1}{2k^2}$ and $\sum_{k=1}^{\infty} \frac{1}{2k^2} = \frac{1}{2} \sum_{k=1}^{\infty} \frac{1}{k^2}$ converges (p-series with $p = 2$.)

The series $\sum_{k=1}^{\infty} \frac{k}{2k^2+k+1}$ diverges, since $k + 1 \leq 2k^2$ for $k \geq 1$, and so $b_k = \frac{k}{2k^2+k+1} \geq \frac{k}{4k^2} = \frac{1}{4k}$ and $\sum_{k=1}^{\infty} \frac{1}{4k}$ diverges (p-series with $p = 1$.) $\square$

While the Comparison Test and p-series concern series with positive terms, Fourier Series contain sines and cosines, and so will have terms changing in sign. We distinguish two types of convergence for series with sign-changing terms:

Definition 8.13 (Absolute and conditional convergence). *A series $\sum_{k=1}^{\infty} c_k$ converges absolutely if $\sum_{k=1}^{\infty} |c_k|$ converges. The series converges conditionally if $\sum_{k=1}^{\infty} c_k$ converges but $\sum_{k=1}^{\infty} |c_k|$ diverges.*

Basically, a conditionally convergent series depends on cancellation between positive and negative terms to converge, while an absolutely convergent series is more robust: its terms tend to zero rapidly enough to ensure convergence without having to count on cancellations.

Example 8.14 (Alternating series). The series

$$\sum_{k=1}^{\infty} (-1)^k \frac{1}{k^p} \tag{8.6}$$

alternates in sign, because of the $(-1)^k$ factor. If $p > 1$, then $|a_k| = 1/k^p$, and the p-series $\sum_{k=1}^{\infty} \frac{1}{k^p}$ converges; thus for $p > 1$ this alternating series converges <u>absolutely</u>. On the other hand, when $0 < p \leq 1$ the series of the absolute values is a <u>divergent</u> p-series, and so the series (8.6) does not converge absolutely. However, any <u>alternating series</u>,

$$\sum_{k=1}^{\infty} (-1)^k b_k, \text{ with } \lim_{k \to \infty} b_k = 0 \text{ and } b_{k+1} \leq b_k \text{ for all } k,$$

is convergent. (See Stewart.) Thus, the series (8.6) converges <u>conditionally</u> when $0 < p \leq 1$; the terms tend to zero, but not rapidly enough for the series to converge without the help of cancellation. $\square$

For absolutely convergent series we can have a good estimate on the rate of convergence, ie, how many terms we need to keep to have a good approximation of the limit by a partial sum. On the other hand, conditional convergence is delicate and the series converges slowly.

Let's apply these ideas to trigonometric Fourier series. For simplicity, we take $L = \pi$, and consider 2π-periodic functions $f(x)$ (which means extending functions on $(-\pi, \pi)$ periodically!), with the usual formula for the coefficients,

$$\left.\begin{aligned}
a_0 &= \frac{1}{\pi} \int_{-\pi}^{\pi} f(x)dx \\
a_k &= \frac{1}{\pi} \int_{-\pi}^{\pi} f(x) \cos(kx)\, dx \\
b_k &= \frac{1}{\pi} \int_{-\pi}^{\pi} f(x) \sin(kx)\, dx,
\end{aligned}\right\} \tag{8.7}$$

$k = 1, 2, 3, \ldots$ The same facts will be true for $2L$-periodic functions (with coefficients given by (8.4)), but the messy formulas will obscure the ideas.

An important distinction is that Fourier series are series of <u>functions</u>, and not just numbers:

$$S(x) = \frac{a_0}{2} + \sum_{k=1}^{\infty}(a_k \cos(kx) + b_k \sin(kx)) = \sum_{k=0}^{\infty} g_k(x).$$

There are several different (and important) notions of convergence for series of functions. The first is easy to grasp: For each fixed value of x, $\sum_{k=1}^{\infty} g_k(x)$ is a numerical series, which converges or doesn't. So we can ask for each individual x whether the series converges or diverges.

Definition 8.15 (Pointwise convergence). *We say that the series $\sum_{k=1}^{\infty} g_k(x)$ converges pointwise on a set $A \in \mathbb{R}$ if the series converges for every individual $x \in A$.*

The notion of poinwise convergence is simple and easy to verify, but it has some drawbacks. In particular, series of continuous functions might converge pointwise to a discontinuous limit function. Also, differentiating or integrating a pointwise convergent series might lead to incorrect answers.

Example 8.16. Consider

$$\sum_{k=1}^{\infty}(1-x)x^k, \qquad x \in [0, 1].$$

Then, we get the following partial sums:

$$S_n = \sum_{k=1}^{n}(1-x)x^k = (1-x)\sum_{k=1}^{n} x^k.$$

If $x \in [0, 1)$, the series converges:

$$\lim_{n\to\infty} S_n(x) = (1-x) \underbrace{\lim_{n\to\infty} \sum_{k=1}^{n} x^k}_{1/(1-x)} = 1$$

However, when $x = 1$, we have $S_n(1) = 0$. So at $x = 1$, the series converges to 0, i.e.

$$\sum_{k=1}^{\infty}(1-x)x^k = \begin{cases} 1 & \text{if } x \in [0,1) \\ 0 & \text{if } x = 1 \end{cases}$$

Therefore, the series converges *pointwise* on the set $A = [0,1]$. Notice that, although each partial sum $S_n(x)$ is a continuous function on A, the series converges to a *discontinuous* limit function! □

A series of continuous functions can converge pointwise to a discontinuous function, and there are examples for which the series of the integrals is not equal to the integral of the series,

$$\int_a^b \left(\sum_{k=1}^{\infty} g_n(x) \right) dx \neq \sum_{k=1}^{\infty} \int_a^b g_n(x)dx.$$

(Notice that when we calculated the Fourier coefficients in (8.4) we were implicitly assuming these would be equal!) So we need to be very careful about doing calculus with a series which is only pointwise convergent.

Fortunately, there is a nice theorem about pointwise convergence of trigonometric Fourier series, which is easy to apply. (However, it is fairly tricky to prove!)

Definition 8.17. *We say that $f(x)$ is piecewise C^1, or piecewise smooth, on $[a,b]$ if (i) f is differentiable and $f'(x)$ is continuous except maybe at finitely many points; (ii) At each exceptional point, $f(x)$ and $f'(x)$ have jump discontinuities.*

At a jump discontinuity x, we denote the left- and right-hand limits by:

$$f\left(x^+\right) = \lim_{t \to x^+} f(t),$$
$$f\left(x^-\right) = \lim_{t \to x^-} f(t).$$

Recall that f is continuous at x if and only if $f\left(x^+\right) = f(x) = f\left(x^-\right)$.

We need to be careful with this definition when dealing with Fourier Series, because even if f is $C^1([-\pi,\pi])$, when we construct a Fourier series we get the 2π-periodic extension of f to $\mathbb{R}$, which might create discontinuities. We saw this happen in Examples 8.6 and 8.7.

Theorem 8.18 (Pointwise Convergence Theorem for Trigonometric Fourier Series). *Assume f is a piecewise C^1, (2π)-periodic function. Then, its trigonometric Fourier Series,*

$$S(x) = \frac{a_0}{2} + \sum_{k=1}^{\infty} \left[a_k \cos(kx) + b_k \sin(kx)\right],$$

(with coefficients given by (8.7)) converges pointwise at every $x \in \mathbb{R}$ to

$$S(x) = \frac{1}{2}\left(f\left(x^+\right) + f\left(x^-\right)\right).$$

In other words, if f is continuous, $S(x) = f(x)$. If $f(x)$ jumps, $S(x)$ averages the jump values.

Remark. It is not sufficient to assume f is continuous to conclude that

$$\lim_{n \to \infty} S_n(x) = f(x),$$

some additional information is needed. There are examples of functions which are continuous (but not piecewise C^1) for which the Fourier Series diverges at some values of x.

Example 8.19. Consider $f(x) = x$, $x \in (-\pi, \pi)$. Then,

$$S(x) = \sum_{k=1}^{\infty} \frac{2(-1)^{k+1}}{k} \sin(kx)$$

$$= x,$$

if $x \in (-\pi, \pi)$, and $S(k\pi) = 0$ for each $k \in \mathbb{Z}$, which averages the value across the jump discontinuities in the 2π-periodic extension of f. $\square$

Example 8.20. Consider $f(x) = x$ for $x \in (-\pi, \pi)$, which is extended 2π-periodically. We already calculated its Fourier Series,

$$S(x) = \sum_{k=1}^{\infty} \frac{2(-1)^{k+1}}{k} \sin(kx).$$

Then, $f(x)$ is piecewise C^1, but it is discontinuous on $\mathbb{R}$, since it must jump at odd multiples of π in order to be periodic. So by the Pointwise Convergence Theorem, it converges at all values $x \in \mathbb{R}$, and agrees with the periodic extension for $x \neq (2m - 1)\pi$, $m \in \mathbb{Z}$. At the odd multiples of π, the Fourier Series takes the midpoint value at the discontinuity,

$$S\left((2m - 1)\pi\right) = \sum_{k=1}^{\infty} \frac{2(-1)^{k+1}}{k} \sin(0) = \sum_{k=1}^{\infty} 0 = 0.$$

Observe that b_k is an alternating sequence, and

$$|b_k| = \left| \frac{2(-1)^{k+1}}{k} \right| = \frac{2}{k}.$$

Since $\sum_{k=1}^{\infty} 2/k$ diverges, the series converges conditionally. We can see how slowly it converges by looking at graphs of S_n, for large n. $\square$

Example 8.21. Consider $f(x) = x^2$ with $x \in (-\pi, \pi)$ extended 2π-periodically. In this case, the extension is piecewise C^1 and also continuous, so the Fourier Series converges to the periodic extension at all values of x, $S(x) = f(x) \, \forall x \in \mathbb{R}$. Further, we find that

$$S(x) = \frac{\pi^2}{3} + \sum_{k=1}^{\infty} \frac{4(-1)^k}{k^2} \cos(kx).$$

Then, by looking at the individual terms,

$$|a_k \cos(kx)| = \left| \frac{4(-1)^k}{k^2} \cos(kx) \right| \leq \frac{4}{k^2},$$

we find that $S(x)$ converges absolutely for all $x \in \mathbb{R}$ by the Comparison Test.

Since it converges for all $x \in \mathbb{R}$, let's try some values. First, when $x = 0$, we get

$$\frac{\pi^2}{3} + \sum_{k=1}^{\infty} \frac{4(-1)^k}{k^2} = 0$$

So we find that

$$\sum_{k=1}^{\infty} \frac{(-1)^k}{k^2} = -\frac{\pi^2}{12}$$

Likewise, when $x = \pi$, we find that

$$\sum_{k=1}^{\infty} \frac{1}{k^2} = \frac{\pi^2}{6}$$

In this way Fourier Series provides us with some exact numerical values for some common series.   □

This example illustrates a second notion of convergence, *uniform convergence*. A uniformly convergent series is one for which the partial sums $S_n(x)$ approximate the limiting function $S(x)$ to within the same error at all points x. If you were to draw a thin strip of uniform width around the graph $y = S(x)$, the graphs $y = S_n(x)$ would all fit completely inside the strip for n large. Figure 8.5 shows how closely the Fourier partial sums approximate x^2 on $[-\pi, \pi]$.

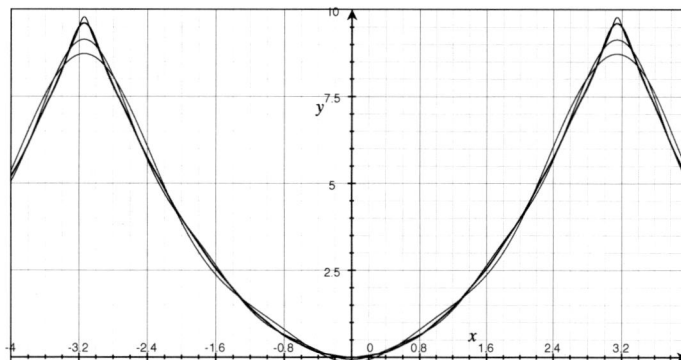

Figure 8.5. Partial sums S_n for $n = 3, 5, 15, 50$ for $f(x) = x^2$ on $(-\pi, \pi)$. The convergence is uniform.

Theorem 8.22 (Uniform Convergence). *Consider $S(x) = \sum_{k=1}^{\infty} g_k(x)$ with $x \in [a, b]$. We say that the series converges uniformly to $S(x)$ if*

$$\lim_{n \to \infty} \left(\max_{x \in [a,b]} \left| S(x) - \sum_{k=1}^{n} g_k(x) \right| \right) = 0.$$

In other words, for any $\epsilon > 0$, there is an N for which

$$\left| S(x) - \sum_{k=1}^{n} g_k(x) \right| < \epsilon \quad \text{for all } x \in [a, b],$$

whenever $n \geq N$.

This looks a bit complicated, but fortunately there is a test for uniform convergence which is easy to apply; it strongly resembles the Comparison Test for numerical series!

Theorem 8.23 (Weierstress). *Assume $g_k(x)$ are continuous on $[a, b]$, where $k = 1, 2, 3, \ldots$.*

- **M-Test.** *If $|g_k(x)| < M_k$, for all $x \in [a, b]$, and $\sum_k M_k$ converges, then $\sum_k g_k(x)$ converges uniformly on $[a, b]$.*

- *If $S(x) = \sum_{k=1}^{\infty} g_k(x)$ converges uniformly on $[a, b]$, then $S(x)$ is continuous, and*

$$\int_a^b S(x)dx = \sum_{k=1}^{\infty} \int_a^b g_k(x)dx$$

When you study Real Analysis you will prove this theorem (which actually is not very difficult!)

Going back to our favorite examples, the series for $f(x) = x$ can not converge uniformly, because $f(x) = x$ extended 2π-periodically is discontinuous, contrary to the Weierstrass theorem. On the other hand, the series for $f(x) = x^2$ extended 2π-periodically does converge uniformly, because

$$|g_k(x)| = \left| \frac{4(-1)^k}{k^2} \cos(kx) \right| \leq \frac{4}{k^2} \; \forall x \in \mathbb{R},$$

and the numerical series $\sum_{k=1}^{\infty} \frac{4}{k^2}$ converges (it's the p-series with $p = 2$.) So we can apply Weierstrass' M-Test with $M_k = \frac{4}{k^2}$ and conclude that the Fourier Series converges uniformly.

For Fourier Series applying Weierstrass' M-Test for uniform convergence is particularly easy, since the variable part of the terms in the series are always $\sin(kx)$ or $\cos(kx)$, and these are easily bounded,

$$|\sin(kx)| \leq 1, \quad |\cos(kx)| \leq 1 \quad \text{for all } x \in \mathbb{R}.$$

Thus, we may always compare the terms of a trigonometric Fourier Series with the numerical series defined by the abolute value of the coefficients,

$$|g_k(x)| = |a_k \cos(kx) + b_k \sin(kx)| \leq |a_k| \, |\cos(kx)| + |b_k| \, |\sin(kx)| \leq |a_k| + |b_k|,$$

for all $x \in \mathbb{R}$. Therefore, the Weierstrass M-Test reduces to the absolute convergence of the series of the coefficients, a_k, b_k:

Corollary 8.24. *Suppose the absolute values of the Fourier coefficients* a_k, b_k *are* <u>*summable*</u>, *that is*

$$\sum_{k=1}^{\infty} (|a_k| + |b_k|) \quad converges.$$

Then the Fourier Series $S(x) = \frac{a_0}{2} + \sum_{k=1}^{\infty} a_k \cos(kx) + b_k \sin(kx)$ *converges uniformly on* $\mathbb{R}$.

From the second part of Theorem 8.23 this can only happen when the 2π-periodic extension of f is continuous.

Example 8.25. Consider $f(x) = |\sin x|$ with $x \in (-\pi, \pi)$. The 2π-periodic extension is even, piecewise C^1, and continuous (graph it, either by hand or using the computer!) Then, because f is even, we must have the sine coefficients vanish, $b_k = 0$ for all $k \in \mathbb{N}$. For the cosine coefficients we use the evenness of f to eliminate the absolute value,

$$
\begin{aligned}
a_k &= \frac{1}{\pi} \int_{-\pi}^{\pi} |\sin x| \cos(kx)\, dx \\
&= \frac{2}{\pi} \int_{0}^{\pi} |\sin x| \cos(kx)\, dx \qquad (f \text{ is even}) \\
&= \frac{2}{\pi} \int_{0}^{\pi} \sin x \cos(kx)\, dx \qquad (\sin x \geq 0 \text{ when } 0 \leq x \leq \pi) \\
&= \frac{1}{\pi} \int_{0}^{\pi} [\sin(1+k)x + \sin(1-k)x]\, dx \\
&= \frac{1}{\pi} \left[\frac{\cos(1+k)x}{(1+k)} + \frac{\cos(1-k)x}{(1-k)} \right]_{0}^{\pi} \qquad (\text{if } k \neq 1!) \\
&= \frac{1}{\pi} \left[\frac{\cos(1+k)\pi - 1}{(1+k)} + \frac{\cos(1-k)\pi - 1}{(1-k)} \right] \\
&= \frac{(-1)^{k+1} - 1}{\pi} \left[\frac{1}{k+1} - \frac{1}{k-1} \right] \\
&= \frac{2}{\pi} \left((-1)^{k+1} - 1 \right) \frac{1}{k^2 - 1} \\
&= \begin{cases} -\frac{4}{\pi} \frac{1}{4j^2 - 1}, & \text{if } k = 2j \text{ is even;} \\ 0, & \text{if } k \text{ is odd.} \end{cases}
\end{aligned}
$$

When $k = 1$, we notice that the second term in the integral in the 4th line is zero, and the first term integrates to zero as well, so $a_1 = 0$. When $k = 1$ there is no division by zero, and so the a_0 term has already been calculated with the other a_k, $a_0 = 4/\pi$. The only surviving terms in the series are a_k with $k = 2j$ an *even* counting number. Therefore, we re-index the series, counting only the even terms, a_{2j}, $j \in \mathbb{N}$,

$$S(x) = \frac{2}{\pi} - \frac{4}{\pi} \sum_{j=1}^{\infty} \frac{1}{4j^2 - 1} \cos(2jx),$$

which converges for each individual x to $f(x)$ by the Pointwise Convergence Theorem.

Since

$$|a_{2j}| = \left| -\frac{4}{\pi} \frac{1}{4j^2 - 1} \right|$$

$$= \frac{4}{\pi(4j^2 - 1)}$$

$$\leq \frac{4}{\pi} \frac{1}{4j^2 - j^2} = \frac{4}{3\pi} \frac{1}{j^2},$$

and $\sum 1/j^2$ converges, the series converges uniformly according to Weierstrass' M-Test. (See figure 8.6.)

We can now use it to calculate some numerical series. When $x = 0$, by the pointwise convergence theorem,

$$0 = f(0) = \frac{2}{\pi} - \frac{4}{\pi} \sum_{j=1}^{\infty} \frac{1}{4j^2 - 1},$$

and so we find the value of another numerical series,

$$\sum_{j=1}^{\infty} \frac{1}{4j^2 - 1} = \frac{1}{2}.$$

When $x = \frac{\pi}{2}$, since $\cos(2jx) = \cos(\pi x) = (-1)^j$, we obtain an alternating numerical series thanks to the pointwise convergence theorem,

$$1 = |\sin(\frac{\pi}{2})| = f\left(\frac{\pi}{2}\right) = \frac{2}{\pi} - \frac{4}{\pi} \sum_{j=1}^{\infty} \frac{(-1)^j}{4j^2 - 1}.$$

Rearranging terms,

$$\sum_{j=1}^{\infty} \frac{(-1)^j}{4j^2 - 1} = \frac{\pi}{4} \left[\frac{2}{\pi} - 1 \right] = \frac{1}{2} - \frac{\pi}{4}.$$

$\square$

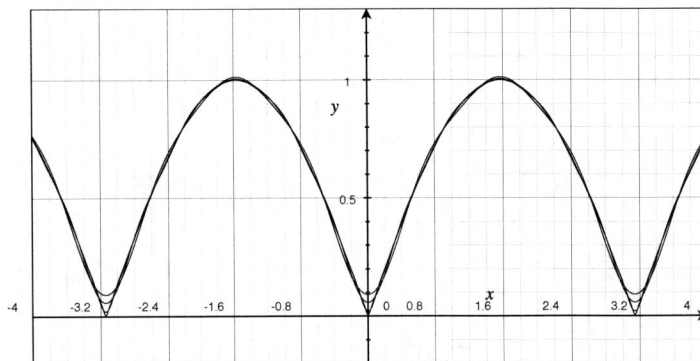

Figure 8.6. Partial sums S_n for $n = 3, 5, 15, 50$ for $f(x) = |\sin x|$ on $(-\pi, \pi)$. The convergence is uniform.

8.5   Orthogonal families

Fourier Series is fundamentally about orthogonality, representing functions in an orthogonal basis. Cosines and sines give only one example of orthogonal families of functions. So where else do orthogonal functions come from? Here are two mechanisms which produce orthogonal families of functions, which are useful and natural in various contexts.

8.5.1   The Gram-Schmidt process

Take a linearly independent collection $\{v_1, v_2, v_3, \dots\}$ in any vector space. The Gram-Scmidt process gives an iterative procedure to create an orthogonal set $\{u_1, u_2, u_3 \dots\}$ by orthogonal projection, which spans the same space as the original collection. (See section 6.3 in Anton & Rorres [AR] to review this concept.)

Take $u_1 = v_1$. Then,

$$u_2 = v_2 - \frac{\langle v_2, u_1 \rangle}{\|u_1\|^2} u_1$$

is orthogonal to u_1. To see this, just take the inner product:

$$\langle u_1, u_2 \rangle = \langle u_1, v_2 \rangle - \left\langle u_1 \frac{\langle v_2, u_1 \rangle}{\|u_1\|^2} u_1 \right\rangle$$

$$= \langle u_1, v_2 \rangle - \frac{\langle v_2, u_1 \rangle}{\|u_1\|^2} \underbrace{\langle u_1, u_1 \rangle}_{\|u_1\|^2}$$

$$= 0.$$

We then iterate the preceeding step, and create the orthogonal family by induction. Assume we already have an orthogonal family with k elements,

$$\{u_1, u_2, \dots, u_k\}.$$

Then, the vector obtained by subtracting off the projections onto the previous orthogonal elements,

$$u_{k+1} = v_{k+1} - \sum_{j=1}^{k} \frac{\langle v_{j+1}, u_j \rangle}{\|u_j\|^2} u_j$$

is orthogonal to $\{u_1, u_2, \dots, u_k\}$, and will have the same span as $\{v_1, v_2, \dots, v_{k+1}\}$.

A common application is to polynomials, $P(x) = a_0 + a_1 x + \cdots + a_n x^n$. A basis of polynomials is $\{1, x, x^2, \dots\}$. For any choice of inner product, we get different orthogonal families of polynomials (named after Legendre, Chebyshev, Bernstein …,) and useful in approximation theory and numerical analysis.

Example 8.26. Take the vector subspace of polynomials, that is the linearly independent set

$$\{1, \ x, \ x^2, \ ,\dots, \ x^k, \ \dots\},$$

on the interval $x \in [-1, 1]$. We choose the familiar L^2 inner product,

$$\langle f, g \rangle = \int_{-1}^{1} f(x)g(x)dx.$$

Start with $P_0(x) = 1$, the constant function. In Problem #12 below, you'll verify that $P_1(x) = x$ and $P_1(x) \perp P_0(x)$. Continuing with Gram-Schmidt, we get the next orthogonal element,

$$P_2(x) = x^2 - \frac{\langle x^2, P_0 \rangle}{\|P_0\|^2} P_0 - -\frac{\langle x^2, P_1 \rangle}{\|P_1\|^2} P_1$$

$$= x^2 - \frac{\int_{-1}^{1} x^2 \cdot 1 dx}{\int_{-1}^{1} 1^2 dx} - \underbrace{\frac{\int_{-1}^{1} x^3 \cdot 1 dx}{\int_{-1}^{1} x^2 dx}}_{=0}$$

$$= x^2 - \frac{1}{3}.$$

This procedure generates the Legendre polynomials on $[-1, 1]$, which are very often used in numerical analysis.

To get other families, we can substitute a different inner product. A common choice is a "weighted" inner product,

$$\langle f, g \rangle = \int_{-1}^{1} f(x)g(x)w(x)dx,$$

where $w(x)$ is a given continuous function. The principle is the same as for the Legendre polynomials, but changing the inner product will change the actual polynomials obtained as an orthogonal family. For example, if we use the weight $w(x) = \frac{1}{\sqrt{1-x^2}}$ on $[-1, 1]$ to define the inner product, we get a different family of polynomials, which will be orthogonal with respect to the weighted inner product, called the Chebyshev polynomials. This looks like a strange choice of a weight function, but the Chebyshev polynomials are extremely useful in numerical analysis!

8.5.2   Eigenvalue problems

This mechanism for generating orthogonal families comes from the basic linear algebra theorems about eigenvalues and eigenvectors of symmetric matrices. Recall that a matrix is symmetric if its transpose $M^t = M$. This is equivalent to symmetry with respect to the inner (dot) product, $(M\vec{u}) \cdot \vec{v} = \vec{u} \cdot (M\vec{v})$, for all vectors $\vec{u}, \vec{v} \in \mathbb{R}^n$. In a general inner product space $\mathcal{V}$ this is the appropriate way to talk about symmetry:

Definition 8.27. *Let M be a linear transformation on an inner product space $\mathcal{V}$. We say M is symmetric if*

$$\langle Mu, v \rangle = \langle u, Mv \rangle, \qquad \text{for all } u, v \in \mathcal{V}.$$

Theorem 8.28. *Let M be a symmetric linear transformation on an inner product space $\mathcal{V}$. If $Mu = \lambda u$ and $Mv = \mu v$ with distinct eigenvalues $\lambda \neq \mu$, then $\langle u, v \rangle = 0$.*

Proof. Notice that due to symmetry, we get

$$\langle \lambda u, v \rangle = \langle Mu, v \rangle = \langle u, Mv \rangle = \langle u, \mu v \rangle$$

So we get $\lambda \langle u, v \rangle = \mu \langle u, v \rangle$. So since $\lambda \neq \mu$, we conclude that $\langle u, v \rangle = 0$. $\square$

In $\mathbb{R}^n$, any symmetric linear transformation (i.e. matrix) provides an orthogonal basis of eigenvectors of M for $\mathbb{R}^n$. Even though $\mathcal{V}$ is infinite dimensional, it turns out that this is still true in the sense of Fourier series.

Now, consider a vector space $\mathcal{V}$ of all C^2 functions,

$$u : [0, L] \to \mathbb{R},$$

satisfying a boundary condition,

$$u(0) = 0 \quad \text{and} \quad u(L) = 0.$$

(Note the similarity to the class of admissible variations, $\mathcal{A}_0$ from the last chapter!) On the vector space $\mathcal{V}$ we use the familiar inner product $\langle u, v \rangle = \int_0^L u(x)v(x)dx$.

Now consider the transformation $Mu = u''(x)$, which takes $u \in \mathcal{V}$ and gives back its the second derivative. By the usual properties of the derivative, if $u_1, u_2 \in \mathcal{V}$ and c_1, c_2 are constants, then

$$M(c_1 u_1 + c_2 u_2) = \frac{d^2}{dx^2}(c_1 u_1 + c_2 u_2) = c_1 u_1''(x) + c_2 u_2''(x) = c_1 Mu_1 + c_2 Mu_2,$$

and so indeed M is a <u>linear</u> transformation on this vector space $\mathcal{V}$.

Lemma 8.29. *M is symmetric with respect to the inner product on $\mathcal{V}$.*

Proof. We integrate by parts, twice:

$$\begin{aligned}
\langle Mu, v \rangle &= \int_0^L u''(x)v(x)dx \\
&= u'(x)v(x)\big|_0^L - \int_0^L u'(x)v'(x)dx \\
&= -v'(x)u(x)\big|_0^L + \int_0^L u(x)v''(x)dx \\
&= \langle u, Mv \rangle
\end{aligned}$$

As in the Calculus of Variations, the endpoint terms all vanish because u, v vanish at $x = 0, L$. $\square$

In particular, by Lemma 8.28 eigenvectors of the transformation M must be orthogonal if their eigenvalues are distinct. But what are the eigenvectors of a linear transformation like M? Just as for matrices, $\lambda \in \mathbb{R}$ is an eigenvalue of M if there exists a nonzero element $u \in \mathcal{V}, u \neq 0$ such that $Mu = \lambda u$. In this context, finding eigenvalues involves solving an ordinary differential equation (ODE) with *boundary conditions* which define the vector space $\mathcal{V}$, $u(0) = 0 = u(L)$. In this case, we refer to $u(x)$ as an <u>eigenfunction</u> of M. One way to do this is to find all solutions of the ODE with the left-hand boundary value $u(0) = 0$ as an initial condition, and check to see if they also solve the right-hand boundary value $u(L) = 0$. When finding the general solution to the ODE we have 3 cases to consider, $\lambda > 0, \lambda = 0, \lambda < 0$, since the form of the general solution to the ODE is different in each case.

When $\lambda > 0$, the general solution to the ODE is

$$u(x) = A \cosh \sqrt{\lambda} x + B \sinh \sqrt{\lambda} x.$$

Since we need $u(0) = 0$, we must have $A = 0$. To satisfy the other boundary condition, $0 = u(L) = \sinh \sqrt{\lambda} L$, but $\sinh x > 0$ whenever $x > 0$ so this can never be satisfied except when $B = 0$ also. So we only get the trivial solution $u(x) \equiv 0$, and so there is no eigenvalue with $\lambda > 0$.

Similarly, when $\lambda = 0$ the general solution to the ODE, $Mu = u''(x) = 0$ is $u(x) = A + Bx$, and the only straight line with $u(0) = 0 = u(L)$ is the trivial one $u(x) \equiv 0$. So $\lambda = 0$ is not an eigenvalue either.

We conclude that for all eigenvalues $\lambda < 0$. For convenience, call $\lambda = -\mu^2$ with $\mu > 0$. Then $u'' + \mu^2 u = 0$ with general solution

$$u(x) = A \cos \mu x + B \sin \mu x.$$

Applying the condition $u(0) = 0$, we have $A = 0$ as before. But at the other endpoint we have nontrivial solutions:

$$0 = u(L) = B \sin \mu L$$

is solved when $\mu L = k\pi$, $k \in \mathbb{N}$, that is $\mu = \mu_k = \frac{k\pi}{L}$. So we get a sequence of eigenvalues and associated eigenfunctions,

$$\lambda_k = -\mu_k^2 = \frac{k^2 \pi^2}{L^2}, \qquad u_k(x) = \sin\left(\frac{k\pi x}{L}\right).$$

By Lemma 8.29 these form an orthogonal family of functions on $[0, L]$. And given $f : [0, L] \to \mathbb{R}$ we can make a Fourier expansion in this family,

$$f(x) \sim S(x) = \sum_{k=1}^{\infty} c_k \phi_k(x),$$

where

$$c_k = \frac{\langle f, \phi_k \rangle}{\|\phi_k\|^2},$$

and the norm is defined via the inner product as usual, $\|f\| = \sqrt{\langle f, f \rangle}$. As for the full trigonometric Fourier Series (sines and cosines), in what sense are $f(x)$ and $S(x)$ equal, and does the series converge?

8.6   Convergence in Norm

We return to questions of convergence of Fourier Series, this time including all orthogonal expansions and not just the classical trigonometric series. The most natural kind of convergence involves the norm $\|v\|$ on the vector space of functions $v \in \mathcal{V}$.

As always, we define the partial sums,

$$S_n(x) = \sum_{k=1}^{n} c_k \phi_k(x). \tag{8.8}$$

Definition 8.30. *We say the series* (8.8) *converges in norm if*

$$\lim_{n \to \infty} \|S_n - f\| = 0.$$

In many cases, the scalar product and norm are defined by definite integrals,

$$\langle f, g \rangle = \int_a^b f(x)\, g(x), dx, \quad \|f\| = \sqrt{\langle f, f \rangle} = \sqrt{\int_a^b [f(x)]^2 \, dx}.$$

These quantities are well-defined for continuous f, but as we've seen, we are often interested in discontinuous functions as well. So it is natural to open up the possibilty of discontinuous f, as long as the integral defining the norm makes sense (and is finite.) We say a function is *square integrable* if $\|f\| < \infty$. (A historically important question in analysis was to identify the proper condition for square integrability, solved by Lebesgue in his theory of integration in 1904!)

Definition 8.31. *We call the family* $\{\phi_k(x)\}$ *complete if for all square integrable functions* f, *the series* (8.8) *converges to* f *in norm, that is,* $\lim_{n \to \infty} \|S_n - f\| = 0.$

Thus, to say the orthogonal family $\{\phi_k(x)\}$ is complete essentially means that it forms an orthogonal basis for all square integrable $f(x)$ on $[a, b]$. This definition just gives a name to a desirable property of orthogonal families. Given a family of orthogonal functions $\{\phi_k\}$, one must show that it is (or isn't) complete, using properties of those functions. It turns out that the two types of examples discussed in the previous section, the Legendre polynomials on $[-1, 1]$ from Section 8.5.1 and eigenfunctions of symmetric boundary-value problems from Section 8.5.2, both yield *complete* sets of orthogonal functions. Proving this is a difficult question in analysis, and we won't address it here.

Nevertheless, let's look at some simple consequences of measuring convergence via the norm. First, let's use orthogonality to actually calculate the square of the error made in approximating f by S_n in the norm. (We have to be careful about indices!)

$$\|S_n - f\|^2 = \langle S_n - f \,,\, S_n - f \rangle = \left\langle \left[\sum_{k=1}^{n} c_k \phi_k - f\right] \,,\, \left[\sum_{j=1}^{n} c_j \phi_j - f\right] \right\rangle$$

$$= \left\langle \sum_{k=1}^{n} c_k \phi_k \,,\, \sum_{j=1}^{n} c_j \phi_j \right\rangle - 2 \left\langle \sum_{k=1}^{n} c_k \phi_k \,,\, f \right\rangle + \|f\|^2$$

$$= \sum_{k=1}^{n} \sum_{j=1}^{n} c_k c_j \langle \phi_k, \phi_j \rangle + 2 \sum_{k=1}^{n} c_k \langle \phi_k, f \rangle + \|f\|^2$$

$$= \sum_{k=1}^{n} c_k^2 \|\phi_k\|^2 - 2 \sum_{k=1}^{n} c_k^2 \|\phi_k\|^2 + \|f\|^2$$

$$= \|f\|^2 - \sum_{k=1}^{n} c_k^2 \|\phi_k\|^2.$$

We draw two conclusions from this computation. The first comes from the observation that the norm $\|S_n - f\|^2 \geq 0$, and so the infinite series

$$\sum_{k=1}^{\infty} c_k^2 \|\phi_k\|^2 = \lim_{n \to \infty} \sum_{k=1}^{n} c_k^2 \|\phi_k\|^2 \leq \|f\|^2 < \infty,$$

so that numerical series $\sum_{k=1}^{n} c_k^2 \|\phi_k\|^2$ converges, to something at most $\|f\|^2$. This fact is called *Bessel's inequality*. The second conclusion is that the Fourier Series converges in norm if and only if

$$0 = \lim_{n \to \infty} \|f - S_n\|^2 = \lim_{n \to \infty} \left[\|f\|^2 - \sum_{k=1}^{n} c_k^2 \|\phi_k\|^2 \right] = \|f\|^2 - \sum_{k=1}^{\infty} c_k^2 \|\phi_k\|^2,$$

that is, if equality holds in Bessel's inequality. So, provided the family $\{\phi_k\}$ is <u>complete</u>, there is a relationship between the norm of the function f and its Fourier coefficients with respect to $\{\phi_k\}$, called **Parseval's identity**,

$$\|f\|^2 = \sum_{k=1}^{\infty} c_k^2 \|\phi_k\|^2.$$

Classical Fourier Series, based on the orthogonal family of trigonometric functions,

$$\{1, \ \cos(kx), \ \sin(kx) \mid k = 1, 2, 3, \dots\},$$

is known to be <u>complete</u>, and so any square-integrable function f on $[-\pi, \pi]$ may be expanded in a Fourier Series which converges in norm:

Theorem 8.32 (Parseval's Theorem). *Suppose $f(x)$ is defined on $[-\pi, \pi]$ and*

$$\int_{-\pi}^{\pi} (f(x))^2 \, dx < \infty.$$

Then, the trigonometric Fourier Series of $f(x)$,

$$S(x) = \frac{a_0}{2} + \sum_{k=1}^{\infty} (a_k \cos(kx) + b_k \sin(kx))$$

converges to $f(x)$ in norm on $[-\pi, \pi]$. In addition,

$$\int_{-\pi}^{\pi} (f(x))^2 \, dx = \pi \left[\frac{a_0^2}{2} + \sum_{k=1}^{\infty} \left(a_k^2 + b_k^2 \right) \right] \tag{8.9}$$

The formula (8.9) is known as *Parseval's Identity*. The proof of Parseval's Theorem is quite intricate, and not appropriate for a course of this level. However, we may appreciate what it says about convergence of Fourier Series, and use it calculate exact values for some more numerical series.

Example 8.33. Consider $f(x) = x$ with $x \in [-\pi, \pi]$. We calculated the coefficients in Example 8.7, and discussed its convergence in Example 8.20. In particular, we noted that it converges pointwise at every $x \in \mathbb{R}$, although it converges to the midpoint of the jump discontinuities at odd multiples of π, and since it is discontinuous as a 2π-periodic function on $\mathbb{R}$, it cannot converge uniformly. On the other hand, $f(x) = x$ is square integrable on $[-\pi, \pi]$, and so its trigonometric Fourier Series does converge in norm. In particular, this shows that convergence in norm is *weaker* than uniform convergence: a series may converge in norm without converging uniformly. Also, convergence in norm permits the series to differ from $f(x)$ at points of discontinuity. From the calculated values of the Fourier coefficients,

$$a_k = 0, \quad b_k = \frac{2}{k}(-1)^{k+1},$$

and Parseval's identity we then obtain an explicit value for a numerical series:

$$\pi \sum_{k=1}^{\infty} \frac{4}{k^2} = \int_{-\pi}^{\pi} x^2 dx = \frac{2}{3}\pi^3$$

$$\sum_{k=1}^{\infty} \frac{1}{k^2} = \frac{\pi^2}{6}.$$

$\square$

Returning to Example 8.25, $f(x) = |\sin x|$ for $x \in (-\pi, \pi)$, and extended as a 2π-periodic function, we had (by evenness) $b_k = 0$ for all k, and

$$a_k = \begin{cases} -\frac{4}{\pi}\frac{1}{4j^2 - 1}, & \text{if } k = 2j \text{ is even;} \\ 0, & \text{if } k \text{ is odd.} \end{cases}$$

Applying Parseval's theorem, we then get the identity,

$$\frac{1}{2}a_0^2 + \sum_{j=1}^{\infty} a_{2j}^2 = \frac{1}{2}\left(\frac{2}{\pi}\right)^2 + \left(\frac{4}{\pi}\right)^2 \sum_{j=1}^{\infty} \frac{1}{(4j^2-1)^2}$$

$$= \frac{1}{\pi}\int_{-\pi}^{\pi} |\sin x|^2 \, dx$$

$$= \frac{1}{\pi}\int_{-\pi}^{\pi} \frac{1}{2}[1 - \cos(2x)] \, dx$$

$$= 1.$$

And so we can evaluate the infinite series,

$$\sum_{j=1}^{\infty} \frac{1}{(4j^2-1)^2} = \frac{\pi^2}{16} - \frac{1}{8}.$$

You can go back to each of the examples we've calculated in class or in the practice problems and apply Parseval's identity to the coefficients to obtain some new identites which give explicit values to various series.

8.7 Application: The vibrating string

To conclude, we look at a problem which is very similar to Fourier's original motivation, the solution of partial differential equations arising in science. Instead of the heat equation, let's look instead at the wave equation, which describes a vibrating string.

Consider a string in a violin, guitar, piano, etc. with length L. Suppose that the string is attached at its endpoints, $x = 0, L$, but is free to vibrate up and down in a vertical plane in between. We call $u(x,t)$ the shape of the string at the point x and time t, so we imagine a snapshot of the string at time t giving us a graph $y = u(x,t)$. The fact that the string is attached at the endpoints means that we are imposing boundary conditions,

$$u(0,t) = 0, \qquad u(L,t) = 0, \qquad \text{for all time } t \in \mathbb{R}. \tag{8.10}$$

The equation of motion for the string is the wave equation,

$$\frac{\partial^2 u}{\partial t^2} = c^2 \frac{\partial^2 u}{\partial x^2},$$

where c is a constant which depends on the density and tension of the string.

We can solve this using Fourier Series! Recall from section 8.5.2 that we obtain an orthogonal family of eigenfunctions by solving a boundary-value problem. For the choice (8.10), these are:

$$v_k(x) = \sin\left(\frac{k\pi}{L}x\right).$$

So we seek a solution in the form of a Fourier Series with time-dependent coefficients,

$$u(x,t) = \sum_{k=1}^{\infty} a_k(t)\, v_k(x).$$

This is already chosen to satisfy the boundary conditions, so we plug into the wave equation to determine the equation satisfied by the coefficients $a_k(t)$ and get:

$$a_k''(t) = -\left(\frac{k\pi c}{L}\right)^2 a_k(t),$$

which has as a general solution

$$a_k(t) = A_k \cos\left(\frac{k\pi c}{L}t + \phi_k\right),$$

where ϕ_k is a phase factor.[1]

To understand what is going on, look at each individual term in the series,

$$a_k(t)\, v_k(x) = A_k \cos\left(\frac{k\pi c}{L}t + \phi_k\right) \sin\left(\frac{k\pi}{L}x\right).$$

Each of these terms is a simple *standing wave*, associated to ϕ_k, a fixed wave form in x multiplied by an oscillatory term in t which makes the wave move up and down but with a fixed profile. The profile comes from $v_k(x)$, which has $(k-1)$ nodes (zeros) inside the string $x \in (0, L)$; see figure 8.7. The time dependence determines the sound produced, which is a single pure frequency:

$$\omega_k = \frac{kc}{2L}, k = 1, 2, 3, \ldots$$

So each term $k = 1, 2, 3, \ldots$ produces a different musical note, and the entire wave makes a sound which is a superposition of these different notes!

The $k = 1$ term gives the *fundamental tone*, $\omega_1 = c/2L$, the lowest note produced by the string. For $k = 2, 3, 4, \ldots$, we get $\omega_k = k\omega_1$, the *overtones*.

Suppose the length, density, and tension in the string are chosen so that the fundamental frequency $\omega_1 = 440$ Hz, which is A_4, the A just above middle-C on a piano. Then, the first overtone $\omega_2 = 880$ Hz gives A_5, which is exactly one octave higher. The next overtone $\omega_3 = 1320$ Hz is E_6, which is a perfect fifth above A_5. Continuing, ω_4 is A_6 (two octaves above the fundamental tone ω_1) and w_5 is $C_7^{\#}$. When you play A_4 on a stringed instrument you are actually hearing a combination of the intended note with a bit of each overtone.

The same principle applies to woodwind instruments. The vibrating string becomes a vibrating column of air, and $u(x,t)$ is the fluctuation of air pressure away from atmospheric pressure in the room. A flute is an air column which is open to the atmosphere on both ends, and so it gives the same boundary condition (8.10) as for a stringed instrument, and

---

[1]You could write it as $a_k(t) = \alpha_k \cos\frac{k\pi c}{L}t + \beta_k \sin\frac{k\pi c}{L}t$, but by a trig identity the two expressions are the same.

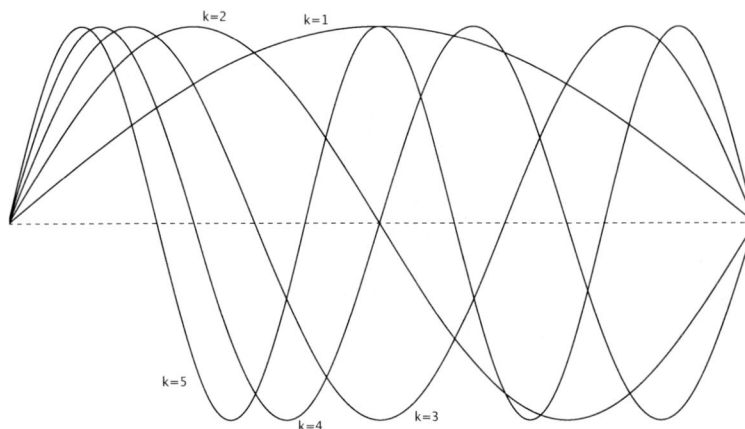

Figure 8.7. The standing wave profiles v_k for the first five harmonics of the vibrating string. Higher frequencies mean more nodes (zeros) in the waveform.

therefore the same harmonic sequence of frequencies. However, clarinets are different: they have an end with a mothpiece and a reed, which are not open to the atmosphere, where the pressure is maximal. This changes the boundary condition at the end $x = 0$ to $u_x(0,t) = 0$. This eigenvalue problem is the subject of Problem 8, below! The consequence is that the orthogonal basis is different, with different eigenvalues, and a completely different harmonic sequence of overtones!

8.8   Practice problems

1. Find the Fourier Series on $[-\pi, \pi]$ of the following functions: $\sin^2 x$, $\sin x \cos x$, $\sin^3 x$, and $\sin^4 x$.

   [Hint: you don't need to calculate any integrals!]

2. Calculate the Fourier Series $S(x)$ of $f(x) = \sin(x/2)$, $-\pi < x < \pi$. What is $S(\pi) =$?

3. Find the Fourier Series of $f(x) = \cosh x$ and $g(x) = \sinh x$, $-1 < x < 1$. What are the values of the Fourier Series at $x = -1$?

4. Find the Fourier Series on $(-\pi, \pi)$ of

$$f(x) = \begin{cases} -\cos x, & \text{if } -\pi < x < 0, \\ \cos x, & \text{if } 0 < x < \pi. \end{cases}$$

At what points in $\mathbb{R}$ is the Fourier Series discontinuous?

5. **(a)** Show that $\{1, \cos(kx) \mid k \in \mathbb{N}\}$ is an orthogonal family on $[0, \pi]$ with inner product

$$\langle f, g \rangle = \int_0^\pi f(x)\, g(x)\, dx.$$

(b) Find the formulas for the coefficients in a Fourier Series in these functions, $f(x) \sim S(x) = \frac{a_0}{2} + \sum_{k=1} a_k \cos(kx)$.

(c) Show that $S(x)$ represents the even, 2π-periodic extension of $f(x)$ from $0 < x < \pi$ to the real line. Draw the graph of $S(x)$ on $-3\pi < x < 3\pi$ when $f(x) = x$.

6. For each numerical series, determine if it diverges, converges conditionally, or converges absolutely.

(a) $\displaystyle\sum_{k=1}^{\infty} \frac{(-1)^k}{2k+1}$

(b) $\displaystyle\sum_{k=1}^{\infty} \frac{\sin(k)}{k^2+2}$

(c) $\displaystyle\sum_{k=1}^{\infty} (-1)^k e^{-3k}$. *[Hint: this is a geometric series.]*

(d) $\displaystyle\sum_{k=1}^{\infty} (-1)^k e^{4k}$.

7. Define a function as a series,

$$S(x) = \sum_{k=1}^{\infty} e^{-kx}.$$

Show that the series diverges for all $x \leq 0$, converges pointwise on the set $(0, \infty)$, and converges uniformly on the set $[1, \infty)$.

8. (a) Calculate the Fourier Series of $f(x) = |x|$, $-\pi < x < \pi$.

(b) Draw the 2π-periodic function which the series converges to, over the interval $-3\pi < x < 3\pi$.

(c) Does the series converge absolutely or conditionally? Does it converge uniformly? Why or why not?

(d) Use your result to calculate $\displaystyle\sum_{k=1}^{\infty} \frac{1}{(2k-1)^2}$ and $\displaystyle\sum_{k=1}^{\infty} \frac{1}{(2k-1)^4}$.

9. Answer (a)–(c) for $f(x) = \cos(x/4)$, $-\pi < x < \pi$. Use the Fourier coefficients to obtain explicit values for the series $\displaystyle\sum_{k=1}^{\infty} \frac{1}{16k^2-1}$, $\displaystyle\sum_{k=1}^{\infty} \frac{(-1)^k}{16k^2-1}$, and $\displaystyle\sum_{k=1}^{\infty} \frac{1}{(16k^2-1)^2}$.

10. Answer (a)–(c) for $f(x) = \sin(x/4)$, $-\pi < x < \pi$. Use the Fourier coefficients to obtain an explicit value for the series $\displaystyle\sum_{k=1}^{\infty} \frac{k^2}{(16k^2-1)^2}$.

11. Consider the vector space V of all C^2 functions $u : [0, L] \to \mathbb{R}$ satisfying the boundary conditions $u'(0) = 0$ and $u(L) = 0$, and the linear transformation $Mu = u''(x)$.

(a) Show that for any $u, v \in V$, $\langle Mu, v \rangle = \langle u, Mv \rangle$.

[Hint: integrate by parts twice, and use the boundary conditions.]

(b) Suppose λ, μ are eigenvalues of M, so there exist nontrivial functions $u, v \in V$, with $Mu = u''(x) = \lambda u(x)$ and $Mv = v''(x) = \mu v$. Show that if $\lambda \neq \mu$, then $\langle u, v \rangle = 0$.

(c) Show that $\left\{ \cos\left(\dfrac{(2k-1)\pi x}{2L} \right) : k = 1, 2, 3, \dots \right\}$ are eigenfunctions of M with distinct eigenvalues $\lambda_k = -(\frac{(2k-1)\pi}{2L})^2$, and conclude that they form an orthogonal family in V.

12. **(a)** Find the Fourier Series $S(x)$ of $f(x) = \cos(x/2)$, $-\pi < x < \pi$.

(b) Graph $S(x)$ for $-3\pi < x < 3\pi$. Does $S(x)$ represent a continuous function on $\mathbb{R}$?

(c) Use (a) to evaluate $\displaystyle\sum_{n=1}^{\infty} \frac{1}{4n^2 - 1}$ and $\displaystyle\sum_{n=1}^{\infty} \frac{(-1)^k}{4n^2 - 1}$.

13. Consider the family of functions $\left\{ \phi_k(x) = \sin\left[(k + \tfrac{1}{2})x \right], \ k = 0, 1, 2, 3, \dots \right\}$ on $x \in [-\pi, \pi]$.

(a) Show that this family is orthogonal with respect to the inner product

$$\langle f, g \rangle = \int_0^\pi f(x)g(x)\, dx.$$

(b) Give the formula for Fourier coefficients for a function $f(x)$ with respect to this family,

$$f(x) \sim S(x) = \sum_{k=0}^{\infty} c_k \phi_k(x).$$

14. For $x \in [-1, 1]$, define the polynomials,

$$P_0(x) = 1, \quad P_1(x) = x, \quad P_2(x) = 3x^2 - 1, \quad P_3(x) = 5x^3 - 3x.$$

(a) Show that these four functions are orthogonal with respect to the inner product

$$\langle f, g \rangle = \int_{-1}^{1} f(x)g(x)\, dx.$$

(b) If $f(x) = a_0 + a_1 x + a_2 x^2 + a_3 x^3 + \cdots + a_n x^n$ is a nontrivial polynomial of degree n, and f is orthogonal to each of P_0, P_1, P_2, P_3, show that the degree $n \geq 4$.

[Hints: Assume for a contradiction that $n \leq 3$, so $f(x) = a_0 + a_1 x + a_2 x^2 + a_3 x^3$, and show $a_0 = 0 = a_1 = a_2 = a_3$ (and so $f(x)$ is the zero polynomial).]

(c) Find a polynomial $P_4(x)$ which is of order 4 and which is orthogonal to each of P_0, P_1, P_2, P_3.

43. A contour diagram of a linear function $f(x, y)$ consists of lines parallel to the x-axis. The contour curve of value c crosses the y-axis at $c/3$. Find $f(x, y)$.

44. Find a formula for a function $f(x, y, z)$ whose level set of value $c = 2$ is the surface $x^2 + y^3 - z = 4$.

45. Find a formula for a function $f(x, y, z)$ whose level surfaces are parallel planes with normal vector $\mathbf{n} = (2, 3, -4)$.

▶ 2.3 LIMITS AND CONTINUITY

Review: Limits of Functions of One Variable

A reader familiar with this material may wish to advance to the next subsection that introduces limits of functions of several variables.

Consider the function $f(x)$ defined by

$$f(x) = \begin{cases} x^2 + 1 & \text{if } x < 1 \\ 2x + 1 & \text{if } x \geq 1. \end{cases}$$

The graph of $f(x)$ is shown in Figure 2.27. The small empty circle means that the point $(1, 2)$ does not belong to the graph. The filled circle at $(1, 3)$ denotes the fact that $f(1) = 3$. Let us try to describe the behavior of f for values of x that are close to $a = 1$.

We start at, say, $x = 0.5$, and, as we walk along the x-axis toward $a = 1$, we compute the corresponding values of the function [keeping in mind that for $x < 1$, $f(x) = x^2 + 1$]. If $x = 0.5$, then $f(0.5) = 1.25$. If $x = 0.9$, then $f(0.9) = 1.81$. Similarly, $f(0.99) = 1.9801$, $f(0.999) = 1.998001$, etc. We see that the values of the function approach 2 as x gets closer and closer to 1. For example, if we need that $f(x)$ be closer to 2 than 1.9999, we can choose any x (substitute $y = 1.9999$ into $y = x^2 + 1$ and solve for x) such that $x > 0.99995$ (and $x < 1$). Let us check a few values: $f(0.99996) = 1.99992$, $f(0.99998) = 1.99996$, etc. The fact that f can be made as close to 2 as needed by choosing $x < 1$ close enough to 1 is written as $\lim_{x \to 1^-} f(x) = 2$, and is called the *left limit of $f(x)$ as x approaches* 1 or the *limit of $f(x)$ as x approaches* 1 *from the left* (the symbol $x \to 1^-$ denotes the fact that x gets closer and closer to 1, and $x < 1$).

A similar investigation shows that $f(x)$ can be made as close to 3 as needed by choosing $x > 1$ to be close enough to 1. This fact is written as $\lim_{x \to 1^+} f(x) = 3$, and represents the *right limit of $f(x)$ as x approaches* 1, or the *limit of $f(x)$ as x approaches* 1 *from the right* (the symbol $x \to 1^+$ is used to denote the fact that x gets close to 1 and $x > 1$). In a

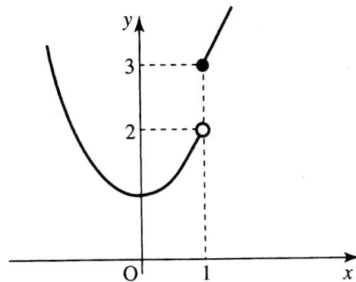

Figure 2.27 Graph of the function $f(x)$ defined above.

situation like this one, when different approaches give different values for the right and the left limits, we say that the *limit* or the *two-sided (or both-sided) limit* does not exist.

The left and right limits are also referred to as the *one-sided* limits. An analogous examination of the behavior of f near $a = 0$ [where $f(x) = x^2 + 1$] would show that $\lim_{x \to 0^+} f(x) = 1$ and $\lim_{x \to 0^-} f(x) = 1$. This time, the one-sided limits agree, and we say that the *two-sided (or both-sided) limit* of $f(x)$ as x approaches 0 exists and is equal to 1, and write $\lim_{x \to 0} f(x) = 1$.

Notice that in our investigation of limits, the value of f at $a = 1$ or at $a = 0$ did not play any role. Let us remember this important fact: when computing limits (as x approaches a), what matters is not the value of the function at $x = a$ (it may not even be defined) but the values of $f(x)$ "near" a (see Exercise 1).

Next, we give precise meaning to phrases like "x approaches a" and "$f(x)$ can be made as close to L as needed." Take an interval $(a - \delta, a + \delta)$ around a, where $\delta > 0$. The phrase "x approaches a" means that no matter what $\delta > 0$ is chosen, we can always find a value x that is inside $(a - \delta, a + \delta)$, and is such that $x \neq a$.

Recalling the fact that the absolute value $|x_1 - x_2|$ gives the distance between x_1 and x_2 on the x-axis, we can rephrase the above statement as follows: "x approaches a" means that no matter what δ is chosen, we can always find an $x \neq a$ whose distance from a is smaller than δ, that is, $|x - a| < \delta$. Since $x \neq a$, the distance between x and a cannot be zero (hence, $|x - a| > 0$) and we write the above as $0 < |x - a| < \delta$.

Here is one way of visualizing this process of "approaching." Assume that "x approaches 5," that is, let $a = 5$. Select a sequence of values for δ, like $\delta = 10^{-1}$, 10^{-2}, 10^{-3}, etc. This sequence defines a sequence of intervals of the form $(a - \delta, a + \delta)$; specifically, the intervals are $(4.9, 5.1)$, $(4.99, 5.01)$, $(4.999, 5.001)$, etc. The phrase "x approaches 5" describes a process of selecting a number x from every interval in this sequence.

The phrase "$f(x)$ can be made as close to L as needed" means that, for any $\epsilon > 0$, the value $f(x)$ lies inside the interval $(L - \epsilon, L + \epsilon)$; that is, the distance $|f(x) - L|$ between $f(x)$ and L is less than ϵ.

Let us go back to our previous example and illustrate what we have just said. We claim that $\lim_{x \to 0} f(x) = \lim_{x \to 0}(x^2 + 1) = 1$ (i.e., $a = 0$ and $L = 1$). Take, for example, $\epsilon = 0.2$ and consider the interval $(L - \epsilon, L + \epsilon) = (0.8, 1.2)$. We should be able to find an interval $(a - \delta, a + \delta) = (-\delta, \delta)$ such that, no matter what nonzero x is selected from that interval, the corresponding value $f(x)$ lies inside $(0.8, 1.2)$. From $|f(x) - 1| < \epsilon = 0.2$, we get $|x^2 + 1 - 1| < 0.2$, so $x^2 < 0.2$; hence, δ can be taken to be $\sqrt{0.2}$. In other words, for any $x \in (-\sqrt{0.2}, \sqrt{0.2})$, $f(x)$ is in $(0.8, 1.2)$. The fact that the limit is 1 means that the above construction of the interval $(a - \delta, a + \delta) = (-\delta, \delta)$ can be carried out for *any* choice of $\epsilon > 0$.

In the same example, we demonstrated that $\lim_{x \to 1} f(x)$ does not exist. Let us think a bit about this: we will show that, for example, $L = 2$ cannot be the limit. Let $\epsilon = 0.1$; that is, consider the interval $(L - \epsilon, L + \epsilon) = (1.9, 2.1)$. Any interval $(a - \delta, a + \delta) = (1 - \delta, 1 + \delta)$, no matter how small, contains a number (call it x_0) to the right of 1. The corresponding value $f(x_0) = 2x_0 + 1$ is greater than 3 (since $x_0 > 1$) and certainly does not belong to $(1.9, 2.1)$; see Figure 2.28. This violates the definition of the limit, and therefore $L = 2$ is not the limit of $f(x)$ as x approaches 1. A similar discussion would rule out any other real number as a candidate for the limit.

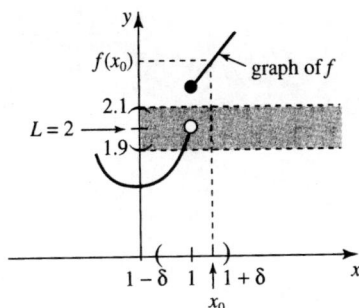

Figure 2.28 Limit of $f(x)$ as x approaches 1 does not exist.

► **EXAMPLE 2.24** "Closeness" and "Approaching" in a Computer Programming Context

Let us relate this "closeness" and "approaching" to a problem sometimes encountered in a computer science class. Suppose that we have to find a real number x such that $x^2 = 2$ (the solutions are infinite nonperiodic decimal numbers $x = \pm\sqrt{2} = \pm 1.4142\ldots$). A bad computer program might try to solve the problem as follows:

```
choose an(other) x
if x² = 2 then done, else choose another x
```

The phrase "choose an(other) x" means that we have a way of selecting a new try for x based on the outcomes of previous passes through the loop (how this is done is not our concern). A program like this has a good chance of never ending! The computer might, for example, get $x^2 = 1.999999$ or $x^2 = 2.000001$ for some choices of x and continue trying with new choices, since neither of the two results is equal to 2. To fix the program, we change it to the following:

```
choose an(other) x
if x² is "close enough to 2" then done, else choose
  another x
```

In this case, the computer will stop when it hits a number x whose square is close to 2, for example, $x^2 = 1.999999$, and will return that x as a solution. Clearly, the result will be an approximation of the solution. If we require that x^2 be even "closer to 2," the approximation will be even better. More precisely, the program

```
let ε = 0.00001
choose an(other) x
if |x² – 2| < ε then done, else choose another x
```

will return an approximate solution. To find a better approximation, all we have to do is to choose a smaller interval (restrict the "tolerance"); that is, take, for example, $\epsilon = 10^{-10}$. ◄

DEFINITION 2.5 Limit of a Function of One Variable

A function $f : \mathbb{R} \to \mathbb{R}$ has limit L as x approaches a, in symbols $\lim_{x \to a} f(x) = L$, if and only if for any given number $\epsilon > 0$ there is a number $\delta > 0$ such that

$$0 < |x - a| < \delta \qquad \text{implies} \qquad |f(x) - L| < \epsilon.$$
◄

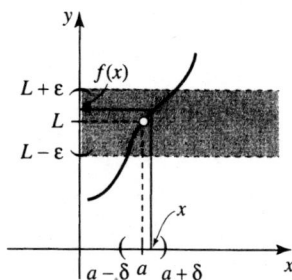

Figure 2.29 L is the limit of a function $y = f(x)$ as $x \to a$.

In other words, given the "tolerance" $\epsilon > 0$, we can find an interval $(a - \delta, a + \delta)$ around a ($\delta > 0$) so that for every $x \neq a$ inside $(a - \delta, a + \delta)$, the corresponding value $f(x)$ lies within the allowed "tolerance" interval $(L - \epsilon, L + \epsilon)$; see Figure 2.29.

Limits of Functions of Several Variables

We are on our way to generalizing the definition of a limit. Since the limit (and continuity) of a vector-valued function is based on the limits (continuity) of its components, it suffices to generalize limits to real-valued functions of several variables. In order to accomplish this task, we have to come up with an analogue of our concept of "closeness": we have to explain what is meant by phrases such as "$\mathbf{x} = (x, y)$ approaches $\mathbf{a} = (a, b)$" or "$\mathbf{x} = (x, y, z)$ approaches $\mathbf{a} = (a, b, c)$," etc. Since "closeness" was defined using open intervals, what we need now is their generalization to higher dimensions.

DEFINITION 2.6 Open Balls in $\mathbb{R}^m$

The *open ball* $B(\mathbf{a}, r) \subseteq \mathbb{R}^m$ with center $\mathbf{a} = (a_1, \ldots, a_m)$ and radius r ($r > 0$) is the set of all points $\mathbf{x}$ in $\mathbb{R}^m$ whose distance from a fixed point $\mathbf{a}$ is smaller than r. In symbols,

$$B(\mathbf{a}, r) = \{\mathbf{x} \in \mathbb{R}^m \mid \|\mathbf{x} - \mathbf{a}\| < r\},$$

where $\mathbf{x} = (x_1, \ldots, x_m)$ and $\|\mathbf{x} - \mathbf{a}\| = \sqrt{(x_1 - a_1)^2 + \cdots + (x_m - a_m)^2}$. ◄

For example, the open ball $B((1, 2), 3) \subseteq \mathbb{R}^2$ consists of all points in $\mathbb{R}^2$ whose distance from $(1, 2)$ is strictly smaller than 3; that is, $\sqrt{(x - 1)^2 + (y - 2)^2} < 3$. It is the inside of the circle of radius 3 centered at the point $(1, 2)$.

Similarly, the open ball $B((0, 0, 0), 2) \subseteq \mathbb{R}^3$ consists of the region inside the sphere of radius 2 centered at the origin. The open ball $B(3, 2) \subseteq \mathbb{R}$ contains all real numbers whose distance from 3 is less than 2; that is, $|x - 3| < 2$. It is the interval $(1, 5)$. The last example shows that, as subsets of $\mathbb{R}$, open balls coincide with open intervals. In particular, the statement $|x - a| < \delta$ (translated as "the distance from x to a is less than δ") can be written as $x \in B(a, \delta)$.

In the case of a function of one variable, the limit as $x \to a$ has been determined by investigating two special approaches, namely the right and left limits. If the two limits were equal, we said that the function had a (two-sided) limit, and its value $\lim_{x \to a} f(x)$ was equal to the common value of the one-sided limits. Consider now the function of two variables

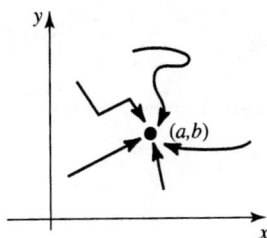

Figure 2.30 Point (a, b) can be approached in infinitely many ways.

(this is a choice of convenience: everything said holds for a function of any number of variables). It is impossible to investigate all possible ways of approaching a selected point $\mathbf{a} = (a, b)$ in $\mathbb{R}^2$: there are infinitely many of them! See Figure 2.30.

There is some good news here: the limit should be (and is) independent of the way we approach $\mathbf{a} = (a, b)$. Therefore, if two different approaches give two different candidates for the limit, we can be sure that the limit does not exist. However, if several approaches to (a, b) all give the same number, this does not prove anything yet: all it says is that, if the limit exists, it must be equal to that number.

We now imitate the one-variable case and define the limit of a function $f \colon U \subseteq \mathbb{R}^m \to \mathbb{R}$ as $\mathbf{x}$ approaches $\mathbf{a}$. The definition (applied to functions of two variables) says that if we can force the values $f(x, y)$ to move arbitrarily close to L as (x, y) gets close to (a, b), the function f has limit L; see Figure 2.31.

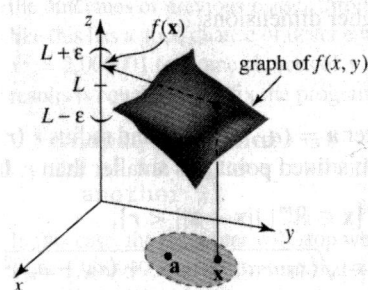

Figure 2.31 Limit of a function of two variables.

DEFINITION 2.7 Limit of a Real-Valued Function of Several Variables

Let $f \colon U \subseteq \mathbb{R}^m \to \mathbb{R}$ be a real-valued function of m variables. We say that the limit of $f(\mathbf{x}) = f(x_1, \ldots, x_m)$ as $\mathbf{x} = (x_1, \ldots, x_m)$ approaches $\mathbf{a} = (a_1, \ldots, a_m)$ is L, in symbols

$$\lim_{\mathbf{x} \to \mathbf{a}} f(\mathbf{x}) = L \quad \text{or} \quad \lim_{(x_1, \ldots, x_m) \to (a_1, \ldots, a_m)} f(x_1, \ldots, x_m) = L,$$

if and only if for every $\epsilon > 0$ there is a number $\delta > 0$ such that $\mathbf{x} \in U$ and

$$0 < \|\mathbf{x} - \mathbf{a}\| < \delta \quad \text{implies} \quad |f(\mathbf{x}) - L| < \epsilon. \tag{2.7}$$

The condition $\|\mathbf{x} - \mathbf{a}\| > 0$ in (2.7) guarantees that $\mathbf{x} \neq \mathbf{a}$. Notice that there is no mention of the way $\mathbf{x}$ is supposed to approach $\mathbf{a}$. The requirement in (2.7) is that the *distance* $||\mathbf{x} - \mathbf{a}||$ between $\mathbf{x}$ and $\mathbf{a}$ becomes smaller and smaller and therefore the definition includes every possible path that brings $\mathbf{x}$ close to $\mathbf{a}$. A convenient way of thinking about the requirement that $||\mathbf{x} - \mathbf{a}|| < \delta$ is to consider a process of selecting a point $\mathbf{x}$ (of course, $\mathbf{x}$ has to belong to the domain U of the function) from the sequence of open balls (all centered at $\mathbf{a}$) that shrink in size (their radii δ becoming smaller and smaller).

Now let $\mathbf{x} = (x, y)$, $\mathbf{a} = (a, b)$, and consider the expression

$$||\mathbf{x} - \mathbf{a}|| = \sqrt{(x - a)^2 + (y - b)^2}. \qquad (2.8)$$

If $\mathbf{x} \to \mathbf{a}$, then the distance $||\mathbf{x} - \mathbf{a}||$ can be made as small (i.e., as close to 0) as needed. But that means the square root, and hence the expression $(x - a)^2 + (y - b)^2$, can be made as close to 0 as needed. Since both summands are positive, it follows that each of $x - a$ and $y - b$ can be made as close to 0 as needed (but only one can actually be made equal to 0). In other words, if $\mathbf{x} \to \mathbf{a}$, then $x \to a$ and $y \to b$. An analogous statement holds in general; that is, if $\mathbf{x} \to \mathbf{a}$, where $\mathbf{x} = (x_1, \ldots, x_m)$ and $\mathbf{a} = (a_1, \ldots, a_m)$, then $x_1 \to a_1, \ldots, x_m \to a_m$ or

$$\lim_{\mathbf{x} \to \mathbf{a}} x_i = a_i \qquad (2.9)$$

for every $i = 1, \ldots, m$.

DEFINITION 2.8 Interior and Boundary Points

A point $\mathbf{a}$ in U is called an *interior point* of U if there is an open ball centered at $\mathbf{a}$ that is completely contained in U. If every open ball centered at $\mathbf{a}$ (this time, $\mathbf{a}$ does not have to be in U) contains not only points in U but also points not in U, then we call $\mathbf{a}$ a *boundary point* of U. ◀

The dashed curves in Figure 2.32 indicate points that do not belong to the set U or to the open balls shown. The points on the "unbroken" curves belong to U. An interior point always belongs to the set. However, a boundary point of U may or may not belong to U, as shown in Figure 2.32(b).

The definition of the limit applies to both interior and boundary points. In approaching a boundary point, we have to make sure that in the process of picking $\mathbf{x}$ from shrinking balls, we always pick only those $\mathbf{x}$ that belong to the domain U of the function. For instance, in computing the limit of $f(x, y) = x^2 \ln y$ as (x, y) approaches $(1, 0)$, we can use any real value for x, but the y values need to be restricted to $y > 0$.

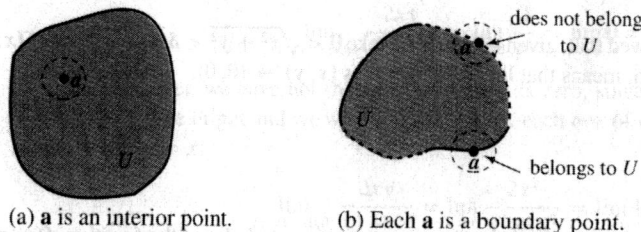

(a) $\mathbf{a}$ is an interior point.   (b) Each $\mathbf{a}$ is a boundary point.

Figure 2.32 Interior and boundary points of a set.

▶ EXAMPLE 2.25

Several level curves of the function $f(x, y) = 3x^2 y/(x^2 + y^2)$ are drawn in Figure 2.33. It looks like the values $f(x, y)$ approach 0 as (x, y) approaches $(0, 0)$. Show that this is indeed true, that is, use Definition 2.7 to prove that $\lim_{(x,y)\to(0,0)} f(x, y) = 0$.

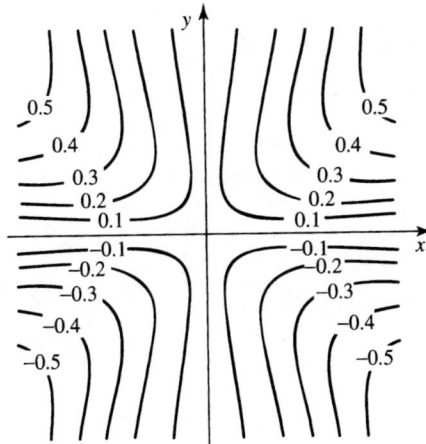

Figure 2.33 Level curves of $f(x, y)$ in Example 2.25.

SOLUTION

Pick any $\epsilon > 0$. We have to find $\delta > 0$ so that (using Definition 2.7 with $L = 0$)

$$|f(x, y) - 0| = \left| \frac{3x^2 y}{x^2 + y^2} - 0 \right| = \frac{3x^2}{x^2 + y^2} |y| < \epsilon,$$

whenever (x, y) satisfies $0 < \sqrt{x^2 + y^2} < \delta$. The latter is the statement $0 < ||\mathbf{x} - \mathbf{a}|| < \delta$, rewritten using the formula (2.8) with $\mathbf{x} = (x, y)$ and $\mathbf{a} = (0, 0)$. The inequality $x^2 \leq x^2 + y^2$ implies that $x^2/(x^2 + y^2) \leq 1$ and thus

$$|f(x, y) - 0| = \frac{3x^2}{x^2 + y^2} |y| \leq 3|y|.$$

So, we need to find $\delta > 0$ that will guarantee $3|y| < \epsilon$. The inequality $\sqrt{x^2 + y^2} < \delta$, combined with $y^2 \leq x^2 + y^2$, gives $|y| = \sqrt{y^2} \leq \sqrt{x^2 + y^2} < \delta$. Therefore, if we take $\delta = \epsilon/3$, we will get

$$|f(x, y) - 0| = \frac{3x^2}{x^2 + y^2} |y| \leq 3|y| < 3\delta = 3\frac{\epsilon}{3} = \epsilon.$$

We just showed that, given $\epsilon > 0$, if we take $0 < \sqrt{x^2 + y^2} < \delta = \epsilon/3$, then $|f(x, y) - 0| < \epsilon$. This, by definition, means that $\lim f(x, y) = 0$ as $(x, y) \to (0, 0)$. ◀

▶ EXAMPLE 2.26

In Section 2.2 we noticed that the computer-generated plot of the function $f(x, y) = 2xy/(x^2 + y^2)$ (see Figure 2.24) could not explain what happens to $f(x, y)$ near $(0, 0)$.

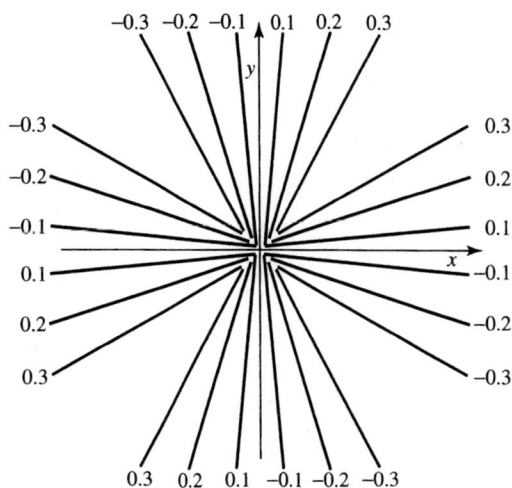

Figure 2.34 Level curves of the function $f(x, y)$ of Example 2.26.

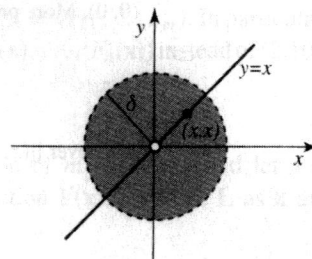

Figure 2.35 Any ball of radius $\delta > 0$ contains some points (x, x), $x \neq 0$.

Using limits, we will now describe the behavior of $f(x, y)$ near (and at) the origin. Figure 2.34 shows the contour diagram of $f(x, y) = 2xy/(x^2 + y^2)$ near $(0, 0)$. The level curves are lines (see Exercise 42 in Section 2.2 for a proof) that "collide" at $(0, 0)$, suggesting that $f(x, y)$ does not have a limit there.

Let us show that $L = 0$ cannot be the limit of $f(x, y)$ as (x, y) approaches $(0, 0)$. Pick an interval around $L = 0$, say, $(-\epsilon, \epsilon)$, for some $0 < \epsilon < 1$. Consider *any* open ball of radius $\delta > 0$ centered at the origin. No matter how small the ball is, it will always contain points that belong to the line $y = x$, for $(x, y) \neq (0, 0)$; see Figure 2.35.

At any point on this line [except at $(0, 0)$], the value of $f(x, y)$ is 1. So, any ball centered at $(0, 0)$ will contain points (x, y) for which $f(x, y)$ does not fall into the interval $(-\epsilon, \epsilon)$. Thus, $L = 0$ is not the limit. In a similar way (see Exercise 4), we can show that no real number is the limit of $f(x, y)$ as (x, y) approaches $(0, 0)$.

Now we present an alternate version (usually, easier to do) of the proof that $f(x, y)$ does not have a limit at $(0, 0)$. The idea lies in the discussion preceding the definition of the limit—all we have to do is to show that different ways of approaching $(0, 0)$ give different results. Let us approach $(0, 0)$ along the x-axis: then $y = 0$, and hence

$$\lim_{(x,y)\to(0,0)} \frac{2xy}{x^2 + y^2} = \lim_{x\to 0} \frac{0}{x^2} = \lim_{x\to 0} 0 = 0.$$

Now let us walk along the y-axis towards $(0, 0)$: in this case $x = 0$, and

$$\lim_{(x,y)\to(0,0)} \frac{2xy}{x^2 + y^2} = \lim_{y\to 0} \frac{0}{y^2} = \lim_{x\to 0} 0 = 0.$$

No luck! Moreover, we have not shown that the limit is zero, since there are infinitely many ways of approaching the origin and we would have to check each one of them. Now look at the approach along the line $y = x$:

$$\lim_{(x,y)\to(0,0)} \frac{2xy}{x^2 + y^2} = \lim_{x\to 0} \frac{2x^2}{x^2 + x^2} = \lim_{x\to 0} 1 = 1.$$

Consequently, the limit of $f(x, y)$ as $(x, y) \to (0, 0)$ does not exist.   ◀

► **EXAMPLE 2.27**

Show that

$$\lim_{(x,y)\to(0,0)} \frac{y^2}{\sqrt{x^2 + y^2}} = 0.$$

SOLUTION

We will show that $y^2/\sqrt{x^2 + y^2} \geq 0$ gets smaller and smaller as (x, y) moves closer and closer to $(0, 0)$. More precisely, for any $\epsilon > 0$, we will prove that

$$\left| \frac{y^2}{\sqrt{x^2 + y^2}} - 0 \right| < \epsilon,$$

whenever $\|(x, y) - (0, 0)\| = \sqrt{x^2 + y^2} < \delta$, for some $\delta > 0$. Since $y^2 \leq x^2 + y^2$, we get

$$\frac{y^2}{\sqrt{x^2 + y^2}} \leq \frac{x^2 + y^2}{\sqrt{x^2 + y^2}} = \sqrt{x^2 + y^2}.$$

Thus, if we take $\delta = \epsilon$, we will obtain

$$\left| \frac{y^2}{\sqrt{x^2 + y^2}} - 0 \right| \leq \sqrt{x^2 + y^2} < \delta = \epsilon,$$

which establishes the desired inequality. ◄

► **EXAMPLE 2.28**

Show that

$$\lim_{(x,y)\to(0,0)} \frac{x^2 y}{x^4 + y^2}$$

does not exist.

SOLUTION

Choose the approach $x = 0$ (that is, along the y-axis):

$$\lim_{(x,y)\to(0,0)} \frac{x^2 y}{x^4 + y^2} = \lim_{y\to 0} \frac{0}{y^2} = \lim_{y\to 0} 0 = 0.$$

Choose the approach $y = x$:

$$\lim_{(x,y)\to(0,0)} \frac{x^2 y}{x^4 + y^2} = \lim_{x\to 0} \frac{x^3}{x^4 + x^2} = \lim_{x\to 0} \frac{x}{x^2 + 1} = 0.$$

Take a (general) line through the origin, $y = mx$ (by varying the values of m we get all lines through the origin, except the y-axis). Then

$$\lim_{(x,y)\to(0,0)} \frac{x^2 y}{x^4 + y^2} = \lim_{x\to 0} \frac{mx^3}{x^4 + m^2 x^2} = \lim_{x\to 0} \frac{mx}{x^2 + m^2} = 0.$$

But we have not exhausted all possible approaches! (We have only exhausted all possible lines.) If we approach the origin along the parabola $y = x^2$, we get

$$\lim_{(x,y)\to(0,0)} \frac{x^2 y}{x^4 + y^2} = \lim_{x\to 0} \frac{x^4}{x^4 + x^4} = \lim_{x\to 0} \frac{x^4}{2x^4} = \frac{1}{2},$$

and the proof is completed. ◄

Our next definition says that the limit of a vector-valued function is computed as the limit of its components. Let $\mathbf{F}: U \subseteq \mathbb{R}^m \to \mathbb{R}^n$ be a vector-valued function of m variables, defined on a set $U \subseteq \mathbb{R}^m$. $\mathbf{F}$ can be written as

$$\mathbf{F}(x_1, \ldots, x_m) = (F_1(x_1, \ldots, x_m), F_2(x_1, \ldots, x_m), \ldots, F_n(x_1, \ldots, x_m)), \qquad (2.10)$$

where $F_i: \mathbb{R}^m \to \mathbb{R}$ is the ith *component of* $\mathbf{F}$, $i = 1, \ldots, n$. Let us emphasize that the components F_i are real-valued functions. In order to keep notation as simple as possible, we will use $\mathbf{x}$, instead of listing all variables $x_1, \ldots, x_m$; i.e., $\mathbf{x} = (x_1, \ldots, x_m)$. In particular, we will write $\mathbf{F}(\mathbf{x})$ instead of $\mathbf{F}(x_1, \ldots, x_m)$, and $\mathbf{F}(\mathbf{x}) = (F_1(\mathbf{x}), \ldots, F_n(\mathbf{x}))$ instead of (2.10).

DEFINITION 2.9 Limit of a Vector-Valued Function

Let $\mathbf{F}(\mathbf{x}) = (F_1(\mathbf{x}), \ldots, F_n(\mathbf{x}))$ be a vector-valued function of m variables, and let $\mathbf{a} = (a_1, \ldots, a_m)$ and $\mathbf{L} = (L_1, \ldots, L_n)$. We say that the function $\mathbf{F}(\mathbf{x})$ has limit $\mathbf{L}$ as $\mathbf{x}$ approaches $\mathbf{a}$, and write $\lim_{\mathbf{x} \to \mathbf{a}} \mathbf{F}(\mathbf{x}) = \mathbf{L}$, if and only if

$$\lim_{\mathbf{x} \to \mathbf{a}} F_1(\mathbf{x}) = L_1, \ldots, \lim_{\mathbf{x} \to \mathbf{a}} F_n(\mathbf{x}) = L_n. \qquad ◀$$

In other words, the limit of a vector-valued function is computed componentwise:

$$\lim_{\mathbf{x} \to \mathbf{a}} \mathbf{F}(\mathbf{x}) = (\lim_{\mathbf{x} \to \mathbf{a}} F_1(\mathbf{x}), \ldots, \lim_{\mathbf{x} \to \mathbf{a}} F_n(\mathbf{x})),$$

provided that all limits on the right side (and those are limits of real-valued functions) exist. The computation of a limit can be simplified by the use of the limit laws and by the use of continuity—that will be discussed later in this section.

THEOREM 2.1 Limit Laws

Let $\mathbf{F}, \mathbf{G}: \mathbb{R}^m \to \mathbb{R}^n$, $f, g: \mathbb{R}^m \to \mathbb{R}$ and assume that $\lim_{\mathbf{x} \to \mathbf{a}} \mathbf{F}(\mathbf{x})$, $\lim_{\mathbf{x} \to \mathbf{a}} \mathbf{G}(\mathbf{x})$, $\lim_{\mathbf{x} \to \mathbf{a}} f(\mathbf{x})$ and $\lim_{\mathbf{x} \to \mathbf{a}} g(\mathbf{x})$ exist. Then

(a) $\lim_{\mathbf{x} \to \mathbf{a}}(\mathbf{F}(\mathbf{x}) + \mathbf{G}(\mathbf{x}))$ and $\lim_{\mathbf{x} \to \mathbf{a}}(\mathbf{F}(\mathbf{x}) - \mathbf{G}(\mathbf{x}))$ exist and

$$\lim_{\mathbf{x} \to \mathbf{a}}(\mathbf{F}(\mathbf{x}) \pm \mathbf{G}(\mathbf{x})) = \lim_{\mathbf{x} \to \mathbf{a}} \mathbf{F}(\mathbf{x}) \pm \lim_{\mathbf{x} \to \mathbf{a}} \mathbf{G}(\mathbf{x}).$$

(b) $\lim_{\mathbf{x} \to \mathbf{a}} f(\mathbf{x})g(\mathbf{x})$ and $\lim_{\mathbf{x} \to \mathbf{a}} c\mathbf{F}(\mathbf{x})$ (for any constant c) exist, and

$$\lim_{\mathbf{x} \to \mathbf{a}} (f(\mathbf{x})g(\mathbf{x})) = \left(\lim_{\mathbf{x} \to \mathbf{a}} f(\mathbf{x})\right)\left(\lim_{\mathbf{x} \to \mathbf{a}} g(\mathbf{x})\right) \qquad \text{and} \qquad \lim_{\mathbf{x} \to \mathbf{a}}(c\mathbf{F}(\mathbf{x})) = c \lim_{\mathbf{x} \to \mathbf{a}} \mathbf{F}(\mathbf{x}).$$

(c) If $\lim_{\mathbf{x} \to \mathbf{a}} g(\mathbf{x}) \neq 0$, then $\lim_{\mathbf{x} \to \mathbf{a}} f(\mathbf{x})/g(\mathbf{x})$ exists, and

$$\lim_{\mathbf{x} \to \mathbf{a}} \frac{f(\mathbf{x})}{g(\mathbf{x})} = \frac{\lim_{\mathbf{x} \to \mathbf{a}} f(\mathbf{x})}{\lim_{\mathbf{x} \to \mathbf{a}} g(\mathbf{x})}.$$

(d) For any $\mathbf{a} \in \mathbb{R}^m$ and any constant $\mathbf{c} \in \mathbb{R}^n$,

$$\lim_{\mathbf{x} \to \mathbf{a}} \mathbf{x} = \mathbf{a} \qquad \text{and} \qquad \lim_{\mathbf{x} \to \mathbf{a}} \mathbf{c} = \mathbf{c}. \qquad ◀$$

In part (d) the symbol $\mathbf{c}$ denotes the function $\mathbf{F}: \mathbb{R}^m \to \mathbb{R}^n$ given by $\mathbf{F}(\mathbf{x}) = \mathbf{c}$ for all $\mathbf{x} \in \mathbb{R}^m$.

SKETCH OF PROOF: Rather than getting involved in arguments involving epsilons and deltas, we will provide more intuitive reasoning. Let $\lim_{x \to a} f(x) = L$ and $\lim_{x \to a} g(x) = M$, and consider part (a). We have to show that $f(x) + g(x)$ can be made as close as needed to $L + M$ by selecting an x close enough to a, $x \neq a$. Since $\lim_{x \to a} f(x) = L$, it is possible to force $f(x)$ to fall as close as needed to L by requiring that x ($x \neq a$) belongs to a ball of a small enough radius δ. Similarly, $\lim_{x \to a} g(x) = M$ means that $g(x)$ can be made as close as needed to M by taking x ($x \neq a$) from the inside of a ball of some small radius δ' centered at a. Taking the smaller of the two balls, we can force both $f(x)$ and $g(x)$ to be as close as needed to L and M, thus making their sum $f(x) + g(x)$ as close to $L + M$ as needed. Other properties are verified analogously.   ◀

▶ EXAMPLE 2.29

Compute $\lim_{(x,y) \to (3,2)} (x^2 - 2 + xy^2)$.

SOLUTION   By the limit laws,

$$
\lim_{(x,y) \to (3,2)} (x^2 - 2 + xy^2) = \lim_{(x,y) \to (3,2)} x^2 - \lim_{(x,y) \to (3,2)} 2 + \lim_{(x,y) \to (3,2)} xy^2
$$

$$
= \left(\lim_{(x,y) \to (3,2)} x \right) \cdot \left(\lim_{(x,y) \to (3,2)} x \right) - \lim_{(x,y) \to (3,2)} 2
$$

$$
+ \left(\lim_{(x,y) \to (3,2)} x \right) \cdot \left(\lim_{(x,y) \to (3,2)} y \right) \cdot \left(\lim_{(x,y) \to (3,2)} y \right) = 9 - 2 + 12 = 19. \quad ◀
$$

Although we need limits to define and understand continuity and derivatives, we do not need to master (fortunately) technical intricacies involved in their computation (as we have seen in the calculus of functions of one variable, we rarely go all the way back to the limit definition of the derivative; instead, we use various formulas and properties, such as the quotient and the chain rules). Some technical issues involving limits are discussed in the exercises.

Continuity

Intuitively speaking, a function is continuous if its graph has no breaks. For a function of one variable this means that the curve (which is its graph) can be drawn on a piece of paper without lifting a pen. A bird flying describes a continuous function: it cannot happen that the bird disappears somewhere and reappears at some other location a moment later. One of the properties of continuous functions states that it is possible to predict their "short-term behavior." For example, assume that the air temperature at this moment is $18°C$; a second later it could be $18.5°C$ or $17°C$ or $19°C$; but it will not be $-100°C$.

On the other hand, having a glance at a traffic light (suppose that it is red) will not help us predict whether, a second later, it will still be red or will change to green. A traffic light's color is a discontinuous function. A hemisphere, or a plane, or the graphs given in Figures 2.20, 2.21, and 2.23, are graphs of continuous functions of two variables. However, the graph of $z = \arctan(0.2y/x)$ is "broken"; that is, f is not continuous at points where $x = 0$; see Figure 2.36.

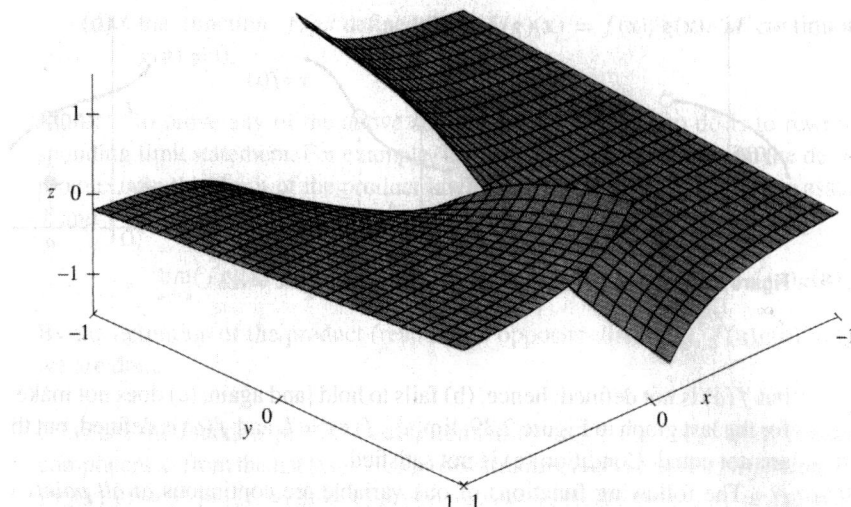

Figure 2.36 Graph of $z = \arctan(0.2y/x)$.

Recall that a function $f: \mathbb{R} \to \mathbb{R}$ is *continuous* at $x = a$ (see Figure 2.37) if and only if

(a) $\lim_{x \to a} f(x)$ exists,

(b) f is defined at a, and

(c) $\lim_{x \to a} f(x) = f(a)$.

We say that a function f is *continuous on an interval* (c, d) if it is continuous at every point a in (c, d). A function f is *continuous on a closed interval* $[c, d]$ if it is continuous on (c, d) and $\lim_{x \to c^+} f(x) = f(c)$ and $\lim_{x \to d^-} f(x) = f(d)$. We are *in* the interval $[c, d]$ and therefore can approach its endpoint c from the right only. Similarly, we can reach d from the left only. Any other point in $[c, d]$ can be reached from both sides; see Figure 2.38.

To understand this definition better, let us consider examples of functions that are not continuous at $x = a$.

The first function in Figure 2.39 does not have a limit as $x \to a$; hence, the condition (a) fails to hold [and (c) does not make sense]. For the second function, $\lim_{x \to a} f(x) = L$,

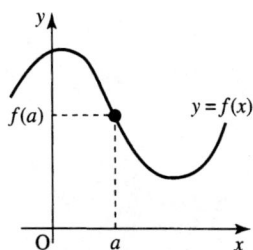

Figure 2.37 $f(x)$ is continuous at $x = a$.

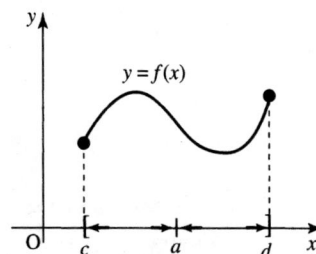

Figure 2.38 $f(x)$ is continuous on $[c, d]$.

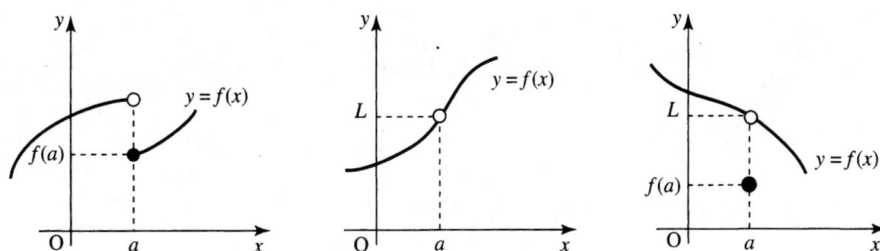

Figure 2.39 All three functions are not continuous at $x = a$.

but $f(a)$ is not defined; hence, (b) fails to hold [and again, (c) does not make sense]. Finally for the last graph in Figure 2.39, $\lim_{x \to a} f(x) = L$ and $f(a)$ is defined, but the two numbers are not equal. Condition (c) is not satisfied.

The following functions of one variable are continuous *at all points where they are defined*: $f(x) = c$, where c is a constant; $f(x) = x^n$, where n denotes any real number; polynomials and rational functions; $f(x) = e^x$, $f(x) = a^x$, for $a > 0$; $f(x) = \ln x$, $f(x) = \log x$; trigonometric and hyperbolic functions and their inverses, the absolute value function $|x|$, etc.

DEFINITION 2.10 Continuity of Functions of Several Variables

A function $f: U \subseteq \mathbb{R}^m \to \mathbb{R}$ is *continuous at* $\mathbf{x} = \mathbf{a}$ if and only if

 (a) $\lim_{\mathbf{x} \to \mathbf{a}} f(\mathbf{x})$ exists,

 (b) f is defined at $\mathbf{a}$, and

 (c) $\lim_{\mathbf{x} \to \mathbf{a}} f(\mathbf{x}) = f(\mathbf{a})$.

We say that f is *continuous on a set* U (or just f is *continuous*) if and only if it is continuous at all points in U. A vector-valued function $\mathbf{F} = (F_1, \ldots, F_n): U \subseteq \mathbb{R}^m \to \mathbb{R}^n$ is *continuous* if and only if its components F_i, $i = 1, \ldots, n$, are continuous. ◀

In light of our definition of the limit of a vector-valued function, a function $\mathbf{F}$ is continuous at $\mathbf{a}$ if and only if $\lim_{\mathbf{x} \to \mathbf{a}} \mathbf{F}(\mathbf{x})$ exists, $\mathbf{F}(\mathbf{a})$ is defined and $\lim_{\mathbf{x} \to \mathbf{a}} \mathbf{F}(\mathbf{x}) = \mathbf{F}(\mathbf{a})$. Let us emphasize that, when testing continuity at boundary points of U (if U has any) by computing the limit as $\mathbf{x} \to \mathbf{a}$, we must approach $\mathbf{a}$ from *within* U: that is, $\mathbf{x} \to \mathbf{a}$ assumes that $\mathbf{x} \in U$ (in the case of one variable, we had to use one-sided limits).

THEOREM 2.2 Properties of Continuous Functions

Let $\mathbf{F}, \mathbf{G}: U \subseteq \mathbb{R}^m \to \mathbb{R}^n$ ($n \geq 1$) and $f, g: U \subseteq \mathbb{R}^m \to \mathbb{R}$ be continuous at $\mathbf{a} \in U$. Then

 (a) the functions $\mathbf{F} \pm \mathbf{G}$, defined by $(\mathbf{F} \pm \mathbf{G})(\mathbf{x}) = \mathbf{F}(\mathbf{x}) \pm \mathbf{G}(\mathbf{x})$, are continuous at $\mathbf{a}$.

 (b) the function $c\mathbf{F}$, defined by $(c\mathbf{F})(\mathbf{x}) = c\mathbf{F}(\mathbf{x})$, is continuous at $\mathbf{a}$.

 (c) the function fg, defined by $(fg)(\mathbf{x}) = f(\mathbf{x})g(\mathbf{x})$, is continuous at $\mathbf{a}$.

(d) the function f/g, defined by $(f/g)(\mathbf{x}) = f(\mathbf{x})/g(\mathbf{x})$, is continuous at $\mathbf{a}$, if $g(\mathbf{a}) \neq 0$.

PROOF: To prove any of the above statements, all we have to do is to rewrite the corresponding limit statement. For example, let us prove part (c). Start with the definition of the product, use the "limit of the product law" (cf. (b), Theorem 2.1) and the assumption that f and g are continuous, thus getting

$$\lim_{\mathbf{x}\to\mathbf{a}}(fg)(\mathbf{x}) = \lim_{\mathbf{x}\to\mathbf{a}} f(\mathbf{x})g(\mathbf{x}) = \left(\lim_{\mathbf{x}\to\mathbf{a}} f(\mathbf{x})\right)\left(\lim_{\mathbf{x}\to\mathbf{a}} g(\mathbf{x})\right) = f(\mathbf{a})g(\mathbf{a}).$$

By the definition of the product (read in the opposite direction), $f(\mathbf{a})g(\mathbf{a}) = (fg)(\mathbf{a})$, and we are done. ◄

Consider the function $pr_i: \mathbb{R}^m \to \mathbb{R}$, defined by $pr_i(x_1, \dots, x_m) = x_i$; it extracts the ith component x_i from the list $(x_1, \dots, x_m)$ of variables, and is called a *projection*. For example, $pr_2(x, y) = y$, $pr_1(x, y, z) = x$, $pr_2(x, y, z) = y$, etc. Now $\lim_{\mathbf{x}\to\mathbf{a}} pr_i(\mathbf{x}) = \lim_{\mathbf{x}\to\mathbf{a}} x_i$ by the definition of the projection, $\lim_{\mathbf{x}\to\mathbf{a}} x_i = a_i$ by (2.9), and $a_i = pr_i(\mathbf{a})$ again by the definition of projection read from right to left. In other words, $\lim_{\mathbf{x}\to\mathbf{a}} pr_i(\mathbf{x}) = pr_i(\mathbf{a})$, and the projection function is continuous. This means that, for example, functions such as $f(x, y) = x$, $f(x, y, z) = z$, etc., are continuous, viewed as functions of *several* variables.

THEOREM 2.3   Continuity of Composition of Functions

Let $\mathbf{F}: U \subseteq \mathbb{R}^m \to \mathbb{R}^n$ and $\mathbf{G}: V \subseteq \mathbb{R}^n \to \mathbb{R}^p$ be such that the range $\mathbf{F}(U)$ of $\mathbf{F}$ is contained in the domain V of $\mathbf{G}$, so that the composition $\mathbf{G} \circ \mathbf{F}$ is defined; see Figure 2.40. If $\mathbf{F}$ is continuous at $\mathbf{a}$ and $\mathbf{G}$ is continuous at $\mathbf{b} = \mathbf{F}(\mathbf{a})$, then $\mathbf{G} \circ \mathbf{F}$ is continuous at $\mathbf{a}$.

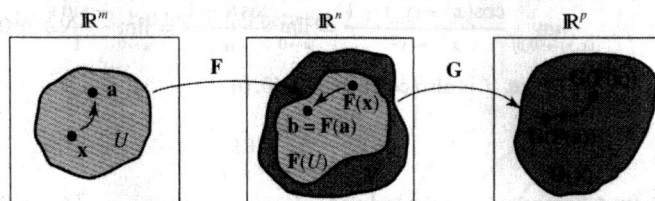

Figure 2.40   Composition of functions $\mathbf{G} \circ \mathbf{F}: U \subseteq \mathbb{R}^m \to \mathbb{R}^p$.

INTUITIVE PROOF: As $\mathbf{x}$ gets closer and closer to $\mathbf{a}$, the values $\mathbf{F}(\mathbf{x})$ get closer and closer to $\mathbf{F}(\mathbf{a})$, since $\mathbf{F}$ is continuous at $\mathbf{a}$. But now $\mathbf{G}$ is continuous at $\mathbf{b} = \mathbf{F}(\mathbf{a})$, and since $\mathbf{F}(\mathbf{x})$ gets closer and closer to $\mathbf{b} = \mathbf{F}(\mathbf{a})$, the values of $\mathbf{G}$, that is, $\mathbf{G}(\mathbf{F}(\mathbf{x}))$, get closer and closer to $\mathbf{G}(\mathbf{F}(\mathbf{a}))$. ◄

The following functions of two variables are continuous *at all points where they are defined*: $f(x, y) = c$, where c is a constant; $f(x, y) = x$, $f(x, y) = y$ (these are the orthogonal projections onto the x-axis and onto the y-axis, respectively); $f(x, y) = x^n$, $f(x, y) = y^n$, where n denotes any real number. Therefore, polynomials and rational functions are continuous (whenever the denominator is not equal to zero), as is a composition involving any of the functions listed here with any function from the one-variable list. A list analogous to this one could be made for functions of m variables.

► **EXAMPLE 2.30**

Show that the function $\mathbf{F}(x, y, z) = (\sin x, x^2 + y^2, e^{xyz})$ is continuous for all $(x, y, z) \in \mathbb{R}^3$.

SOLUTION

We have to analyze the components of $\mathbf{F}$. The first component $F_1(x, y, z) = \sin x$ is the composition of the projection $(x, y, z) \mapsto x$ and the trigonometric function $x \mapsto \sin x$, both of which are continuous. Hence, F_1 is continuous. The component F_2 is a polynomial and hence continuous. The function F_3 is continuous as it is the composition of the polynomial $(x, y, z) \mapsto xyz$ and the exponential function. ◄

► **EXAMPLE 2.31**

Show that the function

$$f(x, y) = \begin{cases} \dfrac{\cos(x^2 + y^2) - 1}{x^2 + y^2} & \text{if } (x, y) \neq (0, 0) \\ 0 & \text{if } (x, y) = (0, 0) \end{cases}$$

is continuous on $\mathbb{R}^2$.

SOLUTION

The function $(x, y) \mapsto x^2 + y^2$ is a polynomial, and hence its composition with the cosine function is continuous. The numerator is continuous as it is the difference of continuous functions [the function $(x, y) \mapsto 1$ is a constant function, and hence continuous]. Since the denominator is continuous and nonzero except when $(x, y) = (0, 0)$, it follows that $f(x, y)$ is continuous at all points $(x, y) \neq (0, 0)$. It remains to check the point $(0, 0)$: by Definition 2.10, it suffices to show that $\lim_{(x,y)\to(0,0)} f(x, y) = f(0, 0) = 0$. To compute the limit, substitute $u = x^2 + y^2$; then $u \to 0$ (since both $x \to 0$ and $y \to 0$) and

$$\lim_{(x,y)\to(0,0)} \frac{\cos(x^2 + y^2) - 1}{x^2 + y^2} = \lim_{u\to 0} \frac{\cos u - 1}{u} = \lim_{u\to 0} \frac{-\sin u}{1} = 0,$$

by L'Hôpital's rule. Hence, f is also continuous at $(0, 0)$. ◄

► **EXAMPLE 2.32**

Find all points of discontinuity of the function

$$f(x, y) = \begin{cases} \dfrac{x^2 y}{x^4 + y^2} & \text{if } (x, y) \neq (0, 0) \\ 0 & \text{if } (x, y) = (0, 0) \end{cases}$$

SOLUTION

The function $f(x, y) = x^2 y / (x^4 + y^2)$ is continuous at all points except possibly at the origin (namely, it is a quotient of continuous functions with a nonzero denominator). It was shown in Example 2.28 that $\lim_{(x,y)\to(0,0)} f(x, y)$ does not exist, and consequently, $f(x, y)$ is not continuous at $(0, 0)$. ◄

► **EXERCISES 2.3**

1. In all three cases shown in Figure 2.41, $\lim_{x\to a} f(x)$ is equal to L. Describe the differences in terms of the behavior of $f(x)$ at a.

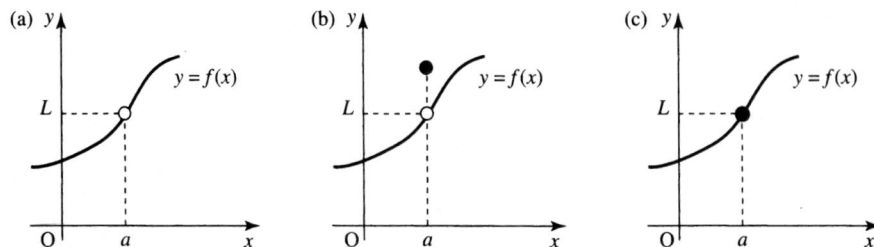

Figure 2.41 Functions from Exercise 1.

2. Consider the function $f \colon \mathbb{R}^2 \to \mathbb{R}$ defined by $f(x, y) = x^2 y^3$. Find the radius of an open ball $B((0, 0), r)$ centered at the origin with the property that $|x^2 y^3| < 0.005$, if $(x, y) \in B((0, 0), r)$. *Hint*: Find a and b such that $-a \le x \le a$ and $-b \le y \le b$ imply $|x^2 y^3| < 0.005$ first. (What region in the xy-plane is represented by $-a \le x \le a$ and $-b \le y \le b$?)

3. Consider the function $f \colon \mathbb{R}^2 \to \mathbb{R}$ defined by $f(x, y) = e^{-(x^2 + y^2)}$. Find an open ball $B((0, 0), r)$ (i.e., find its radius) such that, whenever $(x, y) \in B((0, 0), r)$, f satisfies $|f(x, y) - 1| < 0.01$.

4. Consider the function $f(x, y) = 2xy/(x^2 + y^2)$ of Example 2.26.

(a) Show that $L = 1/2$ cannot be the limit of $f(x, y)$ at $(0, 0)$. (*Hint*: Consider points on the x-axis.)

(b) Show that no number $L_o \neq 0$ can be the limit of $f(x, y)$ at $(0, 0)$.

5. Figure 2.42 shows level curves of a function $f \colon \mathbb{R}^2 \to \mathbb{R}$ whose limit at $(0, 0)$ is 3. Draw a ball $B((0, 0), r_1)$ such that $|f(x, y) - 3| < 0.04$ for every $(x, y) \in B((0, 0), r_1)$. Find another ball $B((0, 0), r_2)$ such that for every $(x, y) \in B((0, 0), r_2)$, $|f(x, y) - 3| < 0.01$. Assume that the values of f in the region between two level curves are between the values of f on those level curves. For example, the value of f at a point in the region between level curves of values 2.92 and 2.96 cannot be 4 or -2, but has to fall between 2.92 and 2.96.

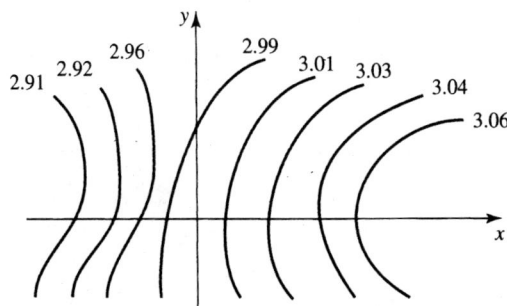

Figure 2.42 Level curves of the function f of Exercise 5.

6. Show that $\lim_{(x,y) \to (-1, 2)} (y - 2)/(x + 1)$ does not exist.

7. Show that $\lim_{(x,y) \to (0,0)} \arctan(0.2x/y)$ does not exist.

Exercises 8 to 13: Find the limit of $f(x, y)$ as $(x, y) \to (0, 0)$, if it exists.

8. $f(x, y) = (x^3 y - xy^3 - x)/(1 - xy)$ **9.** $f(x, y) = 1 - y - e^{-x^2 - y^2} \cos x$

10. $f(x, y) = \sin(3x - 2y + xy)/(3x - 2y + xy)$ (*Hint*: Introduce a new variable $u = 3x - 2y + xy$ and reduce the limit to the one-variable case.)

11. $f(x, y) = (x + y)e^{-1/(x+y)}$

12. $f(x, y) = xy(x^2 + y^2)^{-1/2}$ (*Hint*: Switch to polar coordinates.)

13. $f(x, y) = x^2 y/(x^2 + y^2)$

Exercises 14 to 20: Show that the limit of $f(x, y)$, as $(x, y) \to (0, 0)$, does not exist.

14. $f(x, y) = \dfrac{xy}{(x^2 + y^2)^{3/2}}$

15. $f(x, y) = \dfrac{2x^2 - y^2}{x^2 + 2y^2}$

16. $f(x, y) = \dfrac{3x^2 y + 6xy + 19y^2}{x^2 + 4y^2}$

17. $f(x, y) = \dfrac{2xy}{2x^2 + y^2}$

18. $f(x, y) = \dfrac{x^2 y}{x^4 + y^2}$

19. $f(x, y) = \dfrac{x^3 y}{x^6 + y^2}$

20. $f(x, y) = \dfrac{xy}{x^3 + y^3}$ (*Hint*: Use polar coordinates, simplify and let $r \to 0$.)

21. Evaluate $\lim_{(x,y,z) \to (0,0,0)} \dfrac{xyz}{x^3 + y^3 + z^3}$, if it exists.

22. Prove that the function $\dfrac{\sin x \cos y}{x^2 + y^2 + 1}$ is continuous for every $(x, y) \in \mathbb{R}^2$.

23. Find all points where the function $\mathbf{F}(x, y, z) = (x/(x^2 + y^2 + z^2), y/(x^2 + y^2 + z^2))$ is not continuous.

24. Identify the domain of the function $f(x, y) = (\ln x)^2 + \ln y^2$. Explain why f is continuous at all points in its domain.

25. Find all points of discontinuity of the function $f(x, y) = (1 + \cos^2 x)(3 - \sin x \cos x)^{-1}$.

26. Show that the function $f: \mathbb{R}^m \to \mathbb{R}$, defined by $f(\mathbf{x}) = ||\mathbf{x}||$, is continuous for all $\mathbf{x} \in \mathbb{R}^m$. Find $\lim_{\mathbf{x} \to \mathbf{a}} ||\mathbf{x}||$.

27. Find all $\mathbf{x}$, where the function $f: \mathbb{R}^m \to \mathbb{R}$, defined by $f(\mathbf{x}) = (\mathbf{x} - \mathbf{x}_0)/||\mathbf{x} - \mathbf{x}_0||$, $\mathbf{x}_0 \in \mathbb{R}^m$, is not contunuous.

Exercises 28 to 30: Determine whether or not the limit of $f(x, y)$ as $(x, y) \to (0, 0)$, exists. If possible, define $f(0, 0)$ so as to make f continuous at $(0, 0)$.

28. $f(x, y) = \dfrac{\sin(3x^2 + y^2)}{x^2 + 2y^2}$

29. $f(x, y) = \dfrac{xy^3}{x^2 + y^6}$

30. $f(x, y) = \dfrac{\cos(x^2 + y^2) - 1}{x^2 + y^2}$

31. Find all interior and boundary points of the set $U = \{(x, y) \mid xy \neq 0\}$.

32. Find all interior and boundary points of the set $U = \{(x, y) \mid 1 < x^2 + y^2 \leq 2\}$. What boundary points belong to U?

33. Let $\mathbf{a}$ be a fixed vector in $\mathbb{R}^m$, and let $f: \mathbb{R}^m \to \mathbb{R}$ be a function defined by ($\cdot$ denotes the dot product) $f(\mathbf{x}) = \mathbf{x} \cdot \mathbf{a}$. Show that f is continuous at all $\mathbf{x}$ in $\mathbb{R}^m$.

34. Define a vector-valued function $\mathbf{F}: \mathbb{R}^3 \to \mathbb{R}^3$ by $\mathbf{F}(\mathbf{x}) = \mathbf{x} \times \mathbf{a}$, where $\mathbf{a}$ is a fixed vector in $\mathbb{R}^3$. Find all points where $\mathbf{F}$ is continuous. Find all points where $\mathbf{G}(\mathbf{x}) = \mathbf{x} \times \mathbf{a}/||\mathbf{x} \times \mathbf{a}||$ is continuous.

Exercises 35 to 37: Compute the limit, if it exists, of the function $\mathbf{F}(x, y)$, as (x, y) approaches (a, b). If possible, define $\mathbf{F}(a, b)$ so as to make it continuous at (a, b).

35. $\mathbf{F}(x, y) = \left(\dfrac{y \sin x}{x}, ye^x \right)$, $(a, b) = (0, 2)$

36. $\mathbf{F}(x, y) = \left(\dfrac{x}{\sqrt{x^2 + y^2}}, \dfrac{y}{\sqrt{x^2 + y^2}} \right)$, $(a, b) = (0, 0)$

37. $\mathbf{F}(x, y) = \left(\sin(x + y), \dfrac{\cos y - 1}{xy}, e^{xy} \right)$, $(a, b) = (1, 0)$

Exercises 38 to 40: Compute the limit, if it exists, of the function $f(x, y)$ as (x, y) approaches (a, b). If possible, define $f(a, b)$ so as to make it continuous at (a, b).

38. $f(x, y) = 3x \sin x + y^2 \ln (x - 2y)$, $(a, b) = (2, 1)$

39. $f(x, y) = \dfrac{\sin^2 (xy - 2)}{xy - 2}$, $(a, b) = (-1, -2)$

40. $f(x, y) = \tan (x^2 + y)$, $(a, b) = (0, \pi/2)$

► 2.4 DERIVATIVES

Using limits and continuity we can detect only some important properties of a function. To obtain more information, we make use of another powerful concept: the derivative of a function. For example, the graph of the function $f(x) = e^{-x^2}$ has no breaks [continuity information] and the line $y = 0$ is its horizontal asymptote [limit information]. With the help of the derivative [$f'(x) = -2xe^{-x^2}$] we can say much more: $f(x)$ is increasing for $x \leq 0$ and decreasing for $x \geq 0$; it has a maximum at $x = 0$, etc. Moreover, we can examine *how* $f(x)$ changes (recall that the derivative represents the rate of change): since $f'(-2) = 4e^{-4} \approx 0.0732$ and $f'(-1/2) = e^{-1/4} \approx 0.7788$, it follows that $f(x)$ increases much faster near $-1/2$ than near -2. Similarly, $f'(1) = -2e^{-1} \approx -0.7358$ and $f'(3) = -6e^{-9} \approx -0.0007$ imply that the function f decreases much faster (i.e., loses more per unit change in x) near 1 than near 3.

Recall that the derivative $f'(x)$ of a function $f(x)$ is defined as a limit of difference quotients

$$f'(x) = \lim_{h \to 0} \frac{f(x + h) - f(x)}{h},$$

provided that the limit exists. The number $f'(x_0)$ is the slope of the tangent to the graph of $f(x)$ at the point $(x_0, f(x_0))$.

The function $f'(x)$ is defined on open intervals (a, b) contained in the domain of $f(x)$. We say that the derivative, and, consequently, the tangent, do not exist at "ends" $x = a$ and $x = b$ of a graph. Similarly, the derivative of a function of several variables will be defined on special subsets in the domain: they are called open sets.

DEFINITION 2.11 Open Sets in $\mathbb{R}^m$

A set $U \subseteq \mathbb{R}^m$ is *open in* $\mathbb{R}^m$ if and only if all of its points are interior points.   ◄

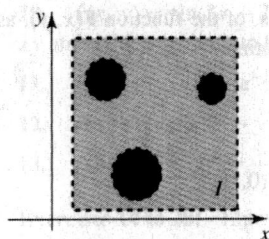

Figure 2.43 The inside of a
square is an open set in $\mathbb{R}^2$.

Figure 2.44 A set that contains a
boundary point cannot be open.

In other words, a set $U \subseteq \mathbb{R}^m$ is open in $\mathbb{R}^m$ if and only if for any point $\mathbf{a} \in U$ there is an open ball centered at $\mathbf{a}$ that is completely contained in U. For example, the inside I of a square (boundary segments not included) is open in $\mathbb{R}^2$: no matter what point in I is chosen, there is always a small open ball that contains it and is contained in I. Clearly, the balls must get smaller and smaller as we approach the edges; see Figure 2.43.

The inside of a circle is an open set in $\mathbb{R}^2$; therefore, the use of the adjective "open" in the definition of the open ball has been justified. All of $\mathbb{R}^2$, or the upper half-plane $\{(x, y) | y > 0\}$ are open in $\mathbb{R}^2$. The first octant without the coordinate planes or the inside of a cube are open sets in $\mathbb{R}^3$.

The interval $(1, 2)$ is open in $\mathbb{R}$ (hence the name open interval). Consider the following two cases as illustration: pick a number in $(1, 2)$, say 1.8; the open ball $(1.7, 1.9)$ contains it, and is contained in $(1, 2)$. Pick, say, 1.9995; the open ball $(1.9992, 1.9998)$ satisfies the requirement of the definition: $1.9995 \in (1.9992, 1.9998) \subseteq (1, 2)$.

On the other hand, if a set U contains any of its boundary points, then it cannot be open: any ball centered at a boundary point, no matter how small, will always contain points outside of U, as shown in Figure 2.44. For example, the interval $[1, 2]$ is not open in $\mathbb{R}$. The set $\{(x, y) | x^2 + y^2 \leq 1\}$ (that contains the circle $x^2 + y^2 = 1$ and the region inside it) is not open in $\mathbb{R}^2$.

Partial Derivatives

We will start our presentation of the derivative by defining a partial derivative of a real-valued function. Throughout this section U denotes an open set.

Consider a function $f(x, y)$ and pick a point (a, b) in its domain U. In order to investigate how f changes at (a, b), we need to specify a direction in which the variables change (for instance, we feel an increase in the temperature as we approach a heater, and a decrease as we walk away from it). In this section, we study two special rates of change, defined by the direction of the coordinate axes. The rates of change in arbitrary directions are discussed in Section 2.7.

The function $g(x) = f(x, b)$ describes the values of f at the points on the line parallel to the x-axis that goes through (a, b). Note that g is a function of one variable. The rate of change of $f(x, y)$ at (a, b) in the direction of the x-axis is given by

$$g'(a) = \lim_{h \to 0} \frac{g(a + h) - g(a)}{h} = \lim_{h \to 0} \frac{f(a + h, b) - f(a, b)}{h},$$

if the limit exists. The expression on the right side is called the *partial derivative of f with respect to x* at (a, b), and is denoted by $(\partial f / \partial x)(a, b)$. In a similar way, we obtain the formula

$$\frac{\partial f}{\partial y}(a, b) = \lim_{h \to 0} \frac{f(a, b + h) - f(a, b)}{h}$$

for the *partial derivative of f with respect to y* at (a, b). Letting the point (a, b) vary, we obtain the functions

$$\frac{\partial f}{\partial x}(x, y) = \lim_{h \to 0} \frac{f(x + h, y) - f(x, y)}{h} \tag{2.11}$$

and

$$\frac{\partial f}{\partial y}(x, y) = \lim_{h \to 0} \frac{f(x, y + h) - f(x, y)}{h} \tag{2.12}$$

which represent *partial derivatives of f with respect to x and y*.

▶ **EXAMPLE 2.33**

Compute $(\partial f / \partial y)(2, 0)$ and $(\partial f / \partial x)(x, y)$ for $f(x, y) = (x - 3)^2 e^y$.

SOLUTION   Following the definition, we get

$$\frac{\partial f}{\partial y}(2, 0) = \lim_{h \to 0} \frac{f(2, h) - f(2, 0)}{h} = \lim_{h \to 0} \frac{e^h - 1}{h} = \lim_{h \to 0} e^h = 1$$

(note that we used L'Hôpital's rule to calculate the limit). Using (2.11),

$$\frac{\partial f}{\partial x}(x, y) = \lim_{h \to 0} \frac{f(x + h, y) - f(x, y)}{h} = \lim_{h \to 0} \frac{(x + h - 3)^2 e^y - (x - 3)^2 e^y}{h}$$
$$= \lim_{h \to 0} \frac{(h^2 + 2xh - 6h)e^y}{h} = \lim_{h \to 0}(h + 2x - 6)e^y = (2x - 6)e^y. \quad ◄$$

Next, we generalize partial derivatives to functions of any number of varibles.

DEFINITION 2.12   Partial Derivative

Let $f: U \subseteq \mathbb{R}^m \to \mathbb{R}$ be a real-valued function of m variables $x_1, \ldots, x_m$, defined on an open set U in $\mathbb{R}^m$. The *partial derivative* of f with respect to x_i (or with respect to the ith variable, $i = 1, \ldots, m$) is a real-valued function $\partial f / \partial x_i$ of m variables, defined by

$$\frac{\partial f}{\partial x_i}(x_1, \ldots, x_m) = \lim_{h \to 0} \frac{f(x_1, \ldots, x_i + h, \ldots, x_m) - f(x_1, \ldots, x_i, \ldots, x_m)}{h},$$

provided that the limit exists.   ◄

In other words, $\partial f / \partial x_i$ can be obtained by regarding all variables except x_i as constants, and applying standard rules for differentiating functions of one variable (in this case, the variable is x_i). If that is not possible, Definition 2.12 has to be used, as in Example 2.35.

Other commonly used symbols for partial derivatives $\partial f / \partial x_i$ are f_{x_i}, f_i, $D_{x_i} f$ and $D_i f$. If a function has a low number of variables, we use $\partial f / \partial x$, f_x, $D_1 f$ or $D_x f$ for the partial derivative of f with respect to x; similarly, the symbols $\partial f/\partial y$, f_y, $D_2 f$ or $D_y f$ denote the partial derivative of f with respect to y, etc.

► **EXAMPLE 2.34**

Let $f(x, y, z) = e^{xy} \sin (y^2 + z^2)$. Compute $\partial f/\partial x$, $\partial f/\partial y$ and $\partial f/\partial z$.

SOLUTION   Regarding y and z as constants, we obtain

$$\frac{\partial f}{\partial x} = e^{xy} y \cdot \sin (y^2 + z^2) = y e^{xy} \sin (y^2 + z^2).$$

Similarly,

$$\frac{\partial f}{\partial y} = e^{xy} x \cdot \sin (y^2 + z^2) + e^{xy} \cos (y^2 + z^2) \cdot 2y$$

$$= e^{xy} (x \sin (y^2 + z^2) + 2y \cos (y^2 + z^2))$$

and

$$\frac{\partial f}{\partial z} = e^{xy} \cdot \cos (y^2 + z^2) \cdot 2z. \qquad \blacktriangleleft$$

► **EXAMPLE 2.35**

Compute $(\partial f/\partial x)(x, y)$ for $f(x, y) = (x^4 + y^4)^{1/3}$.

SOLUTION   The partial derivative

$$\frac{\partial f}{\partial x}(x, y) = \frac{1}{3}(x^4 + y^4)^{-2/3} \cdot 4x^3 = \frac{4x^3}{3(x^4 + y^4)^{2/3}} \qquad (2.13)$$

is defined at all points (x, y) except at the origin. In order to compute $(\partial f/\partial x)(0, 0)$, we use Definition 2.12 or (2.11):

$$\frac{\partial f}{\partial x}(0, 0) = \lim_{h \to 0} \frac{f(h, 0) - f(0, 0)}{h} = \lim_{h \to 0} \frac{(h^4)^{1/3} - 0}{h} = \lim_{h \to 0} h^{1/3} = 0.$$

Therefore, $(\partial f/\partial x)(x, y)$ is given by (2.13) if $(x, y) \neq (0, 0)$, and by $(\partial f/\partial x)(0, 0) = 0$. $\qquad \blacktriangleleft$

To get a better feel for partial derivatives we investigate several functions $f(x, y)$ of two variables. The partial derivative $(\partial f/\partial x)(x, y)$ represents the rate of change of f at (x, y) with respect to x when y is held fixed. A similar interpretation can be given to $(\partial f/\partial y)(x, y)$ [and for that matter, to any partial derivative of a function of any number of variables].

► **EXAMPLE 2.36**

The function $T(x, y) = 33e^{-x^2 - 2y^2}$ describes the air temperature at a location (x, y). Suppose that we start walking away from the origin along the x-axis in the positive direction. What rate of change in temperature do we experience at the moment when we reach the point $(1, 0)$? Compute $T_y(1, 2)$ and give a physical interpretation.

SOLUTION   To answer the first question we have to compute $(\partial T/\partial x)(1, 0)$ (we are walking along the x-axis, so that $y = 0$, and it does not change). Using the chain rule, we get

$$\frac{\partial T}{\partial x} = 33e^{-x^2 - 2y^2}(-2x) = -66x e^{-x^2 - 2y^2}$$

and $(\partial T/\partial x)\,(1, 0) = -66e^{-1} \approx -24.3$. So, we feel that the air is cooling down (the derivative is negative) as we pass through $(1, 0)$. Similarly (the vertical bar is read "evaluated at"),

$$\frac{\partial T}{\partial y}(1, 2) = -132ye^{-x^2-2y^2}\bigg|_{(1,2)} = -264e^{-9} \approx -0.03.$$

In words, at the moment we reach the point $(1, 2)$ on our walk along the vertical line $x = 1$ in the direction of the positive y-axis, we feel a very small decrease in temperature. ◀

▶ **EXAMPLE 2.37**

A contour diagram of a function $f(x, y)$ is shown in Figure 2.45. Estimate the values $(\partial f/\partial x)(10, 1)$ and $(\partial f/\partial y)(10, 1)$.

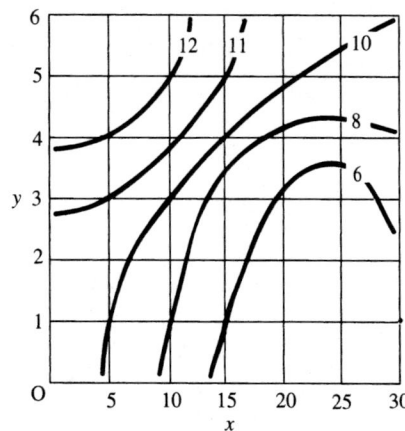

Figure 2.45 Contour diagram of the function $f(x, y)$ of Example 2.37.

SOLUTION To estimate partial derivatives, we use difference quotients; see (2.11) and (2.12). The point $(10, 1)$ lies on the contour of value 8. Moving 5 units to the right, we notice that $F(15, 1) = 6$. So, f decreases by 2 units as x increases by 5 units (and y is kept fixed at 1), and thus $(\partial f/\partial x)(10, 1) \approx -2/5$.

To compute $(\partial f/\partial y)(10, 1)$, we notice that, as y increases from 1 to 3 (with x kept at 10), f increases by 2 units (from 8 to 10). Thus, $(\partial f/\partial y)(10, 1) \approx 2/2 = 1$. ◀

Next, we discuss a geometric interpretation of partial derivatives. Consider a function $z = f(x, y)$ and pick a point (a, b) in its domain. The intersection of the graph of f and the vertical plane $y = b$ is the curve **c** that contains the point $(a, b, f(a, b))$ on the surface. Its equation is $z = f(x, b)$ (z is now a function of one variable) and the partial derivative $(\partial f/\partial x)(a, b)$ is equal to the slope of the tangent to that curve at $(a, b, f(a, b))$; see Figure 2.46.

▶ **EXAMPLE 2.38**

Compute $(\partial f/\partial x)(2, 1)$ for $f(x, y) = 2x^2 + 3xy - y^2$. Find the curve that is the intersection of the graph of $z = f(x, y)$ and the plane $y = 1$ and compute the slope of the tangent to that curve at $x = 2$. Give a geometric interpretation of $(\partial f/\partial x)(2, 1)$.

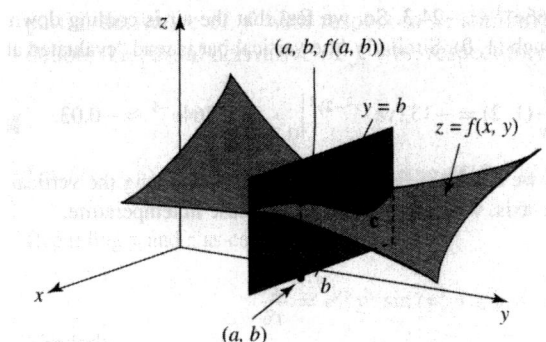

Figure 2.46 Partial derivative is the slope of a tangent.

SOLUTION   The partial derivative is $(\partial f / \partial x)(2, 1) = (4x + 3y)|_{(2,1)} = 11$.

Substitute $y = 1$ into $z = 2x^2 + 3xy - y^2$ to get the curve $z = 2x^2 + 3x - 1$ in the plane $y = 1$. The slope of its tangent line at $x = 2$ is $z'(2) = (4x + 3)|_{x=2} = 11$. The partial derivative of f with respect to x at the point $(2, 1)$ equals the slope of the tangent line at $x = 2$ to the curve that is the intersection of the surface $z = 2x^2 + 3xy - y^2$ and the plane $y = 1$.   ◀

Derivative of a Function of Several Variables

Let $\mathbf{F}$ be a vector-valued function $\mathbf{F}: U \subseteq \mathbb{R}^m \to \mathbb{R}^n$. Recall that $\mathbf{F}$ can be written in terms of its components as

$$\mathbf{F}(x_1, \ldots, x_m) = (F_1(x_1, \ldots, x_m), F_2(x_1, \ldots, x_m), \ldots, F_n(x_1, \ldots, x_m)),$$

or as $\mathbf{F}(\mathbf{x}) = (F_1(\mathbf{x}), F_2(\mathbf{x}), \ldots, F_n(\mathbf{x}))$, where $\mathbf{x} = (x_1, \ldots, x_m)$. In words, we can describe a vector-valued function $\mathbf{F}$ using n real-valued functions of m variables.

By $D\mathbf{F}(\mathbf{x})$ we denote the $n \times m$ matrix of partial derivatives of the components of $\mathbf{F}$ evaluated at $\mathbf{x}$ (provided that all partial derivatives exist at $\mathbf{x}$). Thus,

$$D\mathbf{F}(x) = \begin{bmatrix} \dfrac{\partial F_1}{\partial x_1}(\mathbf{x}) & \dfrac{\partial F_1}{\partial x_2}(\mathbf{x}) & \cdots & \dfrac{\partial F_1}{\partial x_m}(\mathbf{x}) \\[2ex] \dfrac{\partial F_2}{\partial x_1}(\mathbf{x}) & \dfrac{\partial F_2}{\partial x_2}(\mathbf{x}) & \cdots & \dfrac{\partial F_2}{\partial x_m}(\mathbf{x}) \\[1ex] \vdots & \vdots & & \vdots \\[1ex] \dfrac{\partial F_n}{\partial x_1}(\mathbf{x}) & \dfrac{\partial F_n}{\partial x_2}(\mathbf{x}) & \cdots & \dfrac{\partial F_n}{\partial x_m}(\mathbf{x}) \end{bmatrix}. \tag{2.14}$$

The matrix $D\mathbf{F}(\mathbf{x})$ has n rows and m columns (the number of rows is the number of component functions of $\mathbf{F}$, and the number of columns equals the number of variables). The ith row consists of partial derivatives of the ith component F_i of $\mathbf{F}$ with respect to all variables $x_1, \ldots, x_m$, evaluated at $\mathbf{x}$. The ith column is the matrix

$$\frac{\partial \mathbf{F}}{\partial x_i}(\mathbf{x}) = \mathbf{F}_{x_i}(\mathbf{x}) = \begin{bmatrix} \dfrac{\partial F_1}{\partial x_i}(\mathbf{x}) \\ \dfrac{\partial F_2}{\partial x_i}(\mathbf{x}) \\ \vdots \\ \dfrac{\partial F_n}{\partial x_i}(\mathbf{x}) \end{bmatrix},$$

that consists of partial derivatives of the component functions $F_1, \ldots, F_n$ with respect to the same variable x_i, evaluated at $\mathbf{x}$.

► **EXAMPLE 2.39**

Let $\mathbf{F}: \mathbb{R}^3 \to \mathbb{R}^4$ be given by $\mathbf{F}(x, y, z) = (e^{x+yz}, x^2 + 1, \sin(y + z), 4y)$. The components of $\mathbf{F}$ are $F_1(x, y, z) = e^{x+yz}$, $F_2(x, y, z) = x^2 + 1$, $F_3(x, y, z) = \sin(y + z)$, and $F_4(x, y, z) = 4y$. The matrix $D\mathbf{F}(x, y, z)$ is given by

$$D\mathbf{F}(x, y, z) = \begin{bmatrix} e^{x+yz} & ze^{x+yz} & ye^{x+yz} \\ 2x & 0 & 0 \\ 0 & \cos(y+z) & \cos(y+z) \\ 0 & 4 & 0 \end{bmatrix}.$$

The second column of $D\mathbf{F}(x, y, z)$ is equal to

$$\frac{\partial \mathbf{F}}{\partial y}(x, y, z) = \begin{bmatrix} ze^{x+yz} \\ 0 \\ \cos(y+z) \\ 4 \end{bmatrix},$$

which is the matrix of derivatives of component functions with respect to y. ◄

Let us consider several special cases. If $f(x): \mathbb{R} \to \mathbb{R}$, then $Df(x)$ is a 1×1 matrix whose entry is the derivative of (the only component) f with respect to (the only variable) x. Hence, $Df(x)$ is the usual derivative $f'(x)$.

Assume that $f(\mathbf{x}): U \subseteq \mathbb{R}^m \to \mathbb{R}$ is a real-valued function of m variables. Then $Df(\mathbf{x})$ is the $1 \times m$ matrix

$$Df(\mathbf{x}) = \begin{bmatrix} \dfrac{\partial f}{\partial x_1}(\mathbf{x}) & \dfrac{\partial f}{\partial x_2}(\mathbf{x}) & \cdots & \dfrac{\partial f}{\partial x_m}(\mathbf{x}) \end{bmatrix},$$

whose only row consists of partial derivatives of f with respect to all variables $x_1, \ldots, x_m$, evaluated at $\mathbf{x} = (x_1, \ldots, x_m)$. Interpreted as a vector, $Df(\mathbf{x})$ is called the *gradient* of f at $\mathbf{x}$, and is denoted by $grad f(\mathbf{x})$ or $\nabla f(\mathbf{x})$. We will study the gradient in detail in Section 2.7.

146

Let $\mathbf{c} \colon [a, b] \to \mathbb{R}^n$ be a vector-valued function of one variable (we use t rather than x or x_1 to denote the independent variable). In this case, $D\mathbf{c}(t)$ is the $n \times 1$ matrix

$$D\mathbf{c}(t) = \begin{bmatrix} x_1'(t) \\ x_2'(t) \\ \vdots \\ x_n'(t) \end{bmatrix},$$

whose column consists of the derivatives of the components $x_1, \ldots, x_m$ of $\mathbf{c}$ with respect to t [since x_i are functions of one variable, we use x_i' instead of $\partial x_i / \partial t$ to denote the derivative]. Evaluated at a point t_0 and interpreted as a vector, $D\mathbf{c}(t_0)$ is called the *tangent vector* [provided that $D\mathbf{c}(t_0) \neq \mathbf{0}$], or the *velocity vector* of $\mathbf{c}$, and is denoted by $\mathbf{c}'(t_0)$.

The function $\mathbf{c}$ is called a *path* in $\mathbb{R}^n$. We study paths and related concepts (tangent vectors, velocity, etc.) in Section 2.5, and also in Chapter 3.

▶ **EXAMPLE 2.40** Gradient of the Gravitational Potential

Consider the gravitational potential function

$$V(x, y, z) = -\frac{GMm}{\sqrt{x^2 + y^2 + z^2}}$$

discussed in Example 2.10. Compute its gradient $\nabla V(x, y, z)$.

SOLUTION By the chain rule,

$$\frac{\partial V}{\partial x} = \frac{1}{2} GMm (x^2 + y^2 + z^2)^{-3/2} \cdot 2x.$$

The partial derivatives $\partial V / \partial y$ and $\partial V / \partial z$ are computed in the same way. Hence,

$$\nabla V(x, y, z) = DV(x, y, z) = \begin{bmatrix} \dfrac{\partial V}{\partial x} & \dfrac{\partial V}{\partial y} & \dfrac{\partial V}{\partial z} \end{bmatrix}$$

$$= \begin{bmatrix} \dfrac{GMm}{(x^2 + y^2 + z^2)^{3/2}} x & \dfrac{GMm}{(x^2 + y^2 + z^2)^{3/2}} y & \dfrac{GMm}{(x^2 + y^2 + z^2)^{3/2}} z \end{bmatrix}.$$

Rewriting ∇V as a vector, we obtain (write $\mathbf{r} = x\mathbf{i} + y\mathbf{j} + z\mathbf{k}$)

$$\nabla V(x, y, z) = \frac{GMm}{(x^2 + y^2 + z^2)^{3/2}} (x\mathbf{i} + y\mathbf{j} + z\mathbf{k}) = \frac{GMm}{||\mathbf{r}||^3} \mathbf{r}.$$

Note that $GMm\mathbf{r}/||\mathbf{r}||^3$ is the negative of the gravitational force field. ◀

Example 2.40 shows that $\mathbf{F} = -\nabla V$, where $\mathbf{F}$ is the gravitational force field. In general, a force field $\mathbf{F}$ satisfying this formula is called *conservative*, and the scalar function V is the *potential function*. We will study properties of conservative fields and potential functions in Section 5.4.

Derivative and Differentiability

DEFINITION 2.13   Differentiability of a Vector-Valued Function

A vector-valued function $\mathbf{F} = (F_1, \ldots, F_n) \colon U \subseteq \mathbb{R}^m \to \mathbb{R}^n$, defined on an open set $U \subseteq \mathbb{R}^m$, is *differentiable at* $\mathbf{a} \in U$ if

   (a) all partial derivatives of the components $F_1, \ldots, F_n$ of $\mathbf{F}$ exist at $\mathbf{a}$, and

   (b) the matrix of partial derivatives $D\mathbf{F}(\mathbf{a})$ of $\mathbf{F}$ at $\mathbf{a}$ satisfies

$$\lim_{\mathbf{x} \to \mathbf{a}} \frac{||\mathbf{F}(\mathbf{x}) - \mathbf{F}(\mathbf{a}) - D\mathbf{F}(\mathbf{a})(\mathbf{x} - \mathbf{a})||}{||\mathbf{x} - \mathbf{a}||} = 0, \tag{2.15}$$

where $||.||$ in the numerator denotes the length in $\mathbb{R}^n$, and $||.||$ in the denominator is the length in $\mathbb{R}^m$.   ◀

DEFINITION 2.14   Derivative of a Vector-Valued Function

If a vector-valued function $\mathbf{F}$ satisfies the conditions (a) and (b) of Definition 2.13, then the matrix $D\mathbf{F}(\mathbf{a})$ of partial derivatives given by (2.14) is called the *derivative of* $\mathbf{F}$ *at* $\mathbf{a}$.   ◀

The subtractions in the numerator of (2.15) take place in $\mathbb{R}^n$: clearly, $\mathbf{F}(\mathbf{x})$ and $\mathbf{F}(\mathbf{a})$ are in $\mathbb{R}^n$; the third term is the product of the $n \times m$ matrix $D\mathbf{F}(\mathbf{a})$ and the vector (viewed as an $m \times 1$ matrix) $\mathbf{x} - \mathbf{a}$, and is therefore an $n \times 1$ matrix, that is, an element of $\mathbb{R}^n$.

   Let us look more closely at condition (b) in Definition 2.13. Assume that $m = n = 1$; that is, consider the function $f \colon \mathbb{R} \to \mathbb{R}$ (a real-valued function of one variable can be considered as a special case of a general vector-valued function if n is allowed to equal 1).

   Then $Df(x) = f'(x)$ and the statement (b) reads (the symbol $||.||$ is replaced by the absolute value, since all terms involved are real numbers)

$$\lim_{x \to a} \frac{\left| f(x) - \left[f(a) + f'(a)(x - a) \right] \right|}{|x - a|} = 0. \tag{2.16}$$

The expression

$$L_a(x) = f(a) + f'(a)(x - a)$$

appearing in the numerator of (2.16) is called the *linear approximation* or the *linearization* of f at a. Geometrically, L_a represents the equation of the line tangent to the graph of f at a [it is written in point-slope form: the point is $(a, f(a))$, and $f'(a)$ is the slope].

   Since the limit in (2.16) is zero and the denominator goes to zero, it follows that the numerator $|f(x) - L_a(x)|$ has to approach zero as well. Consequently, (2.16) states that $L_a(x)$ approaches $f(x)$ as x approaches a; that is, *near* a the functions $f(x)$ and $L_a(x)$ have approximately the same value. This is not really important: as a matter of fact, *any* line that goes through $(a, f(a))$ satisfies this property. However, formula (2.16) says a lot more than that: if we rewrite it as

$$\lim_{x \to a} \left| \frac{f(x) - f(a) - f'(a)(x - a)}{x - a} \right| = \lim_{x \to a} \left| \frac{f(x) - f(a)}{x - a} - f'(a) \right| = 0,$$

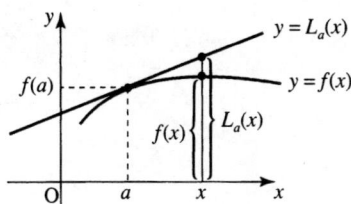

Figure 2.47 The tangent as a linear approximation.

we see that the *slopes* of $f(x)$ and $L_a(x)$ [recall that the slope of $L_a(x)$ is $f'(a)$] must approach each other. And that is true *only* for the tangent line.

In other words, $L_a(x)$ is a *good approximation* to $f(x)$ near a; that is, the tangent line is a *good approximation* to the curve $y = f(x)$ near a; see Figure 2.47.

▶ **EXAMPLE 2.41**

Let $f(x) = xe^{2x}$. Its linearization at $a = 1$ is $[f'(x) = e^{2x} + 2xe^{2x}]$

$$L_1(x) = f(1) + f'(1)(x-1) = e^2 + 3e^2(x-1).$$

Take a point near $a = 1$, say, $x = 1.0001$. Then $L_1(1.0001) = 7.3912728$ approximates the value of the function $f(1.0001) = 7.3912731$.

Clearly, the closer the number x is to 1, the better the approximation. For values of x that are far from 1, the linear approximation does not make any sense. For example, $L_1(0) = -2e^2 = -14.778112$, whereas $f(0) = 0$. ◀

Figure 2.48(a) shows the graph of the function $f(x)$ from the previous example on the interval $[0.5, 1.5]$. As we zoom in on the graph (in Figure 2.48(b), $f(x)$ is shown on the interval $[0.9, 1.1]$, and in Figure 2.48(c) we used $[0.95, 1.05]$), we see that it looks like a straight line.

The fact that $f(x)$ is differentiable at $x = 1$ means that, as we continue zooming in on its graph around $x = 1$, it will resemble, closer and closer, a straight line. That straight line is the linear approximation (the tangent!) of $f(x)$ at $x = 1$. This property is sometimes called a *local linearity*. For instance, assuming that the curve in Figure 2.48(c)

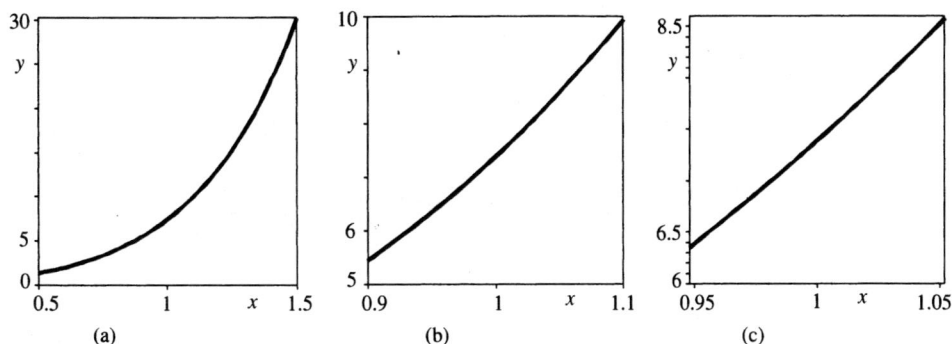

Figure 2.48 Zooming in on the graph of $f(x)$ near $x = 1$.

149

is a straight line, we compute its slope [using the endpoints $(0.95, 6.35)$ and $(1.05, 8.6)$] to be $(8.6 - 6.35)/(1.05 - 0.95) = 22.5$. This is an approximation of the slope $(3e^2 \approx 22.17)$ of the linear approximation of $f(x)$ [and of $f(x)$] at $x = 1$.

Next, we discuss another special case, that of a function $f: \mathbb{R}^2 \to \mathbb{R}$ (i.e., $m = 2$ and $n = 1$). In that case [with the notation $\mathbf{x} = (x, y)$ and $\mathbf{a} = (a, b)$],

$$Df(\mathbf{a})(\mathbf{x} - \mathbf{a}) = \begin{bmatrix} \dfrac{\partial f}{\partial x}(a, b) & \dfrac{\partial f}{\partial y}(a, b) \end{bmatrix} \cdot \begin{bmatrix} x - a \\ y - b \end{bmatrix}$$

$$= \frac{\partial f}{\partial x}(a, b) \cdot (x - a) + \frac{\partial f}{\partial y}(a, b) \cdot (y - b),$$

and hence (2.15) reads

$$\lim_{(x,y) \to (a,b)} \frac{\left| f(x, y) - L_{(a,b)}(x, y) \right|}{\sqrt{(x - a)^2 + (y - b)^2}} = 0, \tag{2.17}$$

where

$$L_{(a,b)}(x, y) = f(a, b) + \frac{\partial f}{\partial x}(a, b) \cdot (x - a) + \frac{\partial f}{\partial y}(a, b) \cdot (y - b) \tag{2.18}$$

is the *linear approximation* or the *linearization* of f at (a, b). It is a *good approximation* of f near (a, b) in the sense that the values of f and $L_{(a,b)}$ for points *near* (a, b) are almost the same; see Figure 2.49. This property does not make $L_{(a,b)}(x, y)$ special. What makes it unique (among all linear functions) is the requirement that it must satisfy (2.17). (For a proof of this fact, see Exercise 45.)

As an illustration, consider $f(x, y) = 1 - x^2 - 2y^2$. Its linearization at $\mathbf{a} = (1, 1)$ is

$$L_{(1,1)}(x, y) = f(1, 1) + (-2x)|_{(1,1)} \cdot (x - 1) + (-4y)|_{(1,1)} \cdot (y - 1) = 4 - 2x - 4y.$$

Take a point near $(1, 1)$, for instance, $\mathbf{x} = (0.96, 1.02)$. The value of the function $f(\mathbf{x}) = f(0.96, 1.02) = 1 - (0.96)^2 - 2(1.02)^2 = -2.0024$ is approximated by the value of its linearization $L_{(1,1)}(\mathbf{x}) = L_{(1,1)}(0.96, 1.02) = -2$.

Geometrically, linear approximation represents the equation of a plane in $\mathbb{R}^3$ (in the previous example, $z = 4 - 2x - 4y$). This plane has the point $(a, b, f(a, b)) = (a, b, L_{(a,b)}(a, b))$ in common with the graph of f (see Figure 2.49) and is a unique plane that satisfies (2.17). A plane with these properties is called a *tangent plane*. It is defined by

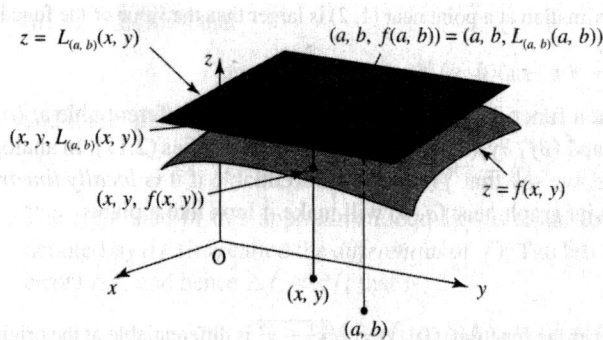

Figure 2.49 Linear approximation $L_{(a,b)}(x, y)$ of a function $f(x, y)$ at (a, b).

the equation

$$z = L_{(a,b)}(x, y) = f(a, b) + \frac{\partial f}{\partial x}(a, b) \cdot (x - a) + \frac{\partial f}{\partial y}(a, b) \cdot (y - b). \qquad (2.19)$$

Based on the two examples we have considered, we say in general that the *linear approximation* $L_{\mathbf{a}}(\mathbf{x})$ of $\mathbf{F}(\mathbf{x})$ at $\mathbf{a}$ or the *linearization* of $\mathbf{F}(\mathbf{x})$ at $\mathbf{a}$, given by

$$L_{\mathbf{a}}(\mathbf{x}) = \mathbf{F}(\mathbf{a}) + D\mathbf{F}(\mathbf{a})(\mathbf{x} - \mathbf{a}), \qquad (2.20)$$

is a *good approximation* of $\mathbf{F}$ near $\mathbf{a}$. Hence, according to Definition 2.13, a vector-valued function $\mathbf{F}$ is differentiable at $\mathbf{a}$ if and only if all partial derivatives of its components exist at $\mathbf{a}$ and its linearization at $\mathbf{a}$ is a *good approximation* in the sense just explained. (Another special case, that of a function $\mathbf{F} \colon \mathbb{R}^2 \to \mathbb{R}^2$, will be studied in Section 6.4.)

► EXAMPLE 2.42

Compute the equation of the plane tangent to the graph of the function $f(x, y) = \arctan(xy)$ at the point $(1, 1)$.

SOLUTION From

$$\frac{\partial f}{\partial x} = \frac{y}{1 + x^2 y^2} \quad \text{and} \quad \frac{\partial f}{\partial y} = \frac{x}{1 + x^2 y^2},$$

we get $(\partial f/\partial x)(1, 1) = 1/2$ and $(\partial f/\partial y)(1, 1) = 1/2$. Since $f(1, 1) = \pi/4$, the equation of the tangent plane is $z = \frac{\pi}{4} + \frac{1}{2}(x - 1) + \frac{1}{2}(y - 1)$, that is, $2x + 2y - 4z + \pi - 4 = 0$. ◄

► EXAMPLE 2.43

Let $f(x, y) = 13 - x^2 - y^2$. Suppose that we use the linear approximation $L_{(1,2)}(x, y)$ of $f(x, y)$ at $(1, 2)$ to approximate the value of f at a point (x, y) near $(1, 2)$. Is this an overestimate or an underestimate of $f(x, y)$?

SOLUTION The level curves $f(x, y) = 13 - x^2 - y^2 = C$ are circles of radius $\sqrt{13 - C}$ for $C < 13$. The intersections of the graph of f with the xz-plane and the yz-plane are the parabolas $z = 13 - x^2$ and $z = 13 - y^2$, both of which are concave down. In other words, the graph of f is a surface built of circles, smaller ones placed on top of the larger ones in such a way that the vertical cross-sections are parabolas. The surface is concave down, so the tangent plane must lie above it. Hence, the value of the linear approximation at a point near $(1, 2)$ is larger than the value of the function. The estimate is an overestimate. ◄

Recall that a function $f(x, y)$ of two variables is differentiable at (a, b) if and only if $(\partial f/\partial x)(a, b)$ and $(\partial f/\partial y)(a, b)$ exist and $f(x, y)$ satisfies (2.17). In analogy with functions of one variable, we say that $f(x, y)$ is differentiable if it is *locally linear* at (a, b); that is, zooming in on its graph near (a, b) will make it look like a plane.

► EXAMPLE 2.44

Determine whether the function $f(x, y) = \sqrt{x^2 + y^2}$ is differentiable at the origin.

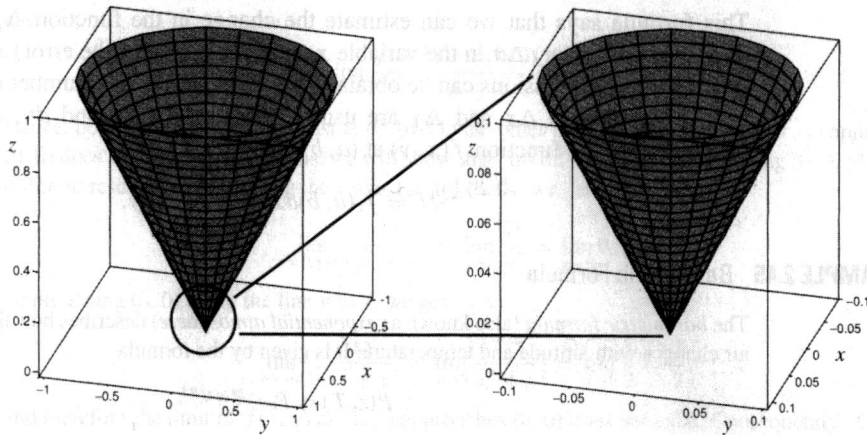

Figure 2.50 Graph of $f(x, y) = \sqrt{x^2 + y^2}$ with a zoom-in near the origin.

SOLUTION

The graph of $f(x, y)$ is a cone whose vertex is at the origin; see Figure 2.50. Zooming in on the graph near the origin, we see that the vertex remains, that is, the graph does not flatten. In other words, local linearity does not hold at the origin. Thus, we believe that f is not differentiable at the origin.

To confirm our intuitive reasoning, we compute

$$\frac{\partial f}{\partial x}(0, 0) = \lim_{h \to 0} \frac{f(h, 0) - f(0, 0)}{h} = \lim_{h \to 0} \frac{\sqrt{h^2} - 0}{h} = \lim_{h \to 0} \frac{|h|}{h}.$$

As $h \to 0^+$, $|h|/h \to 1$, and as $h \to 0^-$, $|h|/h \to -1$; that is, the limit of $|h|/h$ as $h \to 0$ does not exist. So, $(\partial f/\partial x)(0, 0)$ does not exist and thus f is not differentiable at the origin. (See Exercise 46 for an alternate proof.) ◀

Differential

We now discuss another interpretation of the linear approximation formula. Choose a point (a, b) in the domain of a differentiable function $f: \mathbb{R}^2 \to \mathbb{R}$. Measure the value of f at (a, b) and then move to a nearby point $(x, y) = (a + \Delta x, b + \Delta y)$ ("nearby" means that Δx and Δy are small). We would like to compare the value of f at this point with its initial value $f(a, b)$. In other words, we would like to compute or estimate the change (sometimes called the error) Δf in f, defined by $\Delta f = f(x, y) - f(a, b) = f(a + \Delta x, b + \Delta y) - f(a, b)$.

Since $f(x, y) \approx L_{(a,b)}(x, y)$, where $L_{(a,b)}(x, y)$ is the linear approximation of f at (a, b), it follows that

$$f(x, y) \approx f(a, b) + f_x(a, b)(x - a) + f_y(a, b)(y - b),$$

and therefore,

$$f(x, y) - f(a, b) \approx f_x(a, b)(x - a) + f_y(a, b)(y - b). \tag{2.21}$$

The right side of this approximate equality is equal to $f_x(a, b)\Delta x + f_y(a, b)\Delta y$ and is denoted by df (it is called the *differential* of f). The left side in (2.21) is the change (or the error) Δf, and hence $\Delta f \approx df$; that is,

$$\Delta f \approx f_x(a, b)\Delta x + f_y(a, b)\Delta y.$$

This formula says that we can estimate the change in the function Δf in terms of the change (or the error) Δx in the variable x and the change (or the error) Δy in the variable y. Analogous expressions can be obtained for a function of any number of variables.

The quantities Δx and Δy are usually replaced by dx and dy, and we write the differential of the function $f(x, y)$ at (a, b) as

$$df = f_x(a, b)dx + f_y(a, b)dy. \tag{2.22}$$

► **EXAMPLE 2.45** Barometric Formula

The *barometric formula* (also known as *exponential atmosphere*) describes how the pressure P of the air changes with altitude and temperature. It is given by the formula

$$P(z, T) = P_0 e^{-Mg_0 z/RT},$$

where P_0 is the air pressure at sea level, $M = 0.029$ g is the mass of one mole of air, g_0 is the acceleration due to gravity (at sea level), R is the universal gas constant (see Example 2.8), T is the absolute temperature (in degrees Kelvin), and z is the height (in kilometers) above Earth's surface. We compute the differential of P as

$$dP = -\frac{Mg_0 P_0}{RT} e^{-Mg_0 z/RT} dz + \frac{Mg_0 z P_0}{RT^2} e^{-Mg_0 z/RT} dT.$$

The coefficient $-(Mg_0 P_0/RT)e^{-Mg_0 z/RT}$ of dz is negative since an increase in height (with the temperature kept fixed) will decrease air pressure.

The coefficient $(Mg_0 z P_0/RT^2)e^{-Mg_0 z/RT}$ of dT is positive since an increase in temperature (with no change in height) will cause an increase in air pressure.

Although this is a simplified model (it assumes that T does not change with altitude), it is fairly accurate to heights of about 140 km. In parts of the atmosphere where the temperature drops with the height (for instance, $0 \leq z \leq 15$ and $50 \leq z \leq 80$), we conclude that the above model gives an overestimate for the air pressure. ◄

Differentiability and Continuity

In the theory of functions of one variable, one proves that if a function f has a derivative, then it is continuous. The analogous statement ("differentiability implies continuity") also holds for functions of more than one variable; see Theorem 2.4. However, a function whose partial derivatives exist might not be continuous, as the following example shows.

► **EXAMPLE 2.46**

Define $f: \mathbb{R}^2 \to \mathbb{R}$ by

$$f(x, y) = \begin{cases} \dfrac{xy}{x^2 + y^2} & \text{if } (x, y) \neq (0, 0) \\ 0 & \text{if } (x, y) = (0, 0) \end{cases}$$

By definition,

$$\frac{\partial f}{\partial x}(0, 0) = \lim_{h \to 0} \frac{f(h, 0) - f(0, 0)}{h} = \lim_{h \to 0} \frac{0 - 0}{h} = 0$$

and

$$\frac{\partial f}{\partial y}(0, 0) = \lim_{h \to 0} \frac{f(0, h) - f(0, 0)}{h} = \lim_{h \to 0} \frac{0 - 0}{h} = 0.$$

Hence, both partial derivatives exist at $(0, 0)$. On the other hand, the limit of f as (x, y) approaches $(0, 0)$ does not exist. To prove this, we will show that two different ways of reaching $(0, 0)$ yield two different results. Walking along the y-axis toward $(0, 0)$, we get

$$\lim_{x=0, y \to 0} \frac{xy}{x^2 + y^2} = \lim_{y \to 0} \frac{0}{y^2} = \lim_{y \to 0} 0 = 0.$$

Approaching $(0, 0)$ along the line $y = x$, we get

$$\lim_{(x,y) \to (0,0)} \frac{xy}{x^2 + y^2} = \lim_{x \to 0} \frac{x^2}{x^2 + x^2} = \lim_{x \to 0} \frac{1}{2} = \frac{1}{2},$$

and therefore the limit of $f(x, y)$ as (x, y) approaches $(0, 0)$ does not exist. Consequently, f cannot be continuous at $(0, 0)$. ◄

Therefore, the mere existence of partial derivatives does not imply the continuity of a function. However, an extra assumption will fix this problem (see Theorem 2.4).

► **EXAMPLE 2.47**

Show that the function $f(x, y)$ defined in Example 2.46 is not differentiable at $(0, 0)$.

SOLUTION

In Example 2.46 we obtained $(\partial f/\partial x)(0, 0) = 0$ and $(\partial f/\partial y)(0, 0) = 0$; thus, the condition on the existence of partial derivatives of f holds.

Next, we check (2.17). If f had a linear approximation at $(0, 0)$, it would have to be

$$L_{(0,0)} = f(0, 0) + \frac{\partial f}{\partial x}(0, 0)(x - 0) + \frac{\partial f}{\partial y}(0, 0)(y - 0) = 0.$$

The limit in (2.17) is then equal to

$$\lim_{(x,y) \to (0,0)} \frac{\left| \dfrac{xy}{x^2 + y^2} - 0 \right|}{\sqrt{x^2 + y^2}} = \lim_{(x,y) \to (0,0)} \frac{|xy|}{(x^2 + y^2)^{3/2}}.$$

Using the approach $y = x$, we get

$$\lim_{(x,y) \to (0,0)} \frac{|xy|}{(x^2 + y^2)^{3/2}} = \lim_{x \to 0} \frac{x^2}{(2x^2)^{3/2}} = \lim_{x \to 0} \frac{1}{2^{3/2}x}.$$

Since the limit on the right side does not exist, it follows that (2.17) does not hold, and thus f is not differentiable at $(0, 0)$. ◄

THEOREM 2.4   Differentiable Functions Are Continuous

Let $\mathbf{F}: U \subseteq \mathbb{R}^m \to \mathbb{R}^n$ be a vector-valued function and let $\mathbf{a} \in U$. If $\mathbf{F}$ is differentiable at $\mathbf{a}$, then it is continuous at $\mathbf{a}$. ◄

In other words, a function that is not continuous at $\mathbf{a}$ cannot be differentiable there either. Thus, the conclusion that we arrived at in Example 2.46 implies that f is not differentiable at $(0, 0)$ (this is an alternative to the proof presented in Example 2.47).

Theorem 2.4 is the correct generalization of the one-variable case: namely, if the components of **F** have partial derivatives *and* the derivative $D\mathbf{F}$ is a good approximation of **F**, then **F** is continuous. The proof of the theorem is presented in Appendix A.

A function whose partial derivatives exist might not be differentiable (see Examples 2.46 and 2.47). In other words, the existence of partial derivatives does not imply differentiability. However, if all partial derivatives are continuous, the implication is valid, as the following theorem shows.

THEOREM 2.5   Continuity of Partial Derivatives Implies Differentiability

Let $\mathbf{F}: U \subseteq \mathbb{R}^m \to \mathbb{R}^n$ be a vector-valued function with components $F_1, \ldots, F_n: U \subseteq \mathbb{R}^m \to \mathbb{R}$. If all partial derivatives $\partial F_i / \partial x_j$ ($i = 1, \ldots, n$, $j = 1 \ldots, m$) are continuous at **a**, then **F** is differentiable at **a**. ◀

Proving the differentiablity of a function using Definition 2.13 is usually fairly complicated. This theorem gives a more convenient alternative: all we have to do is to check that all partial derivatives exist and are continuous at the point(s) in question.

The proof of Theorem 2.5 is given in Appendix A.

DEFINITION 2.15   Function of Class C^1

A function whose partial derivatives exist and are continuous is said to be *continuously differentiable,* or *of class C^1*. ◀

The definitions and theorems we have stated could be visually represented in a diagram; see Figure 2.51 (containment means implication; i.e., functions contained in one "box" have properties defining any other "box" that contains it).

Let us identify a few facts from the diagram. Functions of class C^1 (those are in the smallest "box") are differentiable (those functions are in the larger box)—that is the statement of Theorem 2.5. Differentiable functions are continuous (Theorem 2.4). If a function has partial derivatives, it might not be differentiable (that was the conclusion of Examples 2.46 and 2.47). Not every differentiable function is of class C^1. A function can be continuous, but its partial derivatives might not exist (see Example 2.44), etc.

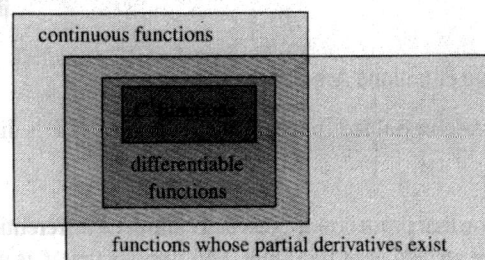

Figure 2.51   Continuity, differentiability, and partial derivatives.

► **EXERCISES 2.4**

Exercises 1 to 6: Determine which of the following sets are open.

1. $U = \{(x, y) \mid 2 < x^2 + y^2 < 3\} \subseteq \mathbb{R}^2$ 2. $U = \{(x, y, z) \mid x \geq 0\} \subseteq \mathbb{R}^3$

3. $U = \{(x, y) \mid x + y = 2\} \subseteq \mathbb{R}^2$ 4. $U = \{(x, y) \mid x + y < 2\} \subseteq \mathbb{R}^2$

5. $U = \{(x, y, z) \mid xyz > 0\} \subseteq \mathbb{R}^3$ 6. $U = \{(x, y, z) \mid x \neq 0, y > 0\} \subseteq \mathbb{R}^3$

7. Consider the function $f(x, y)$ whose contour diagram is shown in Figure 2.45.

(a) Determine the sign of $(\partial f / \partial x)(5, 3)$.

(b) Which of the two numbers, $(\partial f / \partial x)(10, 3)$ or $(\partial f / \partial x)(10, 5)$, is larger?

8. Draw a contour diagram of a function $f(x, y)$ that satisfies $(\partial f / \partial x)(x, y) > 0$ and $(\partial f / \partial y)(x, y) < 0$ for all (x, y).

Exercises 9 to 18: Find the indicated partial derivatives.

9. $f(x, y) = x^y + y \ln x$; f_x, f_y ⑩ $f(x, y, z) = xe^{yz^2}$; f_x, f_y, f_z

11. $f(x, y, z) = \ln (x + y + z^2)$; f_x, f_z 12. $f(x, y) = \arctan (x/y)$; f_x, f_y

13. $f(x, y) = e^{xy} \cos x \sin y$; f_x, f_y ⑭ $f(x, y, z) = x\sqrt{y\sqrt{z}}$; f_x, f_y, f_z

15. $f(x_1, \ldots, x_m) = \sqrt{x_1^2 + \cdots + x_m^2}$; $\partial f / \partial x_i$, $i = 1, \ldots, m$

16. $f(x_1, \ldots, x_m) = e^{x_1 \cdots x_m}$; $\partial f / \partial x_i$, $i = 1, \ldots, m$

17. $f(x, y) = \int_0^x te^{-t^2} dt$; f_x, f_y 18. $f(x, y) = \int_{\ln y}^0 (t + 1)^2 dt$; f_x, f_y

Exercises 19 to 22: The function $z(x, y)$ is defined in terms of two differentiable real-valued functions f and g of one variable. Compute z_x and z_y.

19. $z = f(x) + g(y)$ 20. $z = f(x)g(y)$

21. $z = f(x)/g(y)$ 22. $z = f(x)^{g(y)}$

23. A hiker is standing at the point $(2, 1, 11)$ on a hill whose shape is given by the graph of the function $z = 14 - (x - 3)^2 - 2(y - 2)^4$. Assume that the x-axis points east and the y-axis points north. In which of the two directions (east or north) is the hill steeper?

24. The volume of a certain amount of gas is determined by $V = 0.12TP^{-1}$, where T is the temperature and P is the pressure. Compute and interpret $\partial V / \partial P$ and $\partial V / \partial T$ when $P = 10$ and $T = 370$.

25. Consider the function $f(x, y) = -xe^{-x^2 - 2y^2}$.

(a) Compute $f_y(2, 3)$.

(b) Find the curve that is the intersection of the graph of f and the vertical plane $x = 2$ and compute the slope of its tangent at $y = 3$.

(c) Using (a) and (b), give a geometric interpretation of $f_y(2, 3)$.

26. Let $u(x, y, t) = e^{-2t} \sin (3x) \cos (2y)$ denote the vertical displacement of a vibrating membrane from the point (x, y) in the xy-plane at the time t. Compute $u_x(x, y, t)$, $u_y(x, y, t)$, and $u_t(x, y, t)$ and give physical interpretations of your results.

Exercises 27 to 31: Compute the derivative of the function $\mathbf{F}$ at the point $\mathbf{a}$.

27. $\mathbf{F}(x, y) = (y, x, 11)$, $\mathbf{a} = (0, 0)$ 28. $\mathbf{F}(x, y) = (e^{xy}, x^2 + y^2)$, $\mathbf{a} = (a_1, a_2)$

29. $\mathbf{F}(x, y, z) = (\ln (x^2 + y^2 + z^2), 2xy + z)$, $\mathbf{a} = (1, 1, 0)$

30. $\mathbf{F}(x, y) = (x/\sqrt{x^2 + y^2}, y/\sqrt{x^2 + y^2})$, $\mathbf{a} = (a_1, a_2) \neq (0, 0)$

31. $f(x, y, z) = \|x\mathbf{i} + y\mathbf{j} + z\mathbf{k}\|^2$, $\mathbf{a} = (a_1, a_2, a_3)$

32. Compute $\nabla f(2, 1, -1)$ if $f(x, y, z) = xy \ln (z^2 + xy)$.

33. The electrostatic force field $\mathbf{F}(\mathbf{r})$ and the electrostatic potential $V(\mathbf{r})$ were defined in Example 2.11. Show that $\mathbf{F}(\mathbf{r}) = -\nabla V(\mathbf{r})$. Compare with Example 2.40.

34. Let $f(x, y, z) = xyz(x^2 + y^2 + z^2)^{-2}$. Compute $\nabla f(x, y, z)$ for $(x, y, z) \neq (0, 0, 0)$.

35. Define $f: \mathbb{R}^3 \to \mathbb{R}$ by $f(\mathbf{x}) = \|\mathbf{x}\|$. Find $\nabla f(\mathbf{x})$ and state its domain.

Exercises 36 to 42: Find the linear approximation of the function f at the point $\mathbf{a}$.

36. $f(x, y) = e^{-x^2 - y^2}$, $\mathbf{a} = (0, 0)$

37. $f(x, y) = \ln (3x + 2y)$, $\mathbf{a} = (2, -1)$

38. $f(x, y) = xy(x^2 + y^2)^{-1}$, $\mathbf{a} = (0, 1)$

39. $f(x, y) = x^2 - xy + y^2/2 + 3$, $\mathbf{a} = (3, 2)$

40. $f(x, y, z) = \ln (x^2 - y^2 + z)$, $\mathbf{a} = (3, 3, 1)$

41. $f(x, y, z) = \sqrt{x^2 + y^2 + z^2}$, $\mathbf{a} = (0, 1, 1)$

42. $f(x, y) = \int_x^y e^{-t^2} dt$, $\mathbf{a} = (1, 1)$

43. Verify that $xy(x + y)^{-1} \approx \frac{6}{5} + \frac{9}{25}(x - 2) + \frac{4}{25}(y - 3)$, for (x, y) sufficiently close to $(2, 3)$.

44. Prove that $\ln (2x^2 + 3y - 4) \approx 4x + 3y - 7$, for (x, y) sufficiently close to $(1, 1)$.

45. Assume that $f(x, y)$ is differentiable at (a, b) and let $\overline{L}(x, y) = f(a, b) + m(x - a) + n(y - b)$ be a linear function that satisfies (2.17), that is,

$$\lim_{(x,y) \to (a,b)} \frac{\left| f(x, y) - \overline{L}(x, y) \right|}{\sqrt{(x - a)^2 + (y - b)^2}} = 0.$$

(a) Substitute $y = b$ into the above formula to show that $m = (\partial f/\partial x)(a, b)$.

(b) Prove that $n = (\partial f/\partial y)(a, b)$ and conclude that $\overline{L}$ must be equal to the linear approximation $L_{(a,b)}$.

46. Consider the function $f(x, y) = \sqrt{x^2 + y^2}$ (see Example 2.44) and assume that it has a linear approximation $L_{(0,0)}(x, y)$ at $(0, 0)$.

(a) Explain why $L_{(0,0)}(x, y) = mx + ny$ for some real numbers m and n.

(b) Use (2.17) to show that f is differentiable at the origin if and only if

$$\lim_{(x,y) \to (0,0)} \left(1 - \frac{mx + ny}{\sqrt{x^2 + y^2}} \right) = 0.$$

(c) Use the approach $x \to 0$ and $y = 0$ to show that the above limit is not equal to 0. Conclude that f is not differentiable at the origin.

Exercises 47 to 51: Approximate the value of the given expression and compare it (except in Exercise 51) with the calculator value.

47. $\sqrt{0.99^3 + 2.02^3}$

48. $-0.09\sqrt{4.11^3 - 14.98}$

49. $7.95 \ln 1.02$

50. $\sin (\pi/50) \cos (49\pi/50)$

51. $\int_{0.995}^{1.02} e^{-t^2} dt$

Exercises 52 to 55: Compare the values of Δf and df.

52. $f(x, y) = x^2 - xy + 2y^2 + 1$, $(a, b) = (0, 1)$, $\Delta x = 0.01$, $\Delta y = 0.2$

53. $f(x, y) = e^x - ye^y$, $(a, b) = (0, 1)$, $\Delta x = 0.3$, $\Delta y = 0.01$

54. $f(x, y) = x^3 + xy + y^3$, $(a, b) = (-2, 1)$, $(x, y) = (-2.05, 0.9)$

55. $f(x, y, z) = x^2 y - xyz + z^3$, $(a, b, c) = (1, 2, -1)$, $\Delta x = -0.02$, $\Delta y = 0.01$, $\Delta z = 0.02$

56. Estimate the maximum possible error in computing $f(x, y) = x \cos y$, where $x = 2$ and $y = \pi/3$, with maximum possible errors $\Delta x = 0.2$ and $\Delta y = 0.1$.

57. The pressure in an ideal gas is given by $P(T, V) = RnT/V$; see Example 2.8. Compute the differential of P and explain the signs of the coefficients of dT and dV.

58. Consider the Cobb–Douglas function $P(L, K) = bL^\alpha K^{1-\alpha}$ discussed in Example 2.6. Compute the differential dP and explain the signs of the coefficients of dL and dK.

59. About how accurately can the volume of a cylinder be calculated from the measurements of its height and radius that are in error by 1.5%?

60. The dimensions of a closed rectangular box are measured as 20, 50, and 120 cm, respectively, with a possible error of 0.4 cm in each dimension. Estimate the maximum error in computing the volume and the surface area of the box.

61. The length and the width of a rectangle are measured with a possible error of 2% in length and 3% in width. Approximate the error in computing the area of the rectangle.

62. Let $f(x, y) = 2x^2 y^3$. Estimate the change in the function f if x increases by 3% and y increases by 2%.

63. Find the equation of the tangent plane to the graph of the function $z = 6 - x^2 - y^2$ at the point $(1, 2, 1)$.

64. Find the equation of the tangent plane to the surface $z = 3xy/(x - 2y)$ at the point $(3, 1, 9)$. Check whether the tangent plane contains the origin.

65. Define the function $f: \mathbb{R}^2 \to \mathbb{R}$ by

$$f(x, y) = \begin{cases} y \ln(x^2 + y^2) & \text{if } (x, y) \neq (0, 0) \\ 0 & \text{if } (x, y) = (0, 0) \end{cases}$$

Show that f_x is defined for all (x, y), but that f_x is not continuous at $(0, 0)$.

66. Define the function $f: \mathbb{R}^2 \to \mathbb{R}$ by

$$f(x, y) = \begin{cases} \dfrac{xy^2}{x^2 + y^4} & \text{if } (x, y) \neq (0, 0) \\ 0 & \text{if } (x, y) = (0, 0) \end{cases}$$

(a) Is f continuous at $(0, 0)$?

(b) Compute the linear approximation (if it exists) at $(0, 0)$.

(c) Is f_x continuous at $(0, 0)$?

(d) Is f differentiable?

67. Show that the function $\mathbf{F}(x, y) = (x + y^2, 2xy)$ is differentiable at $(0, 0)$.

68. Show that the function $f(x, y) = (xy)^{1/5}$ is not differentiable at $(0, 0)$.

69. Consider the function

$$f(x, y) = \begin{cases} \ln (x^2 + y^2) & \text{if } (x, y) \neq (0, 0) \\ 0 & \text{if } (x, y) = (0, 0) \end{cases}.$$

(a) Is f differentiable at $(0, 0)$?

(b) Is it possible to conclude from (a) that f is continuous at $(0, 0)$?

(c) Is f continuous at $(0, 0)$?

▶ 2.5 PATHS AND CURVES IN $\mathbb{R}^2$ AND $\mathbb{R}^3$

A trajectory of a moving object, a sound wave, a current in an electric circuit, the conversion between degrees Fahrenheit and Celsius, or the dependence of air pressure on altitude can be visually represented as curves in a plane or in three-dimensional space. Various measurement instruments such as oscilloscopes, heart-beat monitors, computers, and other devices display their data in the form of curves, which are more convenient and easier to interpret than a listing of thousands of numbers. The graph of a real-valued function $y = f(x)$ is a curve. The equation $f(x, y) = 0$ represents a curve described in a slightly different way (it is given "implicitly").

Continuing with vector-valued functions, we now introduce a new way of defining a curve and study its properties (that we will find useful in subsequent sections). We will resume our investigation of curves in Chapter 3. Concepts relevant to integration along curves are discussed in Chapter 5.

We are going to restrict our study to $\mathbb{R}^2$ and $\mathbb{R}^3$, although all statements (except those involving cross products) hold in any dimension.

DEFINITION 2.16 Path and Curve

A *path* in $\mathbb{R}^3$ (or $\mathbb{R}^2$) is a function $\mathbf{c}: [a, b] \to \mathbb{R}^3$ (or $\mathbb{R}^2$), whose domain is a subset $[a, b] \subseteq \mathbb{R}$. The image of $\mathbf{c}$ is called a *curve* in $\mathbb{R}^3$ (or $\mathbb{R}^2$). The function $\mathbf{c}$ is also known as a *parametrization* (or *parametric representation* or *parametric equation*) of the curve. ◀

According to the definition, a path is a function, whereas a geometric object in $\mathbb{R}^3$ (or $\mathbb{R}^2$) that is the image of that function is called a curve. In other words, a path or parametrization (the two are synonyms) represents an analytic way of describing a curve. We will soon witness that a single curve can have infinitely many parametrizations, not all of them characterized by the same properties. The reasons why the distinction between a path and a curve is needed will surface in Chapter 3 and in sections on integration along paths.

On a few occasions we will use the term "curve" to refer to both notions since the context will keep the meaning clear. For example, if we talk about the composition of curves or velocity, we think of a function; on the other hand, the statement "curves are orthogonal to each other" refers to a curve as a geometric object. Likewise, we will use the same notation for both the path and the corresponding curve.

Sometimes, it is useful to extend the domain $[a, b]$ in the definition of a path $\mathbf{c}$ so that $a = -\infty$ or $b = \infty$, or both (i.e., intervals $(-\infty, b]$, $[a, \infty)$ or $(-\infty, \infty) = \mathbb{R}$ are allowed as the domain of **c**). This will enable us to describe, for example, lines (such as the tangent to a curve) as paths in a plane or in space. The variable of **c** is denoted by t and is often referred to as time. In components, we can represent a curve in $\mathbb{R}^2$ as

$$\mathbf{c}(t) = (x(t), y(t)), \qquad t \in [a, b],$$

and a curve in $\mathbb{R}^3$ as

$$\mathbf{c}(t) = (x(t), y(t), z(t)), \qquad t \in [a, b],$$

where $x(t)$, $y(t)$, and $z(t)$ are real-valued functions of t.

► **EXAMPLE 2.48**

The curve $\mathbf{c}_1$ parametrized by $\mathbf{c}_1(t) = (t \cos t, t \sin t)$, $t \in [0, 3\pi]$ in $\mathbb{R}^2$ has been drawn in Figure 2.52. Figure 2.53 shows the plot of the curve $\mathbf{c}_2$ in space given by $\mathbf{c}_2(t) = (\cos t, \sin t, \cos 4t)$, $t \in [0, 2\pi]$.

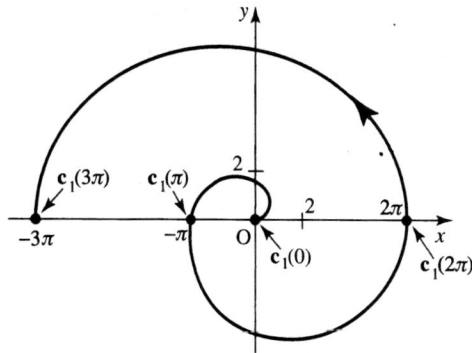

Figure 2.52 Curve $\mathbf{c}_1$ parametrized by $\mathbf{c}_1(t) = (t \cos t, t \sin t)$, $t \in [0, 3\pi]$.

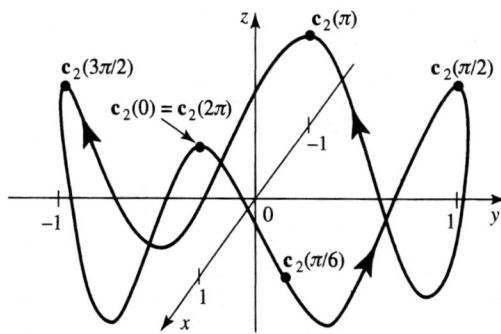

Figure 2.53 Curve $\mathbf{c}_2$ parametrized by $\mathbf{c}_2(t) = (\cos t, \sin t, \cos 4t)$, $t \in [0, 2\pi]$. ◄

A parametric representation of a curve gives a sense of orientation, as explained in the following definition.

DEFINITION 2.17 Orientation

Let $\mathbf{c}(t): [a, b] \to \mathbb{R}^3$ (or $\mathbb{R}^2$) be a path. The point $\mathbf{c}(a)$ is called the *initial point*, and we call $\mathbf{c}(b)$ the *terminal point* of **c**. The initial and the terminal points are called the *endpoints* of **c**. The direction corresponding to increasing values of t gives the *positive orientation*, whereas the opposite direction defines the *negative orientation* of **c**. ◀

If the domain of **c** includes $-\infty$ or ∞ (or both), one (or both) endpoints are not defined. The orientation is indicated in the graph by an arrow; see Figures 2.52 and 2.53. According to the definition, the positive orientation is the direction from the initial point toward the terminal point (if defined).

▶ **EXAMPLE 2.49**

For the path $\mathbf{c}_1(t)$ in Figure 2.52, the initial point is $\mathbf{c}(0) = (0, 0)$, and the terminal point is $\mathbf{c}(3\pi) = (-3\pi, 0)$. The arrows indicate the positive orientation (that can also be described as the counterclockwise orientation). The path $\mathbf{c}_2(t)$ of Figure 2.53 has the same point $\mathbf{c}(0) = \mathbf{c}(2\pi) = (1, 0, 1)$ as its initial and terminal points. To determine the orientation, compute the values of **c** at increasing values of t; for example, $\mathbf{c}(\pi/6) = (\sqrt{3}/2, 1/2, -1/2)$, $\mathbf{c}(\pi/4) = (\sqrt{2}/2, \sqrt{2}/2, -1)$, etc. The positive orientation is given by the direction from $(1, 0, 1)$ to $(\sqrt{3}/2, 1/2, -1/2)$, then to $(\sqrt{2}/2, \sqrt{2}/2, -1)$, etc., as indicated in the graph. ◀

▶ **EXAMPLE 2.50** Parametric Representation of a Line and a Line Segment

A parametric representation of the line segment joining the points $A = (a_1, a_2, a_3)$ and $B = (b_1, b_2, b_3)$ in $\mathbb{R}^3$ is given by $\mathbf{c}(t) = \mathbf{a} + t\mathbf{v}, t \in [0, 1]$, where $\mathbf{a} = (a_1, a_2, a_3)$ and $\mathbf{v} = (b_1 - a_1, b_2 - a_2, b_3 - a_3)$. This parametrization was discussed at the beginning of Section 1.2. The initial point is $A = \mathbf{c}(0)$ and the terminal point is $B = \mathbf{c}(1)$. In coordinates,

$$\mathbf{c}(t) = (a_1 + t(b_1 - a_1), a_2 + t(b_2 - a_2), a_3 + t(b_3 - a_3)), \qquad t \in [0, 1].$$

A line going through $A = (a_1, a_2, a_3)$ in the direction $\mathbf{v} = (v_1, v_2, v_3)$ is represented as

$$\mathbf{c}(t) = \mathbf{a} + t\mathbf{v} = (a_1 + tv_1, a_2 + tv_2, a_3 + tv_3), \qquad t \in \mathbb{R}.$$

As "time" t increases (positive orientation), the point $\mathbf{c}(t)$ moves along the line, away from A, in the direction of **v**. The direction of movement corresponding to decreasing time (negative orientation) corresponds to movement in the direction of $-\mathbf{v}$. ◀

▶ **EXAMPLE 2.51** Parametrization of a Circle and an Ellipse

The curve represented parametrically as

$$\mathbf{c}(t) = (a \cos t, a \sin t), \qquad t \in [0, 2\pi]$$

(where $a > 0$) is the circle in $\mathbb{R}^2$ of radius a centered at the origin ($x(t) = a \cos t$, $y(t) = a \sin t$, and hence $x(t)^2 + y(t)^2 = a^2$); see Figure 2.54. The parameter t represents the angle between the x-axis and the position vector $\mathbf{c}(t)$. The initial point is $\mathbf{c}(0) = (a, 0)$ and the terminal point is $\mathbf{c}(2\pi) = (a, 0) = \mathbf{c}(0)$. Thinking of **c** as a trajectory of a moving object, we see that it takes the object 2π units of time to complete one full revolution and come back to its initial position. The positive orientation (i.e., direction of increasing t) corresponds to counterclockwise motion along the circle. The path

$$\mathbf{c}(t) = (o_1 + a \cos t, o_2 + a \sin t) = (o_1, o_2) + (a \cos t, a \sin t), \qquad t \in [0, 2\pi]$$

represents the circle centered at $O = (o_1, o_2)$ of radius a. The ellipse $x^2/a^2 + y^2/b^2 = 1$ (with semi-axes $a, b > 0$) can be parametrized as $\mathbf{c}(t) = (a \cos t, b \sin t), t \in [0, 2\pi]$. ◀

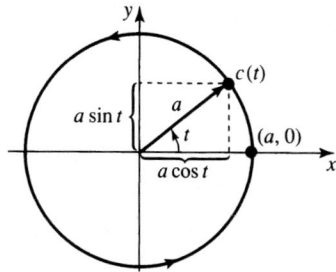

Figure 2.54 Circle $\mathbf{c}(t) = (a \cos t, a \sin t)$, $t \in [0, 2\pi]$.

► **EXAMPLE 2.52** Parametrization of the Graph of $y = f(x)$

The graph of a real-valued function $f \colon [a, b] \to \mathbb{R}$ of one variable defined on an interval $[a, b] \subseteq \mathbb{R}$ is a curve that can be parametrized as $\mathbf{c}(t) = (t, f(t))$, $t \in [a, b]$.

For example, a parametric representation of the graph of $y = x^2$ on $[0, 2]$ is given by $\mathbf{c}(t) = (t, t^2)$, $t \in [0, 2]$. Similarly, $\mathbf{c}(t) = (t, te^{-t})$, $t \in [0, \infty)$, represents the graph of $y = xe^{-x}$ for $x \geq 0$. ◄

Let us for a moment go back to the previous example and compare the two ways of describing the parabola in question. Although both descriptions $y = x^2$, $x \in [0, 2]$, and $\mathbf{c}(t) = (t, t^2)$, $t \in [0, 2]$, do produce (geometrically) the same curve, there are differences. To understand them better, suppose that the curve $\mathbf{c}$ represents the motion of an object. Parametric representation conveys a lot more information than just the geometric curve: for example, the initial point of the motion is $\mathbf{c}(0) = (0, 0)$, and the terminal point is $\mathbf{c}(2) = (2, 4)$. Since $(t_1, t_1^2) \neq (t_2, t_2^2)$ for $0 \leq t_1, t_2 \leq 2$ and $t_1 \neq t_2$, the object moves along the parabola *from* $(0, 0)$ *to* $(2, 4)$, keeping the same direction all the time (i.e., it does not move back and forth; compare with Example 2.54).

From $\mathbf{c}(t) = (t, t^2)$ we can read off the location of the object at *any* time t, $0 \leq t \leq 2$. On the other hand, the graph of $y = x^2$ produces the trajectory of the object without showing any details of the motion. Later in this section, and also in Chapter 3, we will learn how to extract a lot more information from a parametric representation. For example, we will be able to measure the curvature, or determine the acceleration of a motion.

It is important to notice that the values of the parameter t are not built into the graph. In other words, if we select a point on the curve, we cannot read off the value of t that produced it. To somewhat remedy this deficiency, besides plotting a point on the curve, we also indicate the corresponding value of t, as shown in Figure 2.55.

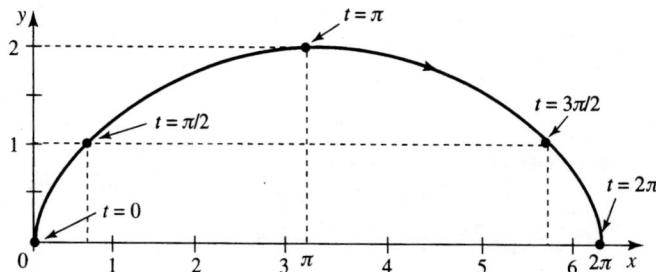

Figure 2.55 Graph of the path $\mathbf{c}(t) = (t - \sin t, 1 - \cos t)$, $t \in [0, 2\pi]$.

► **EXAMPLE 2.53**

Sketch the graph of the function $\mathbf{c}: [0, 3] \to \mathbb{R}^2$ given by $\mathbf{c}(t) = (t^2, 1 - t)$.

SOLUTION

We interpret the values of $\mathbf{c}(t)$ as the coordinates $x(t) = t^2$ and $y(t) = 1 - t$ of a point in $\mathbb{R}^2$. If $t = 0$, then $x(0) = 0$ and $y(0) = 1$. For $t = 1$, we get $x(1) = 1$ and $y(1) = 0$, and similarly, $x(2) = 4$, $y(2) = -1$ and $x(3) = 9$, $y(3) = -2$. Continuing this process and connecting all points thus obtained produce a curve that is the graph of $\mathbf{c}$, see Figure 2.56 (alternative graphing techniques will be discussed later).

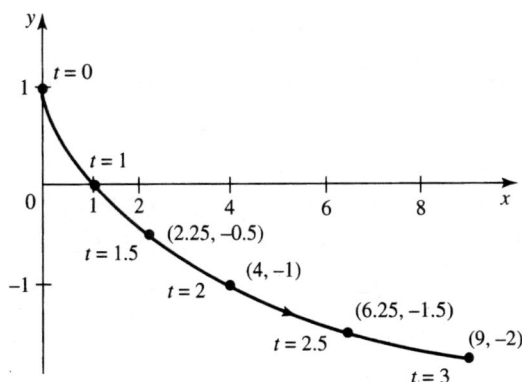

Figure 2.56   Graph of the path . $\mathbf{c}(t) = (t^2, 1 - t)$ for $t \in [0, 3]$.

► **EXAMPLE 2.54**

Consider motions defined by the paths $\mathbf{c}_1(t) = (t, t^2)$, $t \in [-1, 1]$, and $\mathbf{c}_2(t) = (\sin t, (\sin t)^2)$, $t \in [-\pi/2, 5\pi/2]$. Note that both represent the graph of the function $y = x^2$, $-1 \leq x \leq 1$.

From $\mathbf{c}_1(-1) = \mathbf{c}_2(-\pi/2) = (-1, 1)$ and $\mathbf{c}_1(1) = \mathbf{c}_2(5\pi/2) = (1, 1)$, we conclude that both paths have the same initial and terminal points. Since $\mathbf{c}_1(t_1) \neq \mathbf{c}_1(t_2)$ for $t_1 \neq t_2$, it follows that $\mathbf{c}_1$ describes the motion along the graph of $y = x^2$ from $(-1, 1)$ to $(1, 1)$ without retracing any parts of it (i.e., $\mathbf{c}_1$ keeps the same direction all the time).

The motion of an object given by $\mathbf{c}_2$ is different. As t changes from $-\pi/2$ to $\pi/2$, $\sin t$ changes from -1 to 1 (and is one-to-one). Thus, the object moves from $(-1, 1)$ to $(1, 1)$. For $\pi/2 \leq t \leq 3\pi/2$, $\sin t$ decreases from 1 to -1, and so the object moves back along $y = x^2$ from $(1, 1)$ to $(-1, 1)$. Finally, when $3\pi/2 \leq t \leq 5\pi/2$, $\sin t$ increases from -1 to 1, and so the object moves back to $(1, 1)$.   ◄

► **EXAMPLE 2.55**

In Example 2.51 we showed that the path $\mathbf{c}(t) = (\cos t, \sin t)$, $t \in [0, 2\pi]$ represents the circle $x^2 + y^2 = 1$. There are other parametrizations: for instance, $\mathbf{c}_1(t) = (\cos 2t, \sin 2t)$, $t \in [0, \pi]$ satisfies $x(t)^2 + y(t)^2 = 1$ and, since $\mathbf{c}_1(0) = \mathbf{c}_1(\pi) = (1, 0)$, it describes the whole circle. Similarly, we can check that $\mathbf{c}_2(t) = (\sin (t + 3), \cos (t + 3))$, $t \in [0, 2\pi]$, or $\mathbf{c}_3(t) = (-\cos (t/4), \sin (t/4))$, $t \in [0, 8\pi]$, represent the same circle.

As a matter of fact, a curve has infinitely many parametrizations (in terms of Definition 2.16, we say that there are infinitely many *paths* that have the same image; i.e., parametrize the same curve). That is the reason why we made a distinction between a path and a curve. It is worth repeating that a curve is a geometric object and a path is a way of describing it algebraically in terms of a parameter. Parametrizations need not look alike: for example,

$$\mathbf{c}_4(t) = ((4 \cos t + \sin t)/\sqrt{17}, (4 \sin t - \cos t)/\sqrt{17}), \qquad t \in [0, 2\pi]$$

is another representation of the circle $x^2 + y^2 = 1$.   ◄

▶ **EXAMPLE 2.56**

Let $\mathbf{c}$ be the part of the curve $y = 2x^4$ between $(-1, 2)$ and $(1, 2)$. Write down several parametrizations of $\mathbf{c}$.

SOLUTION

As in Example 2.52, we can take $x = t$. Then $y = 2x^4 = 2t^4$, and we obtain the parametrization $\mathbf{c}_1(t) = (t, 2t^4)$, $t \in [-1, 1]$. There is no reason why we have to choose $x = t$. Try $x = mt$, $(m \neq 0)$; then $y = 2x^4 = 2m^4t^4$ and $\mathbf{c}_2(t) = (mt, 2m^4t^4)$, $t \in [-1/|m|, 1/|m|]$. (In defining an interval $[a, b]$, we have to make sure that $a \leq b$; that is why we used the absolute value.) We already have infinitely many parametrizations, one for each nonzero value of m.

Let us list a few more parametrizations [of course, in every case $x(t)$ and $y(t)$ have to satisfy $y(t) = 2x(t)^4$, and the endpoints of the interval for the parameter must give $(-1, 2)$ and $(1, 2)$]: $\mathbf{c}_3(t) = (mt + 1, 2(mt + 1)^4)$, $t \in [-2/m, 0]$ (works for $m > 0$), then $\mathbf{c}_4(t) = (t^{1/3}, 2t^{4/3})$, $t \in [-1, 1]$, or $\mathbf{c}_5(t) = (\tan t, 2\tan^4 t)$, $t \in [-\pi/4, \pi/4]$, etc. On the other hand, $\mathbf{c}_6(t) = (t^2, 2t^8)$, $t \in [-1, 1]$, parametrizes the part of the parabola in the first quadrant only: for example, no value of t gives $(-1, 2)$. ◀

In Chapter 3, and in subsequent chapters, we will learn that there are significant differences between parametrizations. Not every parametrization of a curve can be used to compute its length. Some parametrizations will be more suitable as trajectories of the motion than others. A path integral will be defined for a special class of parametrizations, etc.

▶ **EXAMPLE 2.57**

The parametrizations (paths)

(a) $\mathbf{c}_1(t) = (2\cos t, 2\sin t)$, $t \in [0, \pi]$,

(b) $\mathbf{c}_2(t) = (-2\cos t, 2\sin t)$, $t \in [0, \pi]$,

(c) $\mathbf{c}_3(t) = (2\cos(3t), 2\sin(3t))$, $t \in [0, \pi/3]$,

(d) $\mathbf{c}_4(t) = (-2\cos(t/4), 2\sin(t/4))$, $t \in [0, 4\pi]$,

represent the same curve. Identify the curve and describe the differences between the parametrizations.

SOLUTION

In all four cases, $x(t)^2 + y(t)^2 = 4$ and $y(t) \geq 0$. Next, we compute the endpoints for all paths: $\mathbf{c}_1(0) = (2, 0)$, $\mathbf{c}_1(\pi) = (-2, 0)$, $\mathbf{c}_2(0) = (-2, 0)$, $\mathbf{c}_2(\pi) = (2, 0)$, $\mathbf{c}_3(0) = (2, 0)$, $\mathbf{c}_3(\pi/3) = (-2, 0)$, $\mathbf{c}_4(0) = (-2, 0)$, and $\mathbf{c}_4(4\pi) = (2, 0)$. Consequently, the curve in question is the semicircle of radius 2 (centered at the origin) in the upper half-plane with the endpoints $(2, 0)$ and $(-2, 0)$. Paths $\mathbf{c}_1$ and $\mathbf{c}_3$ are oriented counterclockwise, whereas $\mathbf{c}_2$ and $\mathbf{c}_4$ [having initial points at $(-2, 0)$ and terminal points at $(2, 0)$] are oriented clockwise. Now view t as time and interpret the interval for t as the total time needed to complete the motion along the curve. The motion along $\mathbf{c}_3$ is the fastest, and along $\mathbf{c}_4$ the slowest. Motions along $\mathbf{c}_1$ and $\mathbf{c}_2$ are completed in π units of time. ◀

▶ **EXAMPLE 2.58**

Sketch the curve $\mathbf{c}(t) = (3\cos t, 3\sin t, t)$, $t \in [0, 2\pi]$.

SOLUTION

Since $x = 3\cos t$ and $y = 3\sin t$, it follows that $x^2 + y^2 = 9$, which means that the curve lies on the surface of the cylinder of radius 3 whose axis is the z-axis. Its projection onto the xy-plane (take $z = 0$) is the circle of radius 3 (centered at the origin) oriented counterclockwise. As time t increases, z-coordinates of points on c increase from 0 to 2π. The initial point is $\mathbf{c}(0) = (3, 0, 0)$ and the terminal

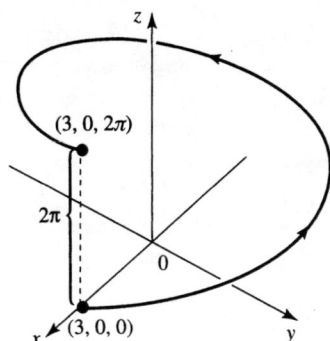

Figure 2.57 The graph of $\mathbf{c}(t) = (3\cos t, 3\sin t, t)$, $t \in [0, 2\pi]$ is a helix of "pitch" 2π.

point is $(3, 0, 2\pi)$. The curve is obtained in the following way: as we move the point along the circle of radius 3 counterclockwise, we simultaneously increase its height (at a constant rate) from 0 to 2π. The curve thus obtained is called a helix; see Figure 2.57. ◀

DEFINITION 2.18 Continuous, Differentiable, and C^1 Paths and Curves

A path (or a parametrization) $\mathbf{c}: [a, b] \to \mathbb{R}^2(\mathbb{R}^3)$ is *continuous* if and only if its component functions $x(t)$ and $y(t)$ (or $x(t)$, $y(t)$ and $z(t)$) are continuous on $[a, b]$. If the component functions of $\mathbf{c}(t)$ are differentiable (respectively C^1), then $\mathbf{c}(t)$ is called a *differentiable* (respectively C^1) path.

A curve is called *continuous* (*differentiable*, C^1) if among all of its parametrizations there is at least one that is continuous (differentiable, C^1). ◀

Let us clarify the meaning of the statements "$f(t)$ is continuous on $[a, b]$" and "$f(t)$ is differentiable on $[a, b]$." Continuity and differentiability are defined in terms of a limit: a function $f(t)$ is continuous at $t_0 \in (a, b)$ if and only if $\lim_{t \to t_0} f(t)$ exists and equals $f(t_0)$; it is differentiable at $t_0 \in (a, b)$ if and only if $\lim_{h \to 0}(f(t_0 + h) - f(t_0))/h$ exists. These definitions apply to any t_0 that lies inside the interval (a, b). To define continuity and differentiability at the endpoints a and b, all we have to do is to replace the (two-sided) limits with the appropriate one-sided limits in such a way that the endpoints are always approached from within the interval. For example, the function $f(t)$ is continuous at $t = b$ if and only if $\lim_{t \to b^-} f(t)$ exists and equals $f(b)$; it is differentiable at $t = a$ if and only if $\lim_{h \to 0^+}(f(a + h) - f(a))/h$ exists.

Recall that a real-valued function of one variable is called C^1 if its derivative is continuous. All curves that have appeared in this section are continuous and differentiable. When we state that "a curve $\mathbf{c}$ is differentiable," we mean to say that some parametric representation of that curve (usually also denoted by $\mathbf{c}$) is differentiable.

The parametrization $\mathbf{c}_4(t) = (t^{1/3}, 2t^{4/3})$, $t \in [-1, 1]$ of Example 2.56 is not differentiable at 0 [the derivative of $x(t)$ is $x'(t) = t^{-2/3}/3$, and hence not defined at 0]. Nevertheless, the parametrizations $\mathbf{c}_1$ (and $\mathbf{c}_2$, $\mathbf{c}_3$, and $\mathbf{c}_5$) are differentiable and C^1, and hence the curve that is the graph of $y = x^4$ on $[-1, 1]$ is differentiable and C^1. The graph of $y = |x|$, $x \in [-1, 1]$ is an example of a continuous, nondifferentiable curve: $|x|$ has a "corner" at

$x = 0$, and consequently, does not have a tangent (i.e., the derivative) there. As a matter of fact, to prove nondifferentiability, we would have to show that no parametrization of $|x|$ is differentiable. We prefer to rely on our intuitive reasoning at this moment.

Let us mention an issue related to notation. Consider the parametrizations $\mathbf{c}_1(t) = (t, 2t^4)$, $t \in [-1, 1]$ and $\mathbf{c}_5(t) = (\tan t, 2\tan^4 t)$, $t \in [-\pi/4, \pi/4]$ of Example 2.56. Strictly speaking, we should have used different symbols for the parameters, since t in $\mathbf{c}_1$ and $\mathbf{c}_5$ is not the same. For example, $\mathbf{c}_1(\pi/4) = (\pi/4, \pi^4/128)$, but $\mathbf{c}_5(\pi/4) = (1, 2)$. However, as t in $\mathbf{c}_1$ changes from -1 to 1, $\mathbf{c}_1$ describes the same curve as $\mathbf{c}_5$ (when its t changes from $-\pi/4$ to $\pi/4$). Beware of this common practice so that it will not become a source of confusion.

Let $\mathbf{c}(t) = (x(t), y(t), z(t))$ be a differentiable path in $\mathbb{R}^3$. The derivative $\mathbf{c}'(t_0) = D\mathbf{c}(t_0)$ of $\mathbf{c}$ at t_0 is the 3×1 matrix

$$\begin{bmatrix} dx/dt \\ dy/dt \\ dz/dt \end{bmatrix}_{at\ t = t_0} = \begin{bmatrix} x'(t_0) \\ y'(t_0) \\ z'(t_0) \end{bmatrix}$$

that can be interpreted as the vector $\mathbf{c}'(t_0) = x'(t_0)\mathbf{i} + y'(t_0)\mathbf{j} + z'(t_0)\mathbf{k}$ in $\mathbb{R}^3$. We visualize $\mathbf{c}'(t_0)$ as a vector whose initial point is located at $\mathbf{c}(t_0)$, as shown in Figure 2.58. To further explore this geometric interpretation, we rewrite $\mathbf{c}'(t_0)$ in the limit form:

$$\mathbf{c}'(t_0) = x'(t_0)\mathbf{i} + y'(t_0)\mathbf{j} + z'(t_0)\mathbf{k}$$

$$= \lim_{h \to 0} \frac{x(t_0 + h) - x(t_0)}{h}\mathbf{i} + \lim_{h \to 0} \frac{y(t_0 + h) - y(t_0)}{h}\mathbf{j} + \lim_{h \to 0} \frac{z(t_0 + h) - z(t_0)}{h}\mathbf{k}$$

$$= \lim_{h \to 0} \frac{(x(t_0 + h)\mathbf{i} + y(t_0 + h)\mathbf{j} + z(t_0 + h)\mathbf{k}) - (x(t_0)\mathbf{i} + y(t_0)\mathbf{j} + z(t_0)\mathbf{k})}{h}$$

$$= \lim_{h \to 0} \frac{\mathbf{c}(t_0 + h) - \mathbf{c}(t_0)}{h}.$$

The vector $(\mathbf{c}(t_0 + h) - \mathbf{c}(t_0))/h$, being parallel to $\mathbf{c}(t_0 + h) - \mathbf{c}(t_0)$, falls in the direction of the secant line joining $\mathbf{c}(t_0 + h)$ and $\mathbf{c}(t_0)$; see Figure 2.58. As $h \to 0$, the point $\mathbf{c}(t_0 + h)$ slides along the curve toward $\mathbf{c}(t_0)$ and the secant line approaches its limit position, the tangent line at $\mathbf{c}(t_0)$. Hence, $\mathbf{c}'(t_0)$ [if $\mathbf{c}'(t_0) \neq \mathbf{0}$] represents the direction of the line tangent to $\mathbf{c}$ at $\mathbf{c}(t_0)$.

A parametric equation of the tangent line (recall that "line = point plus parameter times vector") is given by $\mathbf{l}(t) = \mathbf{c}(t_0) + t\mathbf{c}'(t_0)$, $t \in \mathbb{R}$. This argument justifies the terminology introduced in our next definition.

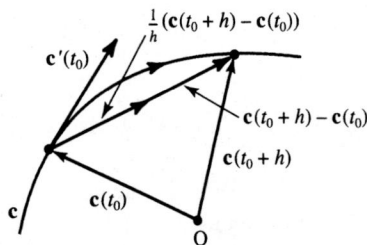

Figure 2.58 $\mathbf{c}'(t_0)$ is in the direction of the tangent line to $\mathbf{c}$ at a point $\mathbf{c}(t_0)$.

DEFINITION 2.19   Tangent Vector and Tangent Line

Let $\mathbf{c}$ be a differentiable path in $\mathbb{R}^2$ or $\mathbb{R}^3$. The vector $\mathbf{c}'(t_0)$ is called a *tangent vector* to $\mathbf{c}$ at $\mathbf{c}(t_0)$. The line tangent to a curve $\mathbf{c}$ [that is represented by a path $\mathbf{c}(t)$] at $\mathbf{c}(t_0)$ is given by $\mathbf{l}(t) = \mathbf{c}(t_0) + t\mathbf{c}'(t_0)$, $t \in \mathbb{R}$, provided that $\mathbf{c}'(t_0) \neq \mathbf{0}$.   ◀

Now suppose that a path $\mathbf{c}(t)$ describes the trajectory of a moving object (and t represents time). Since $\mathbf{c}(t_0 + h) - \mathbf{c}(t_0) = $ (position at time $t_0 + h$) − (position at time t_0), that is,

$$\frac{\mathbf{c}(t_0 + h) - \mathbf{c}(t_0)}{h} = \frac{\text{displacement vector}}{\text{time}},$$

the limit (as time h approaches 0) gives the *instantaneous velocity vector*.

DEFINITION 2.20   Velocity, Speed, and Acceleration

Let $\mathbf{c}(t) = (x(t), y(t), z(t))$ be a differentiable path in $\mathbb{R}^3$. The *velocity* $\mathbf{v}(t)$ at time t is given by the vector-valued function

$$\mathbf{v}(t) = \mathbf{c}'(t) = (x'(t), y'(t), z'(t)).$$

The *speed* is the real-valued function

$$\|\mathbf{v}(t)\| = \sqrt{(x'(t))^2 + (y'(t))^2 + (z'(t))^2},$$

which is the length of the velocity vector. The *acceleration* $\mathbf{a}(t)$ at time t is given by

$$\mathbf{a}(t) = \mathbf{v}'(t) = \mathbf{c}''(t) = (x''(t), y''(t), z''(t)),$$

provided that $\mathbf{c}$ is twice differentiable.   ◀

Usually, we visualize velocity and acceleration as vectors whose tails are located at the point $\mathbf{c}(t)$ on the curve. Example 2.60 will serve as an illustration.

▶ **EXAMPLE 2.59**

Using the notion of speed, we can now confirm our somewhat intuitive reasoning in Example 2.57. Since $\|\mathbf{c}_1'(t)\| = \|\mathbf{c}_2'(t)\| = 2$, $\|\mathbf{c}_3'(t)\| = 6$ and $\|\mathbf{c}_4'(t)\| = 1/2$, it follows (since all parametrizations have constant speed) that the parametrization $\mathbf{c}_3$ is the fastest, $\mathbf{c}_4$ is the slowest, and $\mathbf{c}_1$ and $\mathbf{c}_2$ have the same speed.   ◀

This example shows how speed can be used as a way of describing the differences between parametrizations of the same curve.

▶ **EXAMPLE 2.60**

Assume that the function $\mathbf{c}(t) = (t \sin t, t \cos t, t)$, $1 \leq t \leq 2$, represents the motion of an object in $\mathbb{R}^3$. The matrix

$$D\mathbf{c}(t) = \mathbf{c}'(t) = \begin{bmatrix} \sin t + t \cos t \\ \cos t - t \sin t \\ 1 \end{bmatrix}$$

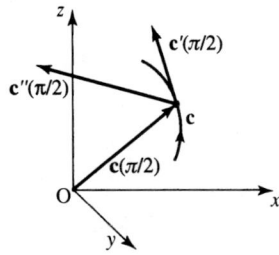

Figure 2.59 Position, velocity, and acceleration vectors of Example 2.60.

(thought of as a vector) gives the velocity of the object. For example, when $t = \pi/2$, the object is located at the point $\mathbf{c}(\pi/2) = (\pi/2, 0, \pi/2)$. Its velocity vector at that moment is computed to be

$$D\mathbf{c}(\pi/2) = \mathbf{c}'(\pi/2) = \begin{bmatrix} 1 \\ -\pi/2 \\ 1 \end{bmatrix},$$

and the acceleration is

$$\mathbf{c}''(\pi/2) = \begin{bmatrix} 2\cos t - \sin t \\ -2\sin t - t\cos t \\ 0 \end{bmatrix}_{at\ t=\pi/2} = \begin{bmatrix} -\pi/2 \\ -2 \\ 0 \end{bmatrix}.$$

We visualize the velocity $\mathbf{c}'(\pi/2)$ and the acceleration $\mathbf{c}''(\pi/2)$ as vectors whose tails are located at the point $\mathbf{c}(\pi/2)$ on the curve; see Figure 2.59. ◀

We will continue our study of tangents, velocity, and acceleration in Chapter 3.

▶ EXERCISES 2.5

Exercises 1 to 9: Find a parametric representation of the given curve:

1. The line segment in $\mathbb{R}^3$ joining the points $(3, 1, -2)$ and $(0, 5, 0)$

2. The line in $\mathbb{R}^2$ going through the point $(3, 2)$ in the direction of the vector $(-1, 1)$

3. The circle in $\mathbb{R}^2$ centered at the origin, of radius $\sqrt{5}$

4. The circle in the plane $z = 4$ centered at the point $(0, 0, 4)$, of radius 4

5. The ellipse in $\mathbb{R}^2$ with semiaxes of length 3 (in the x-direction) and 1 (in the y-direction) whose center is located at the point $(-2, -1)$

6. The graph of $f(x) = 3x^2 - 2$ in $\mathbb{R}^2$ for $-3 \leq x \leq 2$

7. The graph of $x - y^2 = 1$ in $\mathbb{R}^2$ for $0 \leq y \leq 1$

8. The graph of $3x^2 + y^3 = 1$ in $\mathbb{R}^2$ for $x, y \geq 0$

9. The graph of $x^{2/3} + y^{2/3} = 1$ in $\mathbb{R}^2$

10. What curve is represented by $\mathbf{c}(t) = (\cos t, \cos^2 t)$, $t \in \mathbb{R}$?

Exercises 11 to 15: Find an equation of the curve $\mathbf{c}(t)$ in a Cartesian coordinate system and sketch it, indicating its endpoints (if any) and orientation.

11. $\mathbf{c}(t) = (t - 3)\mathbf{i} + t^2\mathbf{j}$, $t \in [0, 2]$ 12. $\mathbf{c}(t) = 3\sin 2t\mathbf{i} + 3\cos 2t\mathbf{j}$, $t \in [0, \pi/2]$

13. $\mathbf{c}(t) = (2\cosh t, 2\sinh t)$, $t \in \mathbb{R}$ (*Hint:* $\cosh^2 t - \sinh^2 t = 1$)

14. $c(t) = (t^3, t^9)$, $t \in [0, 3]$ **15.** $c(t) = (t, e^{3t})$, $t \in [0, \ln 2]$

16. Identify the curve parametrized by $c(t) = (2 - t, 1 + t, t)$, $t \in \mathbb{R}$. If t is replaced by

  (a) $-t$ (b) t^2 (c) t^3 (d) e^t

what does the resulting parametrization represent?

Exercises 17 to 25: Sketch (or describe in words) the curve $c(t)$, indicating its endpoints and orientation.

17. $c(t) = (\cos t, \sin t, 3)$, $t \in [0, 2\pi]$ **18.** $c(t) = (\cos t, \sin t, t)$, $t \in [0, 3\pi]$

19. $c(t) = (\cos t, \sin t, t^3)$, $t \in [0, \pi]$ **20.** $c(t) = (t, \cos t, \sin t)$, $t \in [0, 10\pi]$

21. $c(t) = (t, \arctan t)$, $t \in [-1, 1]$ **22.** $c(t) = \left(1 + t^{-1}\right)\mathbf{i} + \left(1 - t^{-1}\right)\mathbf{j}$, $t \in [1, 2]$

23. $c(t) = \left(t + t^{-1}\right)\mathbf{i} + \left(t - t^{-1}\right)\mathbf{j}$, $t \in [1, 2]$

24. $c(t) = 4\mathbf{i} + (5 + 2\cos t)\mathbf{j} + (1 + 2\sin t)\mathbf{k}$, $t \in [0, 6\pi]$

25. $c(t) = (e^{t/4}\sin t, e^{t/4}\cos t)$, $t \in [0, 2\pi]$

26. The following parametrizations have the same image. Describe their differences.

  (a) $c_1(t) = (t, t^2)$, $t \in [-1, 1]$ (b) $c_2(t) = (\sin t, \sin^2 t)$, $t \in [-\pi/2, \pi/2]$

  (c) $c_3(t) = (\sin t, \sin^2 t)$, $t \in [-\pi/2, 3\pi/2]$

  (d) $c_4(t) = (t^{1/3}, t^{2/3})$, $t \in [-1, 1]$

  (e) $c_5(t) = (2t/\sqrt{1 + t^2}, 4t^2/(1 + t^2))$, $t \in [-1/\sqrt{3}, 1/\sqrt{3}]$

27. Check that the following parametrizations have the same image; that is, that they represent the same curve. Discuss their differences in terms of their speeds and orientations. Find two more parametrizations with the same image as the curves in (a)–(d).

  (a) $c_1(t) = (2\sin t, 2\cos t)$, $t \in [0, 2\pi]$ (b) $c_2(t) = (2\cos t, 2\sin t)$, $t \in [0, 2\pi]$

  (c) $c_3(t) = (2\sin 3t, 2\cos 3t)$, $t \in [0, 2\pi]$

  (d) $c_4(t) = (-2\cos(t/2), 2\sin(t/2))$, $t \in [0, 4\pi]$

28. Show that the path $c(t) = (t^{1/3}, 2t^{2/3})$, $t \in [-1, 1]$ is not differentiable. Identify the curve that is the image of c and prove that it is differentiable.

29. Write down a parametrization of the line $y = 2x$ in $\mathbb{R}^2$ that is not differentiable.

30. The curve $c(t) = (t^2, 1/t)$, $t > 0$, represents the position of an object in the xy-plane. Find its velocity and acceleration at $t = 2$, $t = 1$, and $t = 1/10$. Describe what happens (in terms of magnitudes of the velocity and the acceleration) as t approaches 0.

Exercises 31 to 34: Consider the parametrization $c(t)$ of the curve $y = x^3$, $-1 \le x \le 1$. Determine whether the parametrization is continuous, differentiable or C^1.

31. $c(t) = (t^{1/3}, t)$, $t \in [-1, 1]$ **32.** $c(t) = (2\tan t, 8\tan^3 t)$, $t \in [-\pi/4, \pi/4]$

33. $c(t) = (t|t|, t^3|t|^3)$, $t \in [-1, 1]$ **34.** $c(t) = (e^t - 2, (e^t - 2)^3)$, $t \in [0, \ln 3]$

35. Let $c(t) = (te^t, (1 - t)e^t, e^t)$, $t \in [0, 1]$ describe the position of an object. Find its velocity and acceleration.

36. Show that the parametrization $c_4(t) = ((4\cos t + \sin t)/\sqrt{17}, (4\sin t - \cos t)/\sqrt{17})$, $t \in [0, 2\pi]$ of Example 2.55 represents the circle $x^2 + y^2 = 1$. Identify the initial and the terminal points of $c_4(t)$.

Exercises 37 to 41: The vector function $c(t)$ represents the trajectory of a moving object in $\mathbb{R}^2$ or in $\mathbb{R}^3$. Compute the velocity, speed, and acceleration.

37. $\mathbf{c}(t) = (1 + t^3, t^{-1}, 2)$ **38.** $\mathbf{c}(t) = e^t \cos t \mathbf{i} + e^t \sin t \mathbf{j} + t \mathbf{k}$

39. $\mathbf{c}(t) = e^{2t} \sin(2t)\mathbf{i} + e^{2t} \cos(2t)\mathbf{j}$ **40.** $\mathbf{c}(t) = (\cosh t, \sinh t, t)$

41. $\mathbf{c}(t) = (t^{1/2}, t, t^{3/2})$

▶ 2.6 PROPERTIES OF DERIVATIVES

After presenting the definition of a derivative, the calculus of functions of one variable proceeds by proving theorems that relate the derivatives of combinations of two functions (such as the sum, the product, or the composition) to the derivatives of the functions themselves. For example, the product rule formula $(fg)' = f'g + fg'$ expresses the derivative of the product of f and g in terms of f and g and their derivatives f' and g'. Although it is always possible to use the definition to find the derivative of a function, the computation is usually (technically) hard and quite lengthy. The differentiation rules provide a significantly easier alternative. We start by generalizing these rules to functions of several variables.

THEOREM 2.6   Properties of Derivatives

(a)   Assume that the functions $\mathbf{F}, \mathbf{G} \colon U \subseteq \mathbb{R}^m \to \mathbb{R}^n$ are differentiable at $\mathbf{a} \in U$. Then the sum $\mathbf{F} + \mathbf{G}$ and the difference $\mathbf{F} - \mathbf{G}$ are differentiable at $\mathbf{a}$ and

$$D(\mathbf{F} \pm \mathbf{G})(\mathbf{a}) = D\mathbf{F}(\mathbf{a}) \pm D\mathbf{G}(\mathbf{a}).$$

(b)   If the function $\mathbf{F} \colon U \subseteq \mathbb{R}^m \to \mathbb{R}^n$ is differentiable at $\mathbf{a} \in U$ and $c \in \mathbb{R}$ is a constant, then the product $c\mathbf{F}$ is differentiable at $\mathbf{a}$ and

$$D(c\mathbf{F})(\mathbf{a}) = c\,D\mathbf{F}(\mathbf{a}).$$

(c)   If the real-valued functions $f, g \colon U \subseteq \mathbb{R}^m \to \mathbb{R}$ are differentiable at $\mathbf{a} \in U$, then their product fg is differentiable at $\mathbf{a}$ and

$$D(fg)(\mathbf{a}) = g(\mathbf{a})Df(\mathbf{a}) + f(\mathbf{a})Dg(\mathbf{a}).$$

(d)   If the real-valued functions $f, g \colon U \subseteq \mathbb{R}^m \to \mathbb{R}$ are differentiable at $\mathbf{a} \in U$, and $g(\mathbf{a}) \neq 0$, then their quotient f/g is differentiable at $\mathbf{a}$ and

$$D\left(\frac{f}{g}\right)(\mathbf{a}) = \frac{g(\mathbf{a})Df(\mathbf{a}) - f(\mathbf{a})Dg(\mathbf{a})}{g(\mathbf{a})^2}.$$

(e)   If the vector-valued functions $\mathbf{v}, \mathbf{w} \colon U \subseteq \mathbb{R} \to \mathbb{R}^n$ are differentiable at $a \in U$, then their dot (scalar) product $\mathbf{v} \cdot \mathbf{w}$ is differentiable at a and

$$(\mathbf{v} \cdot \mathbf{w})'(a) = \mathbf{v}'(a) \cdot \mathbf{w}(a) + \mathbf{v}(a) \cdot \mathbf{w}'(a).$$

(f)   If the vector-valued functions $\mathbf{v}, \mathbf{w} \colon U \subseteq \mathbb{R} \to \mathbb{R}^3$ are differentiable at $a \in U$, their cross (vector) product $\mathbf{v} \times \mathbf{w}$ is differentiable at a and

$$(\mathbf{v} \times \mathbf{w})'(a) = \mathbf{v}'(a) \times \mathbf{w}(a) + \mathbf{v}(a) \times \mathbf{w}'(a). \qquad \blacktriangleleft$$

Algebraic operations on the right sides of formulas (a)–(d) are matrix operations. The sum and difference of two matrices appear in (a), (c), and (d) [the matrices are of type

$n \times m$ in (a), and of type $1 \times m$ in (c) and (d)]. The product of a scalar and a matrix appears in (b), (c), and (d) [the fraction in (d) is the product of the scalar $1/g(\mathbf{a})^2$ and the matrix $g(\mathbf{a})Df(\mathbf{a}) - f(\mathbf{a})Dg(\mathbf{a})$]. Using ∇ to denote the gradient, we can rewrite (c) and (d) as

$$\nabla(fg)(\mathbf{a}) = g(\mathbf{a})\nabla f(\mathbf{a}) + f(\mathbf{a})\nabla g(\mathbf{a})$$

and

$$\nabla\left(\frac{f}{g}\right)(\mathbf{a}) = \frac{g(\mathbf{a})\nabla f(\mathbf{a}) - f(\mathbf{a})\nabla g(\mathbf{a})}{g(\mathbf{a})^2}.$$

If $\mathbf{v}$ and $\mathbf{w}$ are vector-valued functions of one variable (that is usually denoted by t), then their dot (or scalar) product is a real-valued function that assigns to every t the real number $\mathbf{v}(t) \cdot \mathbf{w}(t)$. Therefore, the derivative on the left side of (e) is the derivative of a real-valued function of one variable [hence the notation $()'$ instead of D]. Each term on the right side is a dot product of two vectors in $\mathbb{R}^n$. This time, $()'$ denotes the derivative of a vector-valued function of one variable (also called the velocity). All derivatives in (f) are derivatives of vector-valued functions of one variable. The left side is the derivative of the function that assigns a cross product of vectors $\mathbf{v}(t)$ and $\mathbf{w}(t)$ to every t. Since the cross product is defined only in $\mathbb{R}^3$, both $\mathbf{v}$ and $\mathbf{w}$ must have values in $\mathbb{R}^3$.

The proofs of statements (a)–(d) are analogous to the proofs of corresponding statements in the one-variable case. If we write vectors $\mathbf{v}$ and $\mathbf{w}$ in terms of their components, we can reduce the proofs of (e) and (f) again to the one-variable case. For completeness, the proofs are given in Appendix A.

▶ **EXAMPLE 2.61**

Let $f(x, y, z) = xy + e^z$ and $g(x, y, z) = y^2 \sin z$. Compute $D(fg)(0, 1, \pi)$.

SOLUTION

By the product rule (the vertical bar is read "evaluated at"),

$$
\begin{aligned}
D(fg)(0, 1, \pi) &= g(0, 1, \pi)D(f)(0, 1, \pi) + f(0, 1, \pi)D(g)(0, 1, \pi) \\
&= y^2 \sin z|_{(0,1,\pi)}[y \quad x \quad e^z]|_{(0,1,\pi)} + (xy + e^z)|_{(0,1,\pi)}[0 \quad 2y \sin z \quad y^2 \cos z]|_{(0,1,\pi)} \\
&= 0[1 \quad 0 \quad e^\pi] + e^\pi[0 \quad 0 \quad -1] = [0 \quad 0 \quad -e^\pi].
\end{aligned}
$$

Alternatively, we compute the product $(fg)(x, y, z) = xy^3 \sin z + y^2 e^z \sin z$ first, and then differentiate

$$
\begin{aligned}
D(fg)(0, 1, \pi) &= [y^3 \sin z \quad 3xy^2 \sin z + 2ye^z \sin z \quad xy^3 \cos z + y^2 e^z \sin z + y^2 e^z \cos z]\Big|_{(0,1,\pi)} \\
&= [0 \quad 0 \quad -e^\pi].
\end{aligned}
$$
◀

▶ **EXAMPLE 2.62**

Let $\mathbf{v}(t) = t\mathbf{i} + \sin t\mathbf{j} + \cos t\mathbf{k}$ and $\mathbf{w} = 3t\mathbf{i} + 2\mathbf{k}$. Compute $(\mathbf{v} \cdot \mathbf{w})'(t)$ directly (i.e., by first computing the dot product and then differentiating) and check your result by using the product rule (e) from Theorem 2.6.

SOLUTION

We compute the dot product of $\mathbf{v}$ and $\mathbf{w}$ to be

$$(\mathbf{v} \cdot \mathbf{w})(t) = \mathbf{v}(t) \cdot \mathbf{w}(t) = (t\mathbf{i} + \sin t\mathbf{j} + \cos t\mathbf{k}) \cdot (3t\mathbf{i} + 2\mathbf{k}) = 3t^2 + 2\cos t,$$

and thus, $(\mathbf{v} \cdot \mathbf{w})'(t) = 6t - 2\sin t$. Since $\mathbf{v}'(t) = \mathbf{i} + \cos t\mathbf{j} - \sin t\mathbf{k}$ and $\mathbf{w}'(t) = 3\mathbf{i}$, we get

$$\mathbf{v}'(t) \cdot \mathbf{w}(t) + \mathbf{v}(t) \cdot \mathbf{w}'(t) = (\mathbf{i} + \cos t\mathbf{j} - \sin t\mathbf{k}) \cdot (3t\mathbf{i} + 2\mathbf{k}) + (t\mathbf{i} + \sin t\mathbf{j} + \cos t\mathbf{k}) \cdot (3\mathbf{i})$$
$$= 6t - 2\sin t. \qquad ◀$$

▶ **EXAMPLE 2.63**

Compute $\nabla(f/g)(x, y, z)$ if $f(x, y, z) = -x^2y^2$ and $g(x, y, z) = 2yz$.

SOLUTION

Using the quotient rule, we get

$$\nabla(f/g)(x, y, z) = \frac{g(x, y, z)\nabla f(x, y, z) - f(x, y, z)\nabla g(x, y, z)}{g(x, y, z)^2}$$
$$= \frac{2yz[-2xy^2 \quad -2x^2y \quad 0] + x^2y^2[0 \quad 2z \quad 2y]}{4y^2z^2}$$
$$= \frac{[-4xy^3z \quad -2x^2y^2z \quad 2x^2y^3]}{4y^2z^2}$$
$$= \left[\frac{-xy}{z} \quad -\frac{x^2}{2z} \quad \frac{x^2y}{2z^2}\right].$$

In the last step, the matrix in the numerator was multiplied by the function $1/4y^2z^2$. ◀

We could have computed $\nabla(f/g)$ in the previous example without using the quotient rule: since $(f/g)(x, y, z) = -x^2y^2/2yz = -x^2y/2z$, it follows that

$$\nabla(f/g)(x, y, z) = \left[\frac{-xy}{z} \quad -\frac{x^2}{2z} \quad \frac{x^2y}{2z^2}\right].$$

However, in certain situations it will be impossible to avoid using the rules (a)–(f) from Theorem 2.6 (see Examples 2.64 and 2.65).

▶ **EXAMPLE 2.64** Motion of an Object on the Surface of a Sphere

Assume that an object moves in space so that its distance from the origin O remains constant; that is, $||\mathbf{r}(t)|| = c$, where $\mathbf{r}(t)$ is the position vector of the object and $c > 0$. In other words, the object moves along the surface of the sphere with radius c centered at the origin. Now $||\mathbf{r}(t)||^2 = c^2$ is also constant and hence $(d/dt)||\mathbf{r}(t)||^2 = 0$ and (by the product rule)

$$0 = \frac{d}{dt}||\mathbf{r}(t)||^2 = \frac{d}{dt}(\mathbf{r}(t) \cdot \mathbf{r}(t)) = \left(\frac{d}{dt}\mathbf{r}(t)\right) \cdot \mathbf{r}(t) + \mathbf{r}(t) \cdot \left(\frac{d}{dt}\mathbf{r}(t)\right) = 2\mathbf{r}(t) \cdot \mathbf{v}(t),$$

where $\mathbf{v}t = d\mathbf{r}(t)/dt$ is the velocity of the object at time t. Hence, $\mathbf{r}(t) \cdot \mathbf{v}(t) = 0$, so that either $\mathbf{v}(t) = 0$ (which means that the object is at rest), or the velocity vector is always orthogonal to the position vector $\mathbf{r}(t)$; see Figure 2.60.

The converse of the above statement is true as well: if the object moves so that $\mathbf{r}(t) \cdot \mathbf{v}(t) = 0$, then the computation above (read from right to left) shows that $d||\mathbf{r}(t)||^2/dt = 0$; that is, $||\mathbf{r}(t)|| = $ constant. Consequently, the object moves on the surface of a sphere. ◀

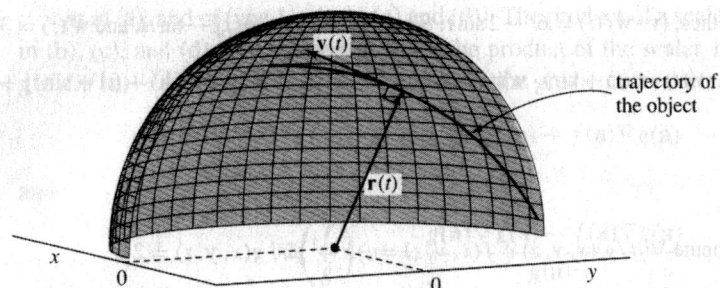

Figure 2.60 For motion on a sphere centered at the origin, the velocity vector is always perpendicular to the position vector.

▶ **EXAMPLE 2.65** Kinetic Energy of a Charged Particle in a Magnetic Field

Consider the motion of a particle [described by the vector function $\mathbf{r}(t)$] of mass m and charge q in a constant magnetic field $\mathbf{B}$, with no electric field present. The electromagnetic force [see formula (2.5), with $\mathbf{E} = \mathbf{0}$], $\mathbf{F}(\mathbf{r}(t)) = q(\mathbf{v}(t) \times \mathbf{B})$ and Newton's Second Law, $\mathbf{F}(\mathbf{r}(t)) = m\mathbf{a}(t) = m\mathbf{v}'(t)$, imply that $m\mathbf{v}'(t) = q(\mathbf{v}(t)) \times \mathbf{B})$. Show that the kinetic energy $K(t) = m||\mathbf{v}(t)||^2/2$ is constant in time.

SOLUTION   We will show that the derivative of $K(t)$ is zero:

$$\left(\frac{1}{2}m||\mathbf{v}(t)||^2\right)' = \frac{1}{2}m(\mathbf{v}(t) \cdot \mathbf{v}(t))' = \frac{1}{2}m(\mathbf{v}(t) \cdot \mathbf{v}'(t) + \mathbf{v}'(t) \cdot \mathbf{v}(t))$$
$$= m\mathbf{v}(t) \cdot \mathbf{v}'(t) = m\left(\mathbf{v}(t) \cdot \frac{q}{m}(\mathbf{v}(t) \times \mathbf{B})\right)$$
$$= q(\mathbf{v}(t) \cdot (\mathbf{v}(t) \times \mathbf{B}))$$

(the product rule was used in the first line, and Newton's Second Law was used in the second line). By definition of the vector product, the vector $\mathbf{v}(t) \times \mathbf{B}$ is perpendicular to $\mathbf{v}(t)$ and hence their scalar product $\mathbf{v}(t) \cdot (\mathbf{v}(t) \times \mathbf{B})$ is zero.

Note that the fact $m||\mathbf{v}(t)||^2/2$ is constant implies that the speed $||\mathbf{v}(t)||$ of the particle is constant.   ◀

The statement of our next theorem is a generalization of the one-variable chain rule.

THEOREM 2.7 Chain Rule

Suppose that $\mathbf{F}: U \subseteq \mathbb{R}^m \to \mathbb{R}^n$ is differentiable at $\mathbf{a} \in U$, U is open in $\mathbb{R}^m$, $\mathbf{G}: V \subseteq \mathbb{R}^n \to \mathbb{R}^p$ is differentiable at $\mathbf{F}(\mathbf{a}) \in V$, V is open in $\mathbb{R}^n$, and $\mathbf{F}(U) \subseteq V$ (so that the composition $\mathbf{G} \circ \mathbf{F}$ is defined). Then $\mathbf{G} \circ \mathbf{F}$ is differentiable at $\mathbf{a}$ and

$$D(\mathbf{G} \circ \mathbf{F})(\mathbf{a}) = D\mathbf{G}(\mathbf{F}(\mathbf{a})) \cdot D\mathbf{F}(\mathbf{a}),$$

where $\cdot$ denotes matrix multiplication.   ◀

This theorem states that the derivative of the composition $\mathbf{G} \circ \mathbf{F}$ at a point $\mathbf{a}$ in U can be computed as a matrix product of the derivative of $\mathbf{G}$ [evaluated at $\mathbf{F}(\mathbf{a})$] and the derivative of $\mathbf{F}$ [evaluated at $\mathbf{a}$]. One easily checks that the matrices on both sides of the chain rule formula are of the same type: since $\mathbf{G} \circ \mathbf{F}: U \subseteq \mathbb{R}^m \to \mathbb{R}^p$, $D(\mathbf{G} \circ \mathbf{F})$ is a $p \times m$ matrix.

The right side is a product of the $p \times n$ matrix $D\mathbf{G}(\mathbf{F}(\mathbf{a}))$ and the $n \times m$ matrix $D\mathbf{F}(\mathbf{a})$, and is hence a $p \times m$ matrix. The proof of this theorem is given in Appendix A.

We now study examples, to gain experience in working with the chain rule.

► **EXAMPLE 2.66**

Let $\mathbf{F}: \mathbb{R}^2 \to \mathbb{R}^3$ be given by $\mathbf{F}(x, y) = (x^3 + y, e^{xy}, 2 + xy)$ and let $\mathbf{G}: \mathbb{R}^3 \to \mathbb{R}^2$ be given by $\mathbf{G}(u, v, w) = (u^2 + v, uv + w^3)$. Compute $D(\mathbf{G} \circ \mathbf{F})(0, 1)$.

SOLUTION By the chain rule,

$$D(\mathbf{G} \circ \mathbf{F})(0, 1) = D\mathbf{G}(\mathbf{F}(0, 1)) \cdot D\mathbf{F}(0, 1) = D\mathbf{G}(1, 1, 2) \cdot D\mathbf{F}(0, 1).$$

The derivatives of F and G are computed to be

$$D\mathbf{F}(0, 1) = \begin{bmatrix} 3x^2 & 1 \\ ye^{xy} & xe^{xy} \\ y & x \end{bmatrix}_{at\ (0,1)} = \begin{bmatrix} 0 & 1 \\ 1 & 0 \\ 1 & 0 \end{bmatrix}$$

and

$$D\mathbf{G}(1, 1, 2) = \begin{bmatrix} 2u & 1 & 0 \\ v & u & 3w^2 \end{bmatrix}_{at\ (1,1,2)} = \begin{bmatrix} 2 & 1 & 0 \\ 1 & 1 & 12 \end{bmatrix},$$

so that

$$D(\mathbf{G} \circ \mathbf{F})(0, 1) = \begin{bmatrix} 2 & 1 & 0 \\ 1 & 1 & 12 \end{bmatrix} \cdot \begin{bmatrix} 0 & 1 \\ 1 & 0 \\ 1 & 0 \end{bmatrix} = \begin{bmatrix} 1 & 2 \\ 13 & 1 \end{bmatrix}.$$

To check the result, compute the composition

$$\begin{aligned}(\mathbf{G} \circ \mathbf{F})(x, y) = \mathbf{G}(\mathbf{F}(x, y)) &= \mathbf{G}(x^3 + y, e^{xy}, 2 + xy) \\ &= ((x^3 + y)^2 + e^{xy}, (x^3 + y)e^{xy} + (2 + xy)^3),\end{aligned}$$

to obtain the function $\mathbf{G} \circ \mathbf{F}: \mathbb{R}^2 \to \mathbb{R}^2$. Its derivative $D(\mathbf{G} \circ \mathbf{F})$ is a 2×2 matrix

$$D(\mathbf{G} \circ \mathbf{F})(x, y) = \begin{bmatrix} 6(x^3 + y)x^2 + ye^{xy} & 2(x^3 + y)^2 + xe^{xy} \\ 3x^2e^{xy} + (x^3 + y)ye^{xy} + 3(2 + xy)^2y & e^{xy} + xye^{xy} + 3(2 + xy)^2x \end{bmatrix},$$

and therefore,

$$D(\mathbf{G} \circ \mathbf{F})(0, 1) = \begin{bmatrix} 1 & 2 \\ 13 & 1 \end{bmatrix}. \quad ◄$$

► **EXAMPLE 2.67**

The composition $(f \circ \mathbf{c})(t)$ of $f: \mathbb{R}^2 \to \mathbb{R}$, $f(x, y) = x^2 + 2y^2$, and $\mathbf{c}: \mathbb{R} \to \mathbb{R}^2$, $\mathbf{c}(t) = (e^t, te^t)$, is a real-valued function of one variable. Compute $(f \circ \mathbf{c})'(0)$.

SOLUTION By the chain rule,

$$(f \circ \mathbf{c})'(0) = D(f \circ \mathbf{c})(0) = Df(\mathbf{c}(0)) \cdot D\mathbf{c}(0) = Df(1, 0) \cdot D\mathbf{c}(0).$$

The function f is a real-valued function of two variables, so its derivative (also called the gradient) is a 1×2 matrix $Df(x, y) = [2x \quad 4y]$. Hence, $Df(1, 0) = [2 \quad 0]$. The function $\mathbf{c}$ (also called a path in $\mathbb{R}^2$) is a function of one variable, and its derivative $D\mathbf{c}(t) = \mathbf{c}'(t)$ is the 2×1 matrix

$$D\mathbf{c}(t) = \begin{bmatrix} e^t \\ e^t + te^t \end{bmatrix}.$$

Consequently,

$$D\mathbf{c}(0) = \begin{bmatrix} 1 \\ 1 \end{bmatrix}$$

and

$$(f \circ \mathbf{c})'(0) = Df(1, 0) \cdot D\mathbf{c}(0) = \begin{bmatrix} 2 & 0 \end{bmatrix} \cdot \begin{bmatrix} 1 \\ 1 \end{bmatrix} = 2.$$

We check this by direct computation: since $(f \circ \mathbf{c})(t) = f(\mathbf{c}(t)) = f(e^t, te^t) = e^{2t} + 2t^2 e^{2t}$, it follows that $(f \circ \mathbf{c})'(t) = 2e^{2t} + 4te^{2t} + 4t^2 e^{2t}$, and, consequently, $(f \circ \mathbf{c})'(0) = 2$. ◀

▶ **EXAMPLE 2.68**

Consider the composition $f \circ \mathbf{c}$, where $f = f(x, y, z)\colon \mathbb{R}^3 \to \mathbb{R}$, and $\mathbf{c}\colon \mathbb{R} \to \mathbb{R}^3$ is given by $\mathbf{c}(t) = (x(t), y(t), z(t))$. Assume that both f and $\mathbf{c}$ are differentiable. Then

$$(f \circ \mathbf{c})(t) = f(\mathbf{c}(t)) = f(x(t), y(t), z(t)),$$

and, by the chain rule,

$$D(f \circ \mathbf{c})(t) = Df(\mathbf{c}(t)) \cdot D\mathbf{c}(t) = \begin{bmatrix} \dfrac{\partial f}{\partial x} & \dfrac{\partial f}{\partial y} & \dfrac{\partial f}{\partial z} \end{bmatrix}_{at\ \mathbf{c}(t)} \cdot \begin{bmatrix} \dfrac{\partial x}{\partial t} \\[1mm] \dfrac{\partial y}{\partial t} \\[1mm] \dfrac{\partial z}{\partial t} \end{bmatrix}_{at\ t}, \tag{2.23}$$

so that

$$D(f \circ \mathbf{c})(t) = \frac{\partial f}{\partial x}(\mathbf{c}(t))\frac{\partial x}{\partial t}(t) + \frac{\partial f}{\partial y}(\mathbf{c}(t))\frac{\partial y}{\partial t}(t) + \frac{\partial f}{\partial z}(\mathbf{c}(t))\frac{\partial z}{\partial t}(t),$$

or (dropping the notation for the dependence on a point)

$$D(f \circ \mathbf{c})(t) = \frac{\partial f}{\partial x}\frac{dx}{dt} + \frac{\partial f}{\partial y}\frac{dy}{dt} + \frac{\partial f}{\partial z}\frac{dz}{dt}. \tag{2.24}$$

We have replaced the partial derivative notation $\partial x/\partial t$, $\partial y/\partial t$, and $\partial z/\partial t$ by dx/dt, dy/dt, and dz/dt, since x, y, and z are functions of one variable (we could have used x', y', and z' instead). The 1×3 matrix in (2.23) is the gradient of f evaluated at $\mathbf{c}(t)$, and the 3×1 matrix is the derivative $\mathbf{c}'(t)$. Hence, (2.24) can be written as

$$D(f \circ \mathbf{c})(t) = \nabla f(\mathbf{c}(t)) \cdot \mathbf{c}'(t), \tag{2.25}$$

where the multiplication on the right side is interpreted either as a matrix multiplication, or as a dot product if both matrices $\nabla f(\mathbf{c}(t))$ and $\mathbf{c}'(t)$ are viewed as vectors in $\mathbb{R}^3$. ◀

Note that the calculations in the previous example can easily be extended to any number of variables. Thus, (2.25) holds for any differentiable function $f : \mathbb{R}^n \to \mathbb{R}$ and any differentiable path $\mathbf{c}\colon \mathbb{R} \to \mathbb{R}^n$.

▶ **EXAMPLE 2.69**

Assume that $f = f(x, y): \mathbb{R}^2 \to \mathbb{R}$ is a differentiable function.

(a) Let $g_1(t) = f(t, t^2)$. Find $g_1'(t)$.

(b) Let $g_2(t) = f(t, f(t, t^2))$. Compute $g_2'(t)$. Assuming that $f(1, 1) = 2$, find $g_2'(1)$.

SOLUTION

(a) Note that $g_1 = f \circ \mathbf{c}$, where $\mathbf{c}(t) = (t, t^2)$. Using (2.25), we obtain

$$g_1'(t) = (f \circ \mathbf{c})'(t) = \nabla f(\mathbf{c}(t)) \cdot \mathbf{c}'(t) = \nabla f(t, t^2) \cdot (1, 2t).$$

Using D_1 and D_2 to denote the partial derivatives of f with respect to its first and second variables, we rewrite the above as

$$g_1'(t) = (D_1 f(t, t^2), D_2 f(t, t^2)) \cdot (1, 2t) = D_1 f(t, t^2) + 2t D_2 f(t, t^2).$$

Alternatively, we compute the derivative directly from $g_1(t) = f(t, t^2)$ using a variant of (2.24) for a function of two variables ("f with respect to its first variable times first variable with respect to t, plus f with respect to its second variable times second variable with respect to t"):

$$g_1'(t) = D_1 f(t, t^2)(t)' + D_2 f(t, t^2)(t^2)' = D_1 f(t, t^2) + 2t D_2 f(t, t^2).$$

(b) Proceeding as above, we start with the chain rule (2.24) for two variables:

$$g_2'(t) = D_1 f(t, f(t, t^2))(t)' + D_2 f(t, f(t, t^2))(f(t, t^2))'$$

Using (a), we obtain

$$g_2'(t) = D_1 f(t, f(t, t^2)) + D_2 f(t, f(t, t^2))(D_1 f(t, t^2) + 2t D_2 f(t, t^2)).$$

Thus, when $t = 1$,

$$g_2'(1) = D_1 f(1, 2) + D_2 f(1, 2)(D_1 f(1, 1) + 2 D_2 f(1, 1)). \qquad \blacktriangleleft$$

▶ **EXAMPLE 2.70**

Let $f: \mathbb{R}^3 \to \mathbb{R}$, and let $\mathbf{G}: \mathbb{R}^3 \to \mathbb{R}^3$ be given by

$$\mathbf{G}(x, y, z) = (u(x, y, z), v(x, y, z), w(x, y, z)).$$

Assume that f and $\mathbf{G}$ are differentiable. Define $h: \mathbb{R}^3 \to \mathbb{R}$ by $h = f \circ \mathbf{G}$, that is,

$$h(x, y, z) = (f \circ \mathbf{G})(x, y, z) = f(\mathbf{G}(x, y, z)) = f(u(x, y, z), v(x, y, z), w(x, y, z)).$$

Compute $\partial h/\partial x$, $\partial h/\partial y$, and $\partial h/\partial z$ using the chain rule.

SOLUTION

The derivative of h (which is a function of x, y, and z) is given by the 1×3 matrix

$$Dh = \begin{bmatrix} \dfrac{\partial h}{\partial x} & \dfrac{\partial h}{\partial y} & \dfrac{\partial h}{\partial z} \end{bmatrix}.$$

Using the symbols $D_1 f$, $D_2 f$, and $D_3 f$ to denote the partial derivatives of f with respect to its variables, we write $Df = [D_1 f \quad D_2 f \quad D_3 f]$. By the chain rule,

$$Dh = Df \cdot DG = [D_1 f \quad D_2 f \quad D_3 f] \cdot \begin{bmatrix} \dfrac{\partial u}{\partial x} & \dfrac{\partial u}{\partial y} & \dfrac{\partial u}{\partial z} \\[2mm] \dfrac{\partial v}{\partial x} & \dfrac{\partial v}{\partial y} & \dfrac{\partial v}{\partial z} \\[2mm] \dfrac{\partial w}{\partial x} & \dfrac{\partial w}{\partial y} & \dfrac{\partial w}{\partial z} \end{bmatrix}.$$

and therefore,

$$\frac{\partial h}{\partial x} = D_1 f \frac{\partial u}{\partial x} + D_2 f \frac{\partial v}{\partial x} + D_3 f \frac{\partial w}{\partial x},$$

$$\frac{\partial h}{\partial y} = D_1 f \frac{\partial u}{\partial y} + D_2 f \frac{\partial v}{\partial y} + D_3 f \frac{\partial w}{\partial y},$$

and

$$\frac{\partial h}{\partial z} = D_1 f \frac{\partial u}{\partial z} + D_2 f \frac{\partial v}{\partial z} + D_3 f \frac{\partial w}{\partial z}. \tag{2.26}$$

Using u, v, and w for the variables of f, we write $D_1 f = \partial f / \partial u$, $D_2 f = \partial f / \partial v$, and $D_3 f = \partial f / \partial w$ and hence,

$$\frac{\partial h}{\partial x} = \frac{\partial f}{\partial u} \frac{\partial u}{\partial x} + \frac{\partial f}{\partial v} \frac{\partial v}{\partial x} + \frac{\partial f}{\partial w} \frac{\partial w}{\partial x}, \tag{2.27}$$

with similar expressions for $\partial h / \partial y$ and $\partial h / \partial z$. ◄

Example 2.70 shows us how to write partial derivatives of f in two different ways. As another exercise in notation, let us compute $\partial h / \partial x$ if $h(x, y) = f(x^2 + y^2, yz, e^x + y)$. We want the partial derivatives of f with respect to its variables, but cannot use expressions like $\partial f / \partial(x^2 + y^2)$ or $\partial f / \partial(yz)$. One approach to solving this notational difficulty is to introduce new variables $u = x^2 + y^2$, $v = yz$, $w = e^x + y$, write $h = f(u, v, w)$, and then use $\partial f / \partial u$, $\partial f / \partial v$, and $\partial f / \partial w$ for partial derivatives. Thus,

$$\frac{\partial h}{\partial x} = \frac{\partial f}{\partial u} \cdot 2x + \frac{\partial f}{\partial v} \cdot 0 + \frac{\partial f}{\partial w} \cdot e^x.$$

Alternatively, using the "D_i" notation for partial derivatives, we write

$$\frac{\partial h}{\partial x} = D_1 f \cdot 2x + D_2 f \cdot 0 + D_3 f \cdot e^x,$$

without explicitly mentioning the names of variables.

Let us make note of a notational convention commonly used in expressions involving the chain rule. Assume that $f = f(x, y)$ is a real-valued function of two variables x and y—take, for example, $f(x, y) = x^2 - 2y^2$ and let $x = u^2 + v^2$ and $y = uv$. Then

$$f(x, y) = f(u^2 + v^2, uv) = (u^2 + v^2)^2 - 2(uv)^2 = u^4 + v^4,$$

so f becomes a function of (new) variables u and v. This process is called *change of variables* and will be discussed in more detail later (e.g., as a technique in integration). It can be described as a composition of functions $h = f \circ \mathbf{P}$, where $\mathbf{P}: \mathbb{R}^2 \to \mathbb{R}^2$ is defined by $\mathbf{P}(u, v) = (u^2 + v^2, uv)$. Let us check this:

$$h(u, v) = (f \circ \mathbf{P})(u, v) = f(\mathbf{P}(u, v)) = f(u^2 + v^2, uv) = u^4 + v^4.$$

Although, strictly speaking, f and h are two different functions (they depend on different variables and, in general, might have different domains), it is a standard practice (especially in applied mathematics) to use the same notation for both. In this context, $f(u, v)$ denotes the function $h(u, v)$, that is, the function f expressed in terms of variables u and v, and $f(x, y)$ denotes, as usual, the function f as a function of x and y. For example, from $f(x, y) = x^2 - 2y^2$, we get $\partial f/\partial x = 2x$, but $\partial f/\partial u$ is not zero, since it does not refer to $f(x, y) = x^2 - 2y^2$ but to $f(u, v) = u^4 + v^4$. Hence, $\partial f/\partial u = 4u^3$.

With this convention in mind, we write the chain rule formula (2.27) as

$$\frac{\partial f}{\partial x} = \frac{\partial f}{\partial u}\frac{\partial u}{\partial x} + \frac{\partial f}{\partial v}\frac{\partial v}{\partial x} + \frac{\partial f}{\partial w}\frac{\partial w}{\partial x}.$$

(f on the left represents f viewed as a function of x, y, and z, and f on the right side is f viewed as a function of u, v, and w.)

► EXAMPLE 2.71

Let $f(u, v, w) = u^2 + v^3 e^w$, where $u = \sin(x + y + z)$, $v = x^2 e^y$, and $w = z$. Compute partial derivatives $\partial f/\partial x$, $\partial f/\partial y$, and $\partial f/\partial z$.

SOLUTION
Using the convention just adopted and formula (2.27), we get

$$\frac{\partial f}{\partial x} = \frac{\partial f}{\partial u}\frac{\partial u}{\partial x} + \frac{\partial f}{\partial v}\frac{\partial v}{\partial x} + \frac{\partial f}{\partial w}\frac{\partial w}{\partial x}$$

[f on the left side is $f(x, y, z) = (\sin(x + y + z))^2 + (x^2 e^y)^3 e^z$, and f on the right side is $f(u, v, w) = u^2 + v^3 e^w$]. Thus,

$$\frac{\partial f}{\partial x} = 2u \cdot \cos(x + y + z) + 3v^2 e^w \cdot 2x e^y + v^3 e^w \cdot 0$$
$$= 2\sin(x + y + z)\cos(x + y + z) + 6x^5 e^{3y+z}.$$

The last line was obtained by substituting the expressions for u, v, and w. Similarly,

$$\frac{\partial f}{\partial y} = \frac{\partial f}{\partial u}\frac{\partial u}{\partial y} + \frac{\partial f}{\partial v}\frac{\partial v}{\partial y} + \frac{\partial f}{\partial w}\frac{\partial w}{\partial y} = 2u \cdot \cos(x + y + z) + 3v^2 e^w \cdot x^2 e^y + v^3 e^w \cdot 0$$
$$= 2\sin(x + y + z)\cos(x + y + z) + 3x^6 e^{3y+z},$$

and

$$\frac{\partial f}{\partial z} = \frac{\partial f}{\partial u}\frac{\partial u}{\partial z} + \frac{\partial f}{\partial v}\frac{\partial v}{\partial z} + \frac{\partial f}{\partial w}\frac{\partial w}{\partial z} = 2u \cdot \cos(x + y + z) + 3v^2 e^w \cdot 0 + v^3 e^w \cdot 1$$
$$= 2\sin(x + y + z)\cos(x + y + z) + x^6 e^{3y+z}. \qquad ◄$$

► EXAMPLE 2.72 Partial Derivatives on a Surface

Let $f = f(x, y, z)$: $\mathbb{R}^3 \to \mathbb{R}$ and $z = g(x, y)$: $\mathbb{R}^2 \to \mathbb{R}$ be differentiable functions [recall that the graph of $z = g(x, y)$ is a surface in $\mathbb{R}^3$]. The function $w = w(x, y) = f(x, y, g(x, y))$: $\mathbb{R}^2 \to \mathbb{R}$ computes the value of f at the points $(x, y, g(x, y))$, which belong to the (surface which is the) graph of $z = g(x, y)$. The function w is called the *restriction* of f to the surface $z = g(x, y)$. Compute $\partial w/\partial x$ and $\partial w/\partial y$.

SOLUTION View w as the composition $w = f \circ \mathbf{G}$, where the function $\mathbf{G}: \mathbb{R}^2 \to \mathbb{R}^3$ is defined by $\mathbf{G}(x, y) = (x, y, g(x, y))$. By the chain rule, $Dw = Df \cdot D\mathbf{G}$, where

$$Dw = \begin{bmatrix} \dfrac{\partial w}{\partial x} & \dfrac{\partial w}{\partial y} \end{bmatrix}.$$

and

$$Df \cdot D\mathbf{G} = \begin{bmatrix} \dfrac{\partial f}{\partial x} & \dfrac{\partial f}{\partial y} & \dfrac{\partial f}{\partial z} \end{bmatrix} \cdot \begin{bmatrix} 1 & 0 \\ 0 & 1 \\ \dfrac{\partial g}{\partial x} & \dfrac{\partial g}{\partial y} \end{bmatrix}.$$

Computing the product $Df \cdot D\mathbf{G}$ and comparing to Dw, we get

$$\frac{\partial w}{\partial x} = \frac{\partial f}{\partial x} + \frac{\partial f}{\partial z}\frac{\partial g}{\partial x},$$

and

$$\frac{\partial w}{\partial y} = \frac{\partial f}{\partial y} + \frac{\partial f}{\partial z}\frac{\partial g}{\partial y}.$$

Alternatively, we could have applied the first formula in (2.26) to $w = f(x, y, z)$, where $z = g(x, y)$, to get

$$\frac{\partial w}{\partial x} = D_1 f \frac{\partial x}{\partial x} + D_2 f \frac{\partial y}{\partial x} + D_3 f \frac{\partial z}{\partial x}.$$

Realizing that $\partial x/\partial x = 1$, $\partial y/\partial x = 0$, and $\partial z/\partial x = \partial g/\partial x$, we can rewrite it as

$$\frac{\partial w}{\partial x} = D_1 f + D_3 f \frac{\partial g}{\partial x}.$$

Finally, using x, y, and z as the variables of f and z to replace $g(x, y)$, we write

$$\frac{\partial w}{\partial x} = \frac{\partial f}{\partial x} + \frac{\partial f}{\partial z}\frac{\partial z}{\partial x}. \qquad \blacktriangleleft$$

▶ EXAMPLE 2.73 Polar Coordinates

Let $x = r\cos\theta$, $y = r\sin\theta$, and let $f = f(x, y)$ be a differentiable function. Express $\partial f/\partial r$ and $\partial f/\partial\theta$ in terms of $\partial f/\partial x$ and $\partial f/\partial y$.

SOLUTION We interpret the change from Cartesian coordinates to polar coordinates as the map $\mathbf{P}: \mathbb{R}^2 \to \mathbb{R}^2$ defined by $\mathbf{P}(r, \theta) = (r\cos\theta, r\sin\theta)$, and consider the composition $h = f \circ \mathbf{P}$. Then

$$h(r, \theta) = f(\mathbf{P}(r, \theta)) = f(r\cos\theta, r\sin\theta);$$

that is, h is the function f "expressed in terms of polar coordinates." The chain rule applied to $h(r, \theta) = (f \circ \mathbf{P})(r, \theta)$ yields

$$Dh(r, \theta) = Df(\mathbf{P}(r, \theta)) \cdot D\mathbf{P}(r, \theta) = Df(x, y) \cdot D\mathbf{P}(r, \theta),$$

and in matrix notation,

$$\begin{bmatrix} \dfrac{\partial h}{\partial r} & \dfrac{\partial h}{\partial \theta} \end{bmatrix} = \begin{bmatrix} \dfrac{\partial f}{\partial x} & \dfrac{\partial f}{\partial y} \end{bmatrix} \cdot \begin{bmatrix} \cos\theta & -r\sin\theta \\ \sin\theta & r\cos\theta \end{bmatrix}.$$

Now, replacing $h(r, \theta)$ by $f(r, \theta)$, following the usual convention, we obtain

$$\frac{\partial f}{\partial r} = \frac{\partial f}{\partial x} \cos\theta + \frac{\partial f}{\partial y} \sin\theta,$$

and

$$\frac{\partial f}{\partial \theta} = \frac{\partial f}{\partial x}(-r\sin\theta) + \frac{\partial f}{\partial y} r\cos\theta.$$ ◄

► EXAMPLE 2.74

Let $x = r\cos\theta$, $y = r\sin\theta$, and $f(x, y) = xe^{x^2+y^2}$. Find $\partial f/\partial r$ and $\partial f/\partial\theta$ directly, and then using the chain rule.

SOLUTION

Since $f(x, y) = xe^{x^2+y^2} = r\cos\theta e^{r^2}$, we get $f(r, \theta) = r\cos\theta e^{r^2}$ (both functions are called f—recall the notational convention!) and hence $\partial f/\partial r = (e^{r^2} + 2r^2 e^{r^2})\cos\theta$ and $\partial f/\partial\theta = -re^{r^2}\sin\theta$. Using the result of the previous example, we obtain

$$\frac{\partial f}{\partial r} = \frac{\partial f}{\partial x}\cos\theta + \frac{\partial f}{\partial y}\sin\theta = (e^{x^2+y^2} + 2x^2 e^{x^2+y^2})\cos\theta + 2xy e^{x^2+y^2}\sin\theta$$

$$= (e^{r^2} + 2r^2\cos^2\theta e^{r^2})\cos\theta + 2r^2 e^{r^2}\sin\theta\cos\theta\sin\theta = (e^{r^2} + 2r^2 e^{r^2})\cos\theta.$$

The expression for $\partial f/\partial\theta$ is obtained similarly. ◄

Notice that in this case the direct computation was faster (and easier). However, there are situations where not only does the chain rule provide a more efficient way, but the direct computation cannot be applied at all; see Exercise 27.

► EXERCISES 2.6

1. Assume that g is a differentiable, real-valued function of two variables and let $f(x, y) = g(x^2 - y^2, y^2 - x^2)$. Prove that $x(\partial f/\partial y) + y(\partial f/\partial x) = 0$.

2. Assume that g is a differentiable real-valued function of one variable, such that $g(1) = 2$ and $g'(1) = 3$.

(a) If $f(x, y) = g(x) + g(x^2)g(y)$, find $(\partial f/\partial x)(x, y)$ and $(\partial f/\partial x)(1, 1)$.

(b) If $f(x, y) = g(x)^{g(y)}$, find $(\partial f/\partial x)(1, 1)$ and $(\partial f/\partial y)(1, 1)$.

3. Find $g'(t)$ if $g(t) = f(t\sin t, t\cos t, t)$, where f is a differentiable function.

4. Assume that f is a differentiable function and let $g(t) = \sin(f(-t, t, 2t))$. Find $g'(t)$.

Exercises 5 to 7: In each case, compute $(f\circ \mathbf{c})'(t)$ in two different ways: by computing the composition first and then differentiating, and by using formula (2.25).

5. $f(x, y) = x^2 y$, $\mathbf{c}(t) = (\sin t, \cos t)$.

6. $f(x, y) = ye^{xy}$, $\mathbf{c}(t) = (t, \ln t)$.

7. $f(x, y, z) = xy + \cos(x^2 + z^2)$, $\mathbf{c}(t) = (t\sin t, t, t\cos t)$.

8. Assume that f is a differentiable function of two variables, and $D_1 f(2, 2) = -2$ and $D_2 f(2, 2) = 4$.

(a) Find $g'(2)$ if $g(x) = f(x, 2)$.

(b) Let $g(x) = f(x, x)$. Find $g'(2)$.

(c) Let $g(x) = f(x^2, x^3)$. Find $g'(x)$.

9. Let $f(x, y) = g(x^2 y, 2x + 5y, x, y)$, where g is a differentiable function of four variables. Find f_x and f_y.

10. Let $f: \mathbb{R}^2 \to \mathbb{R}^3$ be given by $f(x, y) = (h(x), g(y), k(x, y))$, where h, g, and k are differentiable functions of variables indicated. Find Df.

11. Let $F(x, y) = f(h(x), g(y), k(x, y))$, where $f: \mathbb{R}^3 \to \mathbb{R}$, and all functions involved are assumed to be differentiable. Find F_x and F_y.

12. Let $z = f(r)$, where $r = \sqrt{x^2 + y^2}$ and f is a differentiable function. Prove that $yz_x - xz_y = 0$ for all $(x, y) \neq (0, 0)$.

13. Let $f(x, y) = x^2 + xy$ and $g(x, y) = \ln x + \ln y$. Compute $\nabla(fg)(x, y)$ and $\nabla(f/g)(2, 2)$.

14. Let $\mathbf{G}(x, y) = (2xy, y^2 - x^2)$. Compute $D\mathbf{G}(x, y)$ and $D\mathbf{G}(3, 0)$.

15. Let $f(x, y, z) = x^2 + \sin(yz) - 3$. Find $D(f/x)(1, \pi, -1)$ and $D(x^2 y f)(2, 0, 1)$.

16. Let $w = f(x, y, z)$, where $x = r \cos\theta$ and $y = r \sin\theta$. Find $\partial w / \partial r$, $\partial w / \partial \theta$, and $\partial w / \partial z$.

17. Let $w = f(x, y, z)$, where $x = \rho \sin\phi \cos\theta$, $y = \rho \sin\phi \sin\theta$, and $z = \rho \cos\phi$. Find $\partial w / \partial \rho$, $\partial w / \partial \theta$, and $\partial w / \partial \phi$.

18. Let $\mathbf{v}(t) = t\mathbf{i} + (t^2 + 1)\mathbf{j}$ and $\mathbf{w}(t) = \mathbf{i} - 2t\mathbf{j} + e^t\mathbf{k}$. Compute $(\mathbf{v} \cdot \mathbf{w})'(t)$ directly (i.e., by computing the dot product first and then differentiating) and then check your answer using the product rule.

19. Let $\mathbf{v}(t) = t^3\mathbf{i} + te^t\mathbf{k}$ and $\mathbf{w}(t) = -2t\mathbf{j}$. Compute $(\mathbf{v} \times \mathbf{w})'(t)$ directly (i.e., by computing the cross product first) and then check your answer using the product rule.

20. Let $\mathbf{u}(t) = \sin t\,\mathbf{i} + \cos t\,\mathbf{j} + t\mathbf{k}$, $\mathbf{v}(t) = \mathbf{i} + t\mathbf{j} + \mathbf{k}$, and $\mathbf{w}(t) = t^3(\mathbf{i} + \mathbf{j} + \mathbf{k})$. Compute $(\mathbf{u} \cdot (\mathbf{v} \times \mathbf{w}))'(t)$.

21. The function $\mathbf{F}: \mathbb{R}^2 \to \mathbb{R}^3$ is given by $\mathbf{F}(x, y) = (e^x, xy, e^y)$. Compute $D(g \circ \mathbf{F})(0, 0)$, where $g: \mathbb{R}^3 \to \mathbb{R}$ is given by $g(u, v, w) = uw + v^2$.

22. Let $f: \mathbb{R}^3 \to \mathbb{R}$ and $\mathbf{c}: \mathbb{R} \to \mathbb{R}^3$ be given by $f(x, y, z) = \sqrt{x^2 + y^2 + z^2}$ and $\mathbf{c}(t) = (\cos t, \sin t, 1)$. Compute $(f \circ \mathbf{c})'(t)$ and $(f \circ \mathbf{c})'(0)$.

23. Compute $\partial w / \partial x$ and $\partial w / \partial z$ if $w = f(x, y, z)$ and $y = g(x, z)$ are differentiable functions.

24. Let $w = \ln(r^2 + 1)$, where $r = \sqrt{x^2 + y^2}$. Find $\partial w / \partial y$.

25. Define a function $\mathbf{F}: \mathbb{R}^2 \to \mathbb{R}^2$ by $\mathbf{F}(\mathbf{x}) = A \cdot \mathbf{x}$, where A is a 2×2 matrix, and the dot indicates matrix multiplication. Compute $D\mathbf{F}(\mathbf{x})$. Prove that $\mathbf{F}$ is differentiable at any point $(a, b) \in \mathbb{R}^2$.

26. Let A and B be 2×2 matrices. Define $\mathbf{F}, \mathbf{G}: \mathbb{R}^2 \to \mathbb{R}^2$ by $\mathbf{F}(\mathbf{x}) = A \cdot \mathbf{x}$ and $\mathbf{G}(\mathbf{x}) = B \cdot \mathbf{x}$, where $\mathbf{x} \in \mathbb{R}^2$, and the dot indicates matrix multiplication. Find $D(\mathbf{G} \circ \mathbf{F})(\mathbf{x})$.

27. Let $f(x, y) = x^3 y$, where $x^3 + tx = 8$ and $ye^y = t$. Find $(df/dt)(0)$.

28. In Examples 2.46 and 2.47 in Section 2.4, we studied the function

$$f(x, y) = \begin{cases} \dfrac{xy}{x^2 + y^2} & \text{if } (x, y) \neq (0, 0) \\ 0 & \text{if } (x, y) = (0, 0) \end{cases}.$$

Let $\mathbf{c}(t) = (t, t^2)$.

(a) Compute the composition $(f \circ \mathbf{c})(t)$ and show that $(f \circ \mathbf{c})'(0) = 1$.

27. (a) Is the function $f(x, y, z) = x^2 - 2y^2 + z^2$ harmonic? What about $f(x, y, z) = x^2 + y^2 - z^2$?

(b) Laplace's equation for functions of n variables is

$$\frac{\partial^2 f}{\partial x_1^2} + \frac{\partial^2 f}{\partial x_2^2} + \cdots + \frac{\partial^2 f}{\partial x_n^2} = 0.$$

Find an example of a function of n variables that is harmonic, and show that your example is harmonic.

28. Show that the following functions are harmonic:

(a) $f(x, y) = \arctan \frac{y}{x}$

(b) $f(x, y) = \log(x^2 + y^2)$

29. Let f and g be C^2 functions of one variable. Set $\phi = f(x - t) + g(x + t)$.

(a) Prove that ϕ satisfies the wave equation: $\partial^2 \phi / \partial t^2 = \partial^2 \phi / \partial x^2$.

(b) Sketch the graph of ϕ against t and x if $f(x) = x^2$ and $g(x) = 0$.

30. (a) Show that function $g(x, t) = 2 + e^{-t} \sin x$ satisfies the heat equation: $g_t = g_{xx}$. [Here $g(x, t)$ represents the temperature in a metal rod at position x and time t.]

(b) Sketch the graph of g for $t \geq 0$. (HINT: Look at sections by the planes $t = 0$, $t = 1$, and $t = 2$.)

(c) What happens to $g(x, t)$ as $t \to \infty$? Interpret this limit in terms of the behavior of heat in the rod.

31. Show that Newton's potential $V = -GmM/r$ satisfies Laplace's equation

$$\frac{\partial^2 V}{\partial x^2} + \frac{\partial^2 V}{\partial y^2} + \frac{\partial^2 V}{\partial z^2} = 0 \quad \text{for} \quad (x, y, z) \neq (0, 0, 0).$$

32. Let

$$f(x, y) = \begin{cases} xy(x^2 - y^2)/(x^2 + y^2), & (x, y) \neq (0, 0) \\ 0, & (x, y) = (0, 0) \end{cases}$$

(see Figure 3.1.4).

(a) If $(x, y) \neq (0, 0)$, calculate $\partial f / \partial x$ and $\partial f / \partial y$.

(b) Show that $(\partial f / \partial x)(0, 0) = 0 = (\partial f / \partial y)(0, 0)$.

(c) Show that $(\partial^2 f / \partial x \, \partial y)(0, 0) = 1$, $(\partial^2 f / \partial y \, \partial x)(0, 0) = -1$.

(d) What went wrong? Why are the mixed partials not equal?

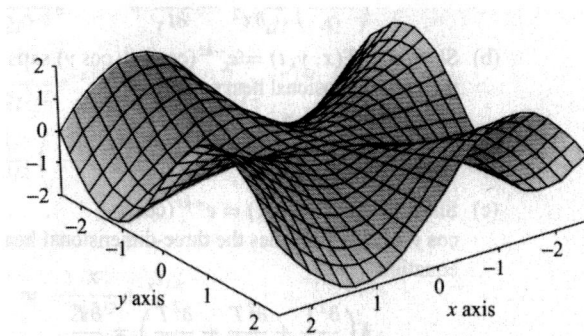

figure **3.1.4** The graph of the function in Exercise 32.

3.2 Taylor's Theorem

When we introduced the derivative in Chapter 2, we saw that the *linear approximation* of a function played an essential role for a geometric reason—finding the equation of a tangent plane—as well as an analytic reason—finding approximate values of functions. Taylor's theorem deals with the important issue of finding *quadratic and higher-order approximations*.

Taylor's theorem is a central tool for finding accurate numerical approximations of functions, and as such plays an important role in many areas of applied and computational mathematics. We shall use it in the next section to develop the second derivative test for maxima and minima of functions of several variables.

The strategy used to prove Taylor's theorem is to reduce it to the one-variable case by probing a function of many variables along lines of the form $l(t) = x_0 + t\mathbf{h}$ emanating from a point x_0 and heading in the direction $\mathbf{h}$. Thus, it will be useful for us to begin by reviewing Taylor's theorem from one-variable calculus.

Single-Variable Taylor Theorem

When recalling a theorem from an earlier course, it is helpful to ask these basic questions: What is the main point of the theorem? What are the key ideas in the proof? Can I understand the result better the second time around?

The main point of the single-variable Taylor theorem is to find approximations of a function near a given point that are accurate to a higher order than the linear approximation. The key idea in the proof is to use the *fundamental theorem of calculus*, followed by *integration by parts*. In fact, just by recalling these basic ideas, we can reconstruct the entire proof. Thinking in this way will help organize all the pieces that need to come together to develop a mastery of Taylor approximations of functions of one and several variables.

For a smooth function $f: \mathbb{R} \to \mathbb{R}$ of one variable, Taylor's theorem asserts that:

$$f(x_0 + h) = f(x_0) + f'(x_0) \cdot h + \frac{f''(x_0)}{2}h^2 + \cdots + \frac{f^{(k)}(x_0)}{k!}h^k + R_k(x_0, h), \quad (1)$$

where

$$R_k(x_0, h) = \int_{x_0}^{x_0+h} \frac{(x_0 + h - \tau)^k}{k!} f^{k+1}(\tau)\, d\tau$$

is the remainder. For small h, this remainder is small to order k in the sense that

$$\lim_{h \to 0} \frac{R_k(x_0, h)}{h^k} = 0. \quad (2)$$

In other words, $R_k(x_0, h)$ is small compared to the already small quantity h^k.

The preceding is the formal statement of Taylor's theorem. What about the proof? As promised, we begin with the fundamental theorem of calculus, written in the form:

$$f(x_0 + h) = f(x_0) + \int_{x_0}^{x_0+h} f'(\tau)\, d\tau.$$

Next, we write $d\tau = -d(x_0 + h - \tau)$ and integrate parts[1] to give:

$$f(x_0 + h) = f(x_0) + f'(x_0)h + \int_{x_0}^{x_0+h} f''(\tau)(x_0 + h - \tau)\, d\tau,$$

which is the first-order Taylor formula. Integrating by parts again:

$$\int_{x_0}^{x_0+h} f''(\tau)(x_0 + h - \tau)\, d\tau$$
$$= -\frac{1}{2}\int_{x_0}^{x_0+h} f''(\tau)\, d(x_0 + h - \tau)^2$$
$$= \frac{1}{2}f''(x_0)h^2 + \frac{1}{2}\int_{x_0}^{x_0+h} f'''(\tau)(x_0 + h - \tau)^2\, d\tau,$$

which, when substituted into the preceding formula, gives the **second-order Taylor formula**:

$$f(x_0 + h) = f(x_0) + f'(x_0)h + \frac{1}{2}f''(x_0)h^2 + \frac{1}{2}\int_{x_0}^{x_0+h} f'''(\tau)(x_0 + h - \tau)^2\, d\tau.$$

This is Taylor's theorem for $k = 2$.

---

[1] Recall that integration by parts (the product rule for the derivative read backward) reads as:

$$\int_a^b u\, dv = uv|_a^b - \int_a^b v\, du.$$

Here we choose $u = f'(\tau)$ and $v = x_0 + h - \tau$.

Taylor's theorem for general k proceeds by repeated integration by parts. The statement (2) that $R_k(x_0, h)/h^k \to 0$ as $h \to 0$ is seen as follows. For τ in the interval $[x_0, x_0 + h]$, we have $|x_0 + h - \tau| \le |h|$, and $f^{k+1}(\tau)$, being continuous, is bounded; say, $|f^{k+1}(\tau)| \le M$. Then:

$$|R_k(x_0, h)| = \left| \int_{x_0}^{x_0+h} \frac{(x_0 + h - \tau)^k}{k!} f^{k+1}(\tau)\, d\tau \right| \le \frac{|h|^{k+1}}{k!} M$$

and, in particular, $|R_k(x_0, h)/h^k| \le |h|\, M/k! \to 0$ as $h \to 0$.

Taylor's Theorem for Many Variables

Our next goal in this section is to prove an analogous theorem that is valid for functions of several variables. We already know a first-order version; that is, when $k = 1$. Indeed, if $f: \mathbb{R}^n \to \mathbb{R}$ is differentiable at $\mathbf{x}_0$ and we define

$$R_1(\mathbf{x}_0, \mathbf{h}) = f(\mathbf{x}_0 + \mathbf{h}) - f(\mathbf{x}_0) - [\mathbf{D}f(\mathbf{x}_0)](\mathbf{h}),$$

so that

$$f(\mathbf{x}_0 + \mathbf{h}) = f(\mathbf{x}_0) + [\mathbf{D}f(\mathbf{x}_0)](\mathbf{h}) + R_1(\mathbf{x}_0, \mathbf{h}),$$

then by the definition of differentiability,

$$\frac{|R_1(\mathbf{x}_0, \mathbf{h})|}{\|\mathbf{h}\|} \to 0 \quad \text{as} \quad \mathbf{h} \to 0;$$

that is, $R_1(\mathbf{x}_0, \mathbf{h})$ vanishes to first order at $\mathbf{x}_0$. In summary, we have:

Theorem 2 First-Order Taylor Formula Let $f: U \subset \mathbb{R}^n \to \mathbb{R}$ be differentiable at $\mathbf{x}_0 \in U$. Then

$$f(\mathbf{x}_0 + \mathbf{h}) = f(\mathbf{x}_0) + \sum_{i=1}^{n} h_i \frac{\partial f}{\partial x_i}(\mathbf{x}_0) + R_1(\mathbf{x}_0, \mathbf{h}),$$

where $R_1(\mathbf{x}_0, \mathbf{h})/\|\mathbf{h}\| \to 0$ as $\mathbf{h} \to 0$ in $\mathbb{R}^n$.

The second-order version is as follows:

Theorem 3 Second-Order Taylor Formula Let $f: U \subset \mathbb{R}^n \to \mathbb{R}$ have continuous partial derivatives of third order.[2] Then we may write

$$f(\mathbf{x}_0 + \mathbf{h}) = f(\mathbf{x}_0) + \sum_{i=1}^{n} h_i \frac{\partial f}{\partial x_i}(\mathbf{x}_0) + \frac{1}{2} \sum_{i,j=1}^{n} h_i h_j \frac{\partial^2 f}{\partial x_i\, \partial x_j}(\mathbf{x}_0) + R_2(\mathbf{x}_0, \mathbf{h}),$$

where $R_2(\mathbf{x}_0, \mathbf{h})/\|\mathbf{h}\|^2 \to 0$ as $\mathbf{h} \to 0$ and the second sum is over all i's and j's between 1 and n (so there are n^2 terms).

---

[2] For the statement of the theorem as given here, f actually needs only to be of class C^2, but for a convenient form of the remainder we assume f is of class C^3.

Notice that this result can be written in matrix form as

$$f(\mathbf{x}_0 + \mathbf{h}) = f(\mathbf{x}_0) + \left[\frac{\partial f}{\partial x_1}, \ldots, \frac{\partial f}{\partial x_n} \right] \begin{bmatrix} h_1 \\ \vdots \\ h_n \end{bmatrix}$$

$$+ \frac{1}{2}[h_1, \ldots, h_n] \begin{bmatrix} \dfrac{\partial^2 f}{\partial x_1 \, \partial x_1} & \dfrac{\partial^2 f}{\partial x_1 \, \partial x_2} & \cdots & \dfrac{\partial^2 f}{\partial x_1 \, \partial x_n} \\ \dfrac{\partial^2 f}{\partial x_2 \, \partial x_1} & \dfrac{\partial^2 f}{\partial x_2 \, \partial x_2} & \cdots & \dfrac{\partial^2 f}{\partial x_2 \, \partial x_n} \\ \vdots & & & \\ \dfrac{\partial^2 f}{\partial x_n \, \partial x_1} & \dfrac{\partial^2 f}{\partial x_n \, \partial x_2} & \cdots & \dfrac{\partial^2 f}{\partial x_n \, \partial x_n} \end{bmatrix} \begin{bmatrix} h_1 \\ h_2 \\ \vdots \\ h_n \end{bmatrix},$$

$$+ R_2(\mathbf{x}_0, \mathbf{h}),$$

where the derivatives of f are evaluated at $\mathbf{x}_0$.

In the course of the proof of the Theorem 3, we shall obtain a useful explicit formula for the remainder, as in the single-variable theorem.

proof of theorem 3 Let $g(t) = f(\mathbf{x}_0 + t\mathbf{h})$ with $\mathbf{x}_0$ and $\mathbf{h}$ fixed, which is a C^3 function of t. Now apply the single-variable Taylor theorem (1) to g, with $k = 2$, to obtain

$$\left. \begin{array}{c} g(1) = g(0) + g'(0) + \dfrac{g''(0)}{2!} + R_2, \\[2em] \text{where} \\[1em] R_2 = \displaystyle\int_0^1 \frac{(t-1)^2}{2!} g'''(t) \, dt. \end{array} \right\}$$

where

By the chain rule,

$$g'(t) = \sum_{i=1}^n \frac{\partial f}{\partial x_i}(\mathbf{x}_0 + t\mathbf{h})\mathbf{h}_i; \qquad g''(t) = \sum_{i,j=1}^n \frac{\partial^2 f}{\partial x_i \, \partial x_j}(\mathbf{x}_0 + t\mathbf{h})h_i h_j,$$

and

$$g'''(t) = \sum_{i,j,k=1}^n \frac{\partial^3 f}{\partial x_i \, \partial x_j \, \partial x_k}(\mathbf{x}_0 + t\mathbf{h})h_i h_j h_k.$$

Writing $R_2 = R_2(\mathbf{x}_0, \mathbf{h})$, we have thus proved:

$$\left. \begin{array}{c} f(\mathbf{x}_0 + \mathbf{h}) = f(\mathbf{x}_0) + \displaystyle\sum_{i=1}^n h_i \frac{\partial f}{\partial x_i}(\mathbf{x}_0) + \frac{1}{2}\sum_{i,j=1}^n h_i h_j \frac{\partial^2 f}{\partial x_i \, \partial x_j}(\mathbf{x}_0) + R_2(\mathbf{x}_0, \mathbf{h}), \\[2em] \text{where} \\[1em] R_2(\mathbf{x}_0, \mathbf{h}) = \displaystyle\sum_{i,j,k=1}^n \int_0^1 \frac{(t-1)^2}{2} \frac{\partial^3 f}{\partial x_i \, \partial x_j \, \partial x_k}(\mathbf{x}_0 + t\mathbf{h})h_i h_j h_k \, dt. \end{array} \right\} \tag{3}$$

The integrand is a continuous function of t and is therefore bounded by a positive constant C on a small neighborhood of $\mathbf{x}_0$ (because it has to be close to its value at $\mathbf{x}_0$). Also note that $|h_i| \leq \|\mathbf{h}\|$, for $\|\mathbf{h}\|$ small, and so

$$|R_2(\mathbf{x}_0, \mathbf{h})| \leq \|\mathbf{h}\|^3 C. \tag{4}$$

In particular,

$$\frac{|R_2(\mathbf{x}_0, \mathbf{h})|}{\|\mathbf{h}\|^2} \leq \|\mathbf{h}\| C \to 0 \quad \text{as} \quad \mathbf{h} \to \mathbf{0},$$

as required by the theorem.

The proof of Theorem 2 follows analogously from the Taylor formula (1) with $k = 1$. A similar argument for R_1 shows that $|R_1(\mathbf{x}_0, \mathbf{h})|/\|\mathbf{h}\| \to 0$ as $\mathbf{h} \to \mathbf{0}$, although this also follows directly from the definition of differentiability. ∎

Forms of the Remainder In Theorem 2,

$$R_1(\mathbf{x}_0, \mathbf{h}) = \sum_{i,j=1}^{n} \int_0^1 (1-t) \frac{\partial^2 f}{\partial x_i \partial x_j}(\mathbf{x}_0 + t\mathbf{h}) h_i h_j \, dt = \sum_{i,j=1}^{n} \frac{1}{2} \frac{\partial^2 f}{\partial x_i \partial x_j}(\mathbf{c}_{ij}) h_i h_j,$$

$$\tag{5}$$

where $\mathbf{c}_{ij}$ lies somewhere on the line joining $\mathbf{x}_0$ to $\mathbf{x}_0 + \mathbf{h}$.

In Theorem 3,

$$R_2(\mathbf{x}_0, \mathbf{h}) = \sum_{i,j,k=1}^{n} \int_0^1 \frac{(t-1)^2}{2} \frac{\partial^3 f}{\partial x_i \, \partial x_j \, \partial x_k}(\mathbf{x}_0 + t\mathbf{h}) h_i h_j h_k \, dt$$

$$= \sum_{i,j,k=1}^{n} \frac{1}{3!} \frac{\partial^3 f}{\partial x_i \, \partial x_j \, \partial x_k}(\mathbf{c}_{ijk}) h_i h_j h_k, \tag{5'}$$

where $\mathbf{c}_{ijk}$ lies somewhere on the line joining $\mathbf{x}_0$ to $\mathbf{x}_0 + \mathbf{h}$.

The formulas involving $\mathbf{c}_{ij}$ and $\mathbf{c}_{ijk}$ (called Lagrange's form of the remainder) are obtained by making use of the *second mean-value theorem for integrals*. This states that

$$\int_a^b h(t)g(t)\, dt = h(c) \int_a^b g(t)\, dt,$$

provided h and g are continuous and $g \geq 0$ on $[a, b]$; here c is some number between a and b.[3] This is applied in formula (4) for the explicit form of the remainder with $h(t) = (\partial^2 f/\partial x_i \partial x_j)(\mathbf{x}_0 + t\mathbf{h})$ and $g(t) = 1 - t$.

---

[3]*Proof* If $g = 0$, the result is clear, so we can suppose $g \neq 0$; thus, we can assume $\int_a^b g(t)\, dt > 0$. Let M and m be the maximum and minimum values of h, achieved at t_M and t_m, respectively. Because $g(t) \geq 0$,

$$m \int_a^b g(t)\, dt \leq \int_a^b h(t)g(t)\, dt \leq M \int_a^b g(t)\, dt.$$

Thus, $\left(\int_a^b h(t)g(t)\, dt \right) / \left(\int_a^b g(t)\, dt \right)$ lies between $m = h(t_m)$ and $M = h(t_M)$ and therefore, by the intermediate-value theorem, equals $h(c)$ for some intermediate c. ∎

The third-order Taylor formula is

$$f(\mathbf{x}_0 + \mathbf{h}) = f(\mathbf{x}_0) + \sum_{i=1}^{n} h_i \frac{\partial f}{\partial x_i}(\mathbf{x}_0) + \frac{1}{2} \sum_{i,j=1}^{n} h_i h_j \frac{\partial^2 f}{\partial x_i\, \partial x_j}(\mathbf{x}_0)$$

$$+ \frac{1}{3!} \sum_{i,j,k=1}^{n} h_i h_j h_k \frac{\partial^3 f}{\partial x_i\, \partial x_j\, \partial x_k}(\mathbf{x}_0) + R_3(\mathbf{x}_0, \mathbf{h}),$$

where $R_3(\mathbf{x}_0, \mathbf{h})/\|\mathbf{h}\|^3 \to 0$ as $\mathbf{h} \to \mathbf{0}$, and so on. The general formula can be proved by induction, using the method of proof already given.

example 1 | Compute the second-order Taylor formula for the function $f(x, y) = \sin(x + 2y)$, about the point $\mathbf{x}_0 = (0, 0)$.

solution | Notice that

$$f(0, 0) = 0,$$

$$\frac{\partial f}{\partial x}(0, 0) = \cos(0 + 2 \cdot 0) = 1, \qquad \frac{\partial f}{\partial y}(0, 0) = 2 \cos(0 + 2 \cdot 0) = 2,$$

$$\frac{\partial^2 f}{\partial x^2}(0, 0) = 0, \qquad \frac{\partial^2 f}{\partial y^2}(0, 0) = 0, \qquad \frac{\partial^2 f}{\partial x\, \partial y}(0, 0) = 0.$$

Thus,

$$f(\mathbf{h}) = f(h_1, h_2) = h_1 + 2h_2 + R_2(\mathbf{0}, \mathbf{h}),$$

where

$$\frac{R_2(\mathbf{0}, \mathbf{h})}{\|\mathbf{h}\|^2} \to 0 \qquad \text{as} \qquad \mathbf{h} \to \mathbf{0}. \qquad \blacktriangle$$

example 2 | Compute the second-order Taylor formula for $f(x, y) = e^x \cos y$ about the point $x_0 = 0$, $y_0 = 0$.

solution | Here

$$f(0, 0) = 1, \qquad \frac{\partial f}{\partial x}(0, 0) = 1, \qquad \frac{\partial f}{\partial y}(0, 0) = 0,$$

$$\frac{\partial^2 f}{\partial x^2}(0, 0) = 1, \qquad \frac{\partial^2 f}{\partial y^2}(0, 0) = -1, \qquad \frac{\partial^2 f}{\partial x\, \partial y}(0, 0) = 0,$$

and so

$$f(\mathbf{h}) = f(h_1, h_2) = 1 + h_1 + \tfrac{1}{2}h_1^2 - \tfrac{1}{2}h_2^2 + R_2(\mathbf{0}, \mathbf{h}),$$

where

$$\frac{R_2(\mathbf{0}, \mathbf{h})}{\|\mathbf{h}\|^2} \to 0 \quad \text{as} \quad \mathbf{h} \to \mathbf{0}. \qquad \blacktriangle$$

In the case of functions of one variable, we can expand $f(x)$ in an infinite power series, called the **Taylor series**:

$$f(x_0 + h) = f(x_0) + f'(x_0)h + \frac{f''(x_0)h^2}{2} + \cdots + \frac{f^{(k)}(x_0)h^k}{k!} + \cdots,$$

provided we can show that $R_k(x_0, h) \to 0$ as $k \to \infty$. Similarly, for functions of several variables, the preceding terms are replaced by the corresponding ones involving partial derivatives, as we have seen in Theorem 3. Again, we can represent such a function by its Taylor series provided we can show that $R_k \to 0$ as $k \to \infty$. This point is examined further in Exercise 13.

The first-, second-, and third-order Taylor polynomials are also called the first-, second-, and third-order Taylor approximations to f, since it is presumed that the remainder is small and gets smaller as the order of the Taylor polynomial increases.

example 3 | Find the first- and second-order Taylor approximations to $f(x, y) = \sin(xy)$ at the point $(x_0, y_0) = (1, \pi/2)$.

solution | Here

$$f(x_0, y_0) = \sin(x_0 y_0) = \sin(\pi/2) = 1$$
$$f_x(x_0, y_0) = y_0 \cos(x_0 y_0) = \frac{\pi}{2} \cos(\pi/2) = 0$$
$$f_y(x_0, y_0) = x_0 \cos(x_0 y_0) = \cos(\pi/2) = 0$$
$$f_{xx}(x_0, y_0) = -y_0^2 \sin(x_0 y_0) = -\frac{\pi^2}{4} \sin(\pi/2) = -\frac{\pi^2}{4}$$
$$f_{xy}(x_0, y_0) = \cos(x_0 y_0) - x_0 y_0 \sin(x_0 y_0) = -\frac{\pi}{2} \sin(\pi/2) = -\frac{\pi}{2}$$
$$f_{yy}(x_0, y_0) = -x_0^2 \sin(x_0 y_0) = -\sin(\pi/2) = -1.$$

Thus, the linear (first-order) approximation is

$$l(x, y) = f(x_0, y_0) + f_x(x_0, y_0)(x - x_0) + f_y(x_0, y_0)(y - y_0)$$
$$= 1 + 0 + 0 = 1,$$

and the second-order (or quadratic) approximation is

$$g(x, y) = 1 + 0 + 0 + \frac{1}{2}\left(-\frac{\pi^2}{4}\right)(x - 1)^2 + \left(-\frac{\pi}{2}\right)(x - 1)\left(y - \frac{\pi}{2}\right)$$
$$+ \frac{1}{2}(-1)\left(y - \frac{\pi}{2}\right)^2$$
$$= 1 - \frac{\pi^2}{8}(x - 1)^2 - \frac{\pi}{2}(x - 1)\left(y - \frac{\pi}{2}\right) - \frac{1}{2}\left(y - \frac{\pi}{2}\right)^2.$$

See Figure 3.2.1. ▲

example 4 | Find linear and quadratic approximations to the expression $(3.98 - 1)^2/(5.97 - 3)^2$. Compare with the exact value.

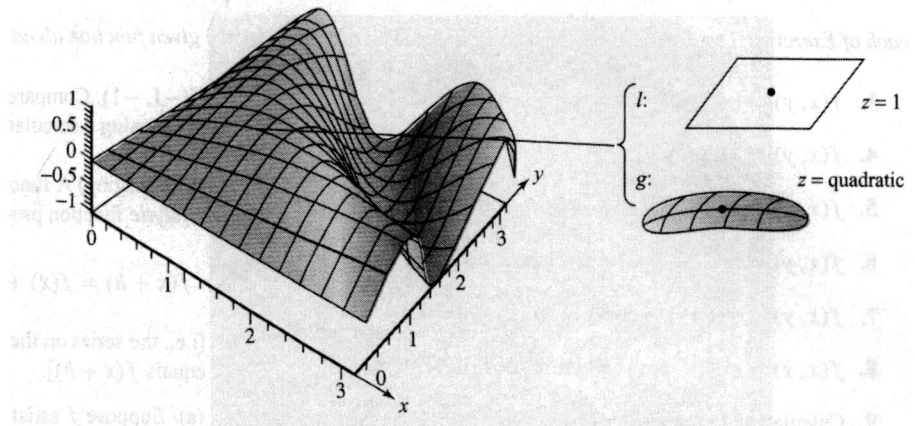

figure **3.2.1** The linear and quadratic approximations to $z = \sin(xy)$ near $(1, \pi/2)$.

solution

Let $f(x, y) = (x - 1)^2/(y - 3)^2$. The desired expression is close to $f(4, 6) = 1$. To find the approximations, we differentiate:

$$f_x = \frac{2(x - 1)}{(y - 3)^2}, \qquad f_y = \frac{-2(x - 1)^2}{(y - 3)^3}$$

$$f_{xy} = f_{yx} = \frac{-4(x - 1)}{(y - 3)^3}, \qquad f_{xx} = \frac{2}{(y - 3)^2}, \qquad f_{yy} = \frac{6(x - 1)^2}{(y - 3)^4}.$$

At the point of approximation, we have

$$f_x(4, 6) = \frac{2}{3}, \qquad f_y = -\frac{2}{3}, \qquad f_{xy} = f_{yx} = -\frac{4}{9}, \qquad f_{xx} = \frac{2}{9}, \qquad f_{yy} = \frac{2}{3}.$$

The linear approximation is then

$$1 + \frac{2}{3}(-0.02) - \frac{2}{3}(-0.03) = 1.00666.$$

The quadratic approximation is

$$1 + \frac{2}{3}(-0.02) - \frac{2}{3}(-0.03) + \frac{2}{9}\frac{(-0.02)^2}{2} - \frac{4}{9}(-0.02)(-0.03) + \frac{2}{3}\frac{(-0.03)^2}{2}$$
$$= 1.00674.$$

The "exact" value using a calculator is 1.00675. ▲

exercises

1. Let $f(x, z) = e^{x+y}$.

   (a) Find the first-order Taylor formula for f at $(0, 0)$.

   (b) Find the second-order Taylor formula for f at $(0, 0)$.

2. Suppose $L: \mathbb{R}^2 \to \mathbb{R}$ is linear, so that L has the form $L(x, y) = ax + by$.

   (a) Find the first-order Taylor approximation for L.

   (b) Find the second-order Taylor approximation for L.

   (c) What will higher-order approximations look like?

In each of Exercises 3 to 8, determine the second-order Taylor formula for the given function about the given point (x_0, y_0).

3. $f(x, y) = (x + y)^2$, where $x_0 = 0$, $y_0 = 0$

4. $f(x, y) = 1/(x^2 + y^2 + 1)$, where $x_0 = 0$, $y_0 = 0$

5. $f(x, y) = e^{x+y}$, where $x_0 = 0$, $y_0 = 0$

6. $f(x, y) = e^{-x^2-y^2} \cos(xy)$, where $x_0 = 0$, $y_0 = 0$

7. $f(x, y) = \sin(xy) + \cos(xy)$, where $x_0 = 0$, $y_0 = 0$

8. $f(x, y) = e^{(x-1)^2} \cos y$, where $x_0 = 1$, $y_0 = 0$

9. Calculate the second-order Taylor approximation to $f(x, y) = \cos x \sin y$ at the point $(\pi, \pi/2)$.

10. Let $f(x, y) = x \cos(\pi y) - y \sin(\pi x)$. Find the second-order Taylor approximation for f at the point $(1, 2)$.

11. Let $g(x, y) = \sin(xy) - 3x^2 \log y + 1$. Find the degree 2 polynomial which best approximates g near the point $(\pi/2, 1)$.

12. For each of the functions in Exercises 3 to 7, use the second-order Taylor formula to approximate

$f(-1, -1)$. Compare your approximation to the exact value using a calculator.

13. (Challenging) A function $f: \mathbb{R} \to \mathbb{R}$ is called an **analytic** function provided

$$f(x + h) = f(x) + f'(x)h + \cdots + \frac{f^{(k)}(x)}{k!}h^k + \cdots$$

[i.e., the series on the right-hand side converges and equals $f(x + h)$].

(a) Suppose f satisfies the following condition: On any closed interval $[a, b]$, there is a constant M such that for all $k = 1, 2, 3, \ldots, |f^{(k)}(x)| \leq M^k$ for all $x \in [a, b]$. Prove that f is analytic.

(b) Let $f(x) = \begin{cases} e^{-1/x} & x > 0 \\ 0 & x \leq 0. \end{cases}$

Show that f is a C^∞ function, but f is not analytic.

(c) Give a definition of analytic functions from $\mathbb{R}^n$ to $\mathbb{R}$. Generalize the proof of part (a) to this class of functions.

(d) Develop $f(x, y) = e^{x+y}$ in a power series about $x_0 = 0$, $y_0 = 0$.

3.3 Extrema of Real-Valued Functions

Historical Note

As we saw in the book's Historical Introduction, the early Greeks sought to mathematize nature and to find, as in the geometric Ptolemaic model of planetary motion, mathematical laws governing the universe. With the revival of Greek learning during the Renaissance, this point of view again took hold and the search for these laws recommenced. In particular, the question was raised as to whether there was *one* law, one mathematical principle that governed and superseded all others, a principle that the Creator used in His Grand Design of the Universe.

MAUPERTUIS' PRINCIPLE. In 1744, the French scientist Pierre-Louis de Maupertuis (see Figure 3.3.1) put forth his grand scheme of the world. The "metaphysical principle" of Maupertuis is the assumption that nature always operates with the greatest possible economy. In short, physical laws are a consequence of a principle of "economy of means"; nature always acts in such a way as to minimize some quantity that Maupertuis called the *action*. Action was nothing more than the expenditure of energy over time, or energy × time. In applications, the type of energy changes with each case. For example, physical systems often try to "rearrange themselves" to have a minimum energy—such as a ball rolling from a mountain peak to a valley, or the primordial irregular earth and a minimum on S. Show that there must be an $\mathbf{x} \in S$ and a $\lambda \neq 0$ such that $A\mathbf{x} = \lambda\mathbf{x}$. (The vector $\mathbf{x}$ is called an ***eigenvector***, while the scalar λ is called an ***eigenvalue***.)

(c) What are the maxima and minima for f on $B = \{(x, y, z) \mid x^2 + y^2 + z^2 \leq 1\}$?

32. Suppose that A in the function f defined in Exercise 31 is not necessarily symmetric.

(a) What is ∇f?

(b) Can we conclude the existence of an eigenvector and eigenvalues as in Exercise 31?

33. (a) Find the critical points of $x + y^2$, subject to the constraint $2x^2 + y^2 = 1$.

(b) Use the bordered Hessian to classify the critical points.

34. Answer the question posed in the last line of Example 9.

35. Try to find the extrema of $xy + yz$ among points satisfying $xz = 1$.

36. A company's production function is $Q(x, y) = xy$. The cost of production is $C(x, y) = 2x + 3y$. If this company can spend $C(x, y) = 10$, what is the maximum quantity that can be produced?

37. Find the point on the curve $(\cos t, \sin t, \sin(t/2))$ that is farthest from the origin.

38. A firm uses wool and cotton fiber to produce cloth. The amount of cloth produced is given by $Q(x, y) = xy - x - y + 1$, where x is the number of pounds of wool, y the number of pounds of cotton, $x > 1$, and $y > 1$. If wool costs p dollars per pound, cotton costs q dollars per pound, and the firm can spend B dollars on material, what should the ratio of cotton and wool be to produce the most cloth?

39. Carry out the analysis of Example 10 for the production function $Q(K, L) = AK^{\alpha}L^{1-\alpha}$, where A and α are positive constants and $0 < \alpha < 1$. This is called a ***Cobb–Douglas production function*** and is sometimes used as a simple model for the national economy. Q is then the aggregate output of the economy for a given input of capital and labor.

3.5 The Implicit Function Theorem (Optional)

In this section we state two versions of the *implicit function theorem*, arguably the most important theorem in all of mathematical analysis. The entire theoretical basis of the idea of a surface as well as the method of Lagrange multipliers depends on it. Moreover, it is a cornerstone of several fields of mathematics, such as differential topology and geometry.

The One-Variable Implicit Function Theorem

In one-variable calculus we learn the importance of the inversion process. For example, $x = \ln y$ is the inverse of $y = e^x$, and $x = \sin^{-1} y$ is the inverse of $y = \sin x$. The inversion process is also important for functions of several variables; for example, the switch between Cartesian and polar coordinates in the plane involves inverting two functions of two variables.

Recall from one-variable calculus that if $y = f(x)$ is a C^1 function and $f'(x_0) \neq 0$, then locally near x_0 we can solve for x to give the inverse function: $x = f^{-1}(y)$. We learn that $(f^{-1})'(y) = 1/f'(x)$; that is, $dx/dy = 1/(dy/dx)$. That $y = f(x)$ can be inverted is plausible because $f'(x_0) \neq 0$ means that the slope of $y = f(x)$ is nonzero, so that the graph is rising or falling near x_0. Thus, if we reflect the graph across the line $y = x$, it is still a graph *near* (x_0, y_0), where $y_0 = f(x_0)$. For example, in Figure 3.5.1, we can invert $y = f(x)$ in the shaded box, so in this range, $x = f^{-1}(y)$ is defined.

A Special Result

We next turn to the situation for real-valued functions of variables $x_1, \ldots, x_n$ and z.

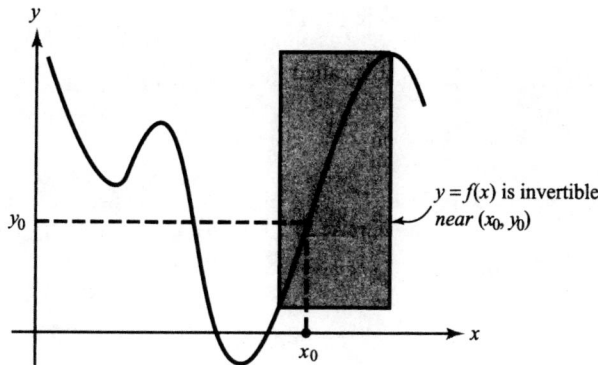

figure **3.5.1** If $f'(x_0) \neq 0$, then $y = f(x)$ is locally invertible.

Theorem 11 Special Implicit Function Theorem Suppose that $F: \mathbb{R}^{n+1} \to \mathbb{R}$ has continuous partial derivatives. Denoting points in $\mathbb{R}^{n+1}$ by $(\mathbf{x}, z)$, where $\mathbf{x} \in \mathbb{R}^n$ and $z \in \mathbb{R}$, assume that $(\mathbf{x}_0, z_0)$ satisfies

$$F(\mathbf{x}_0, z_0) = 0 \quad \text{and} \quad \frac{\partial F}{\partial z}(\mathbf{x}_0, z_0) \neq 0.$$

Then there is a ball U containing $\mathbf{x}_0$ in $\mathbb{R}^n$ and a neighborhood V of z_0 in $\mathbb{R}$ such that there is a unique function $z = g(\mathbf{x})$ defined for $\mathbf{x}$ in U and z in V that satisfies

$$F(\mathbf{x}, g(\mathbf{x})) = 0.$$

Moreover, if $\mathbf{x}$ in U and z in V satisfy $F(\mathbf{x}, z) = 0$, then $z = g(\mathbf{x})$. Finally, $z = g(\mathbf{x})$ is continuously differentiable, with the derivative given by

$$\mathbf{D}g(\mathbf{x}) = -\frac{1}{\dfrac{\partial F}{\partial z}(\mathbf{x}, z)} \, \mathbf{D}_{\mathbf{x}} F(\mathbf{x}, z) \Bigg|_{z=g(\mathbf{x})},$$

where $\mathbf{D}_{\mathbf{x}} F$ denotes the (partial) derivative of F with respect to the variable $\mathbf{x}$—that is, we have $\mathbf{D}_{\mathbf{x}} F = [\partial F / \partial x_1, \ldots, \partial F / \partial x_n]$; in other words,

$$\frac{\partial g}{\partial x_i} = -\frac{\partial F / \partial x_i}{\partial F / \partial z}, \qquad i = 1, \ldots, n. \tag{1}$$

A proof of this theorem is given in the Internet supplement.

Once it is known that $z = g(\mathbf{x})$ exists and is differentiable, formula (1) may be checked by implicit differentiation; to see this, note that the chain rule applied to $F(\mathbf{x}, g(\mathbf{x})) = 0$ gives

$$\mathbf{D}_{\mathbf{x}} F(\mathbf{x}, g(\mathbf{x})) + \left[\frac{\partial F}{\partial z}(\mathbf{x}, g(\mathbf{x}))\right][\mathbf{D}g(\mathbf{x})] = 0,$$

which is equivalent to formula (1).

example 1

In the special implicit function theorem, it is important to recognize the necessity of taking sufficiently small neighborhoods U and V. For example, consider the equation

$$x^2 + z^2 - 1 = 0;$$

that is, $F(x, z) = x^2 + z^2 - 1$, with $n = 1$. Here $(\partial F / \partial z)(x, z) = 2z$, and so the special implicit function theorem applies to a point (x_0, z_0), satisfying $x_0^2 + z_0^2 - 1 = 0$ and $z_0 \neq 0$. Thus, near such points, z is a unique function of x. This function is $z = \sqrt{1 - x^2}$ if $z_0 > 0$ and $z = -\sqrt{1 - x^2}$ if $z_0 < 0$. Note that z is defined for $|x| < 1$ only (U must not be too big) and z is unique only if it is near z_0 (V must not be too big). These facts and the nonexistence of $\partial z / \partial x$ at $z_0 = 0$ are, of course, clear from the fact that $x^2 + z^2 = 1$ defines a circle in the xz plane (Figure 3.5.2).

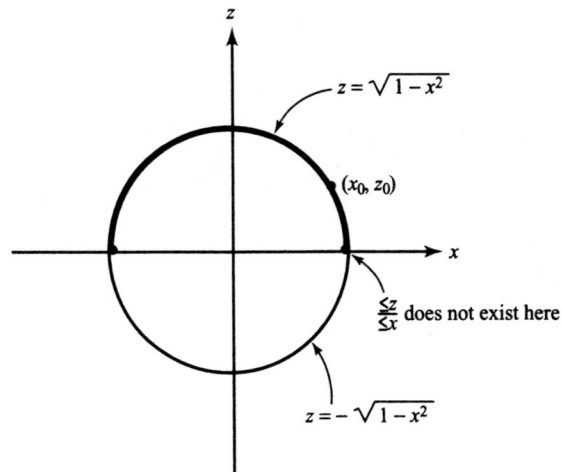

figure **3.5.2** It is necessary to take small neighborhoods in the implicit function theorem. ▲

The Implicit Function Theorem and Surfaces

Let us apply Theorem 11 to the study of surfaces. We are concerned with the level set of a function $g: U \subset \mathbb{R}^n \to \mathbb{R}$; that is, with the surface S consisting of the set of $\mathbf{x}$ satisfying $g(\mathbf{x}) = c_0$, where $c_0 = g(\mathbf{x}_0)$ and where $\mathbf{x}_0$ is given. Let us take $n = 3$ for concreteness. Thus, we are dealing with the level surface of a function $g(x, y, z)$ through a given point (x_0, y_0, z_0). As in the Lagrange multiplier theorem, assume that $\nabla g(x_0, y_0, z_0) \neq \mathbf{0}$. This means that at least one of the partial derivatives of g is nonzero. For definiteness, suppose that $(\partial g / \partial z)(x_0, y_0, z_0) \neq 0$. By applying Theorem 11 to the function $(x, y, z) \mapsto g(x, y, z) - c_0$, we know there is a unique function $z = k(x, y)$ satisfying $g(x, y, k(x, y)) = c_0$ for (x, y) near (x_0, y_0) and z near z_0. Thus, near z_0 the surface S is the graph of the function k. Because k is continuously differentiable, this surface has a tangent plane at (x_0, y_0, z_0) given by

$$z = z_0 + \left[\frac{\partial k}{\partial x}(x_0, y_0) \right](x - x_0) + \left[\frac{\partial k}{\partial y}(x_0, y_0) \right](y - y_0). \tag{2}$$

But by formula (1),

$$\frac{\partial k}{\partial x}(x_0, y_0) = -\frac{\frac{\partial g}{\partial x}(x_0, y_0, z_0)}{\frac{\partial g}{\partial z}(x_0, y_0, z_0)} \quad \text{and} \quad \frac{\partial k}{\partial y}(x_0, y_0) = -\frac{\frac{\partial g}{\partial y}(x_0, y_0, z_0)}{\frac{\partial g}{\partial z}(x_0, y_0, z_0)}.$$

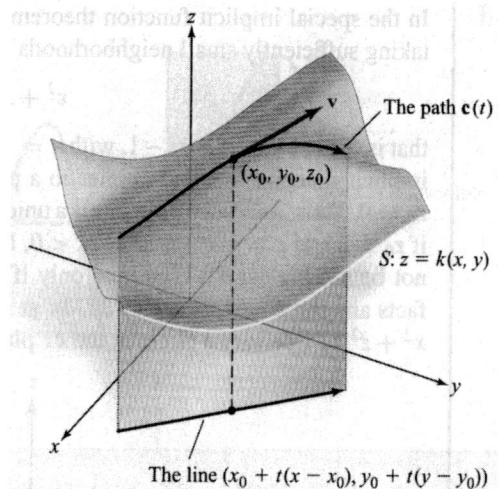

figure **3.5.3** The construction of a path **c**(*t*) in the surface *S* whose tangent vector is **v**.

Substituting these two equations into the equation for the tangent plane gives this equivalent description:

$$0 = (z - z_0)\frac{\partial g}{\partial z}(x_0, y_0, z_0) + (x - x_0)\frac{\partial g}{\partial x}(x_0, y_0, z_0) + (y - y_0)\frac{\partial g}{\partial y}(x_0, y_0, z_0);$$

that is,

$$(x - x_0, y - y_0, z - z_0) \cdot \nabla g(x_0, y_0, z_0) = 0.$$

Thus, the tangent plane to the level surface of g is the orthogonal complement to $\nabla g(x_0, y_0, z_0)$ through the point (x_0, y_0, z_0). This agrees with our characterization of tangent planes to level sets from Chapter 2.

We are now ready to complete the proof of the Lagrange multiplier theorem. To do this, we must show that every vector tangent to S at (x_0, y_0, z_0) is tangent to a curve in S. By Theorem 11, we need only show this for a graph of the form $z = k(x, y)$. However, if $\mathbf{v} = (x - x_0, y - y_0, z - z_0)$ is tangent to the graph [that is, if it satisfies equation (2)], then $\mathbf{v}$ is tangent to the path in S given by

$$\mathbf{c}(t) = (x_0 + t(x - x_0), y_0 + t(y - y_0), k(x_0 + t(x - x_0), y_0 + t(y - y_0)))$$

at $t = 0$. This can be checked by using the chain rule. (See Figure 3.5.3.)

example 2 | Near what points may the surface

$$x^3 + 3y^2 + 8xz^2 - 3z^3y = 1$$

be represented as a graph of a differentiable function $z = k(x, y)$?

solution | Here we take $F(x, y, z) = x^3 + 3y^2 + 8xz^2 - 3z^3y - 1$ and attempt to solve $F(x, y, z) = 0$ for z as a function of (x, y). By Theorem 11, this may be done near a point (x_0, y_0, z_0) if $(\partial F/\partial z)(x_0, y_0, z_0) \neq 0$, that is, if

$$z_0(16x_0 - 9z_0y_0) \neq 0,$$

which means, in turn,

$$z_0 \neq 0 \quad \text{and} \quad 16x_0 \neq 9z_0y_0. \quad \blacktriangle$$

General Implicit Function Theorem

Next we shall state, without proof, the *general implicit function theorem*.[14] Instead of attempting to solve one equation for one variable, we attempt to solve m equations for m variables $z_1, \ldots, z_m$:

$$
\begin{aligned}
F_1(x_1, \ldots, x_n, z_1, \ldots, z_m) &= 0 \\
F_2(x_1, \ldots, x_n, z_1, \ldots, z_m) &= 0 \\
&\vdots \\
F_m(x_1, \ldots, x_n, z_1, \ldots, z_m) &= 0.
\end{aligned}
\tag{3}
$$

In Theorem 11 we had the condition $\partial F/\partial z \neq 0$. The condition appropriate to the general implicit function theorem is that $\Delta \neq 0$,[15] where Δ is the determinant of the $m \times m$ matrix

$$
\begin{bmatrix}
\dfrac{\partial F_1}{\partial z_1} & \cdots & \dfrac{\partial F_1}{\partial z_m} \\
\vdots & & \vdots \\
\dfrac{\partial F_m}{\partial z_1} & \cdots & \dfrac{\partial F_m}{\partial z_m}
\end{bmatrix}
$$

evaluated at the point $(\mathbf{x}_0, \mathbf{z}_0)$; in the neighborhood of such a point, we can uniquely solve for $\mathbf{z}$ in terms of $\mathbf{x}$.

Theorem 12 General Implicit Function Theorem If $\Delta \neq 0$, then near the point $(\mathbf{x}_0, \mathbf{z}_0)$, equation (3) defines unique (smooth) functions

$$
z_i = k_i(x_1, \ldots, x_n) \qquad (i = 1, \ldots, m).
$$

Their derivatives may be computed by implicit differentiation.

---

[14] For three different proofs of the general case, consult:

(a) E. Goursat, *A Course in Mathematical Analysis*, I, Dover, New York, 1959, p. 45. (This proof derives the general theorem by successive application of Theorem 11.)

(b) T. M. Apostol, *Mathematical Analysis*, 2d ed., Addison-Wesley, Reading, Mass., 1974.

(c) J. E. Marsden and M. Hoffman, *Elementary Classical Analysis*, 2d ed., Freeman, New York, 1993.

Of these sources, the last two use more sophisticated ideas that are usually not covered until a junior-level course in analysis. The first, however, is easily understood by the reader who has some knowledge of linear algebra.

[15] For students who have had linear algebra: The condition $\Delta \neq 0$ has a simple interpretation in the case that F *is linear*; namely, $\Delta \neq 0$ is equivalent to the rank of F being equal to m, which in turn is equivalent to the fact that the solution space of $F = 0$ is m-dimensional.

example 3

To show that near the point $(x, y, u, v) = (1, 1, 1, 1)$, we can solve

$$xu + yvu^2 = 2$$
$$xu^3 + y^2v^4 = 2$$

uniquely for u and v as functions of x and y. Compute $\partial u / \partial x$ at the point $(1, 1)$.

solution

To check solvability, we form the equations

$$F_1(x, y, u, v) = xu + yvu^2 - 2$$
$$F_2(x, y, u, v) = xu^3 + y^2v^4 - 2$$

and the determinant

$$\Delta = \begin{vmatrix} \dfrac{\partial F_1}{\partial u} & \dfrac{\partial F_1}{\partial v} \\[2mm] \dfrac{\partial F_2}{\partial u} & \dfrac{\partial F_2}{\partial v} \end{vmatrix} \qquad \text{at} \qquad (1, 1, 1, 1)$$

$$= \begin{vmatrix} x + 2yuv & yu^2 \\[1mm] 3u^2x & 4y^2v^3 \end{vmatrix} \qquad \text{at} \qquad (1, 1, 1, 1)$$

$$= \begin{vmatrix} 3 & 1 \\ 3 & 4 \end{vmatrix} = 9.$$

Because $\Delta \neq 0$, solvability is assured by the general implicit function theorem. To find $\partial u / \partial x$, we implicitly differentiate the given equations in x using the chain rule:

$$x\frac{\partial u}{\partial x} + u + y\frac{\partial v}{\partial x}u^2 + 2yvu\frac{\partial u}{\partial x} = 0$$

$$3xu^2\frac{\partial u}{\partial x} + u^3 + 4y^2v^3\frac{\partial v}{\partial x} = 0.$$

Setting $(x, y, u, v) = (1, 1, 1, 1)$ gives

$$3\frac{\partial u}{\partial x} + \frac{\partial v}{\partial x} = -1$$

$$3\frac{\partial u}{\partial x} + 4\frac{\partial v}{\partial x} = -1.$$

Solving for $\partial u / \partial x$ by multiplying the first equation by 4 and subtracting gives $\partial u / \partial x = -\frac{1}{3}$. ▲

Inverse Function Theorem

A special case of the general implicit function theorem is the *inverse function theorem*. Here we attempt to solve the n equations

$$\left. \begin{array}{c} f_1(x_1, \ldots, x_n) = y_1 \\ \cdots \\ f_n(x_1, \ldots, x_n) = y_n \end{array} \right\} \qquad (4)$$

for $x_1, \ldots, x_n$ as functions of $y_1, \ldots, y_n$; that is, we are trying to invert the equations of system (4). This is analogous to forming the inverses of functions like $\sin x = y$ and $e^x = y$, with which you should be familiar from elementary calculus. Now, however, we are concerned with functions of several variables. The question of solvability is answered by the general implicit function theorem applied to the functions $y_i - f_i(x_1, \ldots, x_n)$ with the unknowns $x_1, \ldots, x_n$ (called $z_1, \ldots, z_n$ earlier). The condition for solvability in a neighborhood of a point $\mathbf{x}_0$ is $\Delta \neq 0$, where Δ is the determinant of the matrix $\mathbf{D}f(\mathbf{x}_0)$, and $f = (f_1, \ldots, f_n)$. The quantity Δ is denoted by $\partial(f_1, \ldots, f_n)/\partial(x_1, \ldots, x_n)$, or $\partial(y_1, \ldots, y_n)/\partial(x_1, \ldots, x_n)$ or $J(f)(\mathbf{x}_0)$ and is called the *Jacobian determinant* of f. Explicitly,

$$\left.\frac{\partial(f_1, \ldots, f_n)}{\partial(x_1, \ldots, x_n)}\right|_{\mathbf{x}=\mathbf{x}_0} = J(f)(\mathbf{x}_0) = \begin{vmatrix} \dfrac{\partial f_1}{\partial x_1}(\mathbf{x}_0) & \cdots & \dfrac{\partial f_1}{\partial x_n}(\mathbf{x}_0) \\ \vdots & & \vdots \\ \dfrac{\partial f_n}{\partial x_1}(\mathbf{x}_0) & \cdots & \dfrac{\partial f_n}{\partial x_n}(\mathbf{x}_0) \end{vmatrix}. \tag{5}$$

Note that in the case when f is linear—for example $f(x) = Ax$, where A is an $n \times n$ matrix—the condition $\Delta \neq 0$ is equivalent to the fact that the determinant of A, det $A \neq 0$, and from Section 1.5 we know that A, and therefore f, has an inverse.

The Jacobian determinant will play an important role in our work on integration (see Chapter 5). The following theorem summarizes this discussion:

Theorem 13 Inverse Function Theorem Let $U \subset \mathbb{R}^n$ be open and let $f_1: U \to \mathbb{R}, \ldots, f_n: U \to \mathbb{R}$ have continuous partial derivatives. Consider equations (4) near a given solution $\mathbf{x}_0, \mathbf{y}_0$. If $J(f)(\mathbf{x}_0)$ [defined by equation (5)] is nonzero, then equation (4) can be solved uniquely as $\mathbf{x} = g(\mathbf{y})$ for $\mathbf{x}$ near $\mathbf{x}_0$ and $\mathbf{y}$ near $\mathbf{y}_0$. Moreover, the function g has continuous partial derivatives.

---

example 4

Consider the equations

$$\frac{x^4 + y^4}{x} = u, \qquad \sin x + \cos y = v.$$

Near which points (x, y), can we solve for x, y in terms of u, v?

solution

Here the functions are $u = f_1(x, y) = (x^4 + y^4)/x$ and $v = f_2(x, y) = \sin x + \cos y$. We want to know the points near which we can solve for x, y as functions of u and v. According to the inverse function theorem, we must first compute the Jacobian determinant $\partial(f_1, f_2)/\partial(x, y)$. We take the domain of $f = (f_1, f_2)$ to be $U = \{(x, y) \in \mathbb{R}^2 \mid x \neq 0\}$. Now

$$\frac{\partial(f_1, f_2)}{\partial(x, y)} = \begin{vmatrix} \dfrac{\partial f_1}{\partial x} & \dfrac{\partial f_1}{\partial y} \\ \dfrac{\partial f_2}{\partial x} & \dfrac{\partial f_2}{\partial y} \end{vmatrix} = \begin{vmatrix} \dfrac{3x^4 - y^4}{x^2} & \dfrac{4y^3}{x} \\ \cos x & -\sin y \end{vmatrix} = \frac{\sin y}{x^2}(y^4 - 3x^4) - \frac{4y^3}{x}\cos x.$$

Therefore, at points where this does not vanish we can solve for x, y in terms of u and v. In other words, we can solve for x, y near those x, y for which $x \neq 0$ and $(\sin y)(y^4 - 3x^4) \neq 4xy^3 \cos x$. Such conditions generally cannot be solved explicitly. For example, if $x_0 = \pi/2$, $y_0 = \pi/2$, we can solve for x, y near (x_0, y_0) because there, $\partial(f_1, f_2)/\partial(x, y) \neq 0$. ▲

exercises

1. Show that the equation $x + y - z + \cos(xyz) = 0$ can be solved for $z = g(x, y)$ near the origin. Find $\dfrac{\partial g}{\partial x}$ and $\dfrac{\partial g}{\partial y}$ at $(0, 0)$.

2. Show that $xy + z + 3xz^5 = 4$ is solvable for z as a function of (x, y) near $(1, 0, 1)$. Compute $\partial z/\partial x$ and $\partial z/\partial y$ at $(1, 0)$.

3. (a) Check directly (i.e., without using Theorem 11) where we can solve the equation $F(x, y) = y^2 + y + 3x + 1 = 0$ for y in terms of x.

   (b) Check that your answer in part (a) agrees with the answer you expect from the implicit function theorem. Compute dy/dx.

4. Repeat Exercise 3 with $F(x, y) = xy^2 - 2y + x^2 + 2 = 0$.

5. Let $F(x, y) = 0$ define a curve in the xy plane through the point (x_0, y_0), where F is C^1. Assume that $(\partial F/\partial y)(x_0, y_0) \neq 0$. Show that this curve can be locally represented by the graph of a function $y = g(x)$. Show that (i) the line orthogonal to $\nabla F(x_0, y_0)$ agrees with (ii) the tangent line to the graph of $y = g(x)$.

6. Consider the surface S given by $3y^2z^2 - 3x = 0$.

   (a) Using the implicit function theorem, verify that we can solve for x as a function of y and z near any point on S. Explicitly write x as a function of y and z.

   (b) Show that near $(1, 1, -1)$ we can solve for either y or z, and give explicit expressions for these variables in terms of the other two.

7. Show that $x^3z^2 - z^3yx = 0$ is solvable for z as a function of (x, y) near $(1, 1, 1)$, but not near the origin. Compute $\partial z/\partial x$ and $\partial z/\partial y$ at $(1, 1)$.

8. Discuss the solvability in the system

$$3x + 2y + z^2 + u + v^2 = 0$$
$$4x + 3y + z + u^2 + v + w + 2 = 0$$
$$x + z + w + u^2 + 2 = 0$$

   for u, v, w in terms of x, y, z near $x = y = z = 0$, $u = v = 0$, and $w = -2$.

9. Discuss the solvability of

$$y + x + uv = 0$$
$$uxy + v = 0$$

for u, v in terms of x, y near $x = y = u = v = 0$ and check directly.

10. Investigate whether or not the system

$$u(x, y, z) = x + xyz$$
$$v(x, y, z) = y + xy$$
$$w(x, y, z) = z + 2x + 3z^2$$

can be solved for x, y, z in terms of u, v, w near $(x, y, z) = (0, 0, 0)$.

11. Consider $f(x, y) = ((x^2 - y^2)/(x^2 + y^2), xy/(x^2 + y^2))$. Does this map of $\mathbb{R}^2 \setminus (0, 0)$ to $\mathbb{R}^2$ have a local inverse near $(x, y) = (0, 1)$?

12. (a) Define $x: \mathbb{R}^2 \to \mathbb{R}$ by $x(r, \theta) = r \cos \theta$ and define $y: \mathbb{R}^2 \to \mathbb{R}$ by $y(r, \theta) = r \sin \theta$. Show that

$$\left. \frac{\partial(x, y)}{\partial(r, \theta)} \right|_{(r_0, \theta_0)} = r_0.$$

   (b) When can we form a smooth inverse function $(r(x, y), \theta(x, y))$? Check directly and with the inverse function theorem.

   (c) Consider the following transformations for spherical coordinates (see Section 1.4):

$$x(\rho, \phi, \theta) = \rho \sin \phi \cos \theta$$
$$x(\rho, \phi, \theta) = \rho \sin \phi \sin \theta$$
$$z(\rho, \phi, \theta) = \rho \cos \phi.$$

   Show that the Jacobian determinant is given by

$$\frac{\partial(x, y, z)}{\partial(\rho, \phi, \theta)} = \rho^2 \sin \phi.$$

   (d) When can we solve for (ρ, ϕ, θ) in terms of (x, y, z)?

13. Let (x_0, y_0, z_0) be a point of the locus defined by $z^2 + xy - a = 0$, $z^2 + x^2 - y^2 - b = 0$, where a and b are constants.

   (a) Under what conditions may the part of the locus near (x_0, y_0, z_0) be represented in the form $x = f(z)$, $y = g(z)$?

   (b) Compute $f'(z)$ and $g'(z)$.

14. Consider the unit sphere S given by $x^2 + y^2 + z^2 = 1$. S intersects the x axis at two points. Which variables can we solve for at these points? What about the points of intersection of S with the y and z axes?

15. Let $F(x, y) = x^3 - y^2$ and let C denote the level curve given by $F(x, y) = 0$.

  (a) Without using the implicit function theorem, show that we can describe C as the graph of x as a function of y near any point.

  (b) Show that $F_x(0, 0) = 0$. Does this contradict the implicit function theorem?

16. Consider the system of equations

$$x^5 v^2 + 2y^3 u = 3$$
$$3yu - xuv^3 = 2.$$

Show that near the point $(x, y, u, v) = (1, 1, 1, 1)$, this system defines u and v implicitly as functions of x and y. For such local functions u and v, define the local function f by $f(x, y) = (u(x, y), v(x, y))$. Find $Df(1, 1)$.

17. Consider the equations

$$x^2 - y^2 - u^3 + v^2 + 4 = 0$$
$$2xy + y^2 - 2u^2 + 3v^4 + 8 = 0.$$

  (a) Show that these equations determine functions $u(x, y)$ and $v(x, y)$ near the point $(x, y, u, v) = (2, -1, 2, 1)$.

  (b) Compute $\frac{\partial u}{\partial x}$ at $(x, y) = (2, -1)$.

18. Is it possible to solve the system of equations

$$xy^2 + xzu + yv^2 = 3$$
$$u^3 yz + 2xv - u^2 v^2 = 2$$

for $u(x, y, z)$, $v(x, y, z)$ near $(x, y, z) = (1, 1, 1)$, $(u, v) = (1, 1)$? Compute $\partial v / \partial y$ at $(x, y, z) = (1, 1, 1)$.

19. The problem of factoring a polynomial $x^n + a_{n-1} x^{n-1} + \cdots + a_0$ into linear factors is, in a sense, an "inverse function" problem. The coefficients a_i may be thought of as functions of the n roots r_j. We would like to find the roots as functions of the coefficients in some region. With $n = 3$, apply the inverse function theorem to this problem and state what it tells you about the possibility of doing this.

---

review exercises for chapter 3

1. Let f be any differentiable function. Show that $u = f(y - kx)$ is a solution to the partial differential equation $\dfrac{\partial u}{\partial x} + k\dfrac{\partial u}{\partial y} = 0$.

2. Prove that if u and v have continuous mixed second partial derivatives and satisfy the Cauchy–Riemann equations

$$\frac{\partial u}{\partial x} = \frac{\partial v}{\partial y}$$
$$\frac{\partial u}{\partial y} = -\frac{\partial v}{\partial x},$$

then both u and v are harmonic.

3. Let $f(x, y) = x^2 - y^2 - xy + 5$. Find all critical points of f and determine whether they are local minima, local maxima, or saddle points.

4. Find the absolute minimum and maximum values of the function $f(x, y) = x^2 + 3xy + y^2 + 5$ on the unit disc $D = \{(x, y) \mid x^2 + y^2 \le 1\}$.

5. Find the second-order Taylor polynomial for $f(x, y) = y^2 e^{-x^2}$ at $(1, 1)$.

6. Let $f(x, y) = ax^2 + bxy + cy^2$.

  (a) Find $g(x, y)$, the second-order Taylor approximation to f at $(0, 0)$.

  (b) What is the relationship between g and f?

  (c) Prove that $R_2(\mathbf{x}_0, \mathbf{h}) = 0$ for all $\mathbf{x}_0$, $\mathbf{h} \in \mathbb{R}^2$. (HINT: Show that f is equal to its second-order Taylor approximation at every point.)

7. Analyze the behavior of the following functions at the indicated points. [Your answer in part (b) may depend on the constant C.]

  (a) $z = x^2 - y^2 + 3xy$, $\quad (x, y) = (0, 0)$

  (b) $z = x^2 - y^2 + Cxy$, $\quad (x, y) = (0, 0)$

8. Find and classify the extreme values (if any) of the functions on $\mathbb{R}^2$ defined by the following expressions:

  (a) $y^2 - x^3$

  (b) $(x - 1)^2 + (x - y)^2$

  (c) $x^2 + xy^2 + y^4$

9. (a) Find the minimum distance from the origin in $\mathbb{R}^3$ to the surface $z = \sqrt{x^2 - 1}$.

  (b) Repeat part (a) for the surface $z = 6xy + 7$.

Chapter 6
Differentiable Mappings

In this chapter we develop the notion of a differentiable map from $\mathbb{R}^n$ to $\mathbb{R}^m$ (or, more generally, from one normed space to another). Starting with this chapter, some linear algebra will be used. At this point, the reader might review the notion of a linear transformation and its matrix representation, since we shall be defining the derivative as a linear mapping. The connection between the general definition and partial derivatives will be found in §6.2. After this we generalize the usual theorems of calculus from the one-variable context treated in §4.7 to the multivariable case (such as the theorem stating that differentiability implies continuity, the chain rule, the mean value theorem, Taylor's theorem, tests for extrema, and so forth).

§6.1 Definition of the Derivative

A function of one variable $f :]a, b[\to \mathbb{R}$ is called *differentiable at* $x_0 \in]a, b[$ if the limit

$$f'(x_0) = \lim_{h \to 0} \frac{f(x_0 + h) - f(x_0)}{h}$$

exists. Equivalently, we may write this formula as

$$\lim_{h \to 0} \frac{f(x_0 + h) - f(x_0) - f'(x_0)h}{h} = 0,$$

that is,

$$\lim_{x \to x_0} \frac{f(x) - f(x_0) - f'(x_0)(x - x_0)}{x - x_0} = 0$$

or, what is the same,

$$\lim_{x \to x_0} \frac{|f(x) - f(x_0) - f'(x_0)(x - x_0)|}{|x - x_0|} = 0.$$

327

201

Chapter 6 Differentiable Mappings

The number $f'(x_0)$ represents the slope of the line tangent to the graph of f at the point $(x_0, f(x_0))$, as in Figure 6.1-1.

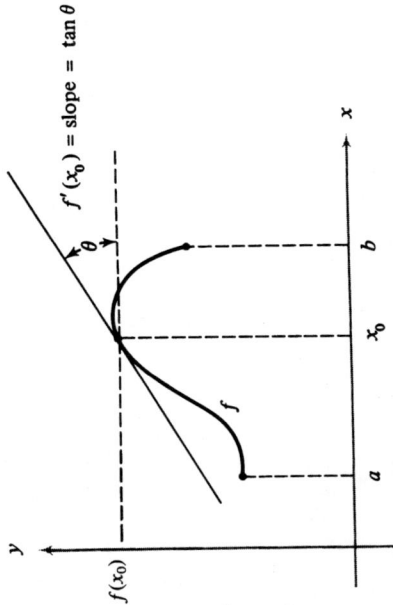

FIGURE 6.1-1   The derivative is the slope of the tangent line

Differentiability of $f: \mathbb{R} \to \mathbb{R}$ at x_0 is equivalent to the existence of a number m such that

$$\lim_{x \to x_0} \frac{|f(x) - f(x_0) - m(x - x_0)|}{|x - x_0|} = 0.$$

The function $T(s) = ms$ is linear: $T(\alpha s + \beta t) = \alpha T(s) + \beta T(t)$ for all real α, β, s, and t. To generalize this notion to maps $f: A \subset \mathbb{R}^n \to \mathbb{R}^m$, we make the following definition.

6.1.1 Definition   A map $f: A \subset \mathbb{R}^n \to \mathbb{R}^m$ *is said to be* **differentiable at** $x_0 \in A$ *if there is a linear function, denoted* $\mathbf{D}f(x_0): \mathbb{R}^n \to \mathbb{R}^m$ *and called the* **derivative** *of f at x_0, such that*

$$\lim_{x \to x_0} \frac{\|f(x) - f(x_0) - \mathbf{D}f(x_0)(x - x_0)\|}{\|x - x_0\|} = 0.$$

In this definition, $\mathbf{D}f(x_0)(x - x_0)$ denotes the value of the linear map $\mathbf{D}f(x_0)$ applied to the vector $x - x_0 \in \mathbb{R}^n$, and so $\mathbf{D}f(x_0)(x - x_0) \in \mathbb{R}^m$. We often write $\mathbf{D}f(x_0) \cdot h$ for $\mathbf{D}f(x_0)(h)$.

We shall be concerned almost exclusively with the Euclidean case, but note right here that if V, W are normed spaces and $f: A \subset V \to W$, then $\mathbf{D}f(x_0): V \to W$, and the definition makes sense.

§6.1 Definition of the Derivative

The definition may be rewritten by saying that for every $\varepsilon > 0$ there is a $\delta > 0$ such that $x \in A$ and $\|x - x_0\| < \delta$ implies

$$\|f(x) - f(x_0) - \mathbf{D}f(x_0)(x - x_0)\| \leq \varepsilon \|x - x_0\|.$$

In **6.1.1** it is implicit that $x \neq x_0$, but in this ε-δ formulation, we can allow $x = x_0$, since then both sides reduce to zero.

Intuitively, $x \mapsto f(x_0) + \mathbf{D}f(x_0)(x - x_0)$ is supposed to be the *best affine approximation* to f near the point x_0. (An affine mapping is a linear mapping plus a constant.) See Figure 6.1-2. In this figure we have indicated the equations of the tangent planes to the graph of f.

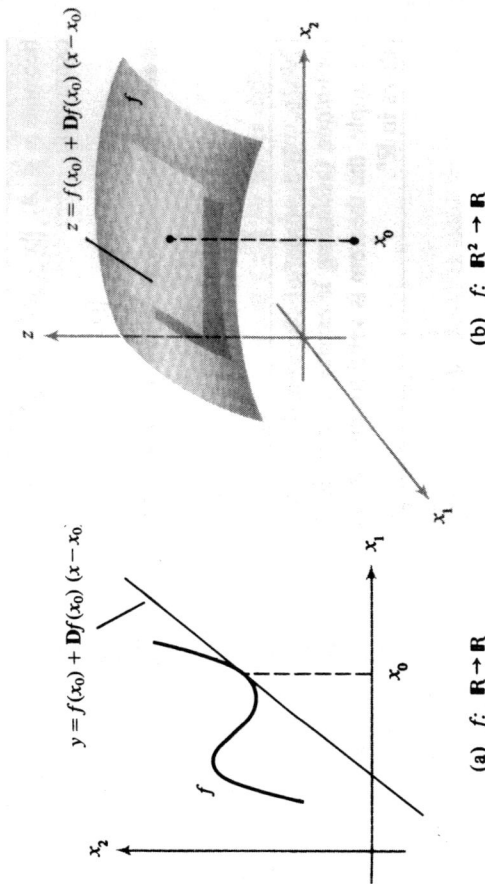

(a) f: $\mathbb{R} \to \mathbb{R}$

(b) f: $\mathbb{R}^2 \to \mathbb{R}$

FIGURE 6.1-2   (a) $f : \mathbb{R} \to \mathbb{R}$; (b) $f : \mathbb{R}^2 \to \mathbb{R}$

If f is a function of one variable and if we compare the definitions of $\mathbf{D}f(x)$ and $df/dx = f'(x)$, we see that $\mathbf{D}f(x)(h) = f'(x) \cdot h$ (the product of the numbers $f'(x)$ and $h \in \mathbb{R}$). Thus the linear map $\mathbf{D}f(x)$ is just multiplication by df/dx, in this case. If f is differentiable at each point of A, we say that f is *differentiable* **on** A. We expect intuitively (as in Figure 6.1-2) that there can be only one best linear approximation. This is in fact true if we assume that A is an open set.

6.1.2 Theorem   *Let A be an open set in $\mathbb{R}^n$ and suppose $f : A \to \mathbb{R}^m$ is differentiable at x_0. Then $\mathbf{D}f(x_0)$ is uniquely determined by f.*

6.1.3 Example *Let* $f : \mathbb{R} \to \mathbb{R}$, $f(x) = x^3$. *Compute* $\mathbf{D}f(x)$ *and* df/dx.

Solution From one-variable calculus, $dx^3/dx = 3x^2$. Thus, in this example, $\mathbf{D}f(x)$ is the linear mapping

$$h \mapsto \mathbf{D}f(x) \cdot h = 3x^2 h. \quad \blacklozenge$$

6.1.4 Example *Show that, in general,* $\mathbf{D}f$ *is not uniquely determined.*

Solution For example, if $A = \{x_0\}$ is a single point, any $\mathbf{D}f(x_0)$ will do, because $x \in A$, $\|x - x_0\| < \delta$ holds only when $x = x_0$, in which case the expression

$$\|f(x) - f(x_0) - \mathbf{D}f(x_0)(x - x_0)\|$$

is zero. The definition is thus fulfilled in a trivial way. $\quad \blacklozenge$

Note. If the proof of Theorem **6.1.2** is examined closely, one sees that $\mathbf{D}f(x)$ is unique (assuming it exists) on a wider range of sets than open sets. For example, the theorem is valid for closed intervals in $\mathbb{R}$ or generally for closed disks in $\mathbb{R}^n$.

Exercises for §6.1

1. Compute $\mathbf{D}f(x)$ for $f : \mathbb{R} \to \mathbb{R}$ defined by $f(x) = x \sin x$.

2. Prove that $\mathbf{D}(f + g) = \mathbf{D}f + \mathbf{D}g$.

3. Let $A = \{(x, y) \in \mathbb{R}^2 \mid 0 \le x \le 1, y = 0\}$. Prove that the conclusion of Theorem **6.1.2** is false for this A.

4. Let $f : \mathbb{R}^n \to \mathbb{R}^m$ and suppose there is a constant M such that for $x \in \mathbb{R}^n$, $\|f(x)\| \le M\|x\|^2$. Prove that f is differentiable at $x_0 = 0$ and that $\mathbf{D}f(x_0) = 0$.

5. If $f : \mathbb{R} \to \mathbb{R}$ is differentiable and $|f(x)| \le |x|$, must $\mathbf{D}f(0) = 0$?

§6.2 Matrix Representation

In addition to the definition of $\mathbf{D}f(x)$, there is another way to differentiate a function f of several variables. We write f in components, $f(x_1, \ldots, x_n) = (f_1(x_1, \ldots, x_n), \ldots, f_m(x_1, \ldots, x_n))$, and compute the partial derivatives $\partial f_j / \partial x_i$ for $j = 1, \ldots, m$ and $i = 1, \ldots, n$, where the notation $\partial f_j / \partial x_i$ means that we compute the usual derivative of f_j with respect to x_i; while keeping the other variables $x_1, \ldots, x_{i-1}, x_{i+1}, \ldots, x_n$ fixed.

6.2.1 Definition $\partial f_j / \partial x_i$ *is given by the following limit, when the limit exists:*

$$\frac{\partial f_j}{\partial x_i}(x_1, \ldots, x_n) = \lim_{h \to 0} \left\{ \frac{f_j(x_1, \ldots, x_i + h, \ldots, x_n) - f_j(x_1, \ldots, x_n)}{h} \right\}.$$

In **§6.1** we saw that $\mathbf{D}f(x)$ for $f : \mathbb{R} \to \mathbb{R}$ is just the linear map "multiplication by df/dx." This fact can be generalized to the following theorem.

6.2.2 Theorem *Suppose* $A \subset \mathbb{R}^n$ *is an open set and* $f : A \to \mathbb{R}^m$ *is differentiable on* A. *Then the partial derivatives* $\partial f_j / \partial x_i$ *exist, and the matrix of the linear map* $\mathbf{D}f(x)$ *with respect to the standard bases in* $\mathbb{R}^n$ *and* $\mathbb{R}^m$ *is given by*

$$\begin{pmatrix} \dfrac{\partial f_1}{\partial x_1} & \dfrac{\partial f_1}{\partial x_2} & \cdots & \dfrac{\partial f_1}{\partial x_n} \\ \dfrac{\partial f_2}{\partial x_1} & \dfrac{\partial f_2}{\partial x_2} & \cdots & \dfrac{\partial f_2}{\partial x_n} \\ \cdots & \cdots & \cdot & \cdots \\ \dfrac{\partial f_m}{\partial x_1} & \dfrac{\partial f_m}{\partial x_2} & \cdots & \dfrac{\partial f_m}{\partial x_n} \end{pmatrix}$$

where each partial derivative is evaluated at $x = (x_1, \ldots, x_n)$. *This matrix is called the Jacobian matrix of* f *or the derivative matrix.*

In doing specific computations, we can usually compute the Jacobian matrix easily, and Theorem **6.2.2** gives us $\mathbf{D}f$. In some books, $\mathbf{D}f$ is called the *differential* or the *total derivative* of f.

When $m = 1$, f is a real-valued function of n variables. Then $\mathbf{D}f$ has the matrix

$$\left(\frac{\partial f}{\partial x_1} \cdots \frac{\partial f}{\partial x_n} \right)$$

and the derivative applied to a vector $e = (a_1, \ldots, a_n)$ is

$$\mathbf{D}f(x) \cdot e = \sum_{i=1}^{n} \frac{\partial f}{\partial x_i} a_i.$$

It should be emphasized that $\mathbf{D}f$ is a linear mapping at each $x \in A$ and *the definition of* $\mathbf{D}f(x)$ *is independent of the basis used.* If we change from the standard basis to another basis, the matrix elements will change. If one examines the definition of the matrix of a linear transformation, it can be seen that the columns of the matrix relative to the new basis will be the derivative $\mathbf{D}f(x)$ applied to the new basis in $\mathbb{R}^n$ with this image vector expressed in the new basis in $\mathbb{R}^m$. Of course, *the linear map* $\mathbf{D}f(x)$ *itself does not change from basis to basis.* In the case $m = 1$, $Df(x)$ is, in the standard basis, a $1 \times n$ matrix, as just shown. The vector whose components are the same as those of $\mathbf{D}f(x)$ is called the *gradient* of f and is denoted grad f or ∇f. Thus, for $f : A \subset \mathbb{R}^n \to \mathbb{R}$,

$$\text{grad } f = \left(\frac{\partial f}{\partial x_1}, \ldots, \frac{\partial f}{\partial x_n} \right).$$

(Sometimes it is said that grad f is just $\mathbf{D}f$ with commas inserted!) To give an intrinsic definition of the gradient requires the use of the inner product. In fact, $\nabla f(x)$ is the vector such that for any $v \in \mathbb{R}^n$,

$$\langle \nabla f(x), v \rangle = \mathbf{D}f(x) \cdot v.$$

An important special case occurs when $f = L$ is already linear. From the definition of the derivative, we see that $\mathbf{D}L = L$, as expected, since the best affine approximation to a linear map has the linear map itself as the linear part (see Example **6.2.4**). Thus, the Jacobian matrix of L is the matrix of L itself in this case. Another case of interest is a constant map. Indeed, one sees that a constant map has derivative zero; zero is the linear map $K : \mathbb{R}^n \to \mathbb{R}^m$ such that $K(x) = 0 = (0, \ldots, 0)$ for all $x \in \mathbb{R}^n$.

6.2.3 Example *Let* $f : \mathbb{R}^2 \to \mathbb{R}^3$ *be defined by* $f(x,y) = (x^2, x^3 y, x^4 y^2)$. *Compute* Df.

Solution According to Theorem **6.2.2**, $\mathbf{D}f(x,y)$ is the linear map whose matrix is

$$\left(\begin{array}{cc} \dfrac{\partial f_1}{\partial x} & \dfrac{\partial f_1}{\partial y} \\ \dfrac{\partial f_2}{\partial x} & \dfrac{\partial f_2}{\partial y} \\ \dfrac{\partial f_3}{\partial x} & \dfrac{\partial f_3}{\partial y} \end{array} \right) = \left(\begin{array}{cc} 2x & 0 \\ 3x^2 y & x^3 \\ 4x^3 y^2 & 2x^4 y \end{array} \right)$$

where $f_1(x,y) = x^2$, $f_2(x,y) = x^3 y$, and $f_3(x,y) = x^4 y^2$. ◆

6.2.4 Example *Let* $L : \mathbb{R}^n \to \mathbb{R}^m$ *be a linear map; that is,* $L(x+y) = L(x) + L(y)$ *and* $L(\alpha x) = \alpha L(x)$. *Show that* $\mathbf{D}L(x) = L$.

Solution Given x_0 and $\varepsilon > 0$, we must find $\delta > 0$ such that $\|x - x_0\| < \delta$ implies

$$\|L(x) - L(x_0) - \mathbf{D}L(x) \cdot (x - x_0)\| \leq \varepsilon \|x - x_0\|.$$

But with $\mathbf{D}L(x) = L$, the left side becomes

$$\|L(x) - L(x_0) - L(x - x_0)\|,$$

which is zero, since $L(x - x_0) = L(x) - L(x_0)$, by linearity of L. Hence, $\mathbf{D}L(x) = L$ satisfies the definition of the derivative (with any $\delta > 0$). ◆

6.2.5 Example *Let* $f(x,y,z) = (x \sin y)/z$. *Compute* grad f.

Solution grad $f = (\partial f / \partial x, \partial f / \partial y, \partial f / \partial z)$, and here

$$\frac{\partial f}{\partial x} = \frac{\sin y}{z}, \quad \frac{\partial f}{\partial y} = \frac{x \cos y}{z}, \quad \frac{\partial f}{\partial z} = -\frac{x \sin y}{z^2},$$

so that

$$\text{grad } f(x,y,z) = \left(\frac{\sin y}{z}, \frac{x \cos y}{z}, -\frac{x \sin y}{z^2} \right).$$

◆

Exercises for §6.2

1. Let $f: \mathbb{R}^3 \to \mathbb{R}^2$, $f(x,y,z) = (x^4y, xe^z)$. Compute Df.

2. Let $f: \mathbb{R}^3 \to \mathbb{R}$, $(x,y,z) \mapsto e^{x^2+y^2+z^2}$. Compute Df and grad f.

3. Let L be a linear map of $\mathbb{R}^n \to \mathbb{R}^m$, let $g: \mathbb{R}^n \to \mathbb{R}^m$ be such that $\|g(x)\| \le M\|x\|^2$, and let $f(x) = L(x) + g(x)$. Prove that $Df(0) = L$.

4. Let $f(x,y) = (xy, y/x)$. Compute Df. Compute the matrix of $Df(x,y)$ with respect to the basis $(1,0), (1,1)$ in $\mathbb{R}^2$.

5. Discuss the possibility of defining Df for f a mapping from one normed space to another.

§6.3 Continuity of Differentiable Mappings; Differentiable Paths

It was shown in §4.7 that a differentiable function of one variable is continuous. This is appealing intuitively, since having a tangent line (or plane) to the graph is stronger than having no breaks in the graph. We recall the proof: Let $f:]a,b[\to \mathbb{R}$ be differentiable at x_0. Then

$$\lim_{x \to x_0}(f(x) - f(x_0)) = \lim_{x \to x_0}\left(\frac{f(x) - f(x_0)}{x - x_0}\right) \cdot (x - x_0)$$
$$= f'(x_0) \cdot \lim_{x \to x_0}(x - x_0) = f'(x_0) \cdot 0 = 0$$

and so $\lim_{x \to x_0}(f(x) - f(x_0)) = 0$, which implies that f is continuous at x_0. This argument generalizes to the case of $f: A \subset \mathbb{R}^n \to \mathbb{R}^m$, as in the next proposition.

6.3.1 Proposition Suppose $A \subset \mathbb{R}^n$ is open and $f: A \to \mathbb{R}^m$ is differentiable on A. Then f is continuous. In fact, for each $x_0 \in A$, there are a constant $M > 0$ and a $\delta_0 > 0$ such that $\|x - x_0\| < \delta_0$ implies $\|f(x) - f(x_0)\| \le M\|x - x_0\|$. (This is called the **local Lipschitz property**.)

Earlier, we examined the special case of real-valued functions, $f: \mathbb{R}^n \to \mathbb{R}$. The case of a function $c: \mathbb{R} \to \mathbb{R}^m$ is also important. Here c represents a

curve or **path** in $\mathbb{R}^m$. In this case, $\mathbf{D}c(t): \mathbb{R} \to \mathbb{R}^m$ is represented by the vector associated with the single column matrix

$$\begin{pmatrix} \dfrac{dc_1}{dt} \\ \vdots \\ \dfrac{dc_m}{dt} \end{pmatrix}$$

where $c(t) = (c_1(t), \ldots, c_m(t))$. This vector is denoted $c'(t)$ and is called the **tangent vector** or **velocity vector** to the curve. If we note that

$$c'(t) = \lim_{h \to 0}\frac{c(t+h) - c(t)}{h}$$

and use the fact that $(c(t+h) - c(t))/h$ is a chord that approximates the tangent line to the curve, we see that $c'(t)$ should represent the exact tangent vector (see Figure 6.3-1). In terms of a moving particle, $(c(t+h)-c(t))/h$ is an approximation to the velocity, since it is displacement/time, and so $c'(t)$ is the *instantaneous velocity*.

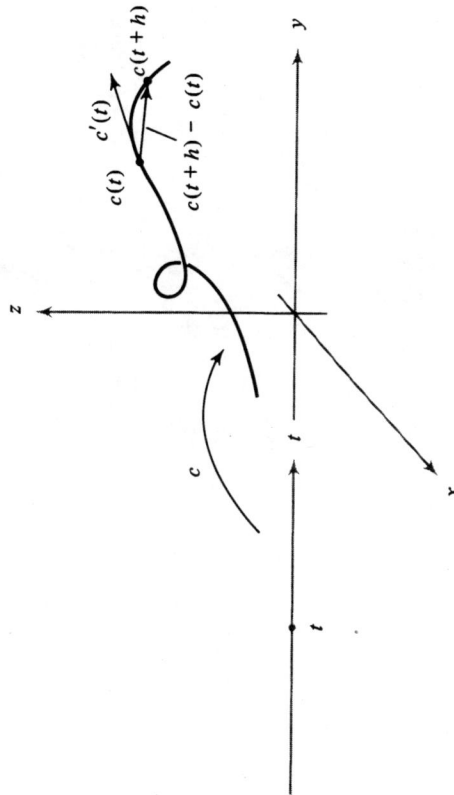

FIGURE 6.3-1   The velocity vector of a curve

Strictly speaking, we should always represent $c'(t)$ as a column vector, since the matrix of $\mathbf{D}c(t)$ is an $m \times 1$ matrix. However, this is typographically awkward, and so we often write $c'(t)$ as a row vector.

6.3.2 Example *Let $c(t) = (t^2, t, \sin t)$. Find the tangent vector to $c(t)$ at $c(0) = (0, 0, 0)$.*

Solution $c'(t) = (2t, 1, \cos t)$. Setting $t = 0$, $c'(0) = (0, 1, 1)$, which is the vector tangent to $c(t)$ at $(0, 0, 0)$. ◆

Next we recall some single-variable ideas from §4.7:

6.3.3 Example *Prove that $f : \mathbb{R} \to \mathbb{R}$ defined by $x \mapsto |x|$ is continuous but not differentiable at 0.*

Solution $f(x) = x$ for $x \geq 0$ and $f(x) = -x$ for $x < 0$, and so f is continuous on $]0, \infty[$ and $]-\infty, 0[$. Since $\lim_{x \to 0} f(x) = 0 = f(0)$, f is also continuous at 0, and so f is continuous at all points. Finally, f is not differentiable at 0, for if it were,

$$\lim_{x \to 0} \frac{f(x) - f(0)}{x - 0} = \lim_{x \to 0} \frac{f(x)}{x}$$

would exist. But for $x > 0$, $f(x)/x$ is $+1$ and for $x < 0$ it is -1, and so the limit cannot exist. ◆

6.3.4 Example *Must the derivative of a function be continuous?*

Solution The answer is no, but an example is not obvious. An example is the function

$$f(x) = x^2 \sin \frac{1}{x} \quad \text{if } x \neq 0,$$

and

$$f(x) = 0 \quad \text{if } x = 0.$$

See Figure 6.3-2.
To demonstrate differentiability at zero, we shall show that

$$\frac{f(x)}{x} \to 0 \quad \text{as } x \to 0.$$

Indeed, $|f(x)/x| = |x \sin(1/x)| \leq |x| = |x \sin(1/x)| \to 0$ as $x \to 0$. Thus, $f'(0)$ exists and is zero. Hence, f is differentiable at 0. By differentiation rules of one-variable calculus,

$$f'(x) = 2x \sin \frac{1}{x} - \cos \frac{1}{x} \quad \text{if } x \neq 0.$$

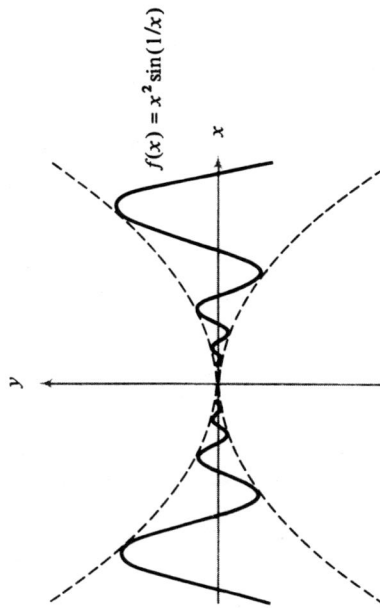

$f(x) = x^2 \sin(1/x)$

FIGURE 6.3-2 This function is differentiable, but the derivative is discontinuous at 0. ◆

As $x \to 0$, the first term tends to 0 but the second term oscillates between $+1$ and -1, and so $\lim_{x \to 0} f'(x)$ does not exist. Thus, f' exists but is not continuous.

Supplement to §6.3

Karl Weierstrass gave an example of a continuous function $f(x)$ of one variable that has no derivative anywhere (see Exercise 20, Chapter 5). Roughly speaking, this function superimposes infinitely many corners like those in Example 6.3.3. One can also ask if such functions arise in any "practical" context. Surprisingly, the answer is yes. One place in which "nowhere differentiable" paths are important is in the study of *Brownian motion*, the erratic motion of small particles suspended in a fluid such as water or air. The American mathematician Norbert Wiener developed an effective model for studying this motion involving integration over a "space" of paths. In this method "most" continuous paths are not differentiable anywhere and have no tangent vectors.

Another context in which nowhere differentiable paths occur is in the study of fractals and dynamical systems. For instance, fix a complex number c and let $f_c : \mathbb{R}^2 \approx \mathbb{C} \to \mathbb{C}$ be defined by $f_c(z) = z^2 + c$. Let $J_c^\infty = \{z \mid f_c^n(z) \to \infty \text{ as } n \to \infty\}$, where f_c^n means f_c composed with itself n times, and let $J_c = \mathrm{bd}(J_c^\infty)$. For $c = 0$, it is clear that J_c is a circle, but for $c \neq 0$ (but close enough to zero) it is known that J_c is a continuous but nowhere differentiable curve! One calls J_c the *Julia set* of f_c; it is shown in Figure 6.3-3.

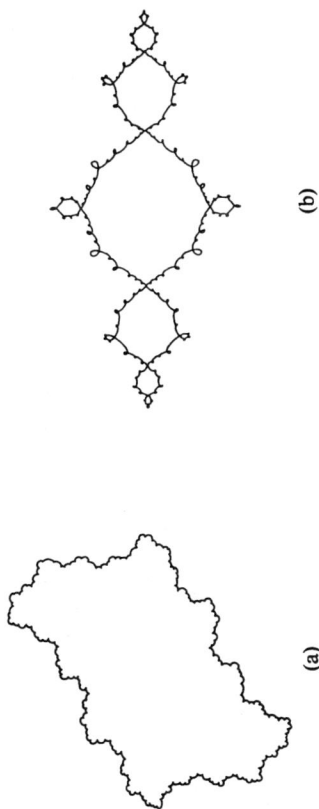

(a)

(b)

FIGURE 6.3-3 (a) The Julia set of $f(z) = z^2 + \frac{1}{2}i$, which is a simple closed curve but is nowhere differentiable; (b) the Julia set of $f(z) = z^2 - 1$, which contains infinitely many closed curves

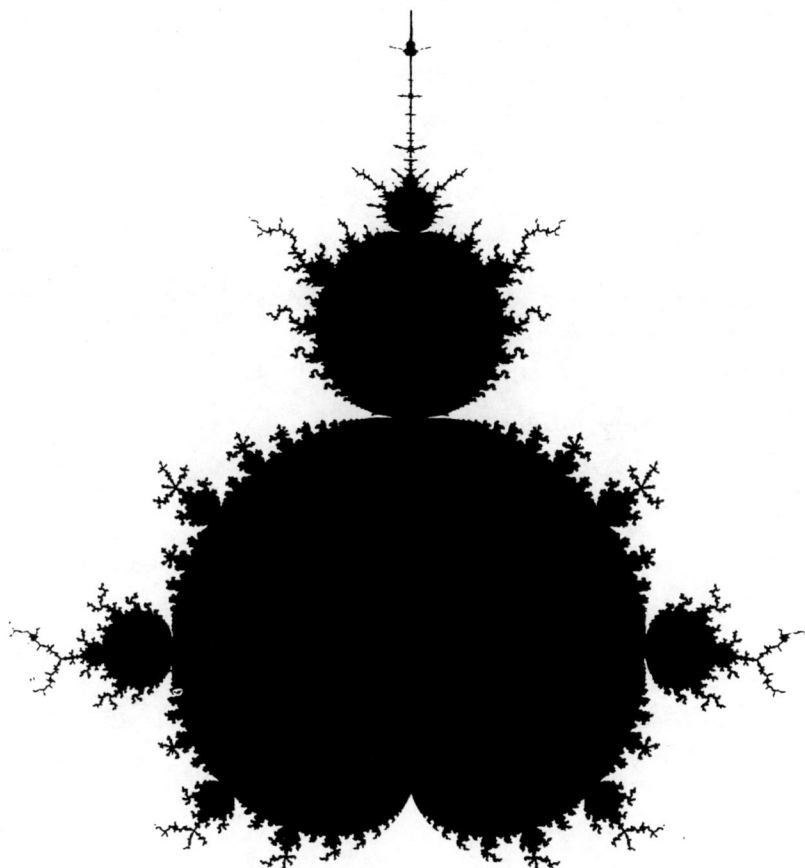

FIGURE 6.3-4 The Mandelbrot set (reprinted by permission, from B. B. Mandelbrot, *The Fractal Geometry of Nature*, W. H. Freeman, New York, 1983)

The set of c for which J_c is path-connected is called the *Mandelbrot set,* shown in Figure 6.3-4. (The Mandelbrot set is also the set of c for which zero does not go to infinity under iteration of f_c—this is not obvious, however.) A deep theorem of Douady and Hubbard is that *the Mandelbrot set is connected.* This is an example of a very complicated set whose connectedness is far from obvious—computer magnification of this set shows how truly subtle it is. For more information, references, and the reasons this subject has some practical importance, see R. Devaney, *An Introduction to Chaotic Dynamical Systems* (Addison-Wesley, Reading, Mass., 1985), and references therein.

Exercises for §6.3

1. Let $f(x) = x^2$ if x is irrational and let $f(x) = 0$ if x is rational. Is f continuous at 0? Is it differentiable at 0?

2. Is the local Lipschitz condition in Theorem **6.3.1** enough to guarantee differentiability?

3. Must the derivative of a continuous function exist at its maximum?

4. Let $f(x) = x \sin(1/x)$, $x \neq 0$, and $f(0) = 0$. Investigate the continuity and differentiability of f at 0.

5. Find the tangent vector to the curve $c(t) = (3t^2, e^t, t + t^2)$ at the point corresponding to $t = 1$.

The partial derivatives of a function measure its rate of change in the special directions parallel to the axes. The *directional derivatives* do this in other directions also.

6.4.2 Definition *Let f be real-valued and defined in a neighborhood of $x_0 \in \mathbb{R}^n$, and let $e \in \mathbb{R}^n$ be a unit vector. Then*

$$\frac{d}{dt} f(x_0 + te)\Big|_{t=0} = \lim_{t \to 0} \frac{f(x_0 + te) - f(x_0)}{t}$$

is called the directional derivative of f at x_0 in the direction e.

From this definition, we see that the directional derivative is the rate of change of f in the direction e and, for $n = 2$, gives the slope of the graph of f in that direction; see Figure 6.4-2.

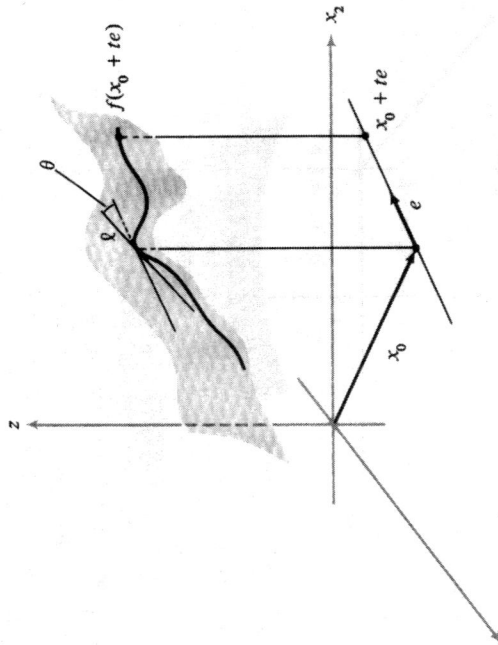

FIGURE 6.4-2   Slope of $l = \tan \theta$ = directional derivative

We claim that *the directional derivative in the direction of e equals* $Df(x_0) \cdot e$. To see this, consider the definition of $Df(x_0)$ with $x = x_0 + te$: Given $\varepsilon > 0$,

$$\left\| \frac{f(x_0 + te) - f(x_0)}{t} - Df(x_0) \cdot e \right\| \leq \varepsilon \|e\|$$

§6.4 Conditions for Differentiability

Since the Jacobian matrix provides an effective computational tool, it would be useful to know if the existence of the usual partial derivatives implies that the derivative Df exists. This is, unfortunately, not true in general. For example, take $f : \mathbb{R}^2 \to \mathbb{R}$ defined by $f(x,y) = x$ when $y = 0$, $f(x,y) = y$ when $x = 0$, and $f(x,y) = 1$ elsewhere. Then $\partial f/\partial x$ and $\partial f/\partial y$ exist at $(0,0)$ and are equal to 1. However, f is not continuous at $(0,0)$ (why?), and so the derivative Df cannot possibly exist at $(0,0)$. See Figure 6.4-1. (See the examples and exercises for more exotic examples.)

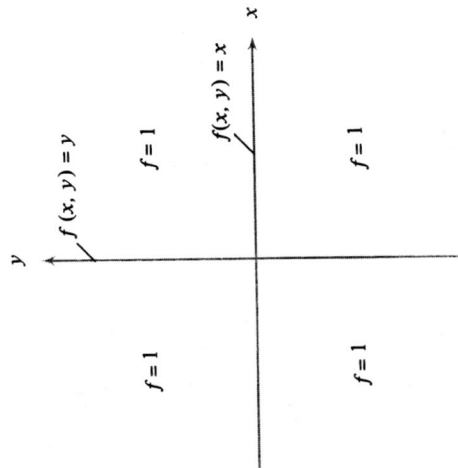

FIGURE 6.4-1   The partial derivatives of this function exist at $(0,0)$, but the function is not continuous at $(0,0)$

It is quite simple to understand such behavior. The partial derivatives depend only on what happens in the directions of the x and y axes, whereas the definition of Df involves the combined behavior of f in a whole neighborhood of a given point. We can, however, assert the following.

6.4.1 Theorem *Let $A \subset \mathbb{R}^n$ be open and $f : A \subset \mathbb{R}^n \to \mathbb{R}^m$. Suppose $f = (f_1, \ldots, f_m)$. If each of the partials $\partial f_j / \partial x_i$ exists and is continuous on A, then f is differentiable on A.*

if $|t|$ is sufficiently small. Thus, if f is differentiable at x_0, then the directional derivatives also exist and are given by

$$\lim_{t\to 0}\frac{f(x_0+te)-f(x_0)}{t}=\mathbf{D}f(x_0)\cdot e.$$

In particular, observe that $\partial f/\partial x_i$ is the derivative of f in the direction of the ith coordinate axis (with $e=e_i=(0,0,\dots,0,1,0,\dots,0)$).

For a function $f:\mathbb{R}^2\to\mathbb{R}$, the directional derivatives $\mathbf{D}f(x_0)\cdot e$ can be used to determine the plane tangent to the graph of f (compare Figure 6.1-2). That is, the line l given by $z=f(x_0)+\mathbf{D}f(x_0)\cdot te$ is tangent to the graph of f, since, as in Figure 6.4-2, $\mathbf{D}f(x_0)\cdot e$ is the rate of change of f in the direction e. Thus, the tangent plane to the graph of f at $(x_0,f(x_0))$ may be described by the equation

$$z=f(x_0)+\mathbf{D}f(x_0)\cdot(x-x_0)$$

(see Figure 6.4-3). Since we have not defined the notion of the tangent plane to a surface, we shall adopt this equation as a *definition* of the tangent plane.

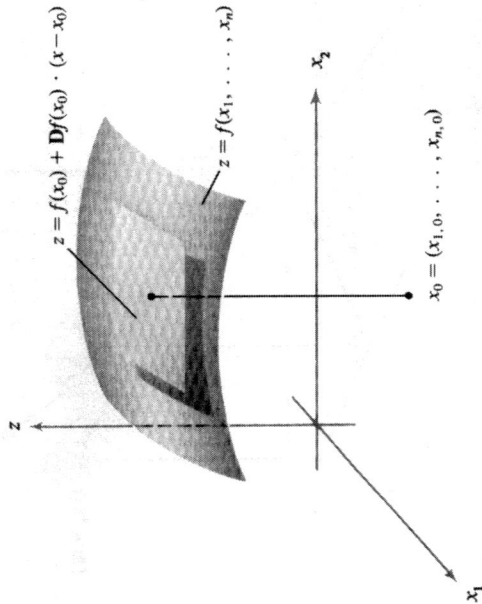

FIGURE 6.4-3 The tangent plane to the graph of a function

6.4.3 Example *Show that the existence of all directional derivatives at a point need not imply differentiability.*

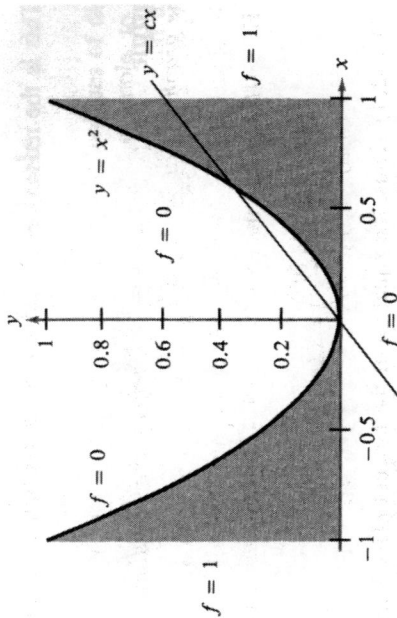

FIGURE 6.4-4 The existence of directional derivatives does not force differentiability or even continuity

Solution Define a function $f:\mathbb{R}^2\to\mathbb{R}$ by $f(x,y)=1$ if $0<y<x^2$ and by $f(x,y)=0$ otherwise. Then f is identically 0 along the horizontal and vertical axes. Any other line through the origin also stays in the region in which $f=0$ for some short distance on both sides of the origin. Thus f is constantly 0 on some interval on both sides of the origin along any such line. This shows that the directional derivative at the origin in the direction of that line is 0. All directional derivatives exist and are 0 at the origin, but the function is not even continuous, much less differentiable, at the origin. See Figure 6.4-4.

A slightly more complicated but similar example is the function $f:\mathbb{R}^2\to\mathbb{R}$ defined by

$$f(x,y)=\frac{xy}{x^2+y}\quad\text{if } x^2\neq -y$$

and

$$f(x,y)=0\quad\text{if } x^2=-y.$$

Letting $e=(e_1,e_2)$, where $e_2\neq 0$,

$$\frac{1}{t}f(te_1,te_2)=\frac{1}{t}\frac{t^2e_1e_2}{t^2e_1^2+te_2}=\frac{e_1e_2}{te_1^2+e_2}\to e_1$$

as $t\to 0$; the case $e_2=0$ gives zero. Thus each directional derivative exists at $(0,0)$. However, f is not continuous at $(0,0)$, since for x^2 near $-y$ with both x,y small, f is very large. (We leave the details to the reader.) ◆

This example shows that the existence of all directional derivatives would *not* be a convenient definition of differentiability, since it would not even imply continuity. This is the reason one adopts the more restrictive notion in Definition 6.1.1.

6.4.4 Example *Let $f(x,y) = x^2 + y$. Compute the equation of the plane tangent to the graph of f at $x = 1$, $y = 2$.*

Solution Here $\mathbf{D}f(x,y)$ has matrix

$$\left(\frac{\partial f}{\partial x}, \frac{\partial f}{\partial y} \right) = (2x, 1),$$

and so $\mathbf{D}f(1,2) = (2, 1)$. Thus, the equation of the tangent plane becomes

$$z = 3 + (2,1)\begin{pmatrix} x-1 \\ y-2 \end{pmatrix} = 3 + 2(x-1) + (y-2);$$

that is,

$$2x + y - z = 1. \quad \blacklozenge$$

Exercises for §6.4

1. Use Theorem 6.4.1 to show that $f(x,y)$ defined by
$$f(x,y) = \frac{(xy)^2}{\sqrt{x^2+y^2}}, \ (x,y) \neq (0,0)$$
and
$$f(x,y) = 0, \ (x,y) = (0,0)$$
is differentiable at $(0,0)$.

2. Investigate the differentiability of
$$f(x,y) = \frac{xy}{\sqrt{x^2+y^2}}$$
at $(0,0)$ if $f(0,0) = 0$.

3. Find the tangent plane to the graph of $z = x^2 + y^2$ at $(0, 0)$.

4. Find the equation of the tangent plane to $z = x^3 + y^4$ at $x = 1$, $y = 3$.

5. Find a function $f : \mathbb{R}^2 \to \mathbb{R}$ that is differentiable at each point but whose partials are not continuous at $(0,0)$.

§6.5 The Chain Rule

As we recalled in §4.7, one of the most important techniques of differentiation is the chain rule ("function of a function" rule). For example, to differentiate $(x^3 + 3)^6$, let $y = x^3 + 3$ and first differentiate y^6, getting $6y^5$, and then multiply by the derivative of $x^3 + 3$ to obtain the final answer $6(x^3 + 3)^5 3x^2$. There is a similar process for functions of several variables. For example, if u, v, and f are real-valued functions of two variables, then

$$\frac{\partial}{\partial x} f(u(x,y), v(x,y)) = \frac{\partial f}{\partial u}\frac{\partial u}{\partial x} + \frac{\partial f}{\partial v}\frac{\partial v}{\partial x}.$$

The following theorem includes all of these as special cases.

6.5.1 Chain Rule *Let $A \subset \mathbb{R}^n$ be open and $f : A \to \mathbb{R}^m$ be differentiable at $x_0 \in A$. Let $B \subset \mathbb{R}^m$ be open, $f(A) \subset B$, and $g : B \to \mathbb{R}^p$ be differentiable at $f(x_0)$. Then the composite $g \circ f$ is differentiable at x_0 and $\mathbf{D}(g \circ f)(x_0) = \mathbf{D}g(f(x_0)) \circ \mathbf{D}f(x_0)$.*

Note that the right-hand side is well defined, because $\mathbf{D}f(x_0) : \mathbb{R}^n \to \mathbb{R}^m$ and $\mathbf{D}g(f(x_0)) : \mathbb{R}^m \to \mathbb{R}^p$ and so their composition as linear transformations is defined. The chain rule is also called the *composite function theorem*, since it tells us how to differentiate composite functions.

Since the product of two matrices corresponds to the composition of the corresponding linear maps they represent, the chain rule can be rephrased by saying that *the Jacobian matrix of $g \circ f$ at $x = (x_1, \ldots, x_n)$ is the product of the Jacobian matrix of g evaluated at $f(x)$ with the Jacobian matrix of f evaluated at x (in that order)*. Thus, if $h = g \circ f$ and $y = f(x)$, then

$$\mathbf{D}h(x) = \begin{pmatrix} \dfrac{\partial g_1}{\partial y_1} & \cdots & \dfrac{\partial g_1}{\partial y_m} \\ \vdots & \ddots & \vdots \\ \dfrac{\partial g_p}{\partial y_1} & \cdots & \dfrac{\partial g_p}{\partial y_m} \end{pmatrix} \begin{pmatrix} \dfrac{\partial f_1}{\partial x_1} & \cdots & \dfrac{\partial f_1}{\partial x_n} \\ \vdots & \ddots & \vdots \\ \dfrac{\partial f_m}{\partial x_1} & \cdots & \dfrac{\partial f_m}{\partial x_n} \end{pmatrix}$$

where the $\partial g_i/\partial y_j$ are evaluated at $y = f(x)$ and the $\partial f_i/\partial x_j$ at x. Writing this out, we obtain, for example,

$$\frac{\partial h_1}{\partial x_1} = \sum_{j=0}^{m} \frac{\partial g_1}{\partial y_j}\frac{\partial f_j}{\partial x_1}.$$

This situation occurs when we "change variables." For example, suppose $f(x, y)$ is a real-valued function and $x = r\cos\theta$, $y = r\sin\theta$ define the new polar coordinate variables r, θ. Form the function

$$h(r, \theta) = f(r\cos\theta, r\sin\theta).$$

Then

$$\frac{\partial h}{\partial r} = \frac{\partial f}{\partial x}\cos\theta + \frac{\partial f}{\partial y}\sin\theta$$

and

$$\frac{\partial h}{\partial \theta} = -\frac{\partial f}{\partial x} r\sin\theta + \frac{\partial f}{\partial y} r\cos\theta.$$

The reader should derive similar formulas for spherical coordinates (r, φ, θ), where $x = r\cos\theta\sin\varphi$, $y = r\sin\theta\sin\varphi$, $z = r\cos\varphi$ (spherical coordinates are discussed further in §9.5).

Another illustration may clarify matters. Suppose we are given functions $u(x, y), v(x, y), w(x, y)$, and $f(u, v, w)$ and we form the function $h(x, y) = f(u(x, y), v(x, y), w(x, y))$. The chain rule gives

$$\frac{\partial h}{\partial x} = \frac{\partial f}{\partial u}\frac{\partial u}{\partial x} + \frac{\partial f}{\partial v}\frac{\partial v}{\partial x} + \frac{\partial f}{\partial w}\frac{\partial w}{\partial x}.$$

The idea behind the proof of this formula (as an illustrative case) is as follows. Write

$$\frac{h(x+\Delta x, y) - h(x, y)}{\Delta x} = \frac{f(u(x+\Delta x, y), v(x+\Delta x, y), w(x+\Delta x, y))}{\Delta x}$$

$$-\frac{f(u(x, y), v(x+\Delta x, y), w(x+\Delta x, y))}{\Delta x}$$

$$+\frac{f(u(x, y), v(x+\Delta x, y), w(x+\Delta x, y))}{\Delta x}$$

$$-\frac{f(u(x, y), v(x, y), w(x+\Delta x, y))}{\Delta x}$$

$$+\frac{f(u(x, y), v(x, y), w(x+\Delta x, y))}{\Delta x}$$

$$-\frac{f(u(x, y), v(x, y), w(x, y))}{\Delta x}.$$

Using $f(u+\Delta u, v, w) - f(u, v, w) \approx \Delta u \,\partial f/\partial u$, we find that the preceding expression is approximately

$$\frac{\partial f}{\partial u}\frac{\Delta u}{\Delta x} + \frac{\partial f}{\partial v}\frac{\Delta v}{\Delta x} + \frac{\partial f}{\partial w}\frac{\Delta w}{\Delta x}.$$

Thus, letting $\Delta x \to 0$ gives the formula. Can you pinpoint what items in this argument need clarifying for the proof to be complete?

6.5.2 Example *Verify the chain rule for $f(u, w) = u^2 v + wv^2$ and $u = xy$, $v = \sin x$, $w = e^x$.*

Solution Here $h(x, y) = f(u(x, y), v(x, y), w(x, y))$ is given by

$$h(x, y) = x^2 y^2 \sin x + e^x \sin^2 x,$$

and so, directly,

$$\frac{\partial h}{\partial x} = 2xy^2 \sin x + x^2 y^2 \cos x + e^x \sin^2 x + e^x\, 2\sin x\cos x.$$

On the other hand, the chain rule gives

$$\frac{\partial f}{\partial u}\frac{\partial u}{\partial x} + \frac{\partial f}{\partial v}\frac{\partial v}{\partial x} + \frac{\partial f}{\partial w}\frac{\partial w}{\partial x} = 2uv\frac{\partial u}{\partial x} + u^2\frac{\partial v}{\partial x} + 2wv\frac{\partial v}{\partial x} + v^2\frac{\partial w}{\partial x}$$

$$= 2xy^2 \sin x + x^2 y^2 \cos x + 2e^x \sin x\cos x + e^x \sin^2 x,$$

which is the same result. The formula for $\partial h/\partial y$ can be checked similarly. ◆

6.5.3 Example *Let $f: \mathbb{R} \to \mathbb{R}$ and $F: \mathbb{R}^2 \to \mathbb{R}$ be given by $F(x, y) = f(xy)$. Verify that*

$$x\frac{\partial F}{\partial x} = y\frac{\partial F}{\partial y}.$$

Solution By the chain rule,

$$\frac{\partial F}{\partial x} = f'(xy)y \quad \text{and} \quad \frac{\partial F}{\partial y} = f'(xy)x,$$

and so the statement is clear. ◆

6.5.4 Example *Suppose that $\gamma: [0, 1] \to \mathbb{R}^n$ is a differentiable parametrization of a curve in $\mathbb{R}^n$ and that f is a differentiable function from $\mathbb{R}^n$ into $\mathbb{R}$. Let $h(t) = f(\gamma(t))$. Show that $h'(t) = \langle \nabla f(\gamma(t)), \gamma'(t)\rangle$ and explain how this generalizes the formula obtained earlier for directional derivatives. (See Figure 6.5-1.)*

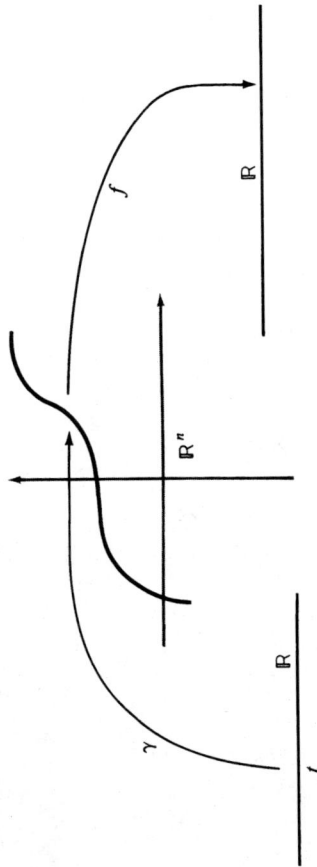

FIGURE 6.5-1   A function defined along a parametrized curve

Solution   Since $h(t) = (f \circ \gamma)(t)$, the chain rule gives

$$h'(t) = \left[\frac{\partial f}{\partial x_1}, \frac{\partial f}{\partial x_2}, \ldots, \frac{\partial f}{\partial x_n}\right] \begin{bmatrix} x_1'(t) \\ x_2'(t) \\ \vdots \\ x_n'(t) \end{bmatrix}$$

$$= \frac{\partial f}{\partial x_1}x_1'(t) + \frac{\partial f}{\partial x_2}x_2'(t) + \cdots + \frac{\partial f}{\partial x_n}x_n'(t).$$

All the partial derivatives are evaluated at the point $\gamma(t) = (x_1(t), x_2(t), \ldots, x_n(t))$. This is exactly the same as the inner product of the gradient of f at that point with the velocity vector $\gamma'(t)$ at that point. The directional derivative of f at the point v_0 in the direction of the unit vector $e = (a_1, a_2, \ldots, a_n)$ is the special case in which the curve is the straight line $\gamma(t) = v_0 + te$. In that case $x_k(t) = \gamma_k(t) = v_{0k} + ta_k$. Thus, we recover the same formula as before:

$$\langle \nabla f(\gamma(0)), \gamma'(0)\rangle = \langle \nabla f(v_0), e\rangle$$

since $\gamma(0) = v_0$, and $\gamma'(t) = e$ for all t. ◆

Exercises for §6.5

1. Write out the chain rule for

$$h(x,y,z) = f(u(x,y,z), v(x,y), w(y,z)).$$

2. Verify the chain rule for

$$u(x,y,z) = xe^y, \quad v(x,y,z) = (\sin x)yz$$

and

$$f(u,v) = u^2 + v\sin u$$

with

$$h(x,y,z) = f(u(x,y,z), v(x,y,z)).$$

3. Let $F(x,y) = f(x^2 + y^2)$. Show that $x(\partial F/\partial y) = y(\partial F/\partial x)$.

4. Write out the chain rule relating rectangular coordinates to spherical coordinates in three dimensions.

5. Let $f: \mathbb{R} \to \mathbb{R}$ and $F: \mathbb{R}^2 \to \mathbb{R}$ be differentiable and satisfy $F(x, f(x)) = 0$ and $\partial F/\partial y \neq 0$. Prove that $f'(x) = -\dfrac{\partial F/\partial x}{\partial F/\partial y}$ where $y = f(x)$.

§6.6 Product Rule and Gradients

Another well-known rule of differential calculus is the *product rule*, or *Leibniz rule*.

6.6.1 Proposition   *Let $A \subset \mathbb{R}^n$ be open and let $f: A \to \mathbb{R}^m$ and $g: A \to \mathbb{R}$ be differentiable functions. Then gf is differentiable, and for $x \in A$, $\mathbf{D}(gf)(x): \mathbb{R}^n \to \mathbb{R}^m$ is given by $\mathbf{D}(gf)(x) \cdot e = g(x)(\mathbf{D}f(x) \cdot e) + (\mathbf{D}g(x) \cdot e)f(x)$ for all $e \in \mathbb{R}^n$. (This makes sense, because $g(x) \in \mathbb{R}$ and $\mathbf{D}g(x) \cdot e \in \mathbb{R}$.)*

We sometimes abbreviate this result by saying that

$$\mathbf{D}(gf) = g\mathbf{D}f + (\mathbf{D}g)f,$$

but the precise meaning is as stated in the proposition. The reader is already familiar with the product rule from §4.7 and elementary calculus. In terms of components, the proposition is in fact just the usual product rule:

$$\frac{\partial}{\partial x_i}(gf_k) = g\frac{\partial f_k}{\partial x_i} + \frac{\partial g}{\partial x_i}f_k.$$

For quotients, we have a similar result. If $g \neq 0$, then

$$\mathbf{D}\left(\frac{f}{g}\right) = \frac{g\mathbf{D}f - (\mathbf{D}g)f}{g^2}.$$

To prove this formula, it suffices, by Proposition 6.6.1, to demonstrate it for the case $1/g$. This reduces it to a problem in elementary calculus, which we asked the reader to deal with in §4.7.

Other rules of differentiation are encompassed in the statement that $\mathbf{D}$ is *linear*, that is, that $\mathbf{D}(f + g) = \mathbf{D}f + \mathbf{D}g$ and $\mathbf{D}(\lambda f) = \lambda \mathbf{D}f$ for $\lambda \in \mathbb{R}$, a constant.

Let us consider the *geometry of gradients* a little further. Let $f : A \subset \mathbb{R}^n \to \mathbb{R}$ be differentiable. The gradient is

$$\operatorname{grad} f(x) = \left(\frac{\partial f}{\partial x_1}, \ldots, \frac{\partial f}{\partial x_n}\right).$$

Hence the directional derivative in the direction h is the inner product

$$\mathbf{D}f(x) \cdot h = \langle \operatorname{grad} f(x), h \rangle$$
$$= \text{rate of change of } f \text{ at the point } x \text{ in direction } h.$$

Consider a "surface" S defined by $f(x) = $ constant. *We will now show that* $\operatorname{grad} f(x)$ *is orthogonal to this surface* (our argument will gloss over the precise nature of this surface—this will be dealt with in §7.7). To prove this, consider a curve $c(t)$ in S with its tangent vector $c'(0)$ where $c(0) = x_0$. We assert that

$$\langle \operatorname{grad} f(x_0), c'(0) \rangle = 0.$$

Since $c(t) \in S$, $f(c(t)) = $ constant in t. Differentiating and using the chain rule, we get

$$\mathbf{D}f(c(t)) \cdot c'(t) = 0.$$

Setting $t = 0$, and using $\mathbf{D}f(x) \cdot h = \langle \operatorname{grad} f(x), h \rangle$, gives the desired relation. See Figure 6.6-1.

We may describe the plane tangent to the surface S defined by $f(x) = $ constant at a point x_0 on S by $\langle \operatorname{grad} f(x_0), x - x_0 \rangle = 0$, since $\operatorname{grad} f(x_0)$ is orthogonal to S. It is also evident from the equation

$$\langle \operatorname{grad} f(x_0), h \rangle = \|\operatorname{grad} f(x_0)\| \cos \theta$$

(where $\|h\| = 1$ and θ is the angle between $\operatorname{grad} f(x_0)$ and h) that the vector $\operatorname{grad} f(x_0)$ points in the direction in which f is changing the fastest. It is not unreasonable, because if we suppose that f represents the height function of a mountain, then $f = $ constant is a level contour. To climb or descend the

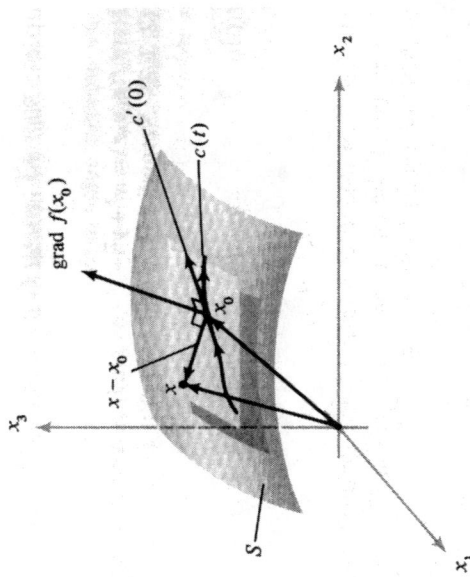

FIGURE 6.6-1   The gradient is orthogonal to level sets

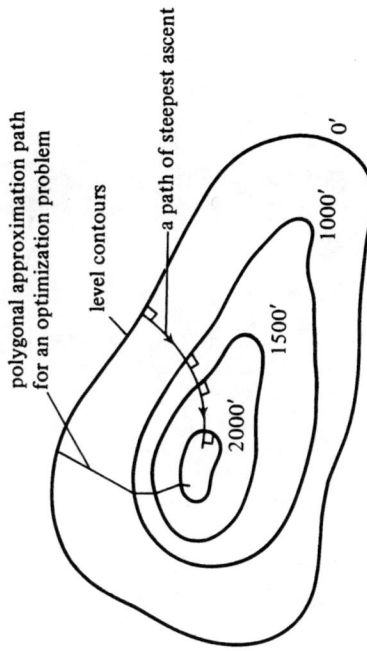

FIGURE 6.6-2   Direction of steepest ascent is orthogonal to the level contours

mountain as quickly as possible, we should walk perpendicular to the level contours (Figure 6.6-2).

These facts can be of value in optimization problems. In such problems, one is given a function $f(x_1, \ldots, x_n)$ and the problem is to maximize or "optimize" f by some practical scheme. A common method is to take a trial point x_0 and proceed along a straight line in the direction of the gradient of f to reach a new point at which f will be larger (at least if we do not go too far), and repeat.

6.6.2 Example   *Find the normal to the surface $x^2 + y^2 + z^2 = 3$ at $(1,1,1)$.*

Solution   Here $f(x,y,z) = x^2 + y^2 + z^2$ has gradient $\text{grad}\, f = (2x, 2y, 2z)$, which at $(1,1,1)$ is $(2,2,2)$. Normalizing, a unit normal is $(1/\sqrt{3}, 1/\sqrt{3}, 1/\sqrt{3})$. ◆

6.6.3 Example   *Find the direction of greatest rate of increase of $f(x,y,z) = x^2 y \sin z$ at $(3,2,0)$.*

Solution   The required direction is that of the gradient vector, which is $(2xy \sin z, x^2 \sin z, x^2 y \cos z)$, which becomes $(0,0,18)$ at $(3,2,0)$. Normalizing, we get the unit direction vector $(0,0,1)$. ◆

6.6.4 Example   *What is the tangent plane to the surface $x^2 - y^2 + xz = 2$ at $(1,0,1)$?*

Solution   Here $\text{grad}\, f(1,0,1) = (3,0,1)$, and so the tangent plane has equation $\langle (x-1, y, z-1), (3,0,1) \rangle = 0$, that is, $3x + z = 4$. ◆

Exercises for §6.6

1. Prove that
$$\frac{d}{dt} f(x_0 + th)\Big|_{t=0} = Df(x_0) \cdot h$$
by using the chain rule, where $f : \mathbb{R}^m \to \mathbb{R}^n$.

2. Find a unit normal to the surface $x^2 - y^2 + xyz = 1$ at $(1, 0, 1)$.

3. Find the equation of the tangent plane to the surface $x^2 - y^2 + xyz = 1$ at $(1, 0, 1)$.

4. In what direction is $f(x,y) = e^{x^2} y$ increasing the fastest?

5. Let $f : \mathbb{R}^n \to \mathbb{R}$, $g : \mathbb{R}^n \to \mathbb{R}$. Show that $\text{grad}\,(fg) = f\,\text{grad}\, g + g\,\text{grad}\, f$.

6. Show that $\text{grad}\, f$, as the normal to the tangent plane, is a more general description of the tangent plane than the description in §6.4.

§6.7 The Mean Value Theorem

Two important calculus theorems are the mean value theorem and Taylor's theorem. First, let us turn our attention to the mean value theorem. In §4.7 we recalled the proof of the mean value theorem of elementary calculus, which stated that if $f : [a,b] \to \mathbb{R}$ is continuous and if f is differentiable on $]a,b[$, there exists a point $c \in]a,b[$ such that $f(b) - f(a) = f'(c)(b-a)$, where $f' = df/dx$.

Unfortunately, for $f : A \subset \mathbb{R}^n \to \mathbb{R}^m$, this version of the mean value theorem, naively interpreted, simply is not true. For example, consider $f : \mathbb{R} \to \mathbb{R}^2$, defined by $f(x) = (x^2, x^3)$. Let us try to find a c such that $0 \leq c \leq 1$ and $f(1) - f(0) = Df(c)(1-0)$. This means that $(1,1) - (0,0) = (2c, 3c^2)$, and thus $2c = 1$ and $3c^2 = 1$. Evidently, there is no c satisfying these equations.

Experience leads us to believe that some restrictive condition might provide a valid theorem. The preceding version will in fact hold *if f is real-valued*. To give the correct theorem, let us first make precise the meaning of "*c* is between x and y" for $c, x, y \in \mathbb{R}^n$. We say c is *on the line segment joining x and y*, or *is between x and y*, if $c = (1-\lambda)x + \lambda y$ for some $0 \leq \lambda \leq 1$, as in Figure 6.7-1.

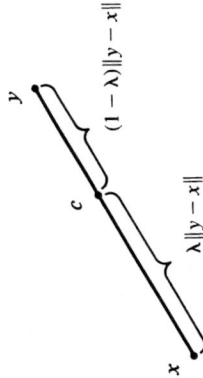

FIGURE 6.7-1   The point c lies on the segment joining x and y

6.7.1 Mean Value Theorem

i. *Suppose $f : A \subset \mathbb{R}^n \to \mathbb{R}$ is differentiable on an open set A. For any $x, y \in A$ such that the line segment joining x and y lies in A (which need not happen for all x,y), there is a point c on that segment such that*
$$f(y) - f(x) = Df(c) \cdot (y - x).$$

ii. *Suppose $f : A \subset \mathbb{R}^n \to \mathbb{R}^m$ is differentiable on the open set A. Suppose the line segment joining x and y lies in A and $f = (f_1, \ldots, f_m)$. Then there exist points $c_1, \ldots, c_m$ on that segment such that*
$$f_i(y) - f_i(x) = Df_i(c_i)(y - x), \quad i = 1, \ldots, m.$$

An alternative formulation of the mean value theorem is given in Worked Example 6.5 at the end of the chapter.

6.7.2 Example *A set $A \subset \mathbb{R}^n$ is said to be convex if for each $x, y \in A$, the segment joining x and y also lies in A. See Figure 6.7-2. Let $A \subset \mathbb{R}^n$ be an open convex set and let $f : A \to \mathbb{R}^m$ be differentiable. If $\mathbf{D}f = 0$ on A, show that f is constant on A.* (Generalizations of this are given in Exercise 9 at the end of the chapter.)

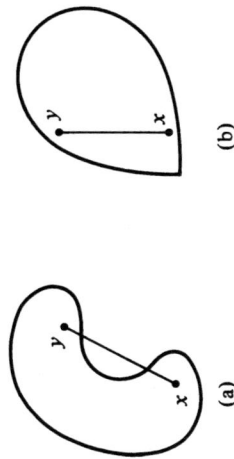

FIGURE 6.7-2 (a) Not convex; (b) convex

Solution If $x, y \in A$, then for each component f_i, there is a vector c_i such that

$$f_i(y) - f_i(x) = \mathbf{D}f_i(c_i)(y - x).$$

Since $\mathbf{D}f = 0$, $\mathbf{D}f_i = 0$ for each i (why?), and so $f_i(y) = f_i(x)$. It follows that $f(y) = f(x)$, which means that f is constant. ◆

6.7.3 Example *Suppose that $f : [0, \infty[\to \mathbb{R}$ is continuous, $f(0) = 0$, f is differentiable on $]0, \infty[$, and f' is nondecreasing. Prove that $g(x) = f(x)/x$ is nondecreasing for $x > 0$.*

Solution From §4.7 or directly from the mean value theorem, we see that a function $h : \mathbb{R} \to \mathbb{R}$ is nondecreasing if $h'(x) \geq 0$, because $x \leq y$ implies that

$$h(y) - h(x) = h'(c)(y - x) \geq 0.$$

Now

$$g'(x) = \frac{xf'(x) - f(x)}{x^2}$$

and there is a c between 0 and x such that

$$f(x) - f(0) = f'(c) \cdot x \leq xf'(x),$$

since $0 < c < x$ implies that $f'(x) \geq f'(c)$. Thus $xf'(x) - f(x) \geq 0$, and so $g' \geq 0$, which implies that g is nondecreasing. ◆

Exercises for §6.7

1. If $f : \mathbb{R} \to \mathbb{R}$ is differentiable and is such that $f'(x) > 0$, prove that f is (strictly) increasing.

2. Prove the following (weak version of) *l'Hôpital's rule:* If f', g' exist at x_0, $g'(x_0) \neq 0$, and $f(x_0) = 0 = g(x_0)$, then $\lim_{x \to x_0} [f(x)/g(x)] = f'(x_0)/g'(x_0)$.

3. Use Exercise 2 to evaluate
   a. $\lim_{x \to 0} [(\sin x)/x]$
   b. $\lim_{x \to 0} [(e^x - 1)/x]$

4. Which of the following sets are convex?
   a. $\{(x, y) \in \mathbb{R}^2 \mid y \geq 0\}$
   b. $\{x \in \mathbb{R}^n \mid 0 < \|x\| < 1\}$
   c. $\mathbb{R} \setminus \{0\}$

5. Let $f : A \subset \mathbb{R}^n \to \mathbb{R}$ be differentiable with A convex, and suppose $\|\text{grad } f(x)\| \leq M$ for $x \in A$. Prove $|f(x) - f(y)| \leq M\|x - y\|$ for $x, y \in A$. Do you think this is true if A is not convex?

6. Let $f : \mathbb{R} \to \mathbb{R}$ be differentiable. Assume that for all $x \in \mathbb{R}$, $0 \leq f'(x) \leq f(x)$. Show that $g(x) = e^{-x}f(x)$ is decreasing. If f vanishes at some point, conclude that f is zero.

§6.8 Taylor's Theorem and Higher Derivatives

Next, we discuss Taylor's formula for functions $f : A \subset \mathbb{R}^n \to \mathbb{R}^m$. To do this, we first discuss derivatives of higher order. For $f : \mathbb{R}^n \to \mathbb{R}$, there is no problem defining partial derivatives of higher order; we just iterate the process of partial differentiation

$$\frac{\partial^2 f}{\partial x_1 \partial x_2} = \frac{\partial}{\partial x_1}\left(\frac{\partial}{\partial x_2} f\right),$$

and so on. However, regarding the derivative as a linear map needs a little more care.

The second derivative is obtained by differentiating **D**f, if it exists, and is accomplished as follows.

6.8.1 Definition Let $L(\mathbb{R}^n, \mathbb{R}^m)$ denote the space of linear maps from $\mathbb{R}^n$ to $\mathbb{R}^m$. (If we choose a basis in $\mathbb{R}^n$ and $\mathbb{R}^m$, then $L(\mathbb{R}^n, \mathbb{R}^m)$ can be identified with the $m \times n$ matrices and hence with $\mathbb{R}^{nm}$.) Now $\mathbf{D}f : A \to L(\mathbb{R}^n, \mathbb{R}^m)$; that is, at each $x \in A$ we get a linear map $\mathbf{D}f(x)$. If we differentiate $\mathbf{D}f$ at x_0, we get a linear map from $\mathbb{R}^n$ to $L(\mathbb{R}^n, \mathbb{R}^m)$, by definition of the derivative. We write $\mathbf{D}(\mathbf{D}f)(x_0) = \mathbf{D}^2 f(x_0)$ and define the map $B_{x_0} : \mathbb{R}^n \times \mathbb{R}^n \to \mathbb{R}^m$ by setting $B_{x_0}(x_1, x_2) = [\mathbf{D}^2 f(x_0)(x_1)](x_2).$

This definition makes sense because $\mathbf{D}^2 f(x_0) : \mathbb{R}^n \to L(\mathbb{R}^n, \mathbb{R}^m)$, and so $\mathbf{D}^2 f(x_0)(x_1) \in L(\mathbb{R}^n, \mathbb{R}^m)$; therefore it can be applied to x_2. The reason we do this is that B_{x_0} avoids the unnecessary use of the conceptually difficult space $L(\mathbb{R}^n, L(\mathbb{R}^n, \mathbb{R}^m))$.

By definition, a **bilinear map** $B : E \times F \to G$, where E, F, G are vector spaces, is a map that is linear in each variable separately; for example, in the first variable this means $B(\alpha e_1 + \beta e_2, f) = \alpha B(e_1, f) + \beta B(e_2, f)$, where $e_1, e_2 \in E$, $f \in F$, and $\alpha, \beta \in \mathbb{R}$. The map B_{x_0} we have defined may be checked to be a bilinear map of $\mathbb{R}^n \times \mathbb{R}^n \to \mathbb{R}^m$.

Given a bilinear map $B : E \times F \to \mathbb{R}$, we can associate a matrix with each choice of basis $e_1, \ldots, e_n$ of E and $f_1, \ldots, f_m$ of F; that is, we can let

$$a_{ij} = B(e_i, f_j).$$

If

$$x = \sum_{i=1}^{n} x_i e_i \quad \text{and} \quad y = \sum_{j=1}^{m} y_j f_j,$$

then

$$B(x,y) = \sum_{ij} a_{ij} x_i y_j = (x_1, \ldots, x_n) \begin{pmatrix} a_{11} & \cdots & a_{1m} \\ \vdots & \ddots & \vdots \\ a_{n1} & \cdots & a_{nm} \end{pmatrix} \begin{pmatrix} y_1 \\ \vdots \\ y_m \end{pmatrix}.$$

Notice that the matrix associated to B depends on the choice of basis of E and F.

Note. For the second derivative, we shall, by abuse of notation, still write $\mathbf{D}^2 f(x_0)$ for the bilinear map B_{x_0} obtained by differentiating $\mathbf{D}f$ at x_0 as described in the preceding paragraphs.

6.8.2 Theorem Let $f : A \subset \mathbb{R}^n \to \mathbb{R}$ be twice differentiable on the open set A. Then the matrix of $\mathbf{D}^2 f(x) : \mathbb{R}^n \times \mathbb{R}^n \to \mathbb{R}$ with respect to the standard basis is given by

$$\begin{pmatrix} \dfrac{\partial^2 f}{\partial x_1 \partial x_1} & \cdots & \dfrac{\partial^2 f}{\partial x_1 \partial x_n} \\ \vdots & \ddots & \vdots \\ \dfrac{\partial^2 f}{\partial x_n \partial x_1} & \cdots & \dfrac{\partial^2 f}{\partial x_n \partial x_n} \end{pmatrix}$$

where each partial derivative is evaluated at the point $x = (x_1, \ldots, x_n)$.

For higher derivatives, we proceed in an analogous manner. For example, $\mathbf{D}^3 f$ gives a trilinear map $\mathbf{D}^3 f(x) : \mathbb{R}^n \times \mathbb{R}^n \times \mathbb{R}^n \to \mathbb{R}^m$ for each x. We do not associate a matrix with this map, but rather the third-order derivatives labeled by four indices: $\partial^3 f_k / \partial x_l \partial x_i \partial x_j$ for each component f_k. (Such quantities are closely related to what are called **tensors**.)

Before proceeding with Taylor's theorem, we give an important property of the second derivative. The matrix in Theorem **6.8.2** is, under fairly mild conditions, symmetric.

6.8.3 Symmetry of Mixed Partials Let $f : A \to \mathbb{R}^m$ be twice differentiable on the open set A with $\mathbf{D}^2 f$ continuous (that is, with the functions $\partial^2 f / \partial x_i \partial x_j$ continuous). Then $\mathbf{D}^2 f$ is symmetric; that is,

$$\mathbf{D}^2 f(x)(x_1, x_2) = \mathbf{D}^2 f(x)(x_2, x_1),$$

or, in terms of components,

$$\frac{\partial^2 f_k}{\partial x_i \partial x_j} = \frac{\partial^2 f_k}{\partial x_j \partial x_i}.$$

Using this, it follows that all the higher derivatives are symmetric as well under analogous conditions.

The symmetry of second derivatives represents a fundamental property not encountered in single-variable calculus. Let us verify the symmetry in a specific example: Suppose $f(x,y,z) = e^{xy}\sin x + x^2 y^4 \cos^2 z$, so that $f : \mathbb{R}^3 \to \mathbb{R}$. Then

$$\frac{\partial f}{\partial x} = e^{xy}\cos x + ye^{xy}\sin x + 2xy^4\cos^2 z,$$

and

$$\frac{\partial f}{\partial y} = xe^{xy}\sin x + 4x^2 y^3 \cos^2 z,$$

$$\frac{\partial^2 f}{\partial y \partial x} = xe^{xy}\cos x + e^{xy}\sin x + xye^{xy}\sin x + 8xy^3\cos^2 z = \frac{\partial^2 f}{\partial x \partial y}.$$

Theorem 6.8.3 is not so obvious intuitively. However, some intuition can be gained from the main idea of the proof. For functions $f(x,y)$, we consider the quantity

$$S = f(x+h, y+k) - f(x+h, y) - f(x, y+k) + f(x,y),$$

which is the difference of the differences in Figure 6.8-1. The algebraic fact that S can be written as the difference of the differences in two ways (horizontal and then vertical, or vice versa) is the reason one has equality of the mixed partials.

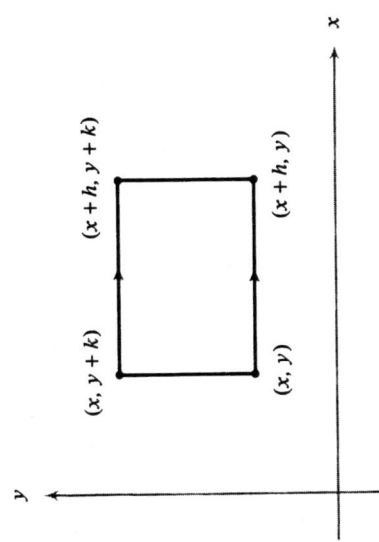

FIGURE 6.8-1   S is a difference of differences

6.8.4 Definition   *A function is said to be of class C^r if the first r derivatives exist and are continuous. (Equivalently, this means that all partial derivatives*

up to order r exist and are continuous.) A function is said to be smooth or of class C^∞ if it is of class C^r for all positive integers r.

Iterative use of the chain rule can be used to show that the composite of C^r functions is also C^r.

6.8.5 Taylor's Theorem   *Let $f : A \to \mathbb{R}$ be of class C^r for $A \subset \mathbb{R}^n$ an open set. Let $x, y \in A$, and suppose that the segment joining x and y lies in A. Then there is a point c on that segment such that*

$$f(y) - f(x) = \sum_{k=1}^{r-1} \frac{1}{k!}\mathbf{D}^k f(x)(y-x,\ldots,y-x) + \frac{1}{r!}\mathbf{D}^r f(c)(y-x,\ldots,y-x)$$

where $\mathbf{D}^k f(x)(y-x,\ldots,y-x)$ denotes $\mathbf{D}^k f(x)$ as a k-linear map applied to the k-tuple $(y-x,\ldots,y-x)$. In coordinates,

$$\mathbf{D}^k f(x)(y-x,\ldots,y-x) = \sum_{i_1,\ldots,i_k=1}^{n} \left(\frac{\partial^k f}{\partial x_{i_1}\cdots \partial x_{i_k}}\right)(y_{i_1} - x_{i_1})\cdots(y_{i_k} - x_{i_k}).$$

Setting $y = x + h$, we can write the Taylor formula as

$$f(x+h) = f(x) + \mathbf{D}f(x)\cdot h + \cdots + \frac{1}{(r-1)!}\mathbf{D}^{r-1}f(x)\cdot(h,\ldots,h) + R_{r-1}(x,h)$$

where $R_{r-1}(x,h)$ is the remainder. Furthermore,

$$\frac{R_{r-1}(x,h)}{\|h\|^{r-1}} \to 0 \quad as \quad h \to 0.$$

Other forms in which the remainder term can be cast are given in the proof of the theorem. This theorem is a generalization of the mean value theorem (in which case r = 1) and of Taylor's theorem encountered in one-variable calculus.

Note.   The last two statements in Taylor's theorem require f to be only C^{r-1}, as is seen by an examination of the proof.

The basic idea of the proof of Taylor's theorem is to use the fundamental theorem of calculus (§4.8) to write

$$f(x+h) - f(x) = \int_0^1 \frac{d}{dt} f(x+th)\, dt$$

and then to repeatedly integrate by parts, generating a series.

From Taylor's theorem, we are led to form the *Taylor series* about x_0,

$$\sum_{k=0}^{\infty} \frac{1}{k!}\mathbf{D}^k f(x_0)(x - x_0, \ldots, x - x_0).$$

This series need not converge to $f(x)$ even if f is C^∞. If it does so in a neighborhood of x_0, we say that f is *real analytic* at x_0. Thus, a function f is real analytic if the remainder term $(1/r!)\,\mathbf{D}^r f(c)(x - x_0, \ldots, x - x_0) \to 0$ as $r \to \infty$. For example, if e^x, $\sin x$, and $\cos x$ are defined in more traditional ways rather than the power series approach we took in §5.4, then this method can be used to establish the power series expansions.

6.8.6 Example *Justify and then verify equality of mixed partials for $f(x,y) = yx^2(\cos y^2)$.*

Solution Since f is C^∞, Theorem 6.8.3 guarantees equality of mixed partials. To see this explicitly, we compute as follows:

$$\frac{\partial f}{\partial x} = 2xy\cos y^2, \quad \frac{\partial^2 f}{\partial y\partial x} = 2x\cos y^2 - 4xy^2\sin y^2;$$

$$\frac{\partial f}{\partial y} = x^2\cos y^2 - 2y^2x^2\sin y^2, \quad \frac{\partial^2 f}{\partial x\partial y} = 2x\cos y^2 - 4y^2x\sin y^2. \quad \blacklozenge$$

6.8.7 Example *If f is C^∞ on $\mathbb{R}$ and for every interval $[a,b]$ there is a constant M such that $|f^{(n)}(x)| \le M^n$ for all n and $x \in [a,b]$, show that f is analytic at each x_0 and*

$$f(x) = \sum_{n=0}^{\infty} \frac{f^{(n)}(x_0)}{n!}(x - x_0)^n.$$

Solution Select b with $-b < x_0 < b$. The remainder is

$$\left| \frac{f^{(n)}(c)}{n!}(x - x_0)^n \right| \le \frac{M^n|x - x_0|^n}{n!},$$

where c is between x and x_0 and $|f^{(n)}(c)| < M^n$ on $[-b, b]$. This tends to 0 as $n \to \infty$, since by the ratio test, the corresponding series converges. Observe that the convergence is uniform on all bounded intervals (why?). $\blacklozenge$

6.8.8 Example *Give an example of a C^∞ function that is not analytic.*

Solution Let

$$f(x) = 0 \quad \text{if } x = 0,$$

and

$$f(x) = e^{-1/x^2} \quad \text{if } x \ne 0.$$

The only place where smoothness of f is in doubt is at $x = 0$. At that point we can use l'Hôpital's rule to evaluate the derivative as the limit of a difference quotient:

$$f'(0) = \lim_{x\to 0} \frac{f(x) - f(0)}{x - 0} = \lim_{x\to 0} \frac{1}{x}e^{-1/x^2} = 0.$$

(Supply the details for the application of l'Hôpital's rule.) Similarly, for $x \ne 0$, we have $f'(x) = (2/x^3)e^{-1/x^2}$ and a similar application of l'Hôpital's rule shows that $f''(0)$ exists and is 0. One proceeds inductively to show that $f^{(n)}(0)$ exists and is 0 for each $n > 0$. Thus f is C^∞. But the Taylor series for f with center at $x_0 = 0$ is identically 0. This Taylor series does not converge to the value of the function in any nontrivial neighborhood of 0, so f is not analytic at 0. $\blacklozenge$

6.8.9 Example *Compute the second-order Taylor formula for $f(x,y) = \cos(x + 2y)$ around $(0,0)$.*

Solution Here $f(0,0) = 1$,

$$\frac{\partial f}{\partial x}(0,0) = -\sin(0 + 2\cdot 0) = 0, \quad \frac{\partial f}{\partial y}(0,0) = -2\sin(0 + 2\cdot 0) = 0,$$

$$\frac{\partial^2 f}{\partial x^2}(0,0) = -\cos(0) = -1, \quad \frac{\partial^2 f}{\partial y^2}(0,0) = -4\cos 0 = -4,$$

and

$$\frac{\partial^2 f}{\partial x\partial y}(0,0) = \frac{\partial^2 f}{\partial y\partial x}(0,0) = -2\cos 0 = -2.$$

Thus
$$f(h,k) = 1 - \frac{1}{2}(h^2 + 4hk + 4k^2) + R_2((0,0),(h,k)),$$

where
$$\frac{R_2((0,0),(h,k))}{\|(h,k)\|^2} \to 0 \quad \text{as } (h,k) \to (0,0). \quad \blacklozenge$$

Exercises for §6.8

1. Verify the equality of mixed partials for $f(x,y) = (e^{x^2+y^2})xy^2$.

2. Use Example 6.8.7 to establish the Taylor series and analyticity of e^x, $\sin x$, and $\cos x$ on all of $\mathbb{R}$, assuming we know their derivatives.

3. Let $f : \mathbb{R} \to \mathbb{R}$ be defined by
$$f(x) = x^2 \sin\left(\frac{1}{x}\right) \qquad \text{if } x \in]-1,1[, x \neq 0$$
and
$$f(x) = 0 \qquad \text{if } x = 0.$$
Investigate the validity of Taylor's theorem for f about the point $x = 0$.

4. Find the Taylor series representation about $x = 0$ for $\log(1-x)$, $-1 < x < 1$, and show that it equals $\log(1-x)$ on $-1 < x < 1$, and also show that it converges uniformly on closed subintervals of $]-1,1[$.

5. Compute the second-order Taylor formula for $f(x,y) = e^x \cos y$ around $(0,0)$.

6. Verify that if the conditions in Example 6.8.7 are met, then we can differentiate the Taylor series term by term to obtain $f'(x)$.

§6.9 Maxima and Minima

An important application of Taylor's theorem is the determination of maxima and minima of real-valued functions. As we might expect from our knowledge of functions of one variable, the criteria involve the second derivative. Let us first recall the real-variable case.

If $f :]a,b[\to \mathbb{R}$ has a local maximum or minimum at x_0 and f is differentiable at x_0, then $f'(x_0) = 0$. Furthermore, if f is twice continuously differentiable and $f''(x_0) < 0$, then x_0 is a local maximum, and if $f''(x_0) > 0$, then x_0 is a local minimum. To generalize these facts to real-valued functions of n variables, we begin by giving the relevant definitions.

6.9.1 Definition *Let $f : A \subset \mathbb{R}^n \to \mathbb{R}$ where A is open. If there is a neighborhood of $x_0 \in A$ on which $f(x_0)$ is a maximum, that is, if $f(x_0) \geq f(x)$ for all x in the neighborhood, we say that x_0 is a* **local maximum point** *and $f(x_0)$ is a* **local maximum value** *for f. Similarly, we can define a* **local minimum** *of f. A point is called* **extreme** *if it is either a local minimum or a local maximum for f. A point x_0 is a* **critical point** *if f is differentiable at x_0 and if $\mathbf{D}f(x_0) = 0$.*

The first basic fact is presented in the next theorem.

6.9.2 Theorem *If $f : A \subset \mathbb{R}^n \to \mathbb{R}$ is differentiable, A is open, and $x_0 \in A$ is an extreme point of f, then $\mathbf{D}f(x_0) = 0$; that is, x_0 is a critical point.*

The proof is much the same as for one-variable calculus. The result is intuitively clear, since at an extreme point the graph of f must have a horizontal tangent plane. However, just being a critical point is not sufficient to guarantee that the point is extreme. For example, consider $f(x) = x^3$. For this function, 0 is a critical point, since $\mathbf{D}f(0) = 0$. But $x^3 > 0$ for $x > 0$ and $x^3 < 0$ for $x < 0$, and so 0 is *not* extreme. Another example is given by $f(x,y) = y^2 - x^2$. Here $0 = (0,0)$ is a critical point, since $\partial f / \partial x = -2x$, $\partial f / \partial y = 2y$, and so $\mathbf{D}f(0,0) = 0$. However, in any neighborhood of 0 we can find points where f is greater than 0 and points where f is less than 0. A critical point that is not a local extreme point is called a *saddle point*. Figure 6.9-1 shows how this terminology originated.

For $f : A \subset \mathbb{R} \to \mathbb{R}$, we have already mentioned that $f(x)$ is a local maximum value if $f'(x) = 0$ and $f''(x) < 0$. This is geometrically clear if we remember that $f''(x) < 0$ means f is concave downward (or that the slopes $f'(x)$ are *decreasing*). To generalize this, the concept of the Hessian of a function g at x_0 is introduced.

6.9.3 Definition *If $g : B \subset \mathbb{R}^n \to \mathbb{R}$ is of class C^2, the* **Hessian** *of g at x_0 is defined to be the bilinear function $H_{x_0}(g) : \mathbb{R}^n \times \mathbb{R}^n \to \mathbb{R}$ given by $H_{x_0}(g)(x,y) = \mathbf{D}^2 g(x_0)(x,y)$. Thus the Hessian is, as a matrix, just the matrix of second partials.*

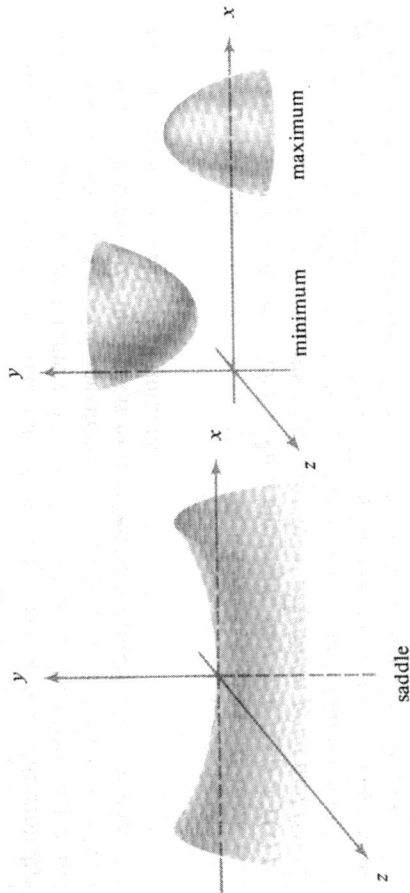

FIGURE 6.9-1 Maximum, minimum, and saddle points

A bilinear form, that is, a bilinear mapping $B : \mathbb{R}^n \times \mathbb{R}^n \to \mathbb{R}$, is called positive definite if $B(x,x) > 0$ for all $x \neq 0$ in $\mathbb{R}^n$ and is called positive semidefinite if $B(x,x) \geq 0$ for all $x \in \mathbb{R}^n$. Negative definite and negative semidefinite bilinear forms are defined similarly.

Now we can make the following generalization to the multivariable case.

6.9.4 Theorem

i.   *If $f : A \subset \mathbb{R}^n \to \mathbb{R}$ is a C^2 function defined on an open set A and x_0 is a critical point of f such that $H_{x_0}(f)$ is negative definite, then f has a local maximum at x_0.*

ii.   *If f has a local maximum at x_0, then $H_{x_0}(f)$ is negative semidefinite.*

The case for minima is covered by changing "negative" to "positive" in Theorem 6.9.4. Note that a minimum of f is a maximum of $-f$.

The second-order Taylor polynomial defines the quadratic function that best fits the graph of the function. The second derivative test then says that we can determine the behavior at a critical point if the second-order term is not degenerate. It is the same as that of the corresponding quadratic surface: a paraboloid opening up or down, or a saddle surface (hyperbolic paraboloid).

The first two correspond to the cases in which the Hessian is positive definite or negative definite, and the third to that in which it is indefinite.

As we have noted, the matrix of $H_{x_0}(f)$ with respect to the standard basis is

$$\begin{pmatrix} \dfrac{\partial^2 f}{\partial x_1 \partial x_1} & \cdots & \dfrac{\partial^2 f}{\partial x_1 \partial x_n} \\ \vdots & \ddots & \vdots \\ \dfrac{\partial^2 f}{\partial x_n \partial x_1} & \cdots & \dfrac{\partial^2 f}{\partial x_n \partial x_n} \end{pmatrix}$$

where the partial derivatives are all evaluated at x_0.

If $n = 1$, Theorem 6.9.4i reduces to the one-variable test $f''(x_0) < 0$; one can have a maximum or a saddle point or a minimum if $f''(x_0) = 0$ (in this case, the test fails). For example, $f(x) = -x^4$ has a maximum, x^5 a saddle point, and x^4 a minimum at $x_0 = 0$, although $f''(0) = 0$.

A few points from linear algebra will be helpful in using Theorem 6.9.4. Let Δ_k be the determinant of the matrix

$$\begin{pmatrix} \dfrac{\partial^2 f}{\partial x_1 \partial x_1} & \cdots & \dfrac{\partial^2 f}{\partial x_1 \partial x_k} \\ \vdots & \ddots & \vdots \\ \dfrac{\partial^2 f}{\partial x_k \partial x_1} & \cdots & \dfrac{\partial^2 f}{\partial x_k \partial x_k} \end{pmatrix}.$$

This is the matrix of the Hessian with the last $n - k$ rows and columns removed. *The symmetric matrix $H_{x_0}(f)$ is positive definite iff $\Delta_k > 0$ for $k = 1, \ldots, n$.* We shall not prove this here in general, but in Example 6.9.5 we prove it for 2×2 matrices. There is also a criterion for the negative definite case given in the next paragraph. *Thus, if $\Delta_k > 0$ for $k = 1, \ldots, n$, then f has a (local) minimum at the critical point x_0.*

If a symmetric matrix is positive semidefinite, then $\Delta_k \geq 0$, so that by 6.9.4ii if $\Delta_k < 0$ for any k, f cannot have a maximum at x_0. Similarly, f has a (local) minimum at x_0 if $H_{x_0}(f)$ is negative definite. By changing the sign of $H_{x_0}(f)$ in the paragraph above and using properties of determinants, it follows that $H_{x_0}(f)$ is negative definite iff $\Delta_k < 0$ for k odd and $\Delta_k > 0$ for k even, and that if $H_{x_0}(f)$ is negative semidefinite, then $\Delta_k \leq 0$ for k odd and $\Delta_k \geq 0$ for k even. Thus f has a minimum at x_0 if $\Delta_k < 0$ for k odd and $\Delta_k > 0$ for k even. If $\Delta_k > 0$ for some odd k or $\Delta_k < 0$ for some even k, then f cannot have a minimum value at x_0. In fact, if $\Delta_k < 0$ for some even k, f can have neither a maximum nor a minimum at x_0, and x_0 must be a saddle point of f (see Exercise 8 at the end of this chapter for an instance of this).

Chapter 6 Differentiable Mappings

Note. This theorem is also useful in economics for optimizing quantities such as profits. It is also used in mechanics when f is the potential of a system, because then a minimum corresponds to stability and the maxima and saddle points correspond to instability. (See Marsden and Tromba, *Vector Calculus*, 3rd ed., W. H. Freeman, New York, 1988, Chap. 4, for details.)

6.9.5 Example   Show that the matrix

$$\begin{pmatrix} a & b \\ b & d \end{pmatrix}$$

is positive definite iff $a > 0$ and $ad - b^2 > 0$.

Solution   Positive definite means that

$$(x,y)\begin{pmatrix} a & b \\ b & d \end{pmatrix}\begin{pmatrix} x \\ y \end{pmatrix} > 0 \quad \text{if } (x,y) \neq (0,0);$$

that is, $ax^2 + 2bxy + dy^2 > 0$. First, suppose this is true for all $(x,y) \neq (0,0)$. Setting $y = 0$, $x = 1$, we get $a > 0$. Setting $y = 1$, we have $ax^2 + 2bx + d > 0$ for all x. This function is a parabola with a minimum (since $a > 0$) at $2ax + 2b = 0$. That is, $x = -b/a$. Hence,

$$a\left(-\frac{b}{a}\right)^2 + 2b\left(-\frac{b}{a}\right) + d > 0;$$

that is, $ad - b^2 > 0$. The converse may be proved in the same way. ◆

6.9.6 Example   Investigate the nature of the critical point $(0,0)$ of

$$f(x,y) = x^2 - xy + y^2.$$

Solution   The partial derivatives are

$$\frac{\partial f}{\partial x} = 2x - y, \quad \frac{\partial^2 f}{\partial x^2} = 2, \quad \frac{\partial^2 f}{\partial x \partial y} = -1, \quad \frac{\partial f}{\partial y} = -x + 2y, \quad \frac{\partial^2 f}{\partial y^2} = 2,$$

---

and so the Hessian evaluated at $x = 0$, $y = 0$ is

$$\begin{pmatrix} 2 & -1 \\ -1 & 2 \end{pmatrix}.$$

Here $\Delta_1 = 2 > 0$ and $\Delta_2 = 4 - 1 = 3 > 0$, and so the Hessian is positive definite. Thus we have a local minimum. ◆

Exercises for §6.9

1. Prove that

$$\begin{pmatrix} a & b \\ b & d \end{pmatrix}$$

   is negative definite iff $a < 0$ and $ad - b^2 > 0$.

2. Investigate the nature of the critical point $(0, 0)$ of $f(x,y) = x^2 + 2xy + y^2 + 6$.

3. Investigate the nature of the critical point $(0, 0, 0)$ of $f(x,y,z) = x^2 + y^2 + 2z^2 + xyz$.

4. (This exercise assumes a knowledge of linear algebra.) Let A be a symmetric matrix. Show that A is positive definite if and only if the eigenvalues of A (which exist and are real, since A is symmetric) are positive. Is this true if A is not symmetric?

5. Check that the matrix

$$\begin{pmatrix} 1 & 0 & 0 \\ 0 & 0 & 0 \\ 0 & 0 & -1 \end{pmatrix}$$

   has $\Delta_i \geq 0$ yet the matrix is *not* semidefinite.

6. Determine the nature of the critical point $(0, 0)$ of the function $x^3 + 2xy^2 - y^4 + x^2 + 3xy + y^2 + 10$.

Theorem Proofs for Chapter 6

6.1.2 Theorem   *Let A be an open set in $\mathbb{R}^n$ and suppose $f : A \to \mathbb{R}^m$ is differentiable at x_0. Then $Df(x_0)$ is uniquely determined by f.*

Proof Let L_1 and L_2 be two linear mappings satisfying conditions of the definition of the derivative. We must show that $L_1 = L_2$. Fix $e \in \mathbb{R}^n$, $\|e\| = 1$, and let $x = x_0 + \lambda e$ for $\lambda \in \mathbb{R}$. Then note that

$$|\lambda| = \|x - x_0\| \quad \text{and} \quad \|L_1 \cdot e - L_2 \cdot e\| = \frac{\|L_1 \cdot \lambda e - L_2 \cdot \lambda e\|}{|\lambda|}.$$

Since A is open, $x \in A$ for λ sufficiently small. By the triangle inequality,

$$\|L_1 \cdot e - L_2 \cdot e\| = \frac{\|L_1(x - x_0) - L_2(x - x_0)\|}{\|x - x_0\|}$$
$$\leq \frac{\|f(x) - f(x_0) - L_1(x - x_0)\|}{\|x - x_0\|}$$
$$+ \frac{\|f(x) - f(x_0) - L_2(x - x_0)\|}{\|x - x_0\|}.$$

As $\lambda \to 0$, these two terms each tend to 0, and so $L_1 \cdot e = L_2 \cdot e$. Our selection of e was arbitrary, except that $\|e\| = 1$. But for any nonzero $y \in \mathbb{R}^n$, $y/\|y\| = e$ has length 1, and, by linearity, if $L_1(e) = L_2(e)$, then $L_1(y) = L_2(y)$. ∎

6.2.2 Theorem *Suppose $A \subset \mathbb{R}^n$ is an open set and $f : A \to \mathbb{R}^m$ is differentiable on A. Then the partial derivatives $\partial f_j/\partial x_i$ exist, and the matrix of the linear map $Df(x)$ with respect to the standard bases in $\mathbb{R}^n$ and $\mathbb{R}^m$ is given by*

$$\begin{pmatrix} \dfrac{\partial f_1}{\partial x_1} & \dfrac{\partial f_1}{\partial x_2} & \cdots & \dfrac{\partial f_1}{\partial x_n} \\[2mm] \dfrac{\partial f_2}{\partial x_1} & \dfrac{\partial f_2}{\partial x_2} & \cdots & \dfrac{\partial f_2}{\partial x_n} \\[2mm] \cdots & \cdots & \ddots & \cdots \\[2mm] \dfrac{\partial f_m}{\partial x_1} & \dfrac{\partial f_m}{\partial x_2} & \cdots & \dfrac{\partial f_m}{\partial x_n} \end{pmatrix}$$

where each partial derivative is evaluated at $x = (x_1, \ldots, x_n)$. This matrix is called the Jacobian matrix of f or the derivative matrix.

Proof By definition of the matrix of a linear mapping, the jth matrix element of $Df(x)$ is the jth component of the vector $Df(x) \cdot e_i = Df(x)$ applied to the ith

standard basis vector, e_i. Call this component a_{ji}. Let $y = x + he_i$ for $h \in \mathbb{R}$ and note that

$$\frac{\|f(y) - f(x) - Df(x) \cdot (y - x)\|}{\|y - x\|}$$
$$= \frac{\|f(x_1, \ldots, x_i + h, \ldots, x_n) - f(x_1, \ldots, x_n) - hDf(x) \cdot e_i\|}{|h|}.$$

Since this tends to 0 as $h \to 0$, then so does the jth component of the numerator, and so, as $h \to 0$,

$$\frac{|f_j(x_1, \ldots, x_i + h, \ldots, x_n) - f_j(x_1, \ldots, x_n) - ha_{ji}|}{|h|} \to 0.$$

Therefore,

$$a_{ji} = \lim_{h \to 0} \frac{f_j(x_1, \ldots, x_i + h, \ldots, x_n) - f_j(x_1, \ldots, x_n)}{h} = \frac{\partial f_j}{\partial x_i}. \quad \blacksquare$$

6.3.1 Proposition *Suppose $A \subset \mathbb{R}^n$ is open and $f : A \to \mathbb{R}^m$ is differentiable on A. Then f is continuous. In fact, for each $x_0 \in A$, there are a constant $M > 0$ and a $\delta_0 > 0$ such that $\|x - x_0\| < \delta_0$ implies $\|f(x) - f(x_0)\| \leq M\|x - x_0\|$. (This is called the **local Lipschitz property**.)*

For the proof, we recall that if $L : \mathbb{R}^n \to \mathbb{R}^m$ is a linear transformation, then there is a constant M_0 such that $\|Lx\| \leq M_0\|x\|$ for all $x \in \mathbb{R}^n$ (see Worked Example 4.4 at the end of Chapter 4). Here we shall be taking $L = Df(x_0)$.

Proof To prove continuity, it suffices to prove the stated Lipschitz property, since, given $\varepsilon > 0$, we can choose $\delta = \min(\delta_0, \varepsilon/M)$. To prove the Lipschitz property, let $\varepsilon = 1$ in the definition of the derivative. Then there is a δ_0 so that $\|x - x_0\| < \delta_0$ implies

$$\|f(x) - f(x_0) - Df(x_0)(x - x_0)\| \leq \|x - x_0\|,$$

which implies

$$\|f(x) - f(x_0)\| \leq \|Df(x_0)(x - x_0)\| + \|x - x_0\|$$

(here we use the triangle inequality in the form $\|y\| - \|z\| \leq \|y - z\|$, which follows by writing $y = (y - z) + z$ and applying the usual form of the triangle inequality). Let $M = M_0 + 1$ and use the fact that $\|Df(x_0)(x - x_0)\| \leq M_0\|x - x_0\|$ to give the result. ∎

6.4.1 Theorem Let $A \subset \mathbb{R}^n$ be open and $f : A \subset \mathbb{R}^n \to \mathbb{R}^m$. Suppose $f = (f_1, \ldots, f_m)$. If each of the partials $\partial f_j / \partial x_i$ exists and is continuous on A, then f is differentiable on A.

Proof If $\mathbf{D}f(x)$ is to exist, its matrix representation must be the Jacobian matrix, by Theorem 6.2.2. We need to show that with $x \in A$ fixed, for any $\epsilon > 0$ there is a $\delta > 0$ such that $\|y - x\| < \delta$, $y \in A$ implies

$$\|f(y) - f(x) - \mathbf{D}f(x)(y-x)\| < \epsilon \|y - x\|.$$

To do this, it suffices to prove this for each component of f separately (why?). Therefore, we can suppose $m = 1$. Write

$$f(y) - f(x) = f(y_1, \ldots, y_n) - f(x_1, y_2, \ldots, y_n) + f(x_1, y_2, \ldots, y_n)$$
$$- f(x_1, x_2, y_3, \ldots, y_n) + f(x_1, x_2, y_3, \ldots, y_n)$$
$$- f(x_1, x_2, x_3, y_4, \ldots, y_n)$$
$$+ \cdots + f(x_1, \ldots, x_{n-1}, y_n) - f(x_1, \ldots, x_n).$$

Now use the mean value theorem, which implies

$$f(y_1, \ldots, y_n) - f(x_1, y_2, \ldots, y_n) = \frac{\partial f}{\partial x_1}(u_1, y_2, \ldots, y_n)(y_1 - x_1).$$

for some u_1 between x_1 and y_1 ($y_2, \ldots, y_n$ are fixed). We write similar expressions for the other terms and get

$$f(y) - f(x) = \left(\frac{\partial f}{\partial x_1}(u_1, y_2, \ldots, y_n) \right)(y_1 - x_1)$$
$$+ \left(\frac{\partial f}{\partial x_2}(x_1, u_2, y_3, \ldots, y_n) \right)(y_2 - x_2)$$
$$+ \cdots + \left(\frac{\partial f}{\partial x_n}(x_1, x_2, \ldots, x_{n-1}, u_n) \right)(y_n - x_n).$$

Since $\mathbf{D}f(x)(y - x) = \sum_{i=1}^n (\partial f / \partial x_i)(x_1, \ldots, x_n)(y_i - x_i)$,

$$\|f(y) - f(x) - \mathbf{D}f(x)(y - x)\| \leq \left\{ \left| \frac{\partial f}{\partial x_1}(u_1, y_2, \ldots, y_n) - \frac{\partial f}{\partial x_1}(x_1, \ldots, x_n) \right| \right.$$
$$+ \cdots + \left. \left| \frac{\partial f}{\partial x_n}(x_1, \ldots, x_{n-1}, u_n) - \frac{\partial f}{\partial x_n}(x_1, \ldots, x_n) \right| \right\} \|y - x\|$$

using the triangle inequality and the fact that $|y_i - x_i| \leq \|y - x\|$. Since the terms $\partial f / \partial x_i$ are continuous and u_i lies between y_i and x_i, there is a $\delta > 0$ such that the term in braces is less than ϵ for $\|y - x\| < \delta$. This estimate proves the assertion. ∎

6.5.1 Chain Rule Let $A \subset \mathbb{R}^n$ be open and $f : A \to \mathbb{R}^m$ be differentiable at $x_0 \in A$. Let $B \subset \mathbb{R}^m$ be open, $f(A) \subset B$, and $g : B \to \mathbb{R}^p$ be differentiable at $f(x_0)$. Then the composite $g \circ f$ is differentiable at x_0 and $\mathbf{D}(g \circ f)(x_0) = \mathbf{D}g(f(x_0)) \circ \mathbf{D}f(x_0)$.

Proof To prove that $\mathbf{D}(g \circ f)(x_0) \cdot y = \mathbf{D}g(f(x_0)) \cdot (\mathbf{D}f(x_0) \cdot y)$, we will show that

$$\lim_{x \to x_0} \frac{\|g \circ f(x) - g \circ f(x_0) - \mathbf{D}g(f(x_0)) \cdot [\mathbf{D}f(x_0)(x - x_0)]\|}{\|x - x_0\|} = 0.$$

To do this, estimate the numerator as follows:

$$\|g \circ f(x) - g \circ f(x_0) - \mathbf{D}g(f(x_0)) \cdot (\mathbf{D}f(x_0)(x - x_0))\|$$
$$= \|g(f(x)) - g(f(x_0)) - \mathbf{D}g(f(x_0))[f(x) - f(x_0)]$$
$$+ \mathbf{D}g(f(x_0))[f(x) - f(x_0) - \mathbf{D}f(x_0)(x - x_0)]\|$$
$$\leq \|g(f(x)) - g(f(x_0)) - \mathbf{D}g(f(x_0))[f(x) - f(x_0)]\|$$
$$+ \|\mathbf{D}g(f(x_0))[f(x) - f(x_0) - \mathbf{D}f(x_0)(x - x_0)]\|$$

by the triangle inequality. Since f is differentiable, there exist a δ_0 and an $M > 0$ such that $\|f(x) - f(x_0)\| \leq M\|x - x_0\|$ whenever $\|x - x_0\| < \delta_0$, by Theorem 6.3.1. Given $\epsilon > 0$, there is, by the definition of the derivative of g, a $\delta_1 > 0$ such that $\|y - f(x_0)\| < \delta_1$ implies

$$\|g(y) - g(f(x_0)) - \mathbf{D}g(f(x_0))[y - f(x_0)]\| < \left(\frac{\epsilon}{2M} \right) \|y - f(x_0)\|.$$

Thus $\|x - x_0\| < \delta_2 = \min\{\delta_0, \delta_1\}$ implies

$$\frac{\|g(f(x)) - g(f(x_0)) - \mathbf{D}g(f(x_0))[f(x) - f(x_0)]\|}{\|x - x_0\|} < \frac{\epsilon}{2}.$$

Since $\mathbf{D}g(f(x_0))$ is a linear map, we know that there is a constant N such that $\|\mathbf{D}g(f(x_0))(y)\| \leq N \cdot \|y\|$ for all $y \in \mathbb{R}^m$, where it can be assumed that $N \neq 0$. Now, by definition of the derivative, there is a $\delta_3 > 0$ such that $\|x - x_0\| < \delta_3$ implies

$$\frac{\|f(x) - f(x_0) - \mathbf{D}f(x_0)(x - x_0)\|}{\|x - x_0\|} < \frac{\epsilon}{2N}.$$

Then $\|x - x_0\| < \delta_3$ implies

$$\frac{\|\mathbf{D}g(f(x_0))[f(x) - f(x_0) - \mathbf{D}f(x_0)(x - x_0)]\|}{\|x - x_0\|}$$
$$\leq \frac{N\|f(x) - f(x_0) - \mathbf{D}f(x_0)(x - x_0)\|}{\|x - x_0\|} < \frac{\epsilon}{2}.$$

Let $\delta = \min\{\delta_2, \delta_3\}$. Thus, $\|x - x_0\| < \delta$ implies

$$\frac{\|g \circ f(x) - g \circ f(x_0) - \mathbf{D}g(f(x_0)) \cdot \mathbf{D}f(x_0)(x - x_0)\|}{\|x - x_0\|}$$

$$\leq \frac{\|g(f(x)) - g(f(x_0)) - \mathbf{D}g(f(x_0))[f(x) - f(x_0)]\|}{\|x - x_0\|}$$

$$+ \frac{\|\mathbf{D}g(f(x_0))[f(x) - f(x_0) - \mathbf{D}f(x_0)(x - x_0)]\|}{\|x - x_0\|} < \frac{\varepsilon}{2} + \frac{\varepsilon}{2} = \varepsilon,$$

which proves the formula. ∎

> **Note.** At this point it might be good for the student to go back to the proof of the chain rule in §4.7 and ask how that proof compares with this one.

6.6.1 Proposition   *Let $A \subset \mathbb{R}^n$ be open and let $f : A \to \mathbb{R}^m$ and $g : A \to \mathbb{R}$ be differentiable functions. Then gf is differentiable, and for $x \in A$, $\mathbf{D}(gf)(x) : \mathbb{R}^n \to \mathbb{R}^m$ is given by $\mathbf{D}(gf)(x) \cdot e = g(x)(\mathbf{D}f(x) \cdot e) + (\mathbf{D}g(x) \cdot e)f(x)$ for all $e \in \mathbb{R}^n$. (This makes sense, because $g(x) \in \mathbb{R}$ and $\mathbf{D}g(x) \cdot e \in \mathbb{R}$.)*

Proof   Given $\varepsilon > 0$ and $x_0 \in A$, choose $\delta > 0$ such that $\|x - x_0\| < \delta$ implies

i. $|g(x)| \leq |g(x_0)| + 1 = M.$

ii. $\|f(x) - f(x_0) - \mathbf{D}f(x_0)(x - x_0)\| \leq \dfrac{\varepsilon}{3M}\|x - x_0\|.$

iii. $\|g(x) - g(x_0) - \mathbf{D}g(x_0)(x - x_0)\| \leq \dfrac{\varepsilon}{3\|f(x_0)\|}\|x - x_0\|.$

iv. $\|g(x) - g(x_0)\| \leq \varepsilon/3M$ where $\|\mathbf{D}f(x_0)y\| \leq M\|y\|$ (iii and iv are needed only if $f(x_0) \neq 0$ and $\mathbf{D}f(x_0) \neq 0$). Why is the choice of δ possible?

With $\|x - x_0\| < \delta$ and using the triangle inequality, we get

$$\|g(x)f(x) - g(x_0)f(x_0) - g(x_0)\mathbf{D}f(x_0)(x - x_0) - [\mathbf{D}g(x_0)(x - x_0)] f(x_0)\|$$

$$\leq \|g(x)f(x) - g(x)f(x_0) - g(x)\mathbf{D}f(x_0)(x - x_0)\|$$

$$+ \|g(x)\mathbf{D}f(x_0)(x - x_0) - g(x_0)\mathbf{D}f(x_0)(x - x_0)\|$$

$$+ \|g(x)f(x_0) - g(x_0)f(x_0) - [\mathbf{D}g(x_0)(x - x_0)] f(x_0)\|$$

$$\leq M \cdot \frac{\varepsilon\|x - x_0\|}{3M} + \frac{\varepsilon}{3M}M\|x - x_0\| + \frac{\varepsilon\|x - x_0\|}{3\|f(x_0)\|} \cdot \|f(x_0)\|$$

$$= \varepsilon\|x - x_0\|. \blacksquare$$

6.7.1 Mean Value Theorem

i. *Suppose $f : A \subset \mathbb{R}^n \to \mathbb{R}$ is differentiable on an open set A. For any $x, y \in A$ such that the line segment joining x and y lies in A (which need not happen for all x, y), there is a point c on that segment such that*

$$f(y) - f(x) = \mathbf{D}f(c) \cdot (y - x).$$

ii. *Suppose $f : A \subset \mathbb{R}^n \to \mathbb{R}^m$ is differentiable on the open set A. Suppose the line segment joining x and y lies in A and $f = (f_1, \ldots, f_m)$. Then there exist points $c_1, \ldots, c_m$ on that segment such that*

$$f_i(y) - f_i(x) = \mathbf{D}f_i(c_i)(y - x), \quad i = 1, \ldots, m.$$

Proof

i. The function $h : [0, 1] \to \mathbb{R}$ defined by $h(t) = f((1 - t)x + ty)$ is differentiable in t on $]0, 1[$. There is a $t_0 \in]0, 1[$ such that $h(1) - h(0) = h'(t_0)(1 - 0)$, by the one-variable mean value theorem. Now $h(1) = f(y)$ and $h(0) = f(x)$. Differentiating using the chain rule, we obtain $h'(t_0) = \mathbf{D}f((1 - t_0)x + t_0 y)(y - x)$, since the derivative of $(1 - t)x + ty$ with respect to t is $y - x$ (explain). Hence we can take $c = (1 - t_0)x + t_0 y$.

ii. This follows by applying i to each component of f separately. ∎

6.8.2 Theorem Let $f : A \subset \mathbb{R}^n \to \mathbb{R}$ be twice differentiable on the open set A. Then the matrix of $\mathbf{D}^2 f(x) : \mathbb{R}^n \times \mathbb{R}^n \to \mathbb{R}$ with respect to the standard basis is given by

$$\begin{pmatrix} \dfrac{\partial^2 f}{\partial x_1 \partial x_1} & \cdots & \dfrac{\partial^2 f}{\partial x_1 \partial x_n} \\ \cdots & \ddots & \cdots \\ \dfrac{\partial^2 f}{\partial x_n \partial x_1} & \cdots & \dfrac{\partial^2 f}{\partial x_n \partial x_n} \end{pmatrix}$$

where each partial derivative is evaluated at the point $x = (x_1, \ldots, x_n)$.

Proof The matrix representation of $\mathbf{D}f : A \to L(\mathbb{R}^n, \mathbb{R})$ is the row vector $(\partial f/\partial x_1, \ldots, \partial f/\partial x_n)$, so that by Theorem **6.2.2**, in a version suitable for row vectors, $\mathbf{D}^2 f : A \to \mathbb{R}^{n^2}$ is given by

$$\begin{pmatrix} \dfrac{\partial^2 f}{\partial x_1 \partial x_1} & \dfrac{\partial^2 f}{\partial x_1 \partial x_2} & \cdots & \dfrac{\partial^2 f}{\partial x_1 \partial x_n} \\ \cdots & & \ddots & \cdots \\ \dfrac{\partial^2 f}{\partial x_n \partial x_1} & \dfrac{\partial^2 f}{\partial x_n \partial x_2} & \cdots & \dfrac{\partial^2 f}{\partial x_n \partial x_n} \end{pmatrix}$$

Regarding $\mathbf{D}^2 f$ as a bilinear map will not change the matrix representation, as a consideration of the definitions shows. ∎

6.8.3 Symmetry of Mixed Partials Let $f : A \to \mathbb{R}^m$ be twice differentiable on the open set A with $\mathbf{D}^2 f$ continuous (that is, with the functions $\partial^2 f/\partial x_i \partial x_j$ continuous). Then $\mathbf{D}^2 f$ is symmetric; that is,

$$\mathbf{D}^2 f(x)(x_1, x_2) = \mathbf{D}^2 f(x)(x_2, x_1),$$

or, in terms of components,

$$\frac{\partial^2 f_k}{\partial x_i \partial x_j} = \frac{\partial^2 f_k}{\partial x_j \partial x_i}.$$

Proof Showing that $\mathbf{D}^2 f(x) \cdot (y, z) = \mathbf{D}^2 f(x) \cdot (z, y)$ is equivalent to stating that

$$\frac{\partial^2 f_k}{\partial x_i \partial x_j} = \frac{\partial^2 f_k}{\partial x_j \partial x_i}.$$

By holding all other variables fixed, we are reduced to the two-dimensional case. Thus we can assume that f is of class C^2 on $A \subset \mathbb{R}^2$ and is real-valued.

As suggested in the text, we consider, for fixed $(x, y) \in A$ and small h, k, the quantity

$$S_{h,k} = [f(x+h, y+k) - f(x+h, y)] - [f(x, y+k) - f(x, y)].$$

Define the function g_k by $g_k(u) = f(u, y+k) - f(u, y)$, and—motivated by Figure 6.8-1—observe that the formula for $S_{h,k}$ can be written

$$S_{h,k} = g_k(x+h) - g_k(x).$$

Thus, by the mean value theorem, $S_{h,k} = g_k'(c_{h,k}) \cdot h$ for some $c_{h,k}$ lying between x and $x+h$. Hence

$$S_{h,k} = \left\{ \frac{\partial f}{\partial x}(c_{h,k}, y+k) - \frac{\partial f}{\partial x}(c_{h,k}, y) \right\} \cdot h = \frac{\partial^2 f}{\partial y \partial x}(c_{h,k}, d_{h,k}) \cdot hk$$

for some $d_{h,k}$ lying between y and $y+k$.

Now $S_{h,k}$ is "symmetrical" in h, k and x, y. By interchanging the two middle terms in $S_{h,k}$, we can derive (in the same way)

$$S_{h,k} = \frac{\partial^2 f}{\partial x \partial y}(\bar{c}_{h,k}, \bar{d}_{h,k}) \cdot hk.$$

Equating these two formulas for $S_{h,k}$, canceling h, k, and letting $h \to 0$, $k \to 0$ (using continuity of $\mathbf{D}^2 f$) gives the result. ∎

Note. A refinement is this: If f is C^1 and $\partial^2 f/\partial x \partial y$ exists and is continuous, then $\partial^2 f/\partial y \partial x$ exists and these are equal. This requires more work than the preceding proof, but the idea is the same. (See Exercise 24 at the end of this chapter.)

6.8.5 Taylor's Theorem Let $f : A \to \mathbb{R}$ be of class C^r for $A \subset \mathbb{R}^n$ an open set. Let $x, y \in A$, and suppose that the segment joining x and y lies in A. Then there is a point c on that segment such that

$$f(y) - f(x) = \sum_{k=1}^{r-1} \frac{1}{k!} \mathbf{D}^k f(x)(y-x, \ldots, y-x) + \frac{1}{r!} \mathbf{D}^r f(c)(y-x, \ldots, y-x)$$

where $\mathbf{D}^k f(x)(y-x, \ldots, y-x)$ denotes $\mathbf{D}^k f(x)$ as a k-linear map applied to the k-tuple $(y-x, \ldots, y-x)$. In coordinates,

$$\mathbf{D}^k f(x)(y-x, \ldots, y-x) = \sum_{i_1, \ldots, i_k=1}^{n} \left(\frac{\partial^k f}{\partial x_{i_1} \cdots \partial x_{i_k}} \right)(y_{i_1} - x_{i_1}) \cdots (y_{i_k} - x_{i_k}).$$

376

Chapter 6 Differentiable Mappings

Setting $y = x + h$, we can write the Taylor formula as

$$f(x+h) = f(x) + \mathbf{D}f(x) \cdot h + \cdots + \frac{1}{(r-1)!} \mathbf{D}^{r-1}f(x) \cdot (h, \ldots, h) + R_{r-1}(x, h)$$

where $R_{r-1}(x, h)$ is the remainder. Furthermore,

$$\frac{R_{r-1}(x,h)}{\|h\|^{r-1}} \to 0 \quad as \quad h \to 0.$$

Proof If we remember that

$$\frac{d}{dt} f(x+th) = \mathbf{D}f(x+th) \cdot h = \sum_{i=1}^{n} \frac{\partial f}{\partial x_i}(x+th) h_i$$

from the chain rule, then we can integrate both sides from $t = 0$ to $t = 1$ to obtain

$$f(x+h) - f(x) = \int_0^1 \sum_{i=1}^{n} \frac{\partial f}{\partial x_i}(x+th) h_i \, dt.$$

Integrate the expression on the right-hand side by parts, using the general formula

$$\int_0^1 u \frac{dv}{dt} dt = - \int_0^1 v \frac{du}{dt} dt + uv \Big|_0^1$$

with $u = (\partial f/\partial x_i)(x+th)h_i$ and $v = t - 1$. Then,

$$\sum_{i=1}^{n} \int_0^1 \frac{\partial f}{\partial x_i}(x+th) h_i \, dt = \sum_{i,k=1}^{n} \int_0^1 (1-t) \frac{\partial^2 f}{\partial x_i \partial x_k}(x+th) h_i h_k \, dt + \sum_{i=1}^{n} h_i \frac{\partial f}{\partial x_i}(x),$$

since

$$\frac{du}{dt} = \frac{\partial^2 f}{\partial x_i \partial x_k}(x+th) h_i h_k,$$

from the chain rule, and

$$uv \Big|_0^1 = (t-1) \frac{\partial f}{\partial x_i}(x+th) h_i \Big|_{t=0}^{1} = \frac{\partial f}{\partial x_i}(x) h_i.$$

Thus we have proved the identity

$$f(x+h) - f(x) = \sum_{i=1}^{n} \frac{\partial f}{\partial x_i}(x) \cdot h_i + R_1(h, x)$$

377

Theorem Proofs for Chapter 6

where

$$R_1(h, x) = \sum_{i,k=1}^{n} \int_0^1 (1-t) \frac{\partial^2 f}{\partial x_i \partial x_k}(x+th) h_i h_k \, dt.$$

Since $|h_i| \le \|h\|$, we get

$$|R_1(h, x_0)| \le \|h\|^2 \left\{ \sum_{i,k=1}^{n} \int_0^1 (1-t) \left| \frac{\partial^2 f}{\partial x_i \partial x_k}(x_0 + th) \right| dt \right\}.$$

If we integrate $R_1(h, x)$ by parts again with

$$u = \frac{\partial^2 f}{\partial x_i \partial x_k}(x+th) h_i h_k \quad and \quad v = -\frac{(t-1)^2}{2},$$

we get

$$R_1(h, x) = \sum_{i,j,k} \int_0^1 \frac{(t-1)^2}{2} \frac{\partial^3 f}{\partial x_i \partial x_j \partial x_k}(x+th) h_i h_j h_k \, dt + \sum_{i,j} \frac{1}{2} \frac{\partial^2 f}{\partial x_i \partial x_j}(x) h_i h_j.$$

Thus we have proved that

$$f(x+h) = f(x) + \sum_{i=1}^{n} h_i \frac{\partial f}{\partial x_i}(x) + \sum_{i,j=1}^{n} \frac{h_i h_j}{2} \frac{\partial^2 f}{\partial x_i \partial x_j}(x) + R_2(h, x),$$

where

$$R_2(h, x) = \sum_{i,j,k} \int_0^1 \frac{(t-1)^2}{2} \frac{\partial^3 f}{\partial x_i \partial x_j \partial x_k}(x+th) h_i h_j h_k \, dt.$$

The integrand in the last formula is a continuous function and is therefore bounded on a small neighborhood of x (remember, it has to be close to the value of the function at x). Thus, for a constant $M \ge 0$ and for $\|h\|$ small, we get

$$|R_2(h, x)| \le \|h\|^3 M.$$

In particular, $R_2(h, x_0)/\|h\|^2 \le \|h\| M \to 0$ as $h \to 0$. The formula stated in the theorem for the remainder (Lagrange's form of the remainder) is obtained by applying the *second mean value theorem* for integrals. Recall that this states that

$$\int_a^b f(x) g(x) \, dx = f(c) \int_a^b g(x) \, dx,$$

provided that f and g are continuous and $g \geq 0$ on $[a, b]$; here c is some number between a and b (see Exercise 45, Chapter 4). Thus,

$$R_1(h, x_0) = \sum_{i,k=1}^{n} \int_0^1 (1-t) \frac{\partial^2 f}{\partial x_i \partial x_k}(x+th)h_i h_k \, dt$$

$$= \int_0^1 (1-t) \mathbf{D}^2(f(x+th))(h,h) \, dt = \frac{1}{2}\mathbf{D}^2 f(c) \cdot (h,h)$$

where c lies somewhere on the line joining x to $y = x + h$. Similarly,

$$R_2(h, x_0) = \sum_{i,j,k=1}^{n} \int_0^1 \frac{(t-1)^2}{2} \frac{\partial^3 f}{\partial x_i \partial x_j \partial x_k}(x+th)h_i h_j h_k \, dt$$

$$= \int_0^1 \frac{(t-1)^2}{2} \mathbf{D}^3 f(x+th) \cdot (h,h,h) \, dt = \frac{1}{3!}\mathbf{D}^3 f(c) \cdot (h,h,h)$$

where c lies somewhere on the line joining x to $y = x + h$. One can proceed by induction using the same method to get the general result. ∎

Remark 1 With a bit more effort, one can prove a stronger theorem: If f is of class C^r, then

$$f(x+h) = f(x) + \sum_{k=1}^{r} \frac{1}{k!}\mathbf{D}^k f(x) \cdot (h, \ldots, h) + R_r(x, h)$$

where

$$\frac{R_r(x,h)}{\|h\|^r} \to 0$$

as $h \to 0$ in $\mathbb{R}^n$. We leave this point to the interested reader.

Remark 2 Another proof that uses Taylor's formula from one-variable calculus is as follows. Let $g(t) = f(x + t(y-x))$ for $x \in [0,1]$. Applying Taylor's formula on $\mathbb{R}$, there is some $\tilde{t} \in [0,1]$ such that

$$g(1) - g(0) = \sum_{k=1}^{r-1} \frac{1}{k!} g^{(k)}(0) + \frac{1}{r!} g^{(r)}(\tilde{t}).$$

Note that $g(1) = f(y)$ and $g(0) = f(x)$. Let $p(t) = x + t(y-x)$. Then $g = f \circ p$ and $\mathbf{D}p(t)(1) = y - x$ for all x, and so, by Exercise 6b at the end of this chapter,

$$g^{(r)}(t) = \mathbf{D}^k g(t)(1, \ldots, 1) = \mathbf{D}^k f(p(t))(\mathbf{D}p(t)(1), \ldots, \mathbf{D}p(t)(1))$$
$$= \mathbf{D}^k f(x + t(y-x))(y-x, \ldots, y-x).$$

Substituting, we get

$$f(y) - f(x) = \sum_{k=1}^{r-1} \frac{1}{k!}\mathbf{D}^k f(x)(y-x, \ldots, y-x) + \frac{1}{r!}\mathbf{D}^r f(x+\tilde{t}(y-x))(y-x, \ldots, y-x),$$

which completes the proof, with $c = x + \tilde{t}(y - x)$.

6.9.2 Theorem If $f : A \subset \mathbb{R}^n \to \mathbb{R}$ is differentiable, A is open, and $x_0 \in A$ is an extreme point for f, then $\mathbf{D}f(x_0) = 0$; that is, x_0 is a critical point.

Proof If $\mathbf{D}f(x_0) \neq 0$, we can find an $x \in \mathbb{R}^n$ such that $\mathbf{D}f(x_0)x = c \neq 0$, say, $c > 0$. Now find a $\delta > 0$ such that if $\|h\| < \delta$, then

$$\|f(x_0 + h) - f(x_0) - \mathbf{D}f(x_0)h\| \leq \frac{c}{2\|x\|}\|h\|.$$

Pick $\lambda > 0$ such that $\lambda\|x\| < \delta$. Choosing $h = \lambda x$ gives $\|f(x_0 + \lambda x) - f(x_0) - \mathbf{D}f(x_0)\lambda x\| \leq c\lambda\|x\|/(2\|x\|) = c\lambda/2$. Since $\mathbf{D}f(x_0)\lambda x = \lambda c$, we get $f(x_0 + \lambda x) - f(x_0) > 0$. Similarly, $\|f(x_0 - \lambda x) - f(x_0) + \mathbf{D}f(x_0)\lambda x\| \leq c\lambda/2$ implies $f(x_0 - \lambda x) - f(x_0) < 0$. Since $f(x_0 + \lambda x) > f(x_0)$ and $f(x_0 - \lambda x) < f(x_0)$, we see that $f(x_0)$ is not a local extreme value. That is, we can find points y arbitrarily close to x_0 such that $f(y) > f(x_0)$, and similarly there are points y arbitrarily close to x_0 such that $f(y) < f(x_0)$. ∎

6.9.4 Theorem

i. If $f : A \subset \mathbb{R}^n \to \mathbb{R}$ is a C^2 function defined on an open set A and x_0 is a critical point of f such that $H_{x_0}(f)$ is negative definite, then f has a local maximum at x_0.

ii. If f has a local maximum at x_0, then $H_{x_0}(f)$ is negative semidefinite.

Proof

i. $H_{x_0}(f)(x,x) < 0$ for all $x \neq 0$ in $\mathbb{R}^n$ implies $\mathbf{D}^2 f(x_0)(x,x) < 0$ for all $x \neq 0$ in $\mathbb{R}^n$. By Worked Example 4.5 at the end of Chapter 4, a bilinear function is continuous, and so $\mathbf{D}^2 f(x_0)(x,x)$ is a continuous function of x. Moreover, $S = \{x \in \mathbb{R}^n \mid \|x\| = 1\}$ is compact, and so there is a point $\bar{x} \in S$ such that $0 > \mathbf{D}^2 f(x_0)(\bar{x}, \bar{x}) \geq \mathbf{D}^2 f(x_0)(x,x)$ for all $x \in S$. Let $\varepsilon = -\mathbf{D}^2 f(x_0)(\bar{x}, \bar{x})$. Then $\mathbf{D}^2 f(x_0)(x,x) = \|x\|^2 \mathbf{D}^2 f(x_0)(x/\|x\|, x/\|x\|) \leq -\varepsilon\|x\|^2$ for any $x \neq 0$ in $\mathbb{R}^n$. Since $\mathbf{D}^2 f$ is continuous, there is a $\delta > 0$ such that $\|y - x_0\| < \delta$

implies $\|D^2f(y) - D^2f(x_0)\| < \varepsilon/2$, and we may also pick our δ such that $D(x_0, \delta) \subset A$. If $y \in D(x_0, \delta)$, Taylor's theorem gives

$$f(y) - f(x_0) = Df(x_0)(y - x_0) + \frac{1}{2}D^2f(c)(y - x_0, y - x_0),$$

where $c \in D(x_0, \delta)$. Thus,

$$\|D^2f(c) - D^2f(x_0)\| < \frac{\varepsilon}{2}.$$

implies

$$D^2f(c)(y - x_0, y - x_0)$$
$$\leq D^2f(x_0)(y - x_0, y - x_0)$$
$$+ \|D^2f(c)(y - x_0, y - x_0) - D^2f(x_0)(y - x_0, y - x_0)\|$$
$$\leq -\varepsilon\|y - x_0\|^2 + \frac{\varepsilon}{2}\|y - x_0\|^2 = -\frac{\varepsilon}{2}\|y - x_0\|^2.$$

Since $Df(x_0) = 0$, Taylor's theorem gives

$$f(y) - f(x_0) = \frac{1}{2}D^2f(c)(y - x_0, y - x_0) \leq \frac{1}{2}\left(-\frac{\varepsilon}{2}\|y - x_0\|^2\right) < 0.$$

Hence $f(y) < f(x_0)$ for all $y \in D(x_0, \delta)$, $y \neq x_0$, and so f has a local maximum at x_0.

ii. To prove this part of the theorem, we argue by contradiction. Let f have a local maximum at x_0 and suppose $D^2f(x_0)(x, x) > 0$ for some $x \in \mathbb{R}^n$. Now consider $g(t) = -f(x_0 + tx)$. Since f is defined in a neighborhood of x_0, g is defined in a neighborhood of 0. We have $D^2g(0)(1, 1) = -D^2f(x_0)(x, x) < 0$. Using the proof of i, there is a δ such that $|t| < \delta$, $t \neq 0$ implies $g(t) < g(0)$. Thus $|t| < \delta$ implies $f(x_0 + tx) > f(x_0)$, and so f does not have a local maximum at x_0. This contradiction implies that $D^2f(x_0)(x, x) \leq 0$ for all $x \in \mathbb{R}^n$. Hence $H_{x_0}(f)(x, x) \leq 0$ for all $x \in \mathbb{R}^n$. ■

Worked Examples for Chapter 6

Example 6.1 *Let $f : B \subset \mathbb{R}^n \to \mathbb{R}$ where $B = \{x \in \mathbb{R}^n \mid \|x\| \leq 1\}$ be continuous and let f be differentiable on int(B). Suppose $f(x) = 0$ on bd(B). Show that there is a point $x_0 \in$ int(B) for which $Df(x_0) = 0$.*

Solution This is the multidimensional version of Rolle's theorem. If f is identically zero, the theorem is trivial. Therefore, suppose $f(x) \neq 0$ for some $x \in$ int(B). Then f attains a maximum, or minimum, at some interior point, since B is compact. Thus there is an extreme point $x_0 \in$ int(B), and hence, by Theorem 6.9.2, $Df(x_0) = 0$. ◆

Example 6.2 *Show that for a bilinear map $f : \mathbb{R}^n \times \mathbb{R}^m \to \mathbb{R}^p$, we have $Df(x_0, y_0)(x, y) = f(x_0, y) + f(x, y_0)$.*

Solution We know that f is differentiable, because from its matrix representation, we see that the partial derivatives are linear and so are continuous. Since $f(x, y_0)$ is a linear function of x, the derivative in the direction $(x, 0)$ is $Df(x_0, y_0)(x, 0) = f(x, y_0)$, as in Example 6.2.4. Similarly, $Df(x_0, y_0)(0, y) = f(x_0, y)$. Since $Df(x_0, y_0)$ is linear and $(x, y) = (x, 0)+(0, y)$, we have $Df(x_0, y_0)(x, y) = f(x_0, y) + f(x, y_0)$. ◆

Example 6.3 *Find the Jacobian of $f(x, y) = (\sin(x \sin y), (x + y)^2)$, $f : \mathbb{R}^2 \to \mathbb{R}^2$.*

Solution We have

$$\frac{\partial f_1}{\partial x} = \frac{\partial}{\partial x}(\sin(x \sin y))$$
$$= \cos(x \sin y)\frac{\partial}{\partial x}(x \sin y) = \sin y \cos(x \sin y);$$
$$\frac{\partial f_2}{\partial x} = 2(x + y)\frac{\partial}{\partial x}(x + y) = 2(x + y);$$
$$\frac{\partial f_1}{\partial y} = \cos(x \sin y)\frac{\partial}{\partial y}(x \sin y) = \cos(x \sin y)x \cos y;$$
$$\frac{\partial f_2}{\partial y} = 2(x + y).$$

Thus, by Theorem 6.2.2, the Jacobian matrix (where $x = x_1$ and $y = x_2$) is

$$\begin{pmatrix} \sin y \cos(x \sin y) & x \cos y \cos(x \sin y) \\ 2(x + y) & 2(x + y) \end{pmatrix}.$$ ◆

Chapter 6 Differentiable Mappings

Note. Jacobian matrices generally are not symmetric and indeed need not even be square. Symmetry is a property only of the *second* derivative of a function $f : \mathbb{R}^n \to \mathbb{R}$.

Example 6.4 *Find the critical points of $f(x,y) = x^3 - 3x^2 + y^2$ and determine whether f has a (local) maximum, (local) minimum, or saddle point at each of these critical points.*

Solution The critical points are precisely those points (x,y) for which

$$\frac{\partial f}{\partial x} = 3x^2 - 6x = 0 \quad \text{and} \quad \frac{\partial f}{\partial y} = 2y = 0.$$

Solving for x, we see that $x = 0$ or $x = 2$. Therefore, the critical points of f are $(0,0)$ and $(2,0)$. The matrix of the Hessian at (x,y) is

$$\begin{pmatrix} \frac{\partial^2 f}{\partial x \partial x} & \frac{\partial^2 f}{\partial x \partial y} \\ \frac{\partial^2 f}{\partial y \partial x} & \frac{\partial^2 f}{\partial y \partial y} \end{pmatrix} = \begin{pmatrix} 6x - 6 & 0 \\ 0 & 2 \end{pmatrix}.$$

At $(0,0)$ the matrix of the Hessian is

$$\begin{pmatrix} -6 & 0 \\ 0 & 2 \end{pmatrix}$$

and $\Delta_1 = -6$, $\Delta_2 = -12$. Hence, f has a saddle point at $(0,0)$. At $(2,0)$, the matrix of the Hessian is

$$\begin{pmatrix} 6 & 0 \\ 0 & 2 \end{pmatrix}$$

and $\Delta_1 = 6$, $\Delta_2 = 12$ and so f has a local minimum. This is confirmed by the computer-drawn graph shown in Figure 6.WE-1.

Example 6.5 *Let A be an open convex set in $\mathbb{R}^n$ and let $f : \mathbb{R}^n \to \mathbb{R}^m$ be differentiable with a continuous derivative. Suppose $\|\mathbf{D}f(x)y\| \leq M\|y\|$ for all $x \in A$, $y \in \mathbb{R}^n$. Prove the **mean value inequality:***

$$\|f(x_1) - f(x_2)\| \leq M\|x_1 - x_2\|.$$

Exercises for Chapter 6 383

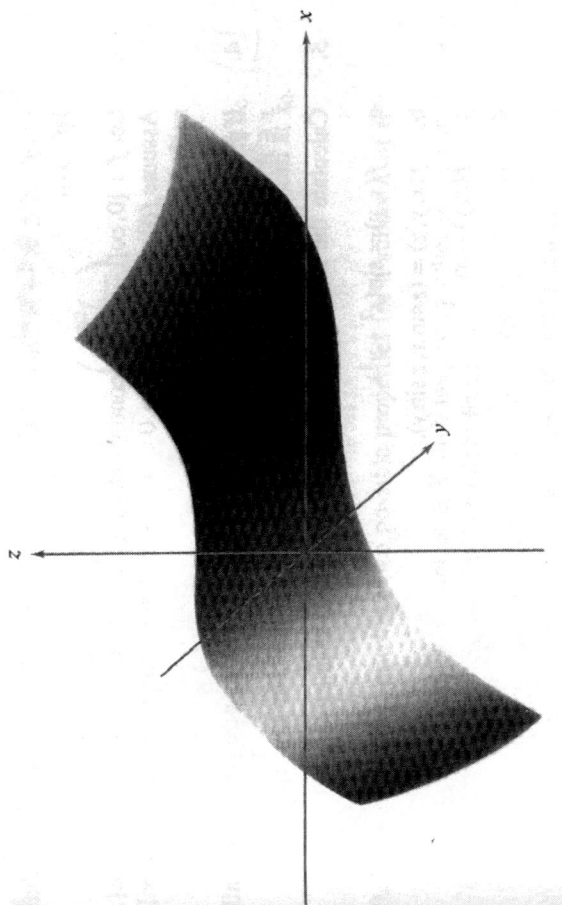

FIGURE 6.WE-1 The graph of $f(x,y) = x^3 - 3x^2 + y^2$.

Solution For $n = 1$, $m = 1$, this follows directly from the mean value theorem. To get the general case, observe that by the chain rule, $(d/dt)\,(f(tx_1 + (1-t)x_2)) = \mathbf{D}f(tx_1 + (1-t)x_2) \cdot (x_1 - x_2)$. Integrate both sides in t from $t = 0$ to $t = 1$ to obtain

$$f(x_1) - f(x_2) = \int_0^1 [\mathbf{D}f(tx_1 + (1-t)x_2) \cdot (x_1 - x_2)]\,dt.$$

The integral here is defined as the integral of the component functions. Taking absolute values and using the hypothesis on $\mathbf{D}f$ now gives the result desired. We used the fact that the absolute value of an integral is less than or equal to the integral of the absolute value—see the remarks following **4.8.5** and note that the case of vector functions is similar. ◆

Exercises for Chapter 6

1. If $f : A \subset \mathbb{R}^n \to \mathbb{R}^m$ and $g : B \subset \mathbb{R}^n \to \mathbb{R}^m$ are differentiable functions on the (open) sets A and B and α, β are constants, prove that $\alpha f + \beta g : A \cap B \subset \mathbb{R}^n \to \mathbb{R}^m$ is differentiable and $\mathbf{D}(\alpha f + \beta g)(x) = \alpha \mathbf{D}f(x) + \beta \mathbf{D}g(x)$.

2. Let $f : A \subset \mathbb{R} \to \mathbb{R}^m$ and assume df_i/dx exists for $i = 1, \dots, m$. Show that $\mathbf{D}f$ exists.

3. Let $f : [0, \infty[\to \mathbb{R}$ be continuous and let f be differentiable on $]0, \infty[$. Assume $f(0) = 0$ and $f(x) \to 0$ as $x \to +\infty$. Show that there is a $c \in]0, \infty[$ such that $f'(c) = 0$.

4. If $f : A \subset \mathbb{R}^n \to \mathbb{R}^n$ is a constant function, show that $\mathbf{D}f(x) = 0$ for all $x \in A$.

5. Calculate the Jacobians of the following functions:

   a. $f(x, y) = \sin(x^2 + y^3)$.

   b. $f(x, y, z) = (z \sin x, z \sin y)$.

   c. $f(x, y) = xy$.

   d. $f(x, y, z) = x^2 + y^2$.

   e. $f(x, y) = (\sin(xy), \cos(xy), x^2y^2)$.

   f. $f(x, y, z) = x^{y+z}$.

   g. $f(x, y, z) = xyz$.

   h. $f(x, y, z) = (z^{xy}, x^2, \tan(xyz))$.

6. **a.** If $f : A \subset \mathbb{R}^n \to \mathbb{R}^m$ and $g : B \subset \mathbb{R}^m \to \mathbb{R}^p$ are twice differentiable and $f(A) \subset B$, then for $x_0 \in A$, $x, y \in \mathbb{R}^n$, show that
$$\mathbf{D}^2(g \circ f)(x_0)(x, y) = \mathbf{D}^2(g(f(x_0)))(\mathbf{D}f(x_0) \cdot x, \mathbf{D}f(x_0) \cdot y)$$
$$+ \mathbf{D}g(f(x_0)) \cdot \mathbf{D}^2 f(x_0)(x, y).$$

   b. If $p : \mathbb{R}^n \to \mathbb{R}^m$ is a linear map plus some constant and $f : A \subset \mathbb{R}^m \to \mathbb{R}^s$ is k times differentiable, prove that
$$\mathbf{D}^k(f \circ p)(x_0)(x_1, \dots, x_k) = \mathbf{D}^k f(p(x_0))(\mathbf{D}p(x_0)(x_1), \dots, \mathbf{D}p(x_0)(x_k)).$$

7. Find the critical points of the following functions and determine whether they are local maxima, local minima, or saddle points:

   a. $f(x, y) = x^3 + 6x^2 + 3y^2 - 12xy + 9x$.

   b. $f(x, y) = \sin x + y^2 - 2y + 1$.

   c. $f(x, y, z) = \cos 2x \cdot \sin y + z^2$.

   d. $f(x, y, z) = (x + y + z)^2$.

---

8. Show that if $f : A \subset \mathbb{R}^2 \to \mathbb{R}$ has a critical point $x_0 \in A$ and we let
$$\Delta = \frac{\partial^2 f}{\partial x_1 \partial x_1} \cdot \frac{\partial^2 f}{\partial x_2 \partial x_2} - \left(\frac{\partial^2 f}{\partial x_1 \partial x_2}\right)^2$$
be evaluated at x_0, then

   a. $\Delta > 0$ and $\partial^2 f / \partial x_1 \partial x_1 > 0$ imply f has a local minimum at x_0.

   b. $\Delta > 0$ and $\partial^2 f / \partial x_1 \partial x_1 < 0$ imply f has a local maximum at x_0.

   c. $\Delta < 0$ implies x_0 is a saddle point of f.

9. Consider the following two possible properties for a subset X of $\mathbb{R}^n$:

   1 There is a point $x_0 \in X$ such that every other point x in X can be joined to x_0 by a straight line in X.

   2 There is a point $x_0 \in X$ such that every other point x in X can be joined to x_0 by a differentiable path in X.

   a. Give examples of each kind of set that are not convex.

   b. Show that if X is an open set in $\mathbb{R}^n$ satisfying either of these conditions and $f : X \to \mathbb{R}$ is a differentiable function with zero derivative, then f is constant.

   c. Show that if X is an open subset of $\mathbb{R}^n$, then the following are equivalent:

     i. Condition **2** above

     ii. Path connectedness of X

     iii. Connectedness of X

10. Prove the analogue of Theorem 6.9.4 for minima.

11. Prove the analogue of Proposition 5.3.3 for $f : A \subset \mathbb{R}^n \to \mathbb{R}^m$.

12. A function $f : \mathbb{R}^n \to \mathbb{R}$ is called *homogeneous of degree* m if $f(tx) = t^m f(x)$ for all $x \in \mathbb{R}^n$ and $t \in \mathbb{R}$. If f is differentiable, show that for $x \in \mathbb{R}^n$,
$$\mathbf{D}f(x)x = mf(x), \quad \text{that is,} \quad \sum_{i=1}^{n} x_i \frac{\partial f}{\partial x_i} = mf(x).$$
Show that maps multilinear in k variables give rise to homogeneous functions of degree k. Give other examples.

Chapter 6 Differentiable Mappings

13. Use the chain rule to find derivatives of the following, where $f(x,y,z) = x^2 + yz$, $g(x,y) = y^3 + xy$, and $h(x) = \sin x$:

    a. $F(x,y,z) = f(h(x), g(x,y), z)$.

    b. $G(x,y,z) = h(f(x,y,z)g(x,y))$.

    c. $H(x,y,z) = g(f(x,y,h(x)), g(z,y))$.

    Also find *general* formulas for the derivatives of F, G, H.

14. a. Extend Worked Example 6.2 to multilinear maps.

    b. Apply the result in a to the case of the determinant map $\det : \mathbb{R}^{n^2} = \mathbb{R}^n \times \cdots \times \mathbb{R}^n \to \mathbb{R}$, to show that $A \in \mathbb{R}^{n^2}$ is a critical point of det iff A has rank $\leq n-2$.

15. Let $f : \mathbb{R} \to \mathbb{R}$ be differentiable. Assume there is *no* $x \in \mathbb{R}$ such that f and f' *both* vanish at x. Show that $S = \{x \mid 0 \leq x \leq 1, f(x) = 0\}$ is finite.

16. If $f : \mathbb{R}^n \to \mathbb{R}^m$ is a differentiable and Df is a constant, show that f is a linear term plus a constant and that the linear part of f is the constant value of Df.

17. If $f : A \subset \mathbb{R}^n \to \mathbb{R}$ is of class C^r and $Df(x_0) = 0$, $D^2 f(x_0) = 0, \ldots,$ $D^{r-1}f(x_0) = 0$ but $D^r f(x_0)(x, \ldots, x) < 0$ for all $x \in \mathbb{R}^n$, $x \neq 0$, then prove that f has a local maximum at x_0.

18. Prove that the equation $x^3 + bx + c = 0$ where $b > 0$ has exactly one solution $x \in \mathbb{R}$.

19. In each of the following problems, determine the second-order Taylor formula for the given function about the given point (x_0, y_0):

    a. $f(x,y) = (x + y)^2$, $x_0 = 0$, $y_0 = 0$.

    b. $f(x,y) = e^{x+y}$, $x_0 = 0$, $y_0 = 0$.

    c. $f(x,y) = 1/(x^2 + y^2 + 1)$, $x_0 = 0$, $y_0 = 0$.

    d. $f(x,y) = e^{-x^2-y^2}\cos(xy)$, $x_0 = 0$, $y_0 = 0$.

    e. $f(x,y) = \sin(xy) + \cos(xy)$, $x_0 = 0$, $y_0 = 0$.

    f. $f(x,y) = e^{(x-1)^2}\cos y$, $x_0 = 1$, $y_0 = 0$.

20. Let $L : \mathbb{R}^n \to \mathbb{R}^m$ be a linear map. Define $\|L\| = \inf\{M \mid \|Lx\| \leq M\|x\|$ for all $x \in \mathbb{R}^n\}$. Show that $\|\cdot\|$ is a norm on the space of linear maps of $\mathbb{R}^n$ to $\mathbb{R}^m$.

Exercises for Chapter 6

21. a. Let $f : A \subset \mathbb{R}^n \to \mathbb{R}$, and assume that for some integer k, $\Delta_k < 0$, where Δ_k is evaluated at x_0. Show that f cannot have a (local) minimum at x_0.

    b. If $\Delta_k < 0$ for some even k, prove that f has a saddle point at x_0.

22. Give an example of a continuous map $f :]0,1[\to \mathbb{R}$ whose graph is not closed. Can this happen for $f : A \subset \mathbb{R} \to \mathbb{R}$ where A is closed?

23. Write down the first four terms in the Taylor expansion of $\log(\cos x)$ about $x = 0$.

24. Let $f(x,y)$ be a real-valued function on $\mathbb{R}^2$. Show that if f is of class C^1 and $\partial^2 f/\partial x \partial y$ exists and is continuous, then $\partial^2 f/\partial y \partial x$ exists and $\partial^2 f/\partial x \partial y = \partial^2 f/\partial y \partial x$ (this is weaker than saying that f is of class C^2). Generalize.

25. Let $f : \mathbb{R}^n \to \mathbb{R}$ and suppose that the partial derivatives $\partial f/\partial x_i$, $i = 1, \ldots, n$, exist and that $\partial f/\partial x_i$, $i = 1, \ldots, n-1$, are continuous. Prove that f is differentiable.

26. a. If $f : \mathbb{R} \to \mathbb{R}$ and f' exists on a neighborhood of $x = a$ and $\lim_{x \to a^+} f'(x) = l$, prove that $f'(a) = l$.

    b. Let $g(x) = 1$ if $x < 0$ and $g(x) = 0$ if $x \geq 0$. Can g be the derivative of any function?

27. Let $f : A \to \mathbb{R}$ be continuous, where $A \subset \mathbb{R}^n$ is open. Assume that all directional derivatives exist and that at each $x_0 \in A$, they determine a linear map. Must f be differentiable?

28. Suppose we define a new type of connectedness as follows: A set $M \subset \mathbb{R}^n$ is "differentiably connected" if every two points $x, y \in M$ can be joined by a differentiable arc $\psi : [0,1] \to \mathbb{R}^n$. What do differentiably connected sets look like? Give an example of a path-connected set that is not differentiably connected. What about open sets?

29. Let $f_n(x) = xe^{-nx}$, $x \in [0, \infty[$, $n = 0, 1, 2, \ldots$.

    a. Show that $f(x) = \sum_{n=0}^{\infty} f_n(x)$ exists. Compute f explicitly.

    b. Is f continuous?

    c. Find a suitable set on which the convergence is uniform.

    d. May we differentiate term by term?

30. Suppose $f : \mathbb{R} \to \mathbb{R}$ is bounded and has a continuous derivative. What is right and what is wrong in the following string of conclusions?

We want to prove that the set T of all points at which f assumes its (absolute) maximum is closed. Since f is differentiable, it is continuous. Hence it assumes its maximum; that is, T is not empty. Denote by S the set of points at which $f'(x) = 0$. Then $T \subset S$. On the other hand, if $x \in S$, then $f'(x) = 0$; hence f achieves either a maximum or a minimum there. If it achieves a maximum, we must have $f(x) \geq 0$. Hence $T = S \cap \{x \mid f(x) \geq 0\}$. Since $\{x \mid f(x) \geq 0\}$ is closed, as is S, T is closed.

Is T really closed, or not?

31. Let $A \subset \mathbb{R}^n$ be compact, and construct the normed space $C(A, \mathbb{R})$ as in Chapter 5. Define, for $x_0 \in A$, $\delta_{x_0} : C(A, \mathbb{R}) \to \mathbb{R}; f \mapsto f(x_0)$. Prove that δ_{x_0} is differentiable.

32. Let $f : \mathbb{R}^2 \to \mathbb{R}$ be defined by

$$f(x,y) = \frac{xy(x^2 - y^2)}{x^2 + y^2}$$

if $(x,y) \neq (0,0)$ and $f(0,0) = 0$. Show that $\partial^2 f / \partial x \partial y$ and $\partial^2 f / \partial y \partial x$ exist at $(0, 0)$ but are not equal.

33. Use Taylor's theorem to prove the binomial theorem,

$$(a + b)^n = \sum_{k=0}^{n} \binom{n}{k} a^k b^{n-k}.$$

34. Consider the sequence of real numbers

$$\frac{1}{2}, \quad \frac{1}{2 + \frac{1}{2}}, \quad \frac{1}{2 + \frac{1}{2 + \frac{1}{2}}}, \ldots,$$

(a continued fraction). Show that it is convergent, and find the limit.

35. Let $f :]a, b[\to \mathbb{R}$ be twice differentiable. Suppose f vanishes at three distinct points. Prove that there is a $c \in]a, b[$ such that $f''(c) = 0$.

36. Suppose $f : [0, 1] \to \mathbb{R}$ is continuous, f is differentiable on $]0, 1[$, and $f(0) = 0$. Assume that $|f'(x)| \leq |f(x)|$, $0 < x < 1$. Prove that $f(x) = 0$ for all $x \in [0, 1]$.

37. A C^2 function $f : \mathbb{R}^2 \to \mathbb{R}$ is called *harmonic* if

$$\frac{\partial^2 f}{\partial x^2} + \frac{\partial^2 f}{\partial y^2} = 0.$$

Assume that (x_0, y_0) is a strict local maximum and f is harmonic. Prove that *all* second derivatives of f vanish at (x_0, y_0).

38. Find the equation of the plane tangent to the following surfaces at the indicated points:

    a. $z = x^2 + y^2$, $(0, 0)$.

    b. $z = x^2 - y^2 + x$, $(1, 0)$.

    c. $z = (x + y)^2$, $(3, 2)$.

39. Analyze the behavior of the following functions at the indicated points:

    a. $z = x^2 - y^2 + 3xy$, $(0, 0)$.

    b. $z = Ax^2 - By^2 + Cxy$, $(0, 0)$.

40. Find the equation of the tangent plane to the surface S given by the graph of

    a. $f(x,y) = \sqrt{x^2 + y^2} + x^2 + y^2$ at $(1, 0, 2)$.

    b. $f(x,y) = \sqrt{x^2 + 2xy - y^2} + 1$ at $(1, 1, \sqrt{3})$.

41. Give an example of a differentiable function $f : \mathbb{R} \to \mathbb{R}$ such that $f(0) = 0$, $f'(0) = 0$ and yet no inequality of the form $|f(x)| \leq Cx^2$ holds in any neighborhood of the origin.